MONTAGE:
INVESTIGATIONS IN LANGUAGE

WILLIAM SPARKE and
CLARK McKOWEN
DIABLO VALLEY COLLEGE
CALIFORNIA

THE
MACMILLAN
COMPANY

COLLIER-MACMILLAN LIMITED, LONDON

First Printing
Library of Congress catalog card number: 69-18253
The Macmillan Company
Collier-Macmillan Canada, Ltd., Toronto, Ontario
Printed in the United States of America

The Publisher wishes to acknowledge with thanks the permission of other publishers to reprint selections in this text. Credits for the individual selections are as follows:

Acknowledgments

ANSEL ADAMS, photograph, pp. 116-117. Reprinted by permission of Ansel Adams. ALEXANDER ALEXEIFF, "Reflections on Motion Picture Animation," and *The Nose,* rough script. Reprinted by permission of Cecile Starr, agent for Alexander Alexeiff. Photograph, pp. 38, 149, 152. Courtesy of AMERICAN ENKA CORP. GUS ARRIOLA, *Gordo.* © United Feature Syndicate, Inc. 1966. AVENGERS #43, pp. 133-4. "Reg. TM, Copyright © 1967 Marvel Comics Group. All Rights Reserved." GIDEON BACHMANN, "Federico Fellini: An interview," from *Film: Book 1,* Robert Hughes, editor. Reprinted by permission of Gideon Bachmann, *Film: Book 1,* and Robert Hughes. JAMES BALDWIN, excerpted from "A Talk to Teachers," Saturday Review Education Supplement, December 21, 1963. Reprinted by permission of Robert Lantz Literary Agency, N.Y. ERIC BERNE, M.D., excerpted from *Games People Play.* Reprinted by permission of Grove Press, Inc. Copyright © 1964 by Eric Berne. RUTH BERNHARD, "Classic Torso," *Contact* Magazine, June, 1960. Reprinted by permission of Ruth Bernhard. AMBROSE BIERCE, "An Occurrence at Owl Creek Bridge," from *In The Midst of Life and Other Tales,* The New American Library of World Literature, Inc. N.Y., 1961. PHILIP BOOTH, "Vermont: Indian Summer." From *Letter From A Distant Land* by Philip Booth. Copyright 1953 by Philip Booth. Originally appeared in *The New Yorker.* Reprinted by permission of The Viking Press, Inc. BILL BRANDT, *Normandy 1959.* Reprinted by permission of Paul Guillumette, Inc. DAVID BUCKLES, poster, p. 383. Reprinted by permission of David Buckles. JOHN W. CAMPBELL, "You Know What I Mean." Reprinted from *Astounding Science Fiction* (now *Analog* Science Fiction-Science Fact); copyright © 1953 by Street & Street Publications, Inc. Reprinted by permission of Condé Nast Publications Inc. ALBERT CAMUS, excerpted from "Create Dangerously." Copyright © 1961 by Alfred A. Knopf, Inc. Reprinted by permission of the publisher from *Resistance, Rebellion and Death* by Albert Camus, trans. by Justin O'Brien. From *Resistance, Rebellion and Death* by Albert Camus, Hamish Hamilton Ltd., London. Reprinted by permission of Hamish Hamilton Ltd. JOHN B. CARROLL, excerpted from *Language and Thought.* John B. Carroll, *Language and Thought,* © 1964. Reprinted by permission of Prentice-Hall, Inc., Englewood Cliffs, N.J. HOWARD L. CHACE, "Hormone Derange," from *The Anguish Languish,* Prentice-Hall, Inc. Copyright by Howard L. Chace. Reprinted by permission of Howard L. Chace. MARC CHAGALL, *A la Russie, aux ânes et aux autres (Russia [Asses and Others]).* Musée National d'Art Moderne. "Clichés des Musés Nationaux." Reprinted by permission of Musée National d'Art Moderne. Permission ADAGP 1967 by French Reproduction Rights Inc. Reprinted by permission of Marc Chagall. EMERSON CHAPLIN, "Kata Kana Can Be Wondafuru." © 1965 by The New York Times Company. Reprinted by permission. Still from CITIZEN KANE, p. 272, bottom. The Museum of Modern Art/Film Stills Archive. 21 West 53rd Street, N.Y.C. JOHN COLLIER, "Ah, The University." Originally appeared in *The New Yorker.* Copyright 1939, 1966 by John Collier. Reprinted by permission of Harold Matson Co., Inc. SISTER MARY CORITA, serigraphs, pp. 126, 127, 131. Reprinted by permission of Group W, Westinghouse Broadcasting Company. MALCOLM COWLEY, excerpted from *Writers At Work.* From *Writers At Work: The Paris Review Interviews,* edited by Malcolm Cowley. Copyright © 1957, 1958 by The Paris Review, Inc. Reprinted by permission of The Viking Press, Inc. Reprinted by permission of Martin Secker & Warburg Limited. E. E. CUMMINGS, "anyone lived in a pretty how town." Copyright, 1940, by E. E. Cummings; "Buffalo Bill's." Copyright, 1923, 1951, by E. E. Cummings. Reprinted from his volume *Poems 1923-1954* by permission of Harcourt, Brace & World, Inc. Reprinted from *Complete Poems* by permission of MacGibbon & Kee, London. Still from DEAR JOHN, p. 276, bottom. Courtesy of Sigma III Corporation. DON DELILLO, "Jump-cut," *The Kenyon Review,* Gambier, Ohio, June, 1966. Reprinted by permission of *The Kenyon Review* and Don DeLillo. VERA DEUTSCH, poster, p. 427. Reprinted by permission of The National Book Committee, N.Y. JOHN DEWEY, *The Limitations and Dangers of Symbols in Relation to Meaning,* excerpted from *How We Think.* From *How We Think,* John Dewey, © 1933. Reprinted by permission of D. C. Heath and Company. LOREN EISELEY, excerpted from "How Flowers Changed the World." Copyright, 1957 by Loren Eiseley. Reprinted by permission of Random House, Inc. from *The Immense Journey,* Vintage Books Edition, by Loren Eiseley. T. S. ELIOT, excerpt from "The Love Song of J. Alfred Prufrock." Reprinted by permission of Harcourt, Brace & World, Inc. from *Collected Poems 1909-1962.* Reprinted by permission of Faber and Faber Ltd., London. ELIOT ELISOFON, photograph, p. 421, from *The Sculpture of*

Africa, Frederick A. Praeger Publishers, N.Y., 1958. Reprinted by permission of Eliot Elisofon. PAUL ENGLE, "Salt Crystals, Spider Webs, and Words," now published as "The Writer on Writing." From the book *On Creative Writing* by Paul Engle. Copyright, ©, 1963, 1964 by Paul Engle. Reprinted by permission of E. P. Dutton & Co., Inc. and William Morris Agency, Inc. " 'AN ESSAY ON WOMEN' and 'AN ESSAY ON BRIDGES' © Columbia Broadcasting System, Inc. 1968. All Rights Reserved." "Published with the permission of Columbia Broadcasting System, Inc. 'An Essay on Women' broadcast on January 24, 1967 and 'An Essay on Bridges' broadcast on February 15, 1965 as part of the program series *Who, What, When, Where, Why,* with Harry Reasoner. Both programs written by Andrew Rooney." EXPO'S FILMS, excerpt. Courtesy *Time,* The Weekly Newsmagazine; Copyright Time Inc. 1967. HENRY FAIRLIE, "The Unreal World of Television News." *Reader's Digest* condensation of "Can You Believe Your Eyes?" by Henry Fairlie (Spring 1967 *Horizon*). © Copyright 1967 by American Heritage Publishing Co., Inc. Reprinted by permission. As condensed in the August 1967 *Reader's Digest.* Used with permission. WILLIAM FAULKNER, excerpted from *Light in August.* Copyright, 1932 by William Faulkner and renewed 1960. Reprinted by permission of Random House from *Light in August,* Modern Library Edition, by William Faulkner. Reprinted by permission of Curtis Brown Ltd. JULES FEIFFER, "Little Girl." Reprinted by permission of Publishers-Hall Syndicate. FEDERICO FELLINI, excerpts from *Juliet of the Spirits,* Orion Press, N.Y., 1965. © 1965 by Grossman Publishers. Translated from *Giulietta degli spiriti* by Federico Fellini. Reprinted by permission of Grossman Publishers, Inc. Still from THE FLY, p. 272, top. Bettmann/Springer Film Archive. 136 East 58th Street. New York, N.Y. 10022. PLaza 8-0362. BOB FRASER, photograph, p. 366, in "The Promised Land," Vol. 24, No. 2 Kaiser Aluminum News. From *The Dynamics of Change* by Don Fabun, Prentice-Hall. Reprinted by permission of Kaiser Aluminum & Chemical Corporation. ROBERT FROST, "Between Prose and Verse." Copyright © 1961 by Robert Frost. The poems included in this essay are from *Complete Poems of Robert Frost.* Reprinted by permission of *The Atlantic Monthly,* Estate of Robert Frost and Holt, Rinehart and Winston, Inc.; "Design." From *Complete Poems of Robert Frost.* Copyright 1936 by Robert Frost. Copyright © 1964 by Lesley Frost Ballantine; "The Span of Life." From *Complete Poems of Robert Frost.* Copyright 1936 by Robert Frost. Copyright © 1964 by Lesley Frost Ballantine. Both reprinted by permission of Holt, Rinehart and Winston, Inc. Both reprinted by permission of Laurence Pollinger Limited from *The Complete Poems of Robert Frost,* Jonathan Cape Limited, London. WAYNE GALLUP, cartoon, p. 356. Reprinted by permission of Wayne Gallup. CLAUDE GASPARI, "La Cour Giacometti" Copyright by Fondation Maeght, St. Paul (A.M.) France. Reprinted by permission of Fondation Maeght. ROBERT GRAVES, "Amergin," excerpted from The Introduction to *The White Goddess.* Reprinted with the permission of Farrar, Straus & Giroux, Inc. from *The White Goddess* by Robert Graves. Copyright 1948 by Robert Graves. Reprinted by permission of Collins-Knowlton-Wing, Inc. Copyright © 1958 by Robert Graves. EDGAR GUEST, "The Call," from *All That Matters,* Reilly & Lee. Reprinted by permission of Henry Regnery Company. DONALD HALL, "Abroad Thoughts from Home," from *New Poets of England and America,* Meridian Books, Inc. Reprinted by permission of Curtis Brown, Ltd. Copyright © 1957 by Donald Hall. FERNAU HALL, excerpted from "An Alphabet of Movement," *New Scientist,* London, October 28, 1965. Reprinted by permission of *New Scientist.* KELSIE T. HARDER, "Toot." Reprinted with permission from *The Saturday Evening Post,* © 1966 The Curtis Publishing Co. Reprinted by permission of Kelsie T. Harder. D. E. HARDING, "The Universe Revalued." Reprinted by permission of D. E. Harding. JOHNNY HART, *B.C.,* pp. 225, 375. By permission of Johnny Hart and Publishers-Hall Syndicate. FERRIS HARTMAN, "The Invasion of English Words," *San Francisco Chronicle,* December 3, 1963. Reprinted by permission of Ferris Hartman and *San Francisco Chronicle.* GROVER HAYNES, "I Fringled a Gnu," Three Penny Press, Studio City, Calif., 1959. Reprinted by permission of Grover Haynes. HEDRICH-BLESSING, "Falling Water." Reprinted by permission of Hedrich-Blessing, Chicago. HAROLD G. HENDERSON, "On Top of Skeletons . . ."; "The Sound"; "To Get to Know Plum Blossoms." From *An Introduction to Haiku* by Harold G. Henderson. Copyright © 1958 by Harold G. Henderson. Reprinted by permission of Doubleday & Company, Inc. JAMES HILL, *Edgar Allan Poe.* Contributed through the courtesy of the John Hancock Mutual Life Insurance Company, Boston, Mass. A. E. HOUSMAN, "Say, lad have you things to do?" From "A Shropshire Lad"—Authorised Edition—from *The Collected Poems of A. E. Housman.* Copyright 1939, 1940, © 1959 by Holt, Rinehart and Winston, Inc. Copyright © 1967, 1968 by Robert E. Symons. Reprinted by permission of Holt, Rinehart and Winston, Inc. Permission to include the poem has been granted by the Society of Authors as the literary representative of the Estate of A. E. Housman, and Messrs. Jonathan Cape Ltd., publishers of A. E. Housman's *Collected Poems.* GEORGE P. HUNT, "Never Takes Notes or Sees a Film Twice—Editor's Note," *Life* Magazine, August 18, 1967. *Life* Magazine © 1967 Time Inc. SHIRO IKEGAWA, picture, p. 339. Courtesy of Container Corporation of America. JAMES INGLIS, "Night Watch," *New Writings in SF3,* Copyright 1965 by John Carnell, London. Reprinted by permission of the author. INITIAL TEACHING ALPHABET CHART. Used by permission of Initial Teaching Alphabet Publications, Inc. New York, N.Y. ISSA, haiku, p. 339. Courtesy of Container Corporation of America. SHIRLEY JACKSON, "The Witch." Reprinted with the permission of Farrar, Straus & Giroux, Inc. from *The Lottery* by Shirley Jackson. Copyright 1949 by Shirley Jackson. Reprinted by permission of Brandt & Brandt, N.Y. ELIZABETH JENNINGS, "Answers." From *A Way of Looking* by Elizabeth Jennings. Copyright © 1955 by Elizabeth Jennings. Reprinted by permission of Holt, Rinehart and Winston, Inc. Reprinted by permission of David Higham Associates, Ltd. JUDSON JEROME, "Negative," from *Light In The West,* The Golden Quill Press, Francestown, N.H., 1962. Reprinted by permission of The Golden Quill Press. Excerpts from THE JERUSALEM BIBLE, copyright © 1966 by Darton, Longman & Todd, Ltd., and Doubleday & Company, Inc. Used by permission of the publishers. NELS JULEUS, excerpted from "Akrestomije, Ergahergahmah, and Ohe." Reprinted by permission from *ETC: A Review of General Semantics,* Vol. XXIII, No. 3; copyright 1966, by the International Society for General Semantics. STEVEN KELMAN, "You Force Kids to Rebel," *The Saturday Evening Post,* November 19, 1966. Reprinted by permission of Steven Kelman. GYORGY KEPES, "Sculptured Volumes, Pencils, and Points," excerpted from "Light as a Creative Medium," *Arts & Architecture,* October, 1966. Copyright by Gyorgy Kepes. Reprinted by permission of Gyorgy Kepes and *Arts & Architecture.* HANK KETCHAM, *Dennis The Menace.* "Reprinted by permission of Publishers-Hall Syndicate. All rights reserved." ALEXANDER KING, excerpted from *Mine Enemy Grows Older,* Signet Books, 1960. Reprinted by permission of Simon and Schuster, Inc. Reprinted by permission of Laurence Pollinger Limited from *Mine Enemy Grows Older,* William Heinnemann Ltd., London. Still from KING KONG, p. 275, bottom. The Museum of Modern Art/Film Stills Archive. 21 West 53rd Street, N.Y.C. RUDYARD KIPLING, "The Story of Muhammad Din." "The Story of Muhammad Din" from *Plain Tales from the Hills* by Rudyard Kipling. Reprinted by permission of Mrs. George Bambridge and Doubleday & Company, Inc., and Macmillan & Company Ltd. PAUL KLEE, *Picture Album (Bilderbogen).* The Phillips Collection, Washington. THEODORA KROEBER, excerpted from *Ishi,* University of California Press, Berkeley, Calif. Reprinted by permission of University of California Press. Still from THE LONELINESS OF A LONG DISTANCE RUNNER, p. 273, bottom. Courtesy of The Walter Reade Organization. LEE FRANK LOWE, "Writers on Learning to Write," *English Journal,* October, 1964. Reprinted with the permission of the National Council of Teachers of English and Lee Frank Lowe. ARCHIBALD MACLEISH, "Hemingway." From *The Wild Old Wicked Man and Other Poems* by Archibald MacLeish, Houghton Mifflin Company, Boston, 1968. Copyright © 1966, 1968 by Archibald MacLeish. Reprinted by permission of Houghton Mifflin Company and Archibald MacLeish. Stills from A MAN AND A WOMAN, pp. 271, bottom; 273, top; 274, top. Courtesy of Allied Artists Pictures Corporation. JOHN MASEFIELD, "Sea Fever." Reprinted with permission of The Macmillan Company from *Poems* by John Masefield. Copyright 1912 by The Macmillan Company renewed 1940 by John Masefield. Permission to include the poem has been granted by the Society of Authors as the literary representative of the Estate of John Masefield. PETER MAYNE, "A Mezedaki in Athens," originally published as "Beware of a Crocodile Bag," from *Pick of Punch,* 1961; *Punch,* November 2, 1960. © Punch Publications Limited. Reprinted by permission of Punch Publications Limited. HENRY MOORE, *Woman* 1957/8. Reprinted by permission of the British Council, London. HENRY MORGAN, "The Comma." From Martin Levin's "Phoenix Nest," *Saturday Review.* Reprinted by permission of Martin Levin. OGDEN NASH, "More About People." Copyright, 1931, by Ogden Nash. From *Verses From 1929 On* by Ogden Nash, by permission of Little, Brown and Co. Reprinted by permission of J. M. Dent & Sons Ltd. HOWARD NEMEROV, "Life Cycle of Common Man." From *New and*

Selected Poems, cprt. by the University of Chicago, 1960. Reprinted by permission of Margot Johnson Agency. NEUSCHWANSTEIN CASTLE. Photograph courtesy of Pan American Airways. NEW PUNCTUATION MARK, excerpt. Courtesy *Time*, The Weekly Newsmagazine; Copyright Time Inc. 1967. Stills from THE NOSE, pp. 242-243. Contemporary Films, Inc. 267 West 25th Street, New York, N.Y. 10001. Used by permission of McGraw-Hill Films. Still from N.Y., N.Y., p. 275, top. The Museum of Modern Art/Film Stills Archive. 21 West 53rd Street, N.Y.C. Stills from AN OCCURRENCE AT OWL CREEK BRIDGE, pp. 54, 210, 213, 214, 215. Contemporary Films, Inc. 267 West 25th Street, New York, N.Y. 10001. Used by permission of McGraw-Hill Films. SEAN O'FAOLAIN, "Admiring the Scenery." From *The Finest Stories of Sean O'Faolain* by Sean O'Faolain, by permission of Atlantic-Little, Brown and Co. Copyright 1932, 1938, by The Viking Press. Copyright 1948, by The Devin-Adair Company. Copyright, ©, 1941, 1949, 1953, 1954, 1956, 1957, by Sean O'Faolain. Reprinted by permission of Mr. Sean O'Faolain and Rupert Hart-Davis Ltd. from *The Finest Stories of Sean O'Faolain.* DICK OLDDEN, cartoon, p. 165, *Look* Magazine, February 21, 1967. Reprinted by permission of Dick Oldden. SUSAN ORR, photograph, p. 104, right. Reprinted by permission of Susan Orr. GEORGE ORWELL, excerpted from "Why I Write." From "Why I Write" in *Such, Such Were The Joys* by George Orwell, copyright, 1945, 1952, 1953, by Sonia Brownell Orwell. Reprinted by permission of Harcourt, Brace & World, Inc. Reprinted by permission of Miss Sonia Brownell Orwell and Secker & Warburg Ltd. from "Why I Write" in *Such, Such Were The Joys* from *Modern Satire.* Reprinted by permission of A. M. Heath & Company Ltd. ROBERT OSBORN, Smile and words from *The Vulgarians*, New York Graphic Society Ltd., Greenwich, Conn. Reprinted by permission of Robert Osborn. PIDGIN AND KRIO, from The Times Literary Supplement, August 10, 1962. Reprinted by permission of The Times Literary Supplement. EZRA POUND, "Ancient Music." Ezra Pound, *Personae.* Copyright 1926, 1954 by Ezra Pound. Reprinted by permission of New Directions Publishing Corporation. Reprinted by permission of Faber and Faber Ltd. MARCEL PROUST, excerpted from "Prologue," from *On Art and Literature.* Copyright © 1958 by Meridian Books, Inc. Translation by Sylvia Townsend Warner © Chatto and Windus Ltd. 1957. Originally published in French by Librairie Gallimard, Paris, 1954, under the title *Contre Sainte-Beuve.* Reprinted by permission of The World Publishing Company. From *By Way of Sainte-Beuve* by Marcel Proust, translated by Sylvia Townsend Warner. Reprinted by permission of Chatto and Windus Ltd., London. Suggested by PAUL REPS, "captured snowflakes suffering," from *Zen Telegrams* by Paul Reps, copyright 1959. Reprinted by permission of Charles E. Tuttle Co., Inc., Rutland, Vt.; "A Cup of Tea," "The Moon Cannot Be Stolen," and "Strawberries," from *Zen Flesh, Zen Bones,* Charles E. Tuttle Co., Inc., Tokyo, 1957. Reprinted by permission of Charles E. Tuttle Co., Inc. KENNETH REXROTH, "A Lemma by Constance Reid." Kenneth Rexroth: *Natural Numbers.* © 1963 by Kenneth Rexroth. Reprinted by permission of New Directions Publishing Corporation. MALVINA REYNOLDS, excerpted from "Little Boxes." Reprinted by permission of Schroder Music Company, Berkeley, Calif. ALBERTO RIZZO, photograph, p. 495. Reprinted from *Mademoiselle*, © 1967, Condé Nast Publications, Inc. Photograph by Alberto Rizzo. THEODORE ROETHKE, "Once More, The Round." "Once More, The Round," copyright © 1962 by Beatrice Roethke as Executrix of the Estate of Theodore Roethke, from *The Collected Poems of Theodore Roethke.* Reprinted by permission of Doubleday & Company, Inc. Reprinted by permission of Faber and Faber Ltd. from *Collected Poems.* CARL SANDBURG, "Buffalo Bill." From *Cornhuskers* by Carl Sandburg Copyright 1918 by Holt, Rinehart and Winston, Inc. Copyright 1946 by Carl Sandburg. Reprinted by permission of Holt, Rinehart and Winston, Inc. Reprinted by permission of Jonathan Cape Ltd. CHARLES SCHULZ, *Peanuts*, p. 41, © United Feature Syndicate, Inc. 1966. P. 316, © United Feature Syndicate, Inc. 1965. ROBERT SERVICE, "The Cremation of Sam McGee." Reprinted by permission of Dodd, Mead & Company, Inc. from *The Collected Poems of Robert Service.* Reprinted by permission of Ernest Benn Limited from *Collected Poems of Robert Service.* Reprinted from *The Collected Poems of Robert Service* by Robert Service, by permission of The Ryerson Press, Toronto. BERNARD SHAW, "The Highest Form of Literature," originally printed as "I Become an Author," and "The Teaching of Art," from *The Wit and Wisdom of Bernard Shaw* by Bernard Shaw, Collier Books, N.Y., 1962. Reprinted by permission of The Macmillan Company, N.Y. WILLIAM SHURTLEFF, excerpted from "Igbo Language 'Delight' To Our Man In Nigeria," *Contra Costa Suns,* Lafayette, Calif., March 3 and 5, 1965. Reprinted by permission of *Contra Costa Suns.* ALFRED SMITH, *Tembo II.* Reprinted by permission of Alfred Smith. W. D. SNODGRASS, "The Marsh." Copyright, © 1957 by W. D. Snodgrass. Reprinted by permission of Alfred A. Knopf, Inc. from *Heart's Needle* by W. D. Snodgrass. "The Marsh" by W. D. Snodgrass is reprinted from *Heart's Needle* by permission of The Marvell Press, Hessle, Yorkshire, England. SAUL STEINBERG, Drawing by Steinberg, p. 84; © 1962. The New Yorker Magazine, Inc.; Drawing by Steinberg, p. 97; © 1963. The New Yorker Magazine, Inc. Reprinted by permission of Saul Steinberg and *The New Yorker.* Still from THE STORY OF A THREE DAY PASS, p. 276, top. Courtesy of Sigma III Corporation. FRANK SULLIVAN, "A Garland of Ibids." Reprinted by permission; Copr. © 1941 The New Yorker Magazine, Inc. MAY SWENSON, "The Key to Everything." "The Key to Everything" (Copyright 1949 May Swenson) is reprinted with the permission of Charles Scribner's Sons from *To Mix With Time* by May Swenson. JOHN SZARKOWSKI, excerpted from *Introduction* from *The Photographer's Eye* by John Szarkowski, copyright 1966 by The Museum of Modern Art, N.Y. Reprinted by permission of The Museum of Modern Art. THE TERTE HAND. Reprinted by permission of The Trustees of The British Museum, London. MIKE THALER, cartoon, p. 377. Reprinted by permission of Mike Thaler. DYLAN THOMAS, "A Dearth of Comic Writers." Dylan Thomas, *Quite Early One Morning.* Copyright 1954 by New Directions. Reprinted by permission of New Directions Publishing Corporation. Reprinted by permission of J. M. Dent & Sons Ltd. and the Trustees for the Copyrights of the late Dylan Thomas. LAWRANCE THOMPSON, excerpted from *Robert Frost: The Early Years.* From *Robert Frost: The Early Years* by Lawrance Thompson. Copyright © 1966 by Lawrance Thompson. Reprinted by permission of Holt, Rinehart and Winston, Inc. Reprinted by permission of Jonathan Cape Limited. THOR, p. 132. "Reg. TM, Copyright © 1967 Marvel Comics Group All Rights Reserved." JAMES THURBER, excerpted from "Draft Board Nights." From "Draft Board Nights," in *My Life and Hard Times,* Copr. © 1933, 1961 James Thurber. Published by Harper and Row. Originally printed in *The New Yorker.* Reprinted by permission of Helen Thurber. And from *Vintage Thurber* by James Thurber copyright © 1963 Hamish Hamilton, London. Reprinted by permission of Hamish Hamilton Ltd. CALVIN TOMKINS, "Zen In The Art Of Tennis." Reprinted by permission; © 1959 The New Yorker Magazine, Inc. Still from THE TRIAL, p. 271, top. Courtesy of Brandon Films. HOMER ULRICH, excerpted from *Music: A Design for Listening,* Harcourt, Brace & World, Inc. Reprinted by permission of Harcourt, Brace & World, Inc. JOHN UPDIKE, excerpted from *The Centaur.* Reprinted by permission of Alfred A. Knopf, Inc. from *The Centaur* by John Updike. Copyright © 1962, 1963 by John Updike. Reprinted by permission of Andre Deutsch Limited; "Wife Wooing." Copyright, © 1960 by John Updike. This story first appeared in *The New Yorker.* Reprinted by permission of Alfred A. Knopf, Inc. from *Pigeon Feathers and Other Stories* by John Updike. Reprinted by permission of Andre Deutsch Limited. WILLIAM CARLOS WILLIAMS, "Smell!" and "Between Walls." William Carlos Williams, *Collected Earlier Poems.* Copyright 1938 by William Carlos Williams. Reprinted by permission of New Directions Publishing Corporation. Reprinted by permission of MacGibbon & Kee Ltd., London. TOM WOLFE, "Clean Fun at Riverhead." From *The Kandy Kolored Tangerine Flake Streamline Baby* by Tom Wolfe, Copyright © 1963 by the Herald Tribune, Inc. Reprinted with the permission of Jonathan Cape Ltd., and Farrar, Straus & Giroux, Inc. Still from WOMAN IN THE DUNES, p. 274, bottom. Courtesy of Contemporary Films/McGraw-Hill. FRANK LLOYD WRIGHT, excerpted from "Faith in your own Individuality." Reprinted by permission of the publisher, Horizon Press, from *Frank Lloyd Wright, His Life, His Work, His Words* by Olgivanna Lloyd Wright. Copyright 1966. WILLIAM BUTLER YEATS, excerpt from "Among School Children." Reprinted with permission of The Macmillan Company from *Collected Poems* by William Butler Yeats. Copyright 1928 by The Macmillan Company, renewed 1956 by Georgie Yeats. Reprinted by permission of Mr. M. B. Yeats and Macmillan & Co. Ltd. CESARE ZAVATTINI, "The Cinema Should Never Turn Back." Reprinted by permission of Cesare Zavattini. Adapted from MERLA ZELLERBACH, "Essence—A New Guess Who Game." Reprinted by permission of *San Francisco Chronicle* and Merla Zellerbach. The authors gratefully acknowledge the following artists who contributed to the book: Aaron Heller, Jeheber & Peace, Inc., Charles Kaplan, Ruth Kaplan, Richard Kaseler, Ray Nania, Ben Schonzeit, and Charles Walker.

a rich, manifold life,
brought close to our eyes

—Johann Wolfgang von Goethe

There is only ONE WAY
in which
a person
acquires a
NEW IDEA:
by the combination
or association
of two or more ideas
he already has
into
a new
JUXTAPOSITION
in such a manner
as to discover
a relationship
among them
of which
he was not previously
aware.
AN IDEA IS A FEAT OF ASSOCIATION.

O body swayed to music,
O brightening glance,
How can we know the dancer
from the dance?

sallipesh
morked
had
his
lampix
bliffles
when
baslurker
the
the
ciptally
plomy
and
up
felmed
coofed
the

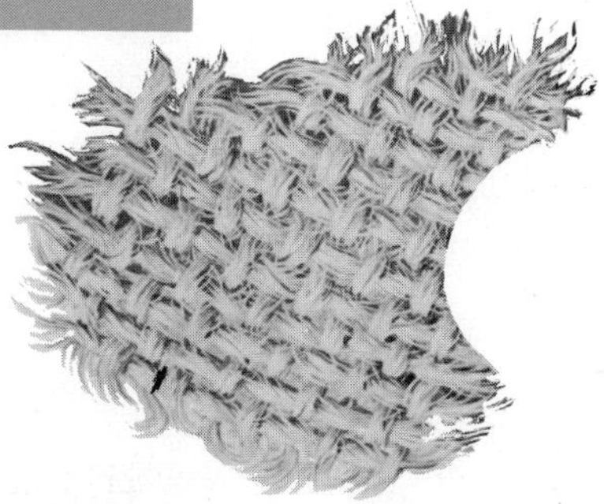

Let us go and make our visit.

Cut out the words in the list and make one English sentence using all the words. Use each word in the list one time only. You should get a seventeen-word sentence that you think sounds like English.

there

When you are finished, explore the significance of the experiment. You will have to allow yourself time to be creative (at least half an hour), to perform "feats of association," to turn things over in your mind. You will develop more stimulating ideas if you free your mind to play with possibilities. If the exploration feels like work, you will probably get rather dull results.

is

If you are not successful after half an hour or so, an exchange of viewpoints with other students may open some new possibilities.

(We would like you to find some connections with the lines of poetry at the top of the page, too.)

only

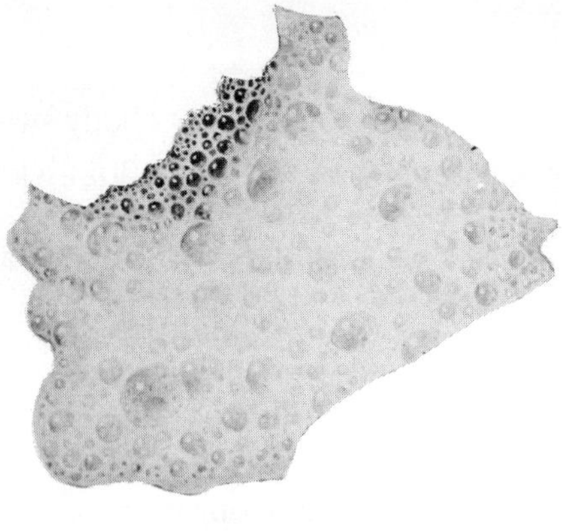

Home Cosmography

one

Here is a contrasting set of words. Try to make a sentence using all the words in the list. Then see what afterthoughts you can create by comparing your experiences with the two lists. See what you and other students can discover (dis-cover, uncover).

wallet
blenk
eventually
frowned
woman
discovered
lawyer
quine
gint
spoke
korg
tiv
lovely
boog
hilo
ideas
klee

way

> The writer can only be fertile if he renews himself and he can only renew himself if his soul is constantly enriched by fresh experiences.

The trouble with fresh experiences is that they tend to fade quickly. Such writers as Joyce, Thoreau, Flaubert, Maugham, Camus kept journals. Many writers regularly collect scraps of interest from their day to day experiences. They use their journals to capture ideas, bits of conversation, insights and images. Writers explore their journals and use them as wells from which to draw when they write.

Journal keeping is a practice not only of writers but of systematic thinkers in all walks of life (Madame Curie, Dag Hammarskjöld, Winston Churchill, Paul Klee, Eric Hoffer) who like to have their thoughts anchored long enough to get at them, tinker with them, combine them, rearrange them, synthesize them. A journal can be a verbal laboratory.

But our students have taught us a further use for a journal: not only can it be a place to record finished ideas or the raw material for ideas; it can also be a place in which to explore and create. We realized after it had happened several times that some of the most stimulating journals from our students had been not a record of their conclusions, but their thoughts *in progress.* We realized that we were being permitted to watch the development of novel ideas. The journal was a record of a student's mental conversation with himself. We could see the excitement of the writer as he approached the flash of insight. As he explored the implications of ideas generated in class, as he turned over various possibilities that occurred, he would write down the progress of his thoughts.

> *Direct your eye right inward, and you'll find*
> *A thousand regions in your mind*
> *Yet undiscovered. Travel them, and be*
> *Expert in home-cosmography.*

Such journals turned out to be certainly the richest in stimulating new views of the material we had been exploring, but they were also well ordered, logically patterned and clearly expressed. They were seldom dull.

in which

the vacant,
vast surrounding

These writers had intuitively worked out a system for focusing their attention on the data, for exploring its implications, for keeping their thoughts from fading away.

filament, filament, filament out of itself

The use of a journal has proven to be such a valuable tool for many of our students that we suggest it as a regular means of exploring and synthesizing the material in this book.

a

Here is what one student said about using a journal:

I have not been thinking in this fashion for very long. About half a semester. I'd like to think that the capacity was always there though.
Occasionally in the past I've had flashes of this new intellectual awakening — they were few and far between. It takes more maturity than I had then to dis-organize the world as I have here.
Feels like? Strange you should ask that because that's just what surprises me most about myself. How I feel about it. It becomes almost physical (but then we can't even separate mental and

physical) but anyway my body reacts. Tension builds sort of. Some of the things I've written staggers me with their implications.

Often I have to go back and see what I've written. The words just pour out, but the more I look at them the better they are. Its almost like an alien mind lurking within me. Probably just lil ole me unfettering itself.

There will be occasions when you will want to examine some particular item closely, others when you feel the need to generalize, to synthesize. Ultimately a synthesis of the whole book should emerge. Toward this end you will find regular journal entries quite helpful.

person

You will probably want to keep a working journal in which you do not let mechanics slow up your thoughts. If you want your instructor to examine your ideas, you should probably prepare a more polished proofread version. Should you be asked to write in other forms such as short stories, poems, or essays, you will find that a regularly kept journal will be a rich collection of ideas and materials.

As for your success with this book, it will depend on your learning to analyze and synthesize and getting the knack of when to do which.

till the ductile anchor hold

seeking the spheres to connect them......

Write out the following passage in modern English. See what you can discover and what relationships you can make.

And the whole earth was of one language and one speech.

And it came to pass, as they journeyed from the east, that they found a plain in the land of Shinar; and they dwelt there.

And they said to one another, Go to, let us make brick, and burn them thoroughly. And they had brick for stone, and slime had they for morter.

And they said, Go to, let us build us a city and a tower, whose top may reach unto heaven; and let us make us a name, lest we be scattered abroad upon the face of the whole earth.

And the Lord came down to see the city and the tower, which the children of men builded.

And the Lord said, Behold, the people is one, and they have all one language; and this they begin to do: and now nothing will be restrained from them, which they have imagined to do.

Go to, let us go down, and there confound their language, that they may not understand one another's speech.

So the Lord scattered them abroad from thence upon the face of all the earth: and they left off to build the city.

Therefore is the name of it called Babel; because the Lord did there confound the language of all the earth: and from thence did the Lord scatter them abroad upon the face of all the earth.

Were all languages one? Where did the thousands of languages spoken around the world come from? Why are there different languages?

ceaselessly musing, venturing, throwing

Casey would waltz with the strawberry blond
And the band played on.

How many shades of meaning for each of the following words can you discover by selecting various contexts for them? For example: I saw a *pink* elephant. He's a *pink*o. I drank a *pink* lady. (Note *lady* in this context also.) He had a bouquet of *pinks*. She has a pair of *pink*ing shears.

acquires

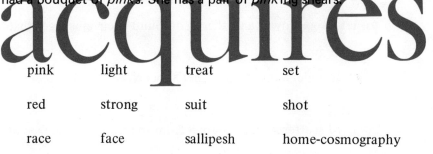

pink	light	treat	set
red	strong	suit	shot
race	face	sallipesh	home-cosmography

a

What other words can you think of that change in degrees of meaning when put in various contexts?

What color *is* "red"? Look around your classroom. Are any two "reds" the same? Is there actually *a* color "red," or does it refer to a range of colors?

As scientists we realise that colour is merely a question of the wave-lengths of aethereal vibrations; but that does not seem to have dispelled the feeling that eyes which reflect light near the wave-length of 4800 are subject for rhapsody whilst those which reflect wave-length 5300 are left unsung.

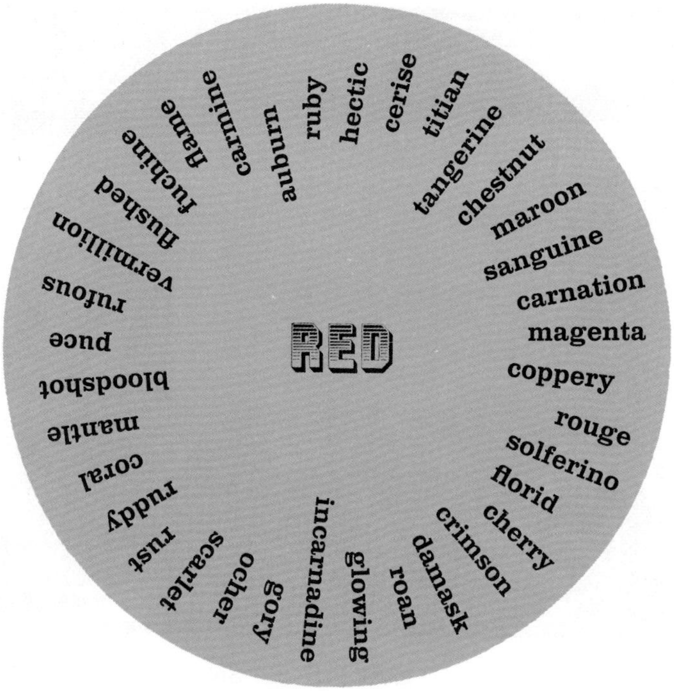

Is definition, or accuracy, the only consideration in language? If so, wouldn't it be more accurate to say, "That sweater is 6500; this tomato is 6400"? Or do we choose words to give the feeling as well? To give the listener an idea of what it is "like"?

When would it be best to speak of wave length 6575?

When *magenta*?

new

When *red*?

Are the important things in our lives poetic or scientific? Or are magenta and wave length 7000 both attempts at accuracy? What is the difference? Do we need both? And what of red? Is it poetic or scientific or what?

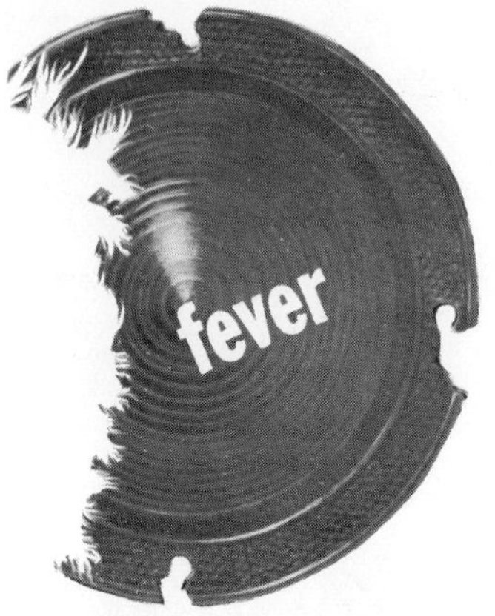

CAPTURED SNOWFLAKES, SUFFERING

idea:

When I "picture" a snowflake (photograph it, draw it, *label* it), do I hold it still, so to speak, to look at it? Does this picturing tend to deny it as a process, something going on?

In what sense are the "snowflakes" above *captured*? In what sense *suffering*?

Are clichés (apple-polisher) captured snowflakes "suffering"?

Are dead metaphors (leg of a table) captured snowflakes "suffering"?

Can you see a way in which language could be thought of as captured snowflakes?

Now turn the whole idea upside down. Can you think of a way in which picturing snowflakes releases them? A way in which language releases the world it refers to?

NATURE IS NOT
AS NATURAL AS IT LOOKS

A CONNEC
ING ORGA

HORSESHOE, INCOME, ISSUE

By the

Try this:

Say this word aloud: *horse*

Now say this: *shoe*

Now listen closely as you say the two together: *horseshoe*

Did you notice what happened to the part spelled *se*?

Say *income.* Then have someone read the sentence "He paid his income tax." In the phrase *income tax* did he pronounce it *ing/come tax*?

In Britain *issue* is often pronounced *iss·you*. In America it often sounds like *ish·you.*

For the three examples above can you figure out why we have a tendency toward the pronunciations pointed out?

Does the picture of the speech organs on page 18 suggest to you a possible physical reason? What happens in your mouth when you go from the *se* in *horse* to the *sh* in *shoe*? In *in/come* versus *ing/come tax*, which position of the tongue is closer to the /k/ sound in *come*, that of *in* or *ing*?

A lot of fun is made of "uneducated" people who slur words or run them together. As you think over the above three examples would you tend to say that these "uneducated" people are responding to the formation of sounds in a natural or unnatural manner? Can an educated person avoid slurring words together in his normal speech as, for example, when he says "horseshoe"? Would he sound normal if he did force a distinction?

Can you see this tendency to simplify pronunciation difficulties at work, for example, in the gradual shift from *day's eye* to *daisy*?

BILIN

The Web of Kinship

The relationship system . . . is based on actual relations of consanguinity and affinity that can be traced by means of the genealogical knowledge preserved by old men and women. The recognition of relationships is so extended that everyone with whom an individual comes in contact in the ordinary course of social life is his relative. It is impossible for a man to have any social relations with anyone who is not his relative because there is no standard by which two persons in this position can regulate their conduct toward one another. I am compelled to treat a person differently according as he is my "brother," "brother-in-law," "father," or "uncle." If I do not know which of these he is, all intercourse is impossible.

When (for example) a stranger comes to a camp that he has never visited before, he does not enter the camp, but remains at some distance. A few of the older men, after a while, approach him, and the first thing they proceed to do is to find out who the stranger is.

on

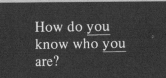

How do *you* know who *you* are?

The commonest question that is put to him is "Who is your *maeli*?" (father's father). The discussion proceeds on genealogical lines until all parties are satisfied of the exact relation of the stranger to each of the natives present in the camp. When this point is reached, the stranger can be admitted to the camp, and the different men and women are pointed out to him and their relation to him defined. I watched two or three of these discussions in

Everything's relative

West Australia. I took with me on my journey a native of the Talainji tribe, and at each native camp we came to, the same process had to be gone through. In one case, after a long discussion, they were still unable to discover any traceable relationship between my servant and the men of the camp. That night my "boy" refused to sleep in the native camp, as was his usual custom, and on talking to him, I found that he was frightened. These men were not his relatives, and they were therefore his enemies. This represents the real feelings of the natives on the matter. If I am a blackfellow and meet another blackfellow, that other must be either my relative or my enemy. If he is my enemy I shall take the first opportunity of killing him, for fear he will kill me.

sociation

A KINSHIP PUZZLE

A couple have four children. The oldest we will designate A, the second B, the third C, and the youngest D. In any language each member of such a family would have some term available by which he might refer to each of his fellows in such a family group. The terms of course differ from language to language. Are there also deeper differences in the bases on which distinctions are made? The following tabulation gives the terms in three languages. Ascertain for each what is the most probable basis of classification.

	English	*Kâte*	*Futuna*
A is B's	brother	hahaʔ	kave
C's	brother	hahaʔ	soa
D's	brother	hahaʔ	kave
B is A's	sister	gba	kave
C's	sister	hahaʔ	kave
D's	sister	hahaʔ	soa
C is A's	brother	gba	soa
B's	brother	gba	kave
D's	brother	hahaʔ	kave
D is A's	sister	gba	kave
B's	sister	gba	soa
C's	sister	gba	kave

Kâte is the language of the Territory of New Guinea. Futuna is spoken in the New Hebrides in the South Pacific.

Consider the problem of translating from each of these languages to the others. What problems would be presented by a simple one-word-equivalent bilingual dictionary between each pair of languages?

a language is, in a sense, a philosophy.
a language is, in a sense, a philosophy.

EVERYTHING'S RELATIVE.

"What is this doing in an English book? This doesn't seem like English. It looks like biology. What does it have to do with *this* course?"

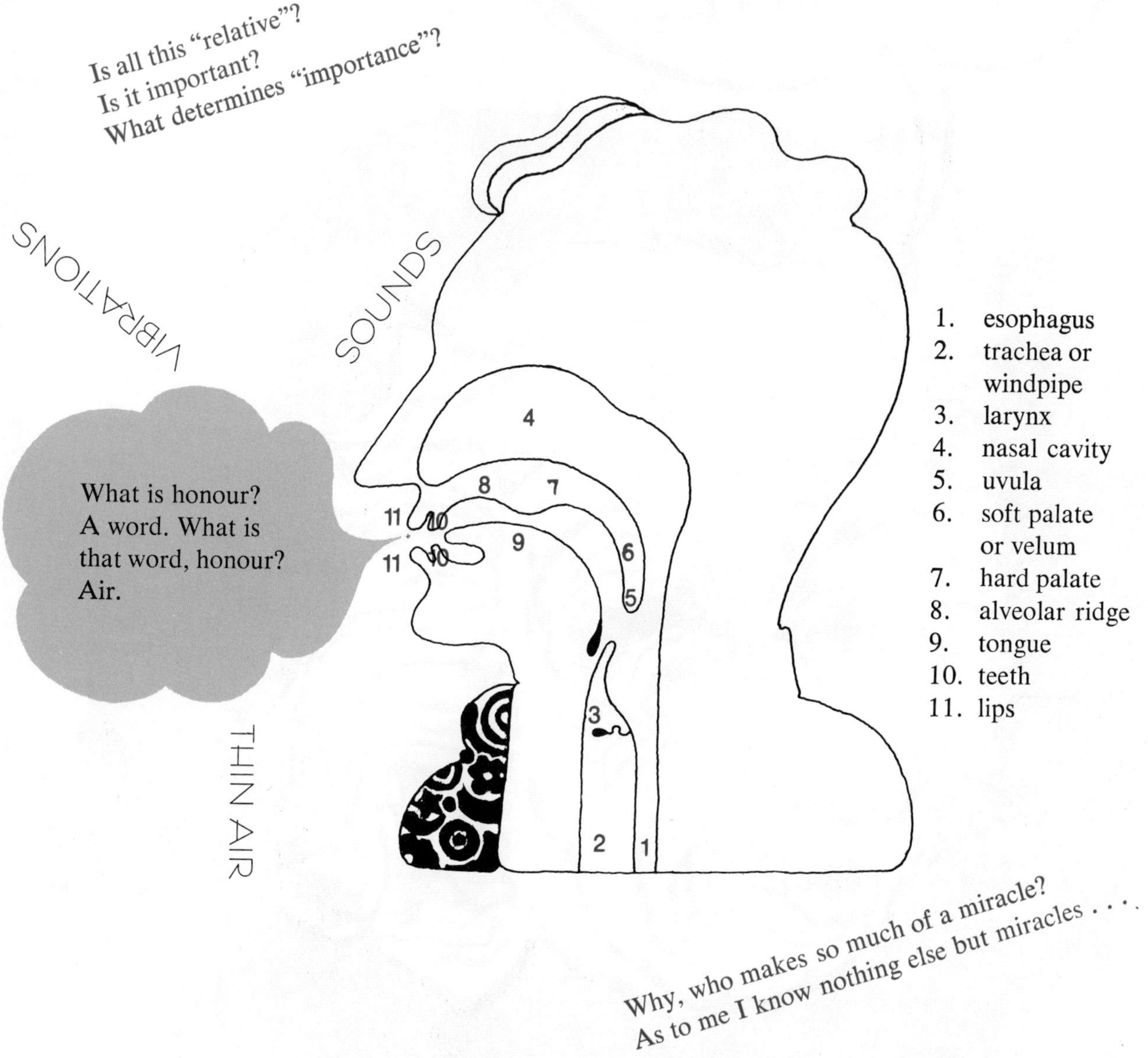

Is all this "relative"?
Is it important?
What determines "importance"?
VIBRATIONS
SOUNDS
What is honour?
A word. What is
that word, honour?
Air.
THIN AIR
1
2
3
4
5
6
7
8
9
10
11
1. esophagus
2. trachea or windpipe
3. larynx
4. nasal cavity
5. uvula
6. soft palate or velum
7. hard palate
8. alveolar ridge
9. tongue
10. teeth
11. lips
Why, who makes so much of a miracle?
As to me I know nothing else but miracles . . . .

Are the physical organs shown here *for* language, or is that use *added* to their *basic* function?

# of two

MIRACLES

Bit and *pit* are pronounced in approximately the same manner, but there is one difference English speakers consider significant. You can discover the specific difference by holding a lighted match about five inches from your mouth as you say first *bit* and then *pit.* (You might have to try this more than once.)

Sip and *zip* are pronounced in approximately the same manner, but there is one difference English speakers consider significant. You can discover what is done differently and where by holding your hands over your ears and saying first *sip* and then *zip.*

You can carry out similar experiments with such pairs as *bad* and *bat, bum* and *bun, thin* and *then.* Where and how are the distinctions made?

How did we learn to make these distinctions?

METAPHOR—An Implied Comparison

Words are things and living things, too.

Is paper or metal in one sense a metaphor for sheep or cows?

Is "bread" for some speakers now a metaphor for money?

> "My diabetes prevents my watching old Shirley Temple movies."

Does this comment rest on a metaphor? Is the metaphor more alive than that in "leg of a table"? (Are *rest* and *alive* used metaphorically here?)

or more

See if you can realize (*real*-ize) metaphors in the following:

hare lip · the iron curtain · saw horse · nerves of steel · eggplant · dust bowl · soft shoulders on a highway · foot of a mountain

Days' Eye   Daisy

Bud·get, from the French *bougette*—wallet, a small leather bag.

Per·son·al·i·ty, from the Latin *persona*—actor's mask. Is your personality you, or is it a mask your self wears?

Does the knowledge of the metaphors asleep in these words tend to enrich them for you? Do you real-ize them more? Is *realize* itself a metaphor?

When I say my heart is a pump, am I speaking metaphorically? What is a pump, then? A heart? (Which came first?) What about the "eye" of a needle? The "eye" of the night? Seeing "eye to eye"?

ideas

Notice the involvement of metaphor in the relatively simple "Bill is mad as a hornet." Isn't "mad" a word applied normally not to hornets but to people? Thus, first a transition of "mad" from people to hornets. The buzzing hornet seems "mad." And then back to people again: "Bill is mad as a hornet."

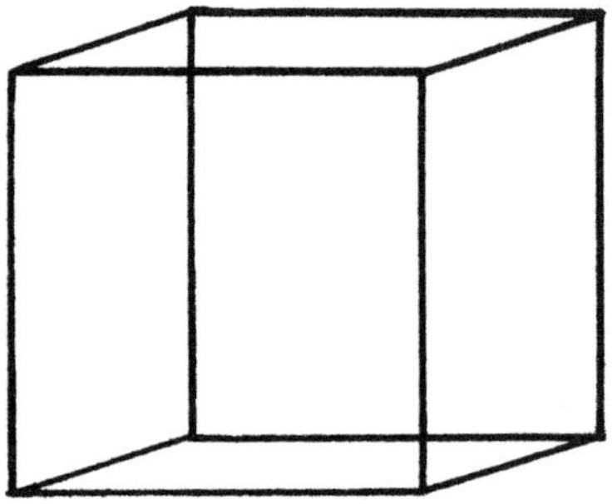

Is there a sense in which the picture above is a metaphor for a box? (Try putting something in it!)

Is *this* also a metaphor for a box?

Where is the land of make-believe?

When we say, "John's a bear this morning," it is easy to see the metaphoric nature of the statement.

But in "John's a boy," can "boy" be thought of in a sense as a metaphor for John? Is there a sense in which "John" itself is a metaphor for the essence to which it points?

he

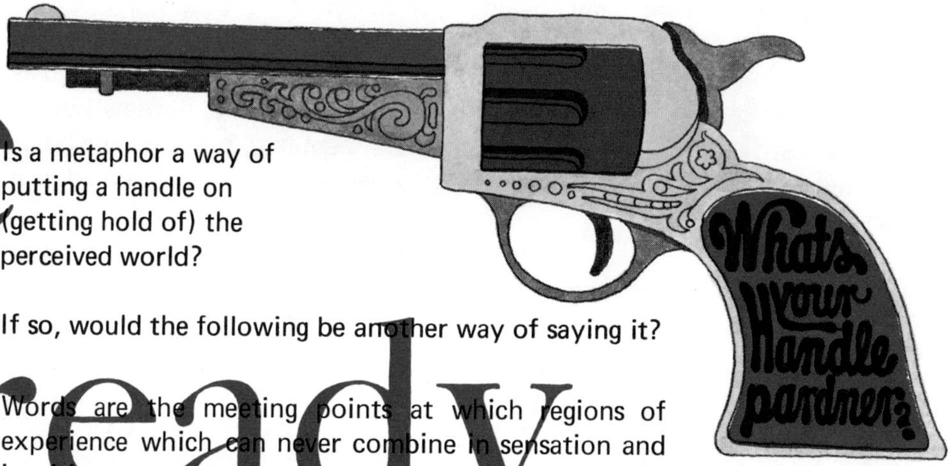
Whats your Handle pardner?

Is a metaphor a way of putting a handle on (getting hold of) the perceived world?

If so, would the following be another way of saying it?

already

Words are the meeting points at which regions of experience which can never combine in sensation and intuition come together.

Does "The fire is *dying*" illustrate the quotation above?

WORDS ARE MATRICES

Is this a metaphor?

An idea is a feat of association.
A metaphor is a feat of association.

Therefore, a metaphor is an idea?

has

Is thinking the process of creating metaphors?

Is thinking creating? Then, is the uncreative person a non-thinker? Or are all people creative?

ON FIRST LOOKING INTO CHAPMAN'S HOMER

Much have I travelled in the realms of gold,
And many goodly states and kingdoms seen;
Round many western islands have I been
Which bards in fealty to Apollo hold.
Oft of one wide expanse had I been told
That deep-browed Homer ruled as his demesne;
Yet did I never breathe its pure serene
Till I heard Chapman speak out loud and bold:
Then felt I like some watcher of the skies
When a new planet swims into his ken;
Or like stout Cortez when with eagle eyes
He stared at the Pacific--and all his men
Looked at each other with a wild surmise--
Silent, upon a peak in Darien.

TO FIST, TO WALL, TO FLASH

Normally we think of a fist as a thing. Could it be thought of as a process? (Make a fist and then relax it. Isn't "fist" something your hand is doing?) Perhaps "to fist" would be more accurate?

Knowing that modern physics sees the world as a system of vibrations, can we think of "walling," as some Indian tribes have it, rather than "the wall"? Could "nounness" be an illusion based on perception which doesn't notice the activity going on?

Are *you* a noun or a verb, something static and permanent or something going on, a process? Does which way you see it make a difference?

When we see a phenomenon in the night sky, is it more logical to say, as English speakers do, "A light flashed," or simply to say as the Nootka do, "flashed"? Is there really any noun quality to what we see going on in the sky? For that matter, is there really any *verb* quality to it?

Is view A of the figure on the left more correct than view B?

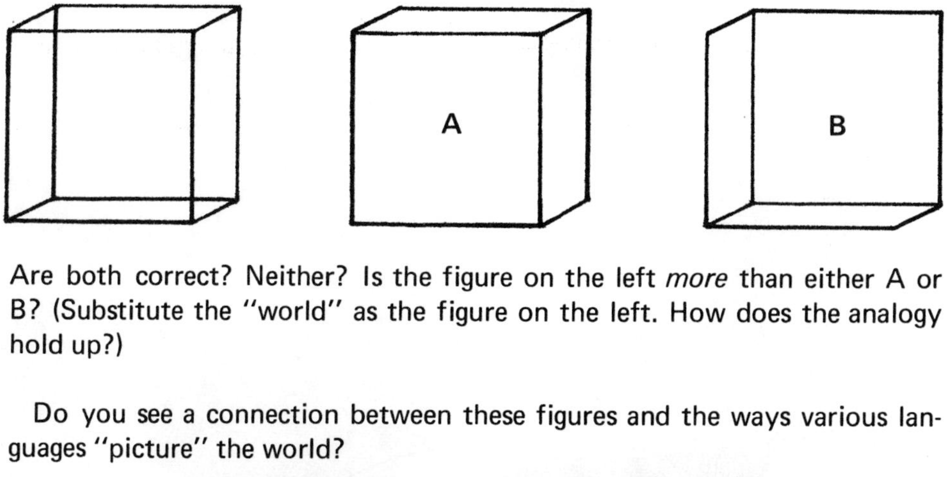

Are both correct? Neither? Is the figure on the left *more* than either A or B? (Substitute the "world" as the figure on the left. How does the analogy hold up?)

Do you see a connection between these figures and the ways various languages "picture" the world?

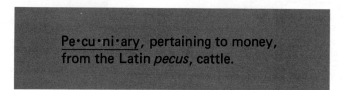

Pe•cu•ni•ary, pertaining to money,
from the Latin *pecus*, cattle.

VOCABULARY QUIZ

____ 1. Fidelity

____ 2. Orphan

____ 3. Birth

____ 4. Happiness

____ 5. Friendship

____ 6. Apologize

____ 7. Novel

____ 8. Learning

____ 9. Success

____ 10. War

____ 11. Truce

____ 12. Martyr

____ 13. Love

____ 14. Conservative

____ 15. Neighbor

____ 16. Mine

____ 17. Faith

A. Friendship.

B. The first and direst of disasters.

C. An agreeable sensation arising from contemplating the misery of another.

D. One whom we are commanded to love as ourselves, and who does all he knows how to make us disobedient.

E. A statesman who is enamored of existing evils, as distinguished from the Liberal, who wishes to replace them with others.

F. Belief without evidence in what is told by one who speaks without knowledge, of things without parallel.

G. A short story padded.

H. The kind of ignorance distinguishing the studious.

I. A ship big enough to carry two in fair weather but only one in foul.

J. Belonging to me if I can hold or seize it.

K. A temporary insanity curable by marriage.

L. The one unpardonable sin against one's fellows.

M. One who moves along the line of least reluctance to a desired death.

N. A by-product of the arts of peace.

O. To lay the foundation for a future offence.

P. A living person whom death has deprived of the power of filial ingratitude.

Q. A virtue peculiar to those who are about to be betrayed.

A Quiz on the Quiz

The lexicographer is a

a. cynic
b. satirist
c. humorist
d. realist
e. romantic
f. all of the above
g. none of the above

WORKING, DANCING, BUTTERFLIES AND WIRE

Certain Indian tribes are said to use the same word for "dancing" and "working". . . In their scheme of things dance and agriculture serve essentially the same purpose of providing the means of livelihood. The growth and prosperity of their crops seem to them to depend as much or more on the correct performance of their dances, their magical and religious ceremonies, than on prompt and proper attention to the soil. . . .

"When the natives along the Swan River in Africa were first introduced to the sacrament of Communion, they called it a dance."

Knowing something of the African uses of the dance, can you see how these Swan River natives might have seen a "logical" connection between the dance and Communion?

Can you see how the Indians might have connected dancing and working as approximately the same thing?

juxtapositio

Can you conclude that all human perception involves "grouping"?

"In the Kâte language which is current in New Guinea, there is a word *bilin* which denotes a certain kind of grass with tough stems and roots that are wedged firmly in the soil; the latter are said to hold the earth together during earthquakes, so that it does not break apart." Obviously, when nails were first introduced by Europeans and when their use became popularly known, the natives called them ____. They called wire and iron rods, in short anything that served the purpose of holding things together ____.

Is this principle operative when a small child calls a stranger "Daddy"? When he sees a peculiarly shaped piece of driftwood and says "Ghost"?

The Cora Indian classes butterflies and airplanes as birds.

Is there a natural logic to all groupings or are they arbitrary—dependent upon connections the viewer "sees"?

Is "boy" such a grouping of many observed "objects" seen as *the same*? Then, is "Mary is a girl" a purely arbitrary grouping? Is "girl" something in nature or something we do *to* nature? A handle on the world?

A SYNTHESIS FOR YOUR JOURNAL

- Think over the area you have been exploring in the last seven pages and see if you can pull it all together into some synthesis *for you*. What are you learning *about*? What happens in you as you explore? Does any sort of feeling accompany your discoveries? Let your mind play over the various observations you have made. What does it mean to you?

in such

Tie this section in with other sections you have explored. Is it related or chaotic? Can you make something meaningful of all you have done so far?

n

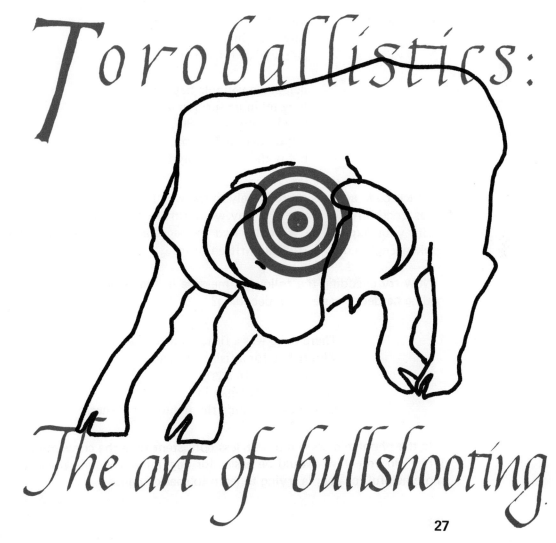

Toroballistics:

The art of bullshooting

Why, who makes much of miracles?

In this code there are thirteen more symbols than in our twenty-six symbol code. Are twenty-six symbols adequate? Should an efficient code have such spelling possibilities as *ghoti* and *ghoughteighteau*? Does this suggest a reason for the additional symbols?

Here are two messages written in the phonemic code. Is their difficulty apparent or real? What does this tell us about old dogs? Try reading the two messages. Most of the consonants are conventional. Write out the messages in our conventional spelling and symbols. If your version differs from your classmates' in some way, see if you can determine the reason.

a manner

betiy hæd ə bit əv bitər bətər
hwic meyd ər bætər bitər.
shiy gat ə bit əv betər bətər
ən meyd ər bitər bætər betər

ðer wəz ə yəŋ felə neymd hɔl
huw fel in ðə spriŋ in ðə fɔl.
twud əv bin ə sæd θiŋ,
if iyd dayd in ðə spriŋ,
bət iy didənt, hiy dayd in ðə fɔl.

Which code adheres more closely to the way English sounds when spoken? Does English really sound the way we normally see it represented in print? From your experience with the two messages above, what are some ways spoken English differs from its written form?

as to

Now try encoding the following message in the phonemic symbols. Is encoding harder or easier than decoding?

There once was a fisher named Fisher
who fished for a fish in a fissure,
but the fish with a grin
pulled the fisherman in;
now they're fishing the fissure for Fisher.

Is the phonemic code more or less consistent than the conventional code? Which do you think would be easier for beginning readers? Which would be more helpful for people trying to learn to speak English?

A PHONEMIC CODE

Symbols used by many linguists in transcribing some of the sounds of English:

/ p /	pin	/ pin /
/ k /	kin	/ kin /
/ b /	bin	/ bin /
/ f /	fin	/ fin /
/ t /	tin	/ tin /
/ d /	din	/ din /
/ g /	gill	/ gil /
/ c /	chin	/ cin /
/ j /	jill	/ jil /
/ v /	veal	/ viyl /
/ r /	rip	/ rip /
/ s /	sip	/ sip /
/ z /	zip	/ zip /
/ š /	shoot	/ šuwt /
/ ž /	pleasure	/ pležər /
/ h /	heel	/ hiyl /
/ m /	mum	/ məm /
/ n /	nun	/ nən /
/ η /	rung	/ rəη /
/ l /	lace	/ leys /
/ w /	wet	/ wet /
/ y /	yet	/ yet /
/ θ /	thin	/ θin /
/ ð /	then	/ ðen /

/ i /	pin, bin	/ pin / , / bin /
/ e /	pet, set	/ pet / , / set /
/ æ /	pat, sat	/ pæt /, /sæt /
/ a /	pot, sot	/ pat / , / sat /
/ ə /	putt, but	/ pət / , / bət /
/ u /	put, foot	/ put / , / fut /
/ o /	boat, moat	/ bot / , / mot /
/ ɔ /	bought, fought	/ bɔt / , / fɔt /
/ ey /	late, bait	/ leyt / , / beyt /
/ iy /	pete, me	/ piyt / , / miy /
/ ay /	buy, tie	/ bay / , / tay /
/ aw /	cow, how	/ kaw / , / haw /
/ ɔy /	toy, joy	/ tɔy / , / jɔy /
/ uw /	boot, you	/ buwt / , / yuw /

discover

In the conventional "code" how many sounds can you recall associated with the symbol *a*? How many does that symbol represent here? In the conventional code do other symbols also represent some of the sounds associated with *a*?

How many sounds in the conventional code are associated with *g*? How many does *g* represent here?

Why are two symbols (θ,ð) provided where only *th* appears in the conventional code?

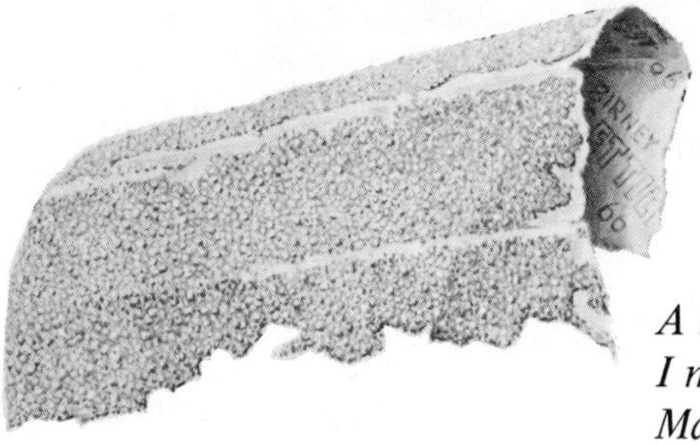

A NOISELESS PATIENT SPIDER

A noiseless patient spider,
I marked where on a little promontory it stood isolated,
Marked how to explore the vacant vast surrounding,
It launched forth filament, filament, filament, out of itself,
Ever unreeling them, ever tirelessly speeding them.

And you O my soul where you stand,
Surrounded, detached, in measureless oceans of space,
Ceaselessly musing, venturing, throwing, seeking the spheres
to connect them,
Till the bridge you will need be form'd, till the ductile anchor
hold,
Till the gossamer thread you fling catch somewhere, O my soul.

a relationship among them

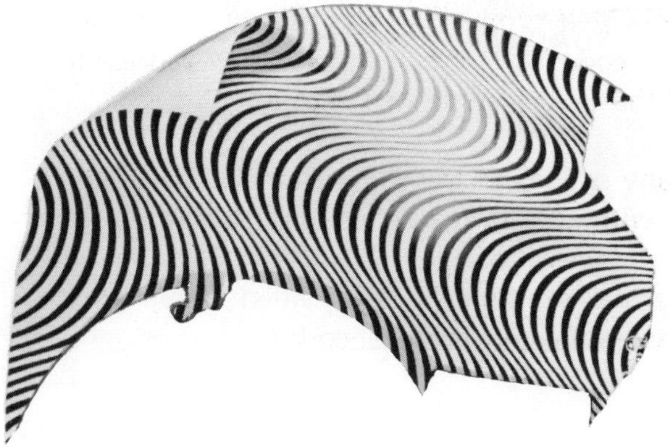

ghoti = fish
gh as in laugh
o as in women
ti as in notion

Ghoughteighteau could spell potato.
Try to figure out why

the dancer from the dance

THE MEDIUM IS THE MESSAGE

# of which

SYNTHESIS

Is there value in man's being aware of the habits he has been programmed for (forming sounds with his teeth, lips, lungs; using an alphabet, using patterns of a language)? Is a man who can only behave automatically in response to his culture really free? How many connections can you find between the investigation of the phonemic code and other investigations we have made? Pull them all together in your journal.

Hallowed be thy name

Oure Fadir

Urne gedæghwamlican

save us from the evil one

Write a passage of approximately thirty-five words. Then refer to a dictionary to discover what the origin of each word is. For example, "Write," ME; OE *writan*. This means that the present form of the word came into Middle English from the Old English word *writan*.

You will probably find that some words have different origins from others. What is the reason for this?

Group together the different kinds of origins. How many do you have of each? Is there one source which appears more dominant in your sample than others? Why do you think this is?

Now compare your list with those of your classmates. What similarities and differences do you notice?

MATRICES

Words cannot, and should not attempt to "hand over sensations bodily"; they have very much more important work to do. So far from verbal language being a "compromise for a language of intuition" – a thin, but better-than-nothing, substitute for real experience, – language, well used, is a completion and does what the intuitions of sensation by themselves cannot do. Words are the meeting points at which regions of experience which can never combine in sensation or intuition, come together. They are the occasion and the means of that growth which is the mind's endless endeavour to order itself. That is why we have language. It is no mere signalling system. It is the instrument of all our distinctively human development, of everything in which we go beyond the other animals.

Thus, to present language as working only through the sensations it reinstates, is to turn the whole process upside down. It overlooks what is important in Mallarmé's dictum that the poet does not write with thoughts (or with ideas or sensations or beliefs or desires or feelings, we may add) but with words. "Are not words," so Coleridge asked, "parts and germinations of the plant? And what is the law of their growth? In something of this sort," he wrote, "I would endeavour to destroy the old antithesis of Words and Things: elevating, as it were, Words into Things and living things too." We must do so if we are to study metaphor profitably. Hulme and the school teachers are forgetting everything that matters most about language in treating it as just a stimulus to visualization. They think the image fills in the meaning of the word; it is rather the other way about and it is the word which brings in the meaning which the image and its original perception lack.

he
was
not

As we look back over the nine hundred years separating Boswell's biography from Alfred's preface, we can see that, while the English language maintained its identity unbroken throughout this long period, it underwent changes which, though gradual, were so great as to be revolutionary. In grammar, it changed from a largely synthetic language, depending principally on inflectional markers to indicate syntactic relations, to an analytic one, depending principally on word order and function words. Its pronunciation went through two periods of radical change, which would make a speaker of Old English, if one should miraculously appear, totally unable to understand the language of Boswell's or our own day. During the first half of this period, the spelling system was adjusted from time to time to reflect the changes in pronunciation. But it became virtually fixed at a point representing the pronunciation of approximately the year 1400, so that modern spelling cannot be learned by ear. Finally, its vocabulary underwent two periods of extensive borrowing, from French in the thirteenth and fourteenth centuries and from Latin in the sixteenth and seventeenth. And even as Boswell wrote, the third period of extensive vocabulary change, resulting from the vast, scientific, intellectual, and technological revolutions of the nineteenth and twentieth centuries, was beginning.

previously aware.

Here are examples of the Lord's Prayer written in Old English, Middle English, Elizabethan English and Modern English:

Fæ̂der ure þu ðe eart on heofonum
si þin nama gehalgod.
Tobecume þin rice.
Gewurðe þin willa on eorðan
swa swa on heofonum.
Urne gedæ̂ghwamlican hlaf syle us to dæ̂g.
And forgyf us ure gyltas
swa swa we forgyfaþ urum gyltendum.
And ne gelæ̂d þu us on costnunge
ac alys us of yfele. Soðlice.

Our Father which art in heaven,
Hallowed be thy name.
Thy kingdom come.
Thy will be done in earth,
as it is in heaven.
Give us this day our daily bread.
And forgive us our debts,
as we forgive our debtors.
And lead us not into temptation,
but deliver us from evil:
For thine is the kingdom,
and the power, and the glory,
for ever. Amen.

Our Father in heaven,
may your name be held holy,
your kingdom come,
your will be done,
on earth as in heaven.
Give us today our daily bread.
And forgive us our debts,
as we have forgiven those who are in debt to us.
And do not put us to the test,
but save us from the evil one.

Oure Fadir that art in heuenes, halwid be thi name; thi kyngdom cumme to; be thi wille don as in heuen and in erthe; gif to vs this day oure breed ouer other substaunce; and forgeve to vs oure dettis, as we forgeve to oure dettours; and leede vs nat in to temptacioun, but delyuere vs fro yuel. Amen.

Below you will see a page of symbols referring to facial expressions from a book on kinesics. Examine the whole list. Then explore our questions which follow.

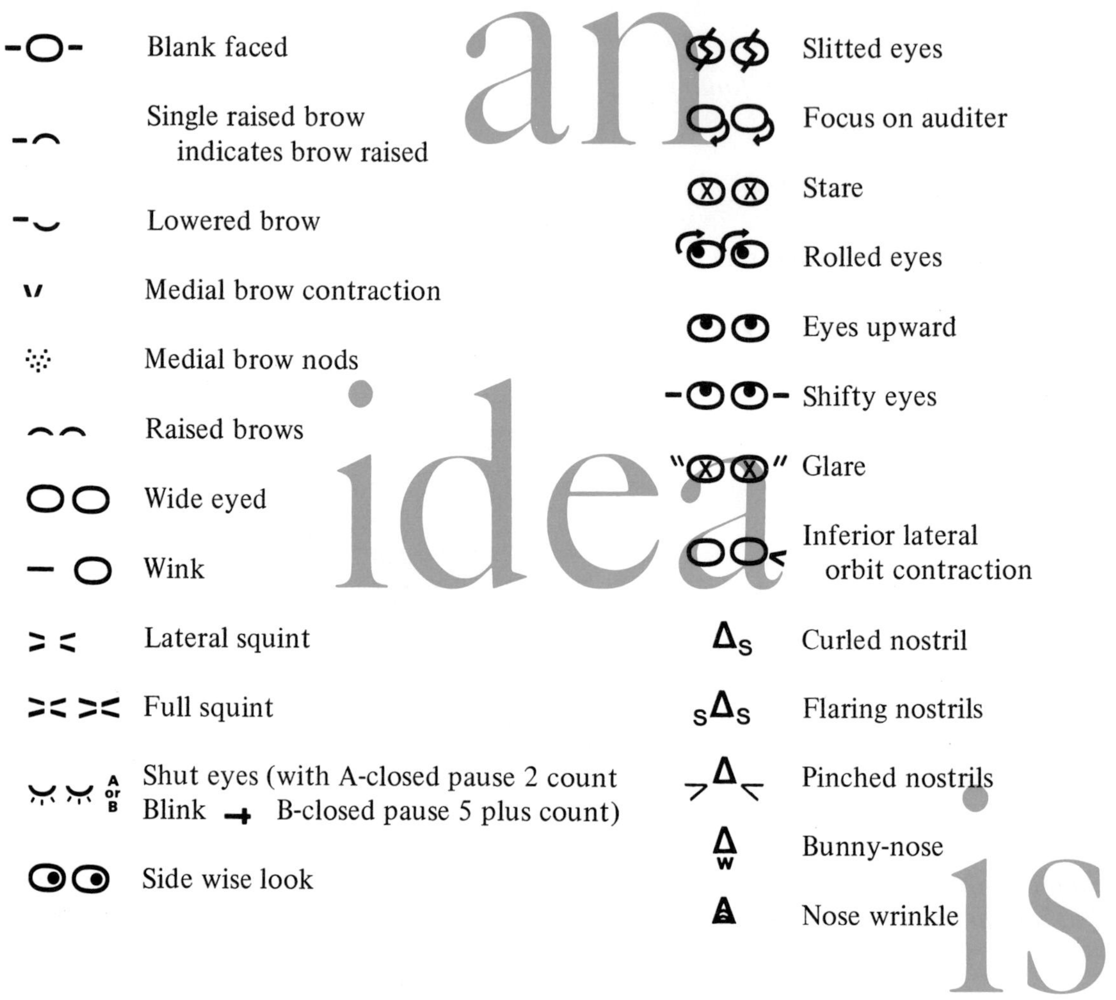

Take it at face value? How much <u>is</u> there in "face value"?

Are the facial expressions to which the chart refers elements of a "language"? Are these elements isolates of larger patterns? (What else goes with a wink?)

Is this a *learned* "language" or is it instinctive? (If any of your classmates have had experience with foreigners, see if they know of any expressions which would have a different meaning in a foreign country.)

How does this "language" affect the meaning of verbal messages?

How important are the patterns, compared with the isolates or "alphabet"?

Are facial expressions a "code"? Do you have to know the "code" in order to understand the meaning of facial expressions?

Try This:

Take ten minutes and write out what you see here so that someone else could imagine what this particular photograph looks like. Then compare your results with those of your classmates.

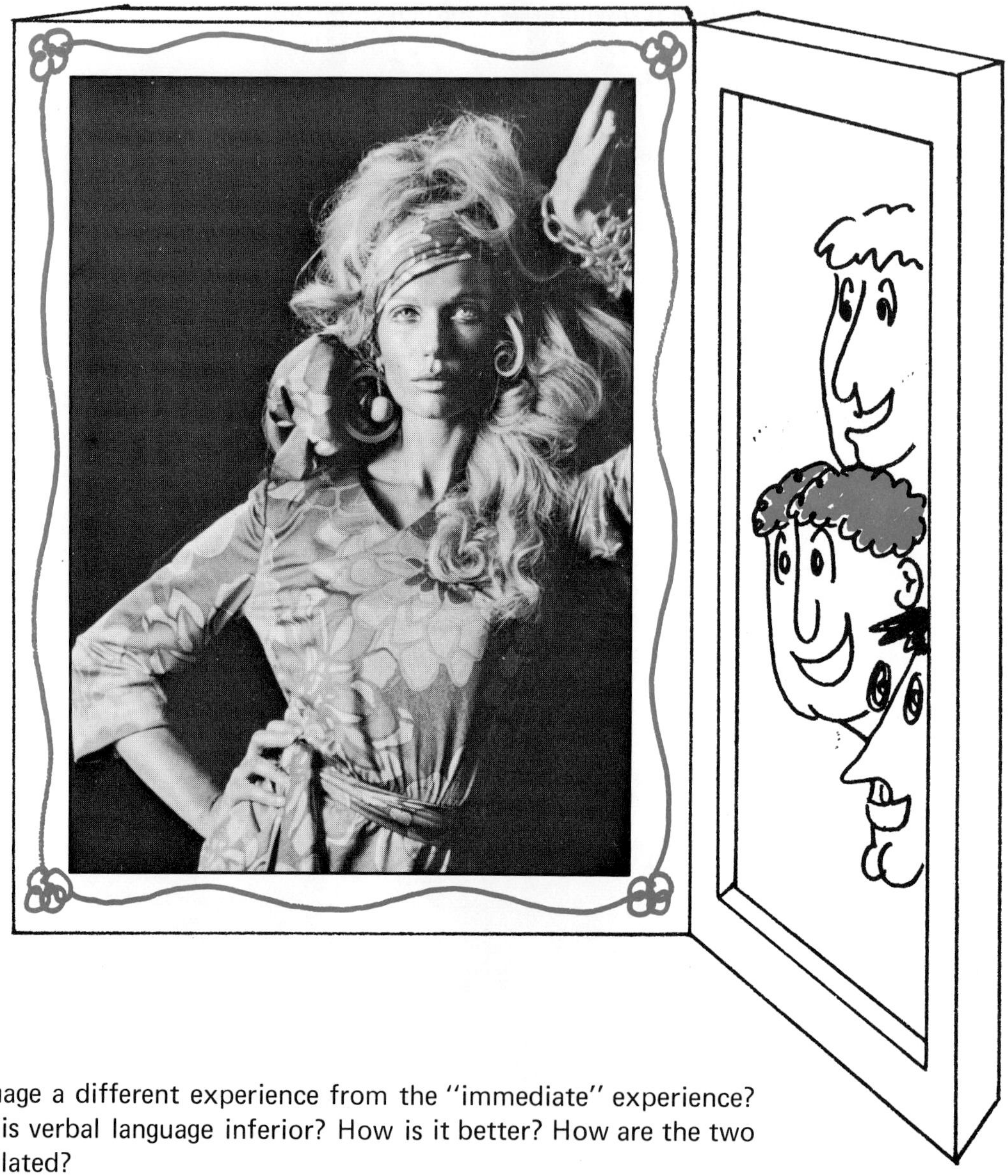

Is verbal language a different experience from the "immediate" experience? In what ways is verbal language inferior? How is it better? How are the two "languages" related?

What nonverbal cues do you perceive in this picture?

How many conventions (clichés) of our society can you find here?

Does the picture's "message" depend on your having learned certain nonverbal cues; that is, do you suppose an Eskimo would get the same message you get from the picture?

Do other members of your class get the same message?

Are there nonverbal "languages"; that is, is the "language" with which you "read" this message an arbitrary system? Do you have to know the code to read the picture?

of

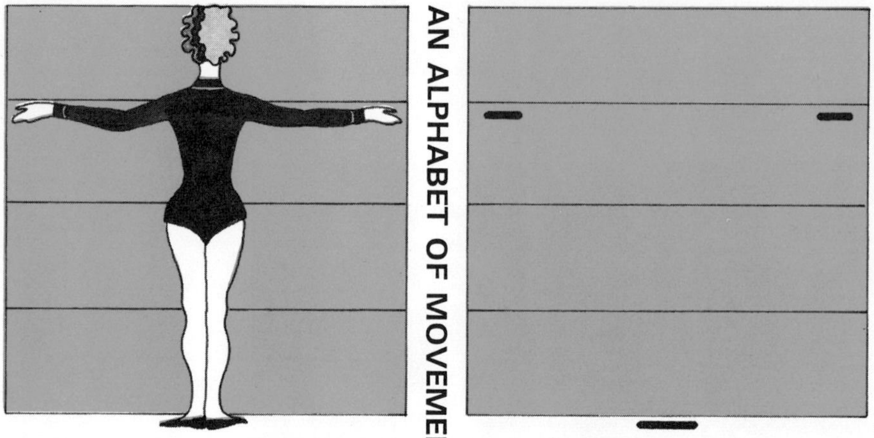

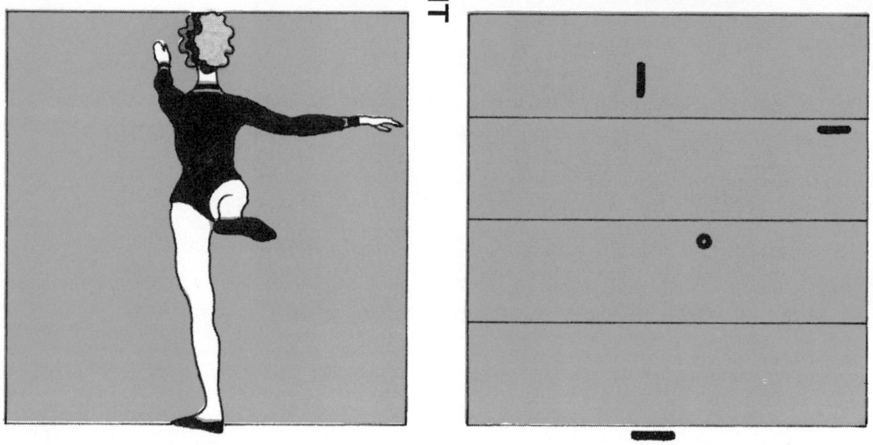

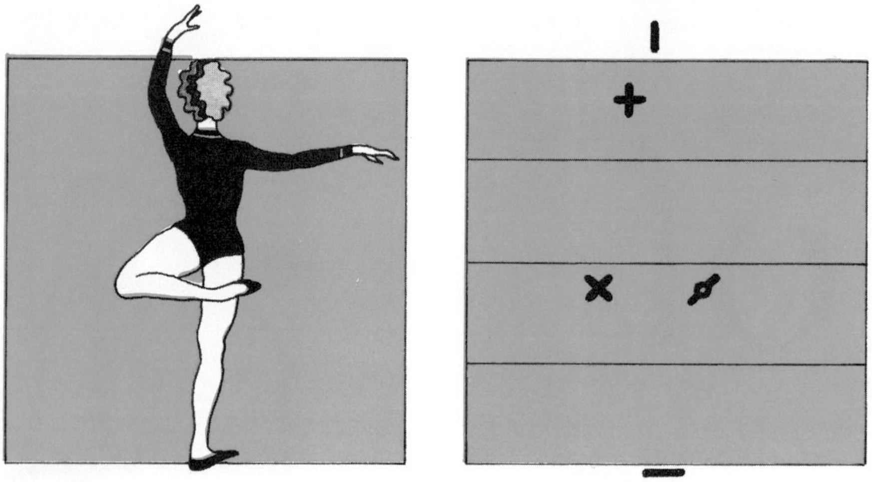

FACE

Level (with the body)	—
In front (of the body)	|
Behind (the body)	•

These three signs gave a complete, precise and nonambiguous record of the line of the limbs if these were straight as in Figure 2. If they were bent as in Figure 3, three other signs were used to mark the position of elbows and knees:

Level	+
In front	†
Behind	×

That was it. The six signs, used in conjunction with music's five line stave.

Figure 1 (top) The five-line stave as a matrix for the human figure

Figure 2 (center) Arabesque, with left arm extending to the front, and right leg to the back

Figure 3 (bottom) Attitude, The left hand and elbow are held slightly in front of the body, so are marked with a vertical line. A tick is put through the dot for the left foot because this crosses over to the right-hand side of the square

Here is a code of ballet movement. For what purpose do you think the code was invented? What might it be used for? Photographs contain more information than drawn figures and drawn figures more than the code. Why create a code? Why not use photographs? (Are the contents of your mind "encoded"? Abstractions?)

Check back through the book to see how many of the other exercises can be said to be dealing with a code. For example, what about the nonsense sentences you tried on pages 3 and 4.

association

What connection can you see between the drawing of a box and the picture of a box on page 21?

Does this *Peanuts* cartoon belong in this section? Is it a code? Is it an abstraction? Is it *better* than a photograph? Why? From what angle might cartooning be thought of as a "language"? What is the "grammar" of cartooning?

DYING WORDS OF DOMINIQUE BOUHOURS, the French Grammarian, (1628-1702): "I am about to—or I am going to—die: either expression is used."

In what sense is a child's drawing a statement? In what sense is it a probe?

Turn over in your mind the following quotations from various sources. Look at each one separately; let your mind play with it. Does it remind you of any of the ideas explored in this chapter? Is there any sense in which you can see it as true?

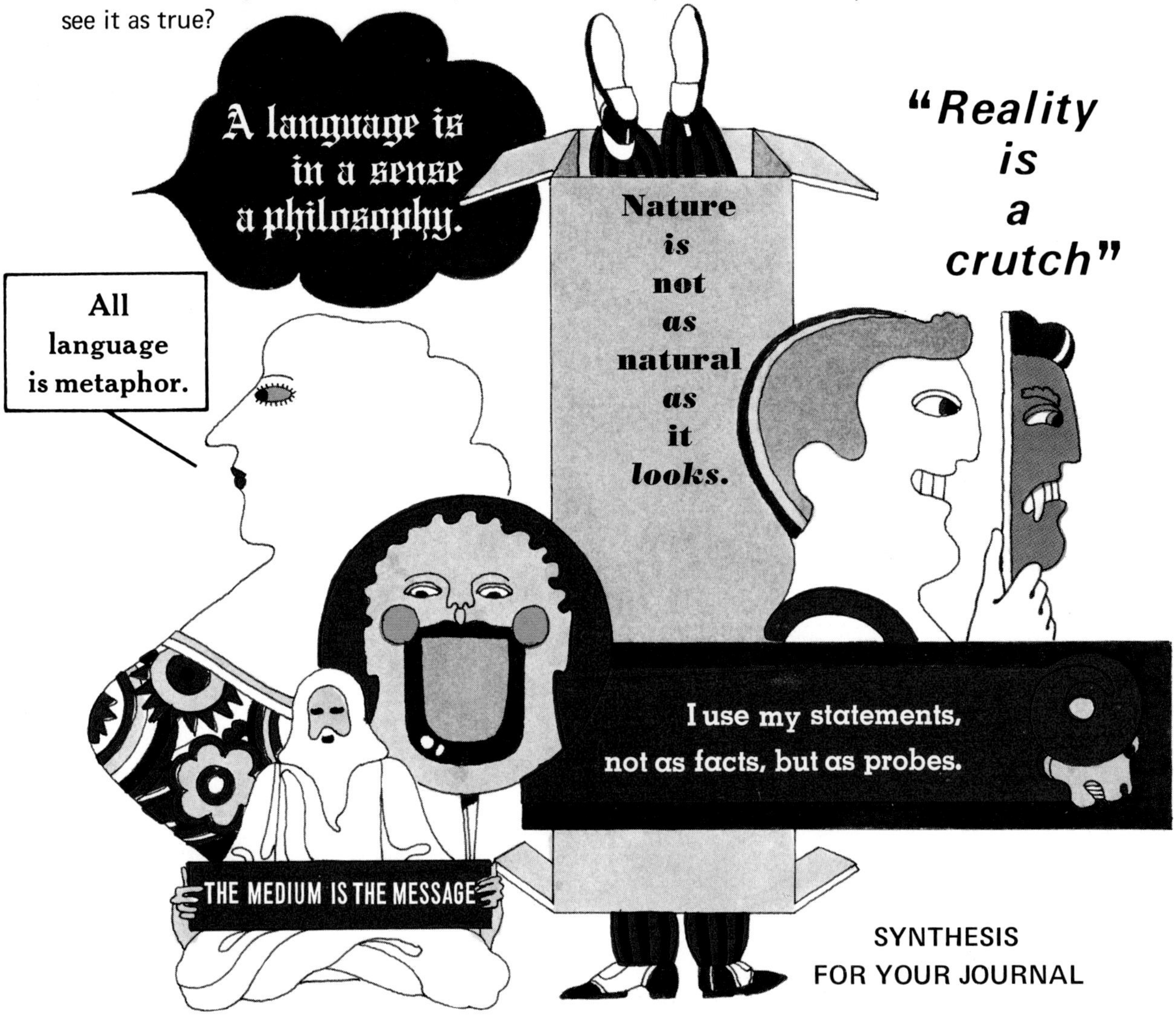
A language is in a sense a philosophy.
All language is metaphor.
Nature is not as natural as it looks.
"Reality is a crutch"
I use my statements, not as facts, but as probes.
THE MEDIUM IS THE MESSAGE

SYNTHESIS FOR YOUR JOURNAL

As your mind plays with these ideas see what they add up to; what picture is your mind forming?

Are your statements probes or clichés? What is the intent behind a cliché? What is the intent behind a probe?

Combination

A SYNTHESIS

After reading the story over once or twice and thinking about the various relationships, see if you can interrelate them in some meaningful way. Can the story be thought of as a synthesis for the whole section? In what ways does it extend the meaning of this section?

WIFE-WOOING

OH MY LOVE. Yes. Here we sit, on warm broad floorboards, before a fire, the children between us, in a crescent, eating. The girl and I share one half-pint of French fried potatoes; you and the boy share another; and in the center, sharing nothing, making simple reflections within himself like a jewel, the baby, mounted in an Easybaby, sucks at his bottle with frowning mastery, his selfish, contemplative eyes stealing glitter from the center of the flames. And you. You. You allow your skirt, the same black skirt in which this morning you with woman's soft bravery mounted a bicycle and sallied forth to play hymns in difficult keys on the Sunday school's old piano—you allow this black skirt to slide off your raised knees down your thighs, slide *up* your thighs in your body's absolute geography, so the parallel whiteness of their undersides is exposed to the fire's warmth and to my sight. Oh. There is a line of Joyce. I try to recover it from the legendary, imperfectly explored grottoes of *Ulysses:* a garter snapped, to please Blazes Boylan, in a deep Dublin den. What? Smackwarm. That was the crucial word. Smacked smackwarm on her smackable warm woman's thighs. Something like that. A splendid man, to feel that. Smackwarm woman's. Splendid also to feel the curious and potent, inexplicable and irrefutably magical life language leads within itself. What soul took thought and knew that adding "wo" to man would make a woman? The difference exactly. The wide w, the receptive o. Womb. In our crescent the children for all their size seem to come out of you toward me, wet fingers and eyes, tinted bronze. Three children, five persons, seven years. Seven years since I wed wide warm woman, white-thighed. Wooed and wed. Wife. A knife of a word that for all its final bite did not end the wooing. To my wonderment.

We eat meat, meat I wrestled warm from the raw hands of the hamburger girl in the diner a mile away, a ferocious place, slick with savagery, wild with chrome; young predators snarling dirty jokes menaced me, old men reached for me with coffee-warmed paws; I wielded my wallet, and won my way back. The fat brown bag of buns was warm beside me in the cold car; the smaller bag holding the two tiny cartons of French-fries emitted an even more urgent heat. Back through the black winter air to the fire, the intimate cave, where halloos and hurrahs greeted me, the deer, mouth agape and its cotton throat gushing, stretched dead across my shoulders. And now you, beside the white O of the plate upon which the children discarded with squeals of disgust, the rings of translucent onion that came squeezed into the hamburgers—you push your toes an inch closer to the blaze, and the ashy white of the inside of your deep thigh is lazily laid bare, and the eternally elastic garter snaps smackwarm against my hidden heart.

Who would have thought, wide wife, back there in the white tremble of the ceremony (in the corner of my eye I held, despite the distracting hail of ominous vows, the vibration of the cluster of stephanotis clutched against your waist), that seven years would bring us no distance, through all those warm beds, to the same trembling point, of beginning? The cells change every seven years and down in the atom, apparently there is a strange discontinuity; as if God wills the universe anew every instant. (Ah God, dear God, tall friend of my childhood, I will never forget you, though they say dreadful things. They say rose windows in cathedrals are vaginal symbols.) Your legs, exposed as fully as by a bathing suit, yearn deeper into the amber wash of heat. Well: begin. A green jet of flame spits out sideways from a pocket of resin in a log, crying, and the orange shadows on the ceiling sway with fresh life. Begin.

"Remember, on our honeymoon, how the top of the kerosene heater made a great big rose window on the ceiling?"

"Vnn." Your chin goes to your knees, your shins draw in, all is retracted. Not much to remember, perhaps, for you; blood badly spilled, clumsiness of all sorts. "It was cold for June."

"Mommy, what was cold? What did you say?" the girl asks, enunciating angrily, determined not to let language slip on her tongue and tumble her so that we laugh.

"A house where Daddy and I stayed one time."

"I don't like dat," the boy says, and throws a half bun painted with chartreuse mustard onto the floor.

You pick it up and with beautiful sombre musing ask, "Isn't that funny? Did any of the others have mustard on them?"

"I *hate* dat," the boy insists; he is two. Language is to him thick vague handles swirling by; he grabs what he can.

"Here. He can have mine. Give me his." I pass my hamburger over, you take it, he takes it from you, there is nowhere a ripple of gratitude. There is no more praise of my heroism in fetching Sunday supper, saving you labor. Cunning, you sense, and sense that I sense your knowledge, that I had hoped to hoard your energy toward a more ecstatic spending.

We sense everything between us, every ripple, existent and nonexistent; it is tiring. Courting a wife takes tenfold the strength of winning an ignorant girl. The fire shifts, shattering fragments of newspaper that carry in lighter gray the ghost of the ink of their message. You huddle your legs and bring the skirt back over them. With a sizzling noise like the sighs of the exhausted logs, the baby sucks the last from his bottle, drops it to the floor with its distasteful hoax of vacant suds, and begins to cry. His egotist's mouth opens; the delicate membrane of his satisfaction tears. You pick him up and stand. You love the baby more than me.

Who would have thought, blood once spilled, that no barrier would be broken, that you would be each time healed into a virgin again? Tall, fair, obscure, remote, and courteous.

We put the children to bed, one by one, in reverse order of birth. I am limitlessly patient, paternal, good. Yet you know. We watch the paper bags and cartons ignite on the breathing pillow of embers, read, watch television, eat crackers, it does not matter. Eleven comes. For a tingling moment you stand on the bedroom rug in your underpants, untangling your nightie; oh, fat white sweet fat fatness. In bed you read. About Richard Nixon. He fascinates you; you hate him. You know how he defeated Jerry Voorhis, martyred Mrs. Douglas, how he played poker in the Navy despite being a Quaker, every fiendish trick, every low adaptation. Oh my Lord. Let's let the poor man go to bed. We're none of us perfect. "Hey let's turn out the light."

"Wait. He's just about to get Hiss convicted. It's very strange. It says he acted honorably."

"I'm sure he did." I reach for the switch.

"No. Wait. Just till I finish this chapter. I'm sure there'll be something at the end."

"Honey, Hiss was guilty. We're all guilty. Conceived in concupiscence, we die unrepentant." Once my ornate words wooed you.

I lie against your filmy convex back. You read sideways, a sleepy trick. I see the page through the fringe of your hair; sharp and white as a wedge of crystal. Suddenly it slips. The book has slipped from your hand. You are asleep. Oh cunning trick, cunning. In the darkness I consider. Cunning. The headlights of cars accidentally slide fanning slits of light around our walls and ceiling. The great rose window was projected upward through the petal-shaped perforations in the top of the kerosene stove, which we stood in the center of the floor. As the flame on the circular wick flickered, the wide soft star of interlocked penumbrae moved and waved as if it were printed on a silk cloth being gently tugged or slowly blown. Its color soft blurred blood. We pay dear in blood for our peaceful homes.

In the morning, to my relief, you are ugly. Monday's wan breakfast light bleaches you blotchily, drains the goodness from your thickness, makes the bathrobe a limp stained tube flapping disconsolately, exposing a sallow décolletage. The skin between your breasts a sad yellow. I feast with the coffee on your drabness. Every wrinkle and sickly tint a relief and a revenge. The children yammer. The toaster sticks. Seven years have worn this woman.

The man, he arrows off to work, jousting for right-of-way, veering on the thin hard edge of the legal speed limit. Out of domestic muddle, softness, pallor, flaccidity: into the city. Stone is his province. The winning of coin.

The maneuvering of abstractions. Making heartless things run. Oh the inanimate, adamant joys of job!

I return with my head enmeshed in a machine. A technicality it would take weeks to explain to you snags my brain; I fiddle with phrases and numbers all the blind evening. You serve me supper as a waitress—as less than a waitress, for I have known you. The children touch me timidly, as they would a steep girder bolted into a framework whose height they don't understand. They drift into sleep securely. We survive their passing in calm parallelity. My thoughts rework in chronic right angles the same snagging circuits on the same professional grid. You rustle the book about Nixon; vanish upstairs into the plumbing; the bathtub pipes cry. In my head I seem to have found the stuck switch at last: I push at it; it jams; I push; it is jammed. I grow dizzy, churning with cigarettes. I circle the room aimlessly.

So I am taken by surprise at a turning when at the meaningful hour of ten you come with a kiss of toothpaste to me moist and girlish and quick; the momentous moral of this story being, An expected gift is not worth giving.

a rich, manifold life?

Authors' version of the limerick on page 28:

ðer wənts wəz ə fišər neymd fišər
huw fišt fər ə fiš in ə fišər,
bət ðə fiš wiθ ə grin
puld ðə fišərmən in;
naw ðer fisiŋ ðə fišər fər fišər.

Do you and your classmates agree on all the symbols? If not, how do you account for the differences?

Does this essay suggest a reason for the approach used in this book? Is autonomy desirable? Is it necessary? Do most texts value autonomy? Does this one?

AUTONOMY

The attainment of autonomy is manifested by the release of three capacities: awareness, spontaneity and intimacy.

Awareness: Awareness means the capacity to see a coffeepot and hear the birds sing in one's own way, and not the way one was taught.

out of itself

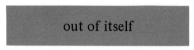

It may be assumed on good grounds that seeing and hearing have a different quality for infants than for grownups, and that they are more esthetic and less intellectual in the first years of life. A little boy sees and hears birds with delight. Then the "good father" comes along and feels he should "share" the experience and help his son "develop." He says: "That's a jay, and this is a sparrow." The moment the little boy is concerned with which is a jay and which is a sparrow, he can no longer see the birds or hear them sing. He has to see and hear them the way his father wants him to. Father has good reasons on his side, since few people can afford to go through life listening to the birds sing, and the sooner the little boy starts his "education" the better. Maybe he will be an ornithologist when he grows up. A few people, however, can still see and hear in the old way. But most of the members of the human race have lost the capacity to be painters, poets or musicians, and are not left the option of seeing and hearing directly even if they can afford to: they must get it secondhand.

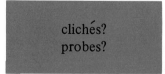

clichés?
probes?

The recovery of this ability is called here "awareness." Physiologically awareness is eidetic perception, allied to eidetic imagery. Perhaps there is also eidetic perception, at least in certain individuals, in the spheres of taste, smell and kinesthesia, giving us the artists in those fields: chefs, perfumers and dancers, whose eternal problem is to find audiences capable of appreciating their products.

> Oh strong ridged and deeply
> hollowed nose of mine . . . .

Awareness requires living in the here and now, and not in the elsewhere, the past or the future. A good illustration of possibilities, in American life, is driving to work in the morning in a hurry. The decisive question is: "Where is the mind when the body is here?" and there are three common cases.

1. The man whose chief preoccupation is being on time is the one who is furthest out. With his body at the wheel of his car, his mind is at the door of his office, and he is oblivious to his immediate surroundings except insofar as they are obstacles to the moment when his soma will catch up with his psyche. This is the Jerk, whose chief concern is how it will look to the boss.

> Are you reading
> this book like
> a jerk?

If he is late, he will take pains to arrive out of breath. The compliant Child is in command, and his game is "Look How Hard I've Tried." While he is driving, he is almost completely lacking in autonomy, and as a human being he is in essence more dead than alive. It is quite possible that this is the most favorable condition for the development of hypertension or coronary disease.

2. The Sulk, on the other hand, is not so much concerned with arriving on time as in collecting excuses for being late. Mishaps, badly timed lights and poor driving or stupidity on the part of others fit well into his scheme

and are secretly welcomed as contributions to his rebellious Child or righteous Parent game of "Look What They Made Me Do." He, too, is oblivious to his surroundings except as they subscribe to his game, so that he is only half alive. His body is in his car, but his mind is out searching for blemishes and injustices.

"I answered the questions,
didn't I?"

3. Less common is the "natural driver," the man to whom driving a car is a congenial science and art. As he makes his way swiftly and skillfully through the traffic, he is at one with his vehicle. He, too, is oblivious of his surroundings except as they offer scope for the craftsmanship which is its own reward, but he is very much aware of himself and the machine which he controls so well, and to that extent he is alive. Such driving is formally an Adult pastime from which his Child and Parent may also derive satisfaction.

The technician,
An A student.

4. The fourth case is the person who is aware, and who will not hurry because he is living in the present moment with the environment which is here: the sky and the trees as well as the feeling of motion. To hurry is to neglect that environment and to be conscious only of something that is still out of sight down the road, or of mere obstacles, or solely of oneself. A Chinese man started to get into a local subway train, when his Caucasian companion pointed out that they could save twenty minutes by taking an express, which they did. When they got off at Central Park, the Chinese man sat down on a bench, much to his friend's surprise. "Well," explained the former, "since we saved twenty minutes, we can afford to sit here that long and enjoy our surroundings."

"How will you get readers
to sit down and let themselves be creative?"

The aware person is alive because he knows how he feels, where he is and when it is. He knows that after he dies the trees will still be there, but he will not be there to look at them again, so he wants to see them now with as much poignancy as possible.

Spontaneity: Spontaneity means option, the freedom to choose and express one's feelings from the assortment available (Parent feelings, Adult feelings and Child feelings). It means liberation, liberation from the compulsion to play games and have only the feelings one was taught to have.

Can I liberate myself if the chains are invisible?

Intimacy: Intimacy means the spontaneous, game-free candidness of an aware person, the liberation of the eidetically perceptive, uncorrupted Child in all its naivete living in the here and now. It can be shown experimentally that eidetic perception evokes affection, and that candidness mobilizes positive feelings, so that there is even such a thing as "onesided intimacy"—a phenomenon well known, although not by that name, to professional seducers, who are able to capture their partners without becoming involved themselves. This they do by encouraging the other person to look at them directly and to talk freely, while the male or female seducer makes only a well-guarded pretense of reciprocating.

Who are you reading this *for*?

Because intimacy is essentially a function of the natural Child (although expressed in a matrix of psychological and social complications), it tends to turn out well if not disturbed by the intervention of games. Usually the adaptation to Parental influences is what spoils it, and most unfortunately this is almost a universal occurrence. But before, unless and until they are corrupted, most infants seem to be loving, and that is the essential nature of intimacy, as shown experimentally.

HOW FLOWERS CHANGED THE WORLD

A few nights ago it was brought home vividly to me that the world has changed since that far epoch [the close of the Age of Reptiles]. I was awakened out of sleep by an unknown sound in my living room. Not a small sound—not a creaking timber or a mouse's scurry—but a sharp, rending explosion as though an unwary foot had been put down upon a wine glass. I had come instantly out of sleep and lay tense, unbreathing. I listened for another step. There was none.

Unable to stand the suspense any longer, I turned on the light and passed from room to room glancing uneasily behind chairs and into closets. Nothing seemed disturbed, and I stood puzzled in the center of the living room floor. Then a small button-shaped object upon the rug caught my eye. It was hard and polished and glistening. Scattered over the length of the room were several more shining up at me like wary little eyes. A pine cone that had been lying in a dish had been blown the length of the coffee table. The dish itself could hardly have been the source of the explosion. Beside it I found two ribbon-like strips of a velvety-green. I tried to place the two strips together to make a pod. They twisted resolutely away from each other and would no longer fit.

I relaxed in a chair, then, for I had reached a solution of the midnight disturbance. The twisted strips were wistaria pods that I had brought in a day or two previously and placed in the dish. They had chosen midnight to explode and distribute their multiplying fund of life down the length of the room. A plant, a fixed, rooted thing, immobolized in a single spot, had devised a way of propelling its offspring across open space. Immediately there passed before my eyes the million airy troopers of the milkweed pod and the clutching hooks of the sandburs. Seeds on the coyote's tail, seeds on the hunter's coat, thistledown mounting on the winds—all were somehow triumphing over life's limitations. Yet the ability to do this had not been with them at the beginning. It was the product of endless effort and experiment.

The seeds on my carpet were not going to lie stiffly where they had dropped like their antiquated cousins, the naked seeds on the pine-cone scales. They were travelers. Struck by the thought, I went out next day and collected several other varieties. I line them up now in a row on my desk—so many little capsules of life, winged, hooked or spiked. Every one is an angiosperm, a product of the true flowering plants. Contained in these little boxes is the secret of that far-off Cretaceous explosion of a hundred million years ago that changed the face of the planet. And somewhere in here, I think, as I poke seriously at one particularly resistant seedcase of a wild grass, was once man himself.

When the first simple flower bloomed on some raw upland late in the Dinosaur Age, it was wind pollinated, just like its early pine-cone relatives. It was a very inconspicuous flower because it had not yet evolved the idea of using the surer attraction of birds and insects to achieve the transportation of pollen. It sowed its own pollen and received the pollen of other flowers by the simple vagaries of the wind. Many plants in regions where insect life is scant still follow this principle today. Nevertheless, the true flower—and the seed that it produced—was a profound innovation in the world of life.

In a way, this event parallels, in the plant

world, what happened among animals. Consider the relative chance for survival of the exteriorly deposited egg of a fish in contrast with the fertilized egg of a mammal, carefully retained for months in the mother's body until the young animal (or human being) is developed to a point where it may survive. The biological wastage is less—and so it is with the flowering plants. The primitive spore, a single cell fertilized in the beginning by a swimming sperm, did not promote rapid distribution, and the young plant, moreover, had to struggle up from nothing. No one had left it any food except what it could get by its own unaided efforts.

By contrast, the true flowering plants (angiosperm itself means "encased seed") grew a seed in the heart of a flower, a seed whose development was initiated by a fertilizing pollen grain independent of outside moisture. But the seed, unlike the developing spore, is already a fully equipped *embryonic plant* packed in a little enclosed box stuffed full of nutritious food. Moreover, by featherdown attachments, as in dandelion or milkweed seed, it can be wafted upward on gusts and ride the wind for miles; or with hooks it can cling to a bear's or a rabbit's hide, or like some of the berries, it can be covered with a juicy, attractive fruit to lure birds, pass undigested through their intestinal tracts and be voided miles away.

The ramifications of this biological invention were endless. Plants traveled as they had never traveled before. They got into strange environments heretofore never entered by the old spore plants or stiff pine-cone-seed plants. The well-fed, carefully cherished little embryos raised their heads everywhere. Many of the older plants with more primitive reproductive mechanisms began to fade away under this unequal contest. They contracted their range into secluded environments. Some, like the giant redwoods, lingered on as relics; many vanished entirely.

The world of the giants was a dying world. These fantastic little seeds skipping and hopping and flying about the woods and valleys brought with them an amazing adaptability. If our whole lives had not been spent in the midst of it, it would astound us. The old, stiff, sky-reaching wooden world had changed into something that glowed here and there with strange colors, put out queer, unheard-of fruits and little intricately carved seed cases, and, most important of all, produced concentrated foods in a way that the land had never seen before, or dreamed of back in the fish-eating, leaf-crunching days of the dinosaurs.

That food came from three sources, all produced by the reproductive system of the flowering plants. There were the tantalizing nectars and pollens intended to draw insects for pollenizing purposes, and which are responsible also for that wonderful jeweled creation, the hummingbird. There were the juicy and enticing fruits to attract larger animals, and in which tough-coated seeds were concealed, as in the tomato, for example. Then, as if this were not enough, there was the food in the actual seed itself, the food intended to nourish the embryo. All over the world, like hot corn in a popper, these incredible elaborations of the flowering plants kept exploding. In a movement that was almost instantaneous, geologically-speaking, the angiosperms had taken over the world. Grass was beginning to cover the bare earth until, today, there are over six thousand species. All kinds of vines and bushes squirmed and writhed under new trees with flying seeds.

The explosion was having its effect on animal life also. Specialized groups of insects were arising to feed on the new sources of food and, incidentally and unknowingly, to pollinate the plant. The flowers bloomed and bloomed in ever larger and more spectacular varieties. Some were pale unearthly night flowers intended to lure moths in the evening twilight, some among the orchids even took the shape of female spiders in order to attract wandering males, some flamed redly in the light of noon or twinkled modestly in the meadow grasses. Intricate mechanisms splashed pollen on the breasts of hummingbirds, or stamped it on the bellies of black, grumbling bees droning assiduously from blossom to blossom. Honey ran, insects multiplied, and even the descendants of that toothed and ancient lizard-bird had become strangely altered. Equipped with prodding beaks instead of biting teeth they pecked the seeds and gobbled the insects that were really converted nectar.

Across the planet grasslands were now spreading. A slow continental upthrust which had been a part of the early Age of Flowers had cooled the world's climates. The stalking reptiles and the leather-winged black imps of the seashore cliffs had vanished. Only birds roamed the air now, hot-blooded and high-speed metabolic machines.

The mammals, too, had survived and were venturing into new domains, staring about perhaps a bit bewildered at their sudden eminence now that the thunder lizards were gone. Many of them, beginning as small browsers upon leaves in the forest, began to venture out upon this new sunlit world of the grass. Grass has a high silica content and demands a new type of very tough and resistant tooth enamel, but the seeds taken incidentally in the cropping of the grass are highly nutritious. A new world had opened out for the warm-blooded mammals. Great herbivores like the mammoths, horses and bisons appeared. Skulking about them had arisen savage flesh-eating carnivores like the now extinct dire wolves and the saber-toothed tiger.

Flesh eaters though these creatures were, they were being sustained on nutritious grasses one step removed. Their fierce energy was being maintained on a high, effective level, through hot days and frosty nights, by the concentrated energy of the angiosperms. That energy, thirty per cent or more of the weight of the entire plant among some of the cereal grasses, was being accumulated and concentrated in the rich proteins and fats of the enormous game herds of the grasslands.

On the edge of the forest, a strange, old-fashioned animal still hesitated. His body was the body of a tree dweller, and though tough and knotty by human standards, he was, in terms of that world into which he gazed, a weakling. His teeth, though strong for chewing on the tough fruits of the forest, or for crunching an occasional unwary bird caught with his prehensile hands, were not the tearing sabers of the great cats. He had a passion for lifting himself up to see about, in his restless, roving curiosity. He would run a little stiffly and uncertainly, perhaps, on his hind legs, but only in those rare moments when he ventured out upon the ground. All this was the legacy of his climbing days; he had a hand with flexible fingers and no fine specialized hoofs upon which to gallop like the wind.

If he had any idea of competing in that new world, he had better forget it, teeth or hooves, he was much too late for either. He was a ne'er-do-well, an in-betweener. Nature had not done well by him. It was as if she had hesitated and never quite made up her mind. Perhaps as a consequence he had a malicious gleam in his eye, the gleam of an outcast who has been left nothing and knows he is going to have to take what he gets. One day a little bands of these odd apes—for apes they were—shambled out upon the grass; the human story had begun.

Apes were to become men, in the inscrutable wisdom of nature, because flowers had produced seeds and fruits in such tremendous quantities that a new and totally different store of energy had become available in concentrated form. Impressive as the slow-moving, dim-brained dinosaurs had been, it is doubtful if their age had supported anything like the diversity of life that now rioted across the planet or flashed in and out among the trees. Down on the grass by a streamside, one of those apes with inquisitive fingers turned over a stone and hefted it vaguely. The group clucked together in a throaty tongue and moved off through the tall grass foraging for seeds and insects. The one still held, sniffed, and hefted the stone he had found. He liked the feel of it in his fingers. The attack on the animal world was about to begin.

If one could run the story of that first human group like a speeded-up motion picture through a million years of time, one might see the stone in the hand change to the flint ax and the torch. All that swarming grassland world with its giant bison and trumpeting mammoths would go down in ruin to feed the insatiable and growing numbers of a carnivore who, like the great cats before him, was taking his energy directly from the grass. Later he found fire and it altered the tough meats and drained their energy even faster into a stomach ill adapted for the ferocious turn man's habits had taken.

His limbs grew longer, he strode more purposefully over the grass. The stolen energy that would take man across the continents would fail him at last. The great Ice Age herds were destined to vanish. When they did so, another hand like the hand that grasped the stone by the river long ago would pluck a handful of grass seed and hold it contemplatively.

In that moment, the golden towers of man, his swarming millions, his turning wheels, the vast learning of his packed libraries, would glimmer dimly there in the ancestor of wheat, a few seeds held in a muddy hand. Without the gift of flowers and the infinite diversity of their fruits, man and bird, if they had continued to exist at all, would be today unrecognizable. Archaeopteryx, the lizard bird, might still be snapping at beetles on a sequoia limb; man might still be a nocturnal insectivore gnawing a roach in the dark. The weight of a petal has changed the face of the world and made it ours.

GOING PLACES SEEING THINGS?

THE MEDIUM

odyssey

Explore inner space

I have travelled much in Concord.

safari

No matter where you go, there you are.

How many novels, stories, movies, and TV shows are about people going somewhere?

Why do people go on journeys?

Why *see* things?

Why admire the scenery?

You are here. Where is that?

Home-cosmography

Turn off your mind, relax and float downstream.

Significance is an afterthought

PILGRIMAGE

No matter how far some people go, they never get there.

ADVENTURE

No matter how far you go, you stay where you are.

TOUR

Awareness means the capacity to see a coffeepot and hear the birds sing in one's own way, and not the way one was taught.

ABROAD THOUGHTS FROM HOME

My history extends
Where moved my tourist hands,
Who traveled on their own
Without a helping brain.

My hands that domineered
My body lacking mind
Pulled me around the globe
Like any country rube.

No more automaton,
Smarter and settled down,
I choose to move my hands
Which way my will extends.

I marvel now to mark
The geographic work
Done by my brainless touch
On every foreign latch.

In active consciousness
I now rehearse those trips
Which I no longer take
And only partly took.

How is your tour through this book progressing?

Are significant journeys mental or physical

A MELANCHOLY ACCIDENT

One says to me, "I wonder that you do not lay up money; you love to travel; you might take the cars and go to Fitchburg to-day and see the country." But I am wiser than that. I have learned that the swiftest traveller is he that goes afoot. I say to my friend, Suppose we try who will get there first. The distance is thirty miles; the fare ninety cents. That is almost a day's wages. I remember when wages were sixty cents a day for laborers on this very road. Well, I start now on foot, and get there before night; I have travelled at that rate by the week together. You will in the meanwhile have earned your fare, and arrive there some time to-morrow, or possibly this evening, if you are lucky enough to get a job in season. Instead of going to Fitchburg, you will be working here the greater part of the day. And so, if the railroad reached round the world, I think that I should keep ahead of you; and as for seeing the country and getting experience of that kind, I should have to cut your acquaintance altogether.

Such is the universal law, which no man can ever outwit, and with regard to the railroad even we may say it is as broad as it is long. To make a railroad round the world available to all mankind is equivalent to grading the whole surface of the planet. Men have an indistinct notion that if they keep up this activity of joint stocks and spades long enough all will at length ride somewhere, in next to no time, and for nothing; but though a crowd rushes to the depot, and the conductor shouts "All aboard!" when the smoke is blown away and the vapor condensed, it will be perceived that a few are riding, but the rest are run over,—and it will be called, and will be, "A melancholy accident." No doubt they can ride at last who shall have earned their fare, that is, if they survive so long, but they will probably have lost their elasticity and desire to travel by that time. . . . "What!" exclaim a million Irishmen starting up from all the shanties in the land, "is not this railroad which we have built a good thing?" Yes, I answer, *comparatively* good, that is, you might have done worse; but I wish, as you are brothers of mine, that you could have spent your time better than digging in this dirt.

AND ONLY PARTLY TOOK.

THE REAL THING

Phoebe came West for the first time at the age of fifty-six. We met her in the terminal near the postcard rack. She seemed glad enough to see us but gladder to find a postcard of the spot where we were standing. That was to be her pattern for the next two weeks. We took her to all the places that delight tourists: the Fairmont, the Top of the Mark, Sausalito, cable cars, Fisherman's Wharf, Golden Gate Bridge, The Tea Garden, Cliff House. But her enthusiasm remained muted until she spotted a postcard rack. Then she came alive. We would try to get her to notice the original, but she would give only the scantiest attention and turn back to the cards. She left our part of California with 187 cards, a vacant cast to her eye, and probably only the dimmest memory of us: We should have been in pictures.

a rich, manifold life,
brought close to our eyes
—Johann Wolfgang von Goethe

From between the little wayside platforms the railway shot two shining arrows off into the vast bogland where they vanished over a rise that might have been imperceptible without them. It was just before sunset in early spring, a soft evening of evaporating moisture and tentative bird song; for the birds seemed to be practicing rather than singing, twirling and stopping, and twirling and stopping, and when the bold thrush rolled out a whirl of sound he might have been mocking all the other eager, stupid little fellows, like the bullfinch or the tits, who had not yet learned their songs.

The three men, leaning on the wooden railing along the platform, looked at the blush of the sun on the last drifted snow of the mountains, and though every rail was cut into an A shape on top, uncomfortable for arm or elbow, they found it restful to lean and look over the bog, speaking hardly at all. They had been walking all day and now were dog tired. They were waiting for the last train to take them into the country town where they all three taught in the diocesan college.

The priest stood in the middle, a young man, too fat for his years, with drooping lids, puffed lips, and a red face as if he suffered from blood pressure. The same features on another man might have suggested a sensual nature, but there was in his heavily-lidded eyes a look that was sometimes whimsical and sometimes sad, and that look, with the gentle turn to his mouth when he smiled, gave him the appearance of a man who had gone through many struggles and finally solved his problems in a spirit of good-humored regret. So, now, as he pulled at his pipe and looked down into a cold bog stream that flowed beneath them, his chin and his piggy jowls rested on his Roman collar, expanded around his little mouth as if he might at any moment break into a little, silent chuckle. Only, you might have felt, those tired eyes would not even then have changed: they would have mocked his own smile.

On his left, carrying the haversack, was a small dark man, with a slim small body and a button of a head and clipped dark moustaches. The main thing about him was that he did break occasionally into sudden talk, and when he did he banged the hard railings repeatedly or lifted his two fists in the air and slapped his forehead. He did all these things, suddenly, when he cried out:

"Why on earth is this ten-thousand-times-accursed station three miles from the village? What's it here for at all? My God, what a country! What - is - it - for?"

"To take us home," said the third man, and the priest's belly shook a little, too tired to expel laughter.

There was nothing remarkable about this third man except that he had handlebar moustaches and a long black coat and a black hat that came down low on his forehead and and shaded his melancholy face; when he spoke, however, his face was gentle as the fluting of a dove. There was nothing resigned about him; his oblong face was blackberry-colored where he shaved and delicate as a woman's where he did not. His eyes were lined with a myriad of fine wrinkles. They were cranky, tormented eyes, and his mouth was thin and cold and hard.

"I know," cried the small man. "It's some

bloody czar that did it. Some fool of an under-secretary long ago or some ass of a flaming lord-lieutenant who took a ruler and drew a line across Ireland and said, 'That shall be the route of the new railway!' God, what a flaming country!"

"I wonder," said the sad man, Hanafan, in his slow voice, "do the common people ever admire scenery?"

"Now that's very interesting, Hanafan," cried the small man across the priest's chest. "That's a most extraordinary thing. I often thought of that. Isn't that a coincidence!"

"Well," said the sad Hanafan, blushing modestly, "it's a common enough idea, you know."

"Of course they do," said the deep basso of the priest.

"But do they, do they, do they?" shouted the little man, hammering the railing.

The priest nodded, never taking his eyes from the stream or his pipe from his little mouth.

"How do you know?" demanded the small man, leaping backward and whirling his head left, right, and up in the air, as if the answer were a bird.

"Why wouldn't they?" grunted the priest.

"I know what you mean," interrupted the small man, and he wagged his finger into the priest's face. "I know. I met men like that. Our gardener at home, for example. I'd say to him —he was an awful old drunkard—he'd be lying of a hot summer's afternoon under an apple tree—a lazy old ruffian—'Grand day, Murphy,' I'd say. 'Oh, a grand day, God bless it,' he'd say, 'and isn't it good to be alive?' But that's not admiring the scenery," went on the small man. "It's not being *conscious* of it. It isn't, if you understand me, projecting the idea of the beauty of the scene, the idea, into one's own consciousness. Is it, now, Hanafan? And that's what you mean by admiring the scenery."

"Well," said Hanafan, and his words were like prize pigeons that he released one by one from his hands, "I don't know. I'm not sure I mean that."

"Then what the hell *do* you mean?"

"If a man said to me," went on Hanafan, in his downy voice, "'I do be sometimes sitting here, Mr. Hanafan, enjoying the cool of the evening,' I'd say that that man was enjoying the scenery even though he might not know he was doing so at all."

The priest nodded. The small man looked contemptuously at Hanafan, who now began to quote from Gray's "Elegy" in his round, womanly voice, all the time looking sadly at the warmth of the sun fading from the distant grains of snow, and the mountains becoming black and cold:

"The lowing herd winds slowly o'er the lea. . ."

"I know, I know," interrupted the other, but Hanafan went on quietly:

"The plowman homeward plods his weary way,
And leaves the world to darkness and to me."

"You see, I feel," he said, "that the plowman responded to the sense of the end of the day, and the way the fields were all gentle, and dark, and quiet. Just like that bog there. . .is. . . all. . ."

His voice died out.

"Ah, damn it," said the small man in disgust, "that has nothing to do with it."

"It has, Mr. Governey," murmured the priest. "In a sense it has."

"Every man," cried Hanafan, aroused with such vigor that the other two glanced at him, "lives out his own imagination of himself. And every imagination must have a background. I'll tell you a queer thing. It's about the station-master in this station a few years ago."

The priest nodded and chuckled aloud.

"He was nearly sixty-five," said Hanafan. "And he was married, and had a grown-up son in New York, and a daughter, a nun in South America."

"I sent her there," said the priest. "A nice poor girl she was, God rest her."

"Did she die?" asked Hanafan, and when the priest said, "Yes," he fell silent and forgot his story until the other teacher reminded him crossly.

"Yes," said Hanafan. But, again, he stopped because the station porter came out with two oil lamps, one of which he put into the frame of the standard near them.

"It's a grand evening, Father," he said as he turned up the wick.

"Is she late again?" asked the priest, and the porter looked up the line at the signal, and said:

"Aye, she's a trifle behindhand, I'm thinking."

He got down and drew a great silver watch from his corduroy vest and held it up to the setting sun, peering through the yellow celluloid guard.

"She's due, bedad. Ah, she'll be here in a quarter of an hour all right."

The small man groaned and said, "What a country!" The other two looked up at the lamp and then away, and Hanafan said:

"Isn't it dark!"

The porter had walked away.

"Well," resumed Hanafan suddenly, "this old stationmaster! His name was Boyhan. He thought he had a great voice for singing. He was stationed at Newtown and he used to come and sing in the choir with us. That was before your time, Mr. Governey. And he sang in the parish choir. And he'd have sung in the Protestant choir and the Wesleyan choir and the tin-hut choir if they let him. There was not a concert in Newtown that he wasn't the head and tail of it, and he always sang twice and three times, and it was all they could do to keep him from giving encores all night long. For," sighed the teacher, "he had no sense and the people used to make a hare of him. He couldn't sing any more than I could. He had a small voice, a small range too, but it had no strength or sweetness; there was no richness in it."

The teacher said these words, *strength, sweetness, richness*, with a luscious curl of his thin lips around the fruit of sound. His eyes widened. Clearly he was seeing nothing but the old stationmaster. Earnestly he went on, a small glow on each cheek:

"That was all right until they shifted poor Boyhan to this Godforsaken place. And if Newtown is a lonely hole, this is the back of beyond. At the same time they started the new broadcasting station in Dublin and Boyhan conceived a great ambition to sing there. He formed the idea that some day or other a passenger would be on his way to Dublin, or from Dublin, and he would hear him singing and say, 'My heavens, who is that with the grand voice?' And he would make inquiries—some director or government official—and stop the train and seek out Boyhan and say to him, 'What's the meaning of this neglect? Why haven't you been asked to sing over the radio?' Then there would be paragraphs in the newspapers about Discovery of Great Irish Baritone, and Romance of a Chance-heard Voice, and so on.

"The result of this was that whenever a train rolled in, Boyhan used always to come out of his office singing. He'd be singing little trills up and down the scale, or a bar of 'The Moon Hath Raised Her Lamp Above.' He was known to all the passengers and, sure, they used to be looking for him. And there he would always be, rubbing his hands and pretending he was doing his do-sol-mi-do just for delight and jollity.

"Well, one hard, moonlight night in December, I was here, like this, waiting for the last train back to Newtown. The snow was white on the hills. It was blazing. There wasn't a sound but the wind in the telegraph wires. The clouds were in flitters, in bits. I well remember it. A rich night. A deep, rich night, and no harm in the winds, but they puffing and blowing."

Again Hanafan's cold thin lips sucked the sound of those words, *rich, deep,* and his eyes dilated under his black hat with the image of his memory. His eyes were not cranky now, but soft and big.

"I was here with a—a—I was here with a—a friend."

He stopped for a second. The small man's eyes pounced on him, observing at once his strange embarrassment. He glanced at the priest, but he had lowered his face and his mouth was clamped. In that hesitant second he saw at once a piece of Hanafan's secret life revealed, a memory of something known also to the priest; the thought of a dead friend —or perhaps a woman—something or somebody that made the memory of that night so precious to Hanafan that he could not speak of it openly.

"Was this long ago?" probed the small man inquisitively.

"We walked up and down," said Hanafan, "looking at the snow under the moon and the clouds tumbling. Then Boyhan came out and he took us across the line. He had a fire and we sat around it. The smell of the peat, thick and slab, was stuck into everything in the room."

"Was it only two of you?" prodded the small man, eager to know if it was a woman.

"He showed us photographs of his daughter, the nun, and of his son, Timsy, with, as he said, a lawn tennis in his hand. He had no wife. She was dead. And there he was living alone, in the station, three miles from the village and his only two children in the world away in exile. I quoted Sir Thomas Browne for him, the passage in *The Quincunx.* We all looked out the little window at the stars of the Plow. 'Think!' said I. *'The quincunx of heaven runs low and 'tis time to close the five ports of knowledge. . . . The huntsmen are up in America and they are already past their first sleep in Persia. But who can be drowsy at that hour which freed us from everlasting sleep, or have slumbering thoughts at that time, when sleep itself must end. . . .'*

"Then, by way of no harm, he began to talk about music and singing and he gave us one song after another. He sang us 'Oft in the Stilly Night' —and, you know, he sang it well. He sang 'The Moon Hath Raised Her Lamp Above.' I heard the signal bell ring as he was in the middle of it and far away the train began to purr. He was singing it so heartily we didn't like to interrupt him, and as the train became a roar across the bog and the lights went flashing across the window, he rose and went out to the platform. By heavens, that man saw the trainload as a vast audience whirled before him. He stood out on the platform singing to them.

"We rushed for the bridge, we had no tickets, he gave us no tickets, and as I ran I shouted back to him, 'Hold the train!' He paid no heed, and when we were up on the middle of the bridge he got to the grand burst, the last crescendo, of 'I come!. . .My heart's delight . . .' and waved the train on. We were left looking at it vanishing up the line. I roared at him for a fool, and a vain fool, but he only bowed to us, and he bowed to the porter, and he bowed his way backward to the office like a Caruso. The train purred into the distance and there we two were with the wind in the wires and the white moon on mountains.

"I went back to abuse him—it was the last train—but he only looked at me like a child you'd strike and said he couldn't hold back a train for anyone. The porter paid no heed to us. He outed the lamps and locked the place up. We left the old fellow alone in the station. We had to walk home. It was a grand, bright night. A lovely, thick night. . . ."

Hanafan's voice broke. Just then a signal bell rang. It was dark over the bog where far away the train murmured and it could easily be heard because the birds had stopped singing. There was nothing but the deep scent of the night air, and below them in a marsh, still deep from the March rains, a prattling as of a thousand tiny frogs.

"This is a lonely place he lived in," whispered Hanafan. "A lonely life. No children. No wife."

The priest rose up and knocked out the ashes of his pipe as the train roared nearer.

"Yes," he agreed.

"But," cried Governey, "what has all that got to do with admiring the scenery?"

"He sang to the night," cried Hanafan passionately. "He sang to the whole night. The moon was up."

His voice fell and they barely heard him over the rumbling train at the end of the platform.

"We saw the moon in the flags of the Liffey as we left the station. In the flags of the river, through the trees."

"Still and all," cried the small man, "He didn't form any intellectual concept. . . ."

The train drowned his voice and its lights flitted across their faces. When they climbed into a carriage the windows were speckled with rain and the three men inside, who leaned back to let them pass, had a cold, damp look. They had been talking when the train stopped, but when they saw the priest they fell silent; looked at him under their brows; and shyly tripped their hats.

"Raining up the line?" asked the priest in a friendly voice.

"Oh, pouring in Dublin, Father," said one of the three men—an elderly, soldierly-looking man, probably a warder in the jail at Maryborough.

The three teachers fell silent, sensing that they had interrupted a conversation. Then they were rolling through the night, looking at the lights racing along the little hedges beside the line. Suddenly the rain that had hit Dublin half an hour before swept down on them across the mountains, slapping the windows like a bucket of water. It kept trickling and shining on the windows.

"He died there last year," said Hanafan suddenly, looking at the trickle outside the pane.

"I once asked him," the priest leaned forward to say to the small man, "what his favorite song was. Do you know what he said?

'Scenes That Are Brightest.' "

The priest leaned back and gave a merry little laugh.

"Still," cried the small man, thumping his knee, "I can't see what this has to do with the question we were discussing!"

The priest looked at him, and kept looking at him as he swayed with the carriage, but he said nothing. Angrily the small man looked back, and then he looked angrily at Hanafan, whose eyes had become cranky and tormented once more. He began to wonder why Hanafan was always so sour, and why he remained on in Newtown if he didn't like the place, and why he had never married. His eye lit up a bit at that and he determined to get it all out of the priest when they were next alone. He tapped Hanafan on the knee and he began to ask him some question, but when he saw that Hanafan's eyes were closed he leaned back again. The priest was still looking at him, so he nodded towards Hanafan and winked. The priest's lidded eyes were as immovable as an owl's.

As they rolled on through the bog the small man kept looking around him restlessly, and at last he shifted over to the three countrymen, determined to find out if the common people really do admire the scenery. He started a conversation about turf cutting, but before he could lead up to the question the train halted at a small station and the strangers got out. Then the three friends were left alone in the cold, damp carriage, listening to the battering rain. Tired and sleepy, nobody noticed that, in his corner, Hanafan was weeping to himself, the drops creeping through his tightly closed eyes.

"Do the common people ever admire scenery?"

THOUGHT AND SIGHT

The great mechanical impulses of the age, of which most of us are so proud, are a mere passing fever, half speculative, half childish. People will discover at last that royal roads to anything can no more be laid in iron than they can in dust; that there are, in fact, no royal roads to anywhere worth going to; that if there were, it would that instant cease to be worth going to, I mean so far as the things to be obtained are in any way estimable in terms of *price.* For there are two classes of precious things in the world: those that God gives us for nothing—sun, air, and life (both mortal life and immortal); and the secondarily precious things which He gives us for a price: these secondarily precious things, worldly wine and milk, can only be bought for definite money; they never can be cheapened. No cheating or bargaining will ever get a single thing out of nature's "establishment" at half-price. Do we want to be strong?—we must work. To be hungry?—we must starve. To be happy?—we must be kind. To be wise?—we must look and think. No changing of place at a hundred miles an hour, nor making of stuffs a thousand yards a minute, will make us one whit stronger, happier, or wiser. There was always more in the world than men could see, walked they ever so slowly; they will see it no better for going fast. And they will at last, and soon, too, find out that their grand inventions for conquering (as they think) space and time do in reality conquer nothing; for space and time are, in their own essence, unconquerable, and besides did not want any sort of conquering; they wanted *using.* A fool always wants to shorten space and time: a wise man wants to lengthen both. A fool wants to kill space and kill time: a wise man, first to gain them, then to animate them. Your railroad, when you come to understand it, is only a device for making the world smaller: and as for being able to talk from place to place, that is, indeed, well and convenient; but suppose you have, originally, nothing to say. We shall be obliged at last to confess, what we should long ago have known, that the really precious things are thought and sight, not pace. It does a bullet no good to go fast; and a man, if he be truly a man, no harm to go slow; for his glory is not at all in going, but in being. . . .

FACE VALUE

If the page which reads "Going places Seeing things" did not come alive for you, make up a page like it using one of the slogans in this book. Take your letters from one magazine but use only one letter from each ad or article.

THE UNIVERSE REVALUED

Every age has its world-picture, its taken-for-granted view of the universe and man's place in it. Ours is *supposed* to be based on science, and no longer on religion or superstition. But is it really the growth of science which has made a cosmology like Plato's or Shakespeare's incredible, and our own the only possible one? Is our modern, educated layman's estimate of the universe really founded on facts, or on prejudice?

It is certainly unlike the old estimate. Men once used to think of the universe as full of life, of the sun and stars and even the earth as visible deities, and of the blue sky as the country of the blessed. Priests and astronomers pointed up to the same encircling heavens, to celestial realms whose divinity was proportional to their distance from man at their center. Physical height matched spiritual status.

All of this has now, we imagine, been finally disproved. Instead of a universe of concentric spheres, we have a centerless one, a cosmic potato instead of a cosmic onion. Instead of an aristocratic universe, we have a leveled-down one, whose principalities and powers have long ago lost all their influence. Instead of awesome star gods looking down on us, we have so many celestial firecrackers or blast furnaces blazing away in the night sky.

Instead of a tremendously alive universe, we have an inanimate one in which sentient beings, lost like the finest of needles in the vastest of haystacks, manage to scrape a brief living. Instead of a meaningful creation—a proper place for man—we have a vast expanse of mindless space in which living things are the rarest accidents, or anomalies. And, in the last resort, even they are accidental collocations of particles.

Such, more or less, is the new world-myth. Roughly speaking, this is how most of us educated nonscientists regard the universe. And we are under the impression that science makes any other view impossible. Does it, in fact?

First let us note that, truly speaking, there is nothing about the universe which forbids our taking this earth—or the sun, or any other convenient spot—as its center. On the contrary, we have only to use our eyes to see that the universe is always arranged as a nest of concentric regions—occupied by such things as pipe bowls and spectacle rims, hands and feet, men and animals, clouds and aircraft, moon and sun and stars—around the ever-central observer. To discount altogether this eminently verifiable fact, in favor of some theory — however useful—of uniform space, is unrealistic. In practice, the dead and centerless cosmic potato is found to be a cosmic onion, whose observer-core is the very focus of life and mind.

Nor are the outer layers of this onionlike universe necessarily without life. True, we have direct evidence of only one inhabited heavenly body — our own. Nevertheless, according to recent scientific theories, a significant proportion of the stars are likely to have developed into solar systems resembling ours, and again a significant proportion of these systems are likely to contain planets which are suitable homes for the living. And where the right conditions arise—the right ingredients and temperatures—there, scientists assure us, life will follow.

Consequently, the number and variety of

inhabited worlds may well beggar imagination.

At any rate, then, we have better reason than Shakespeare for feeling, on starlit nights, that we are looking up into heavens well-sprinkled with life, some of it far surpassing our own. And the chances are that, to find the more superhuman of these inhabited worlds, we should need to probe farther and farther afield from our earth-center. For the realm of the nine planets plainly holds less promise than the remoter realm of the stars—the hundreds of millions of stars of our own Galaxy—containing who knows how many earth-encircled suns. Nor is this realm a millionth part so rich in celestial possibilities as the still remoter realm of the galaxies, with its unthinkably great star population.

Thus science itself not only hints at the existence of the superhuman but links it with distance from ourselves. We are even warned that the more exalted of the worlds above could be influencing us all the while in unsuspected ways—say by telepathy; the laboratory evidence for this faculty is impressive and, apparently, distance is no bar to its operation. In short, we are already back to something like the ancient world-picture, which science was supposed to have destroyed once and for all!

Clearly, then, we laymen can hardly claim the support of science for our pseudoscientific world-picture. But consistency is not our strong point. For instance, we talk as if it were somehow to our discredit that our universe home is on so splendid a scale, and as if we had lost and not found ourselves in it. We think of ourselves as mere pin points in the universe, as if our inability to weigh more than one or two hundred pounds apiece were somehow more significant than our scientists' ability to weigh the stars. Again, we speak of this "vast expanse of mindless space" as if it were anything but our life's source, saturated with and saturating our own mind if no other. We are urged to fight nature, as if we packed a secret supernatural weapon. As for the human self-portrait as an "accidental collocation of particles," and one moreover that walks around blandly describing itself as such—now there's a delightful spectacle! If this is a sample of what our idiotic universe can throw off *accidentally* (whatever that can mean), think of what it could do if ever it got around, by some particularly happy accident, to doing it *intentionally!* And, in fact, we don't have to go far to find intention in what it does. It does *us*, who are full of intention. At any rate, a certain part of the universe called "I" intends itself, and a good deal besides. And so, presumably, does every other star dweller who is not on the point of suicide. How this universe can be so steeped in intention, yet remain merely accidental, we do not explain.

Evidently we science-invoking moderns think of "living matter" as if it were somehow freakish, irrelevant to the nature of the universe. Yet science says that the physical basis of inert objects like heavenly bodies is the same as that of the creatures which come to life in them, formed of their substance. The difference does not lie in the raw material, but its organization. Thus the lowliest particles everywhere are capable of assuming the highest living forms. Potentially, all the stuff of all the stars is alive, purposeful and, indeed, superhuman. And even if such exalted functions could actually emerge only for a moment in only one spot, they would still reveal for all time the hidden nature of all matter. One small flower is enough to identify the biggest plant. It follows that there is no sense whatever in our description of the universe as lifeless and mindless.

The scale of this immense thing is what tricks us. We are not deceived when we consider a creature of handy size; for then we take its whole life history into account, and especially the more developed stages. Thus the plant is a *flowering* plant, even as a seedling; and the caterpillar is no mere worm, but a moth in the making, even if it should never come out in its true colors. *Flower* seeds, *mosquito* larvae, *human* embryos: the higher functions are always the most significant for us—provided our specimen weighs no more than a few hundred tons and survives no more than a few hundred years! Our unhappy cosmos lacks both qualifications. Its scale is wrong; therefore its higher functions tell us nothing important about it; we see it as defunct, and only *infested* with life! No matter what myriads of living worlds and species and individuals our universe-tree may sport, no matter how luxuriant its blossoms of mind and values (all arising naturally, science assures us), we still reckon it a *flowerless* tree! Worse, it is no tree at all; it is not even a branching vase in which we, mere cut flowers, are tastefully displayed, but merely their indifferent or threatening background! Thus, idiotically, do we human flowers deny the life of our cosmic plant because it is not *all* flower, but enormous leaves and stem and root, also!

The analogy is a false one. It does not go half far enough. A rose plucked from the bush is still a rose, but a man plucked from the universe is an absurdity. Yet this absurdity is the very core of our modern myth, which sees man as the clue to what the universe is *not* like!

To say the least, then, the ancient notion of a living cosmos is neither ridiculous nor inconsistent with science. But whatever we think of the universe as a whole, we feel quite sure that its bigger parts are not alive. The bulkiest organisms we recognize are the big trees of California and Oregon and the blue whale.

This is rather odd. For we have, extending from ultimate particles through atoms and molecules and cells up to man who includes them all, a well-filled scale or hierarchy of unitary beings; and then, immeasurably above man, the living whole. Why this cosmic gap? If the vast interval between man and his minutest particles is filled by a series of increasingly subhuman parts, surely the principle of nature's continuity suggests that the equally vast interval between man and the totality may be filled by a series of increasingly superhuman wholes. If these have so far escaped our notice, could that be because we have eyes only for our equals in the cosmic hierarchy?

Have we ever looked for our superiors? Would we recognize them if we saw them? It is notoriously difficult to find a thing one has no idea of. Therefore let us assume that this gap in the natural order is not empty. Let us posit a creature who outbulks a man as a man outbulks a cell, and ask how such a giant would have to differ from ourselves in order to live at all.

Apparently there are limits to the size of a terrestrial organism. If it is too big it is unlikely to survive. In that case, we can only assume that our giant takes flight from his parent heavenly body and sets up as a heavenly body on his own account. Then he not only can be very massive, but *needs* to be; otherwise, he can neither incorporate his own atmosphere and water supply, nor keep a firm gravitational hold upon them; and without water and oxygen, and atmosphere shells to shield him from meteorites and dangerous radiation and extreme temperatures, he cannot make the heavens his home. And once there, he cannot just wander at will, but must attach himself to some star for warmth and energy, keeping a safe distance and turning continually to avoid freezing behind and roasting in front. And he is certainly a lucky giant. As soon as he starts spinning and circling round his star, the laws of gravity and inertia see that he goes on doing so without effort or deviation.

As for his physique, what would he want with legs or arms, hands or feet, or even wings? Nose and tongue and ears, a mouth and rows of teeth, a stomach and bowels and an anus—anything like these could surely be an encumbrance and a laughingstock in the heavens. We are left, apparently, with some vast rounded body, its whole surface drinking in solar energy.

And supposing there were no convenient star to feed on? Well, if he cannot *find* what he needs, he must *be* it. Our starless sky dweller must himself incorporate a starlike source of energy—a great blazing heart to sustain the smaller and cooler peripheral body we have described;

To sum up: if we greatly enlarge the creatures we know, adjusting their physique and behavior to suit their size, we get creatures that are indistinguishable from planets and stars. If they exist, they are probably a familiar sight. Many a star shining in the sky could in fact be a living thing, a fit inhabitant of heaven. And so the scale of creatures does not necessarily end with us. The seeming gap could arise from a defect of vision instead of a defect in the universe.

A celestial detective story with no solution! Perhaps it is time we came down to earth again, to the life we know.

But *do* we know it? A living thing (scientists tell us) is an organization of nonliving ones. The salts of our blood, the acid of our stomachs, and the calcium phosphate of our bones are clearly not alive; but neither are the atoms comprising all our living cells. What is physics or chemistry at one observational level is a man at another, and at once alive and not alive. All depends on whether this thing is taken to pieces or not.

But if the pieces (as pieces) are lifeless, where shall we set the boundaries of the living whole? If by the whole man we mean one who is independent and self-contained, we can hardly leave out the air in his lungs and the saliva in his mouth and the chyme in his guts—at least, nobody has pointed out where these cease to be environment and become organism. And if *they* are caught up in the living whole of him, why not the tools without which he would starve to death and the clothes without which he would freeze to death? After all, he is far more dependent upon his shoes than his toenails, and upon his good false teeth than his bad real ones. They have become part of his life.

That is how he describes them, and that is what they feel like. He identifies himself with his possessions and is not himself without them. He may be more vain of his façade than his face, and more hurt by the loss of a few tiles than many hairs. Until he feels so all-of-a-piece with the clothes he wears, and the horse he rides, and the financial or political power he wields, that they no longer seem outside him, he has still to learn their use. The expert is one who, having incorporated his tools, is unaware of them. They have temporarily vanished into his physique. He doesn't sit on the seat of his pants, or even on a seat in a boat that sails on the sea. *He* sails, *he* is at sea. He doesn't grasp a handle that holds a blade that cuts bread. *He* cuts bread. That is how a man speaks because that is what he is—an endlessly elastic organization of "dead" parts, mostly outside his skin. Thanks to them, he can drink at the lake and browse in the field while attending a concert on the far side of the world — all without setting foot outside his own porch. Instead of going out to these places, he grows out to them.

Nor do these artificial but vital extensions complete his physique. To cut man off from the other creatures is homicidal, for species neither occur nor survive nor develop as things apart, but in great interlocking patterns of mutual dependence. Just as our muscle cells make no sense without our blood cells, so the bee's tongue makes nonsense without the flower's nectary; and so on indefinitely—the more you study one bit of life the more you must take the others into account so that really to know one would be to know the lot. If, then, we seek the living whole—and life, we have seen, is a question of wholeness—nothing short of the entire network of terrestrial organisms, growing up as one living thing from the start, really deserves such a title. And even this vast spherical organization is not yet a complete organism. This living earth-skin in still far from being self-contained—for without rock and water and topsoil and air it is as dead as the least of its parts.

In short, nothing less than the whole Earth is genuinely alive! Here indeed is a visible god or goddess. The giant we were seeking in the heavens was down here all the while!

Whose life is in doubt? Hers, or ours which is hers or nothing? The only *complete* living thing of which we have inside knowledge turns out to be a heavenly body — our Earth. And the *only* heavenly body of which we have inside knowledge turns out to be a living thing—again, our Earth. In fact, it is not *living* heavenly bodies which call for proof, so much as *dead* ones!

The behavior and build of such a creature are so odd that we need a new word for this high-level vitality, this superlife which is at least planetary. Oddity, however, must be expected here. The living cell is a very different story from one of its molecules, and man from one of his cells. It would be strange if the living Earth were not, in turn, unlike her animal and subanimal parts.

All the same, the Earth is no foreign body, living some mysterious life apart from ours. Admittedly her life-preserving maneuvers in the sky are less varied than ours in her; but if to act deliberately is to know with scientific precision what you do and why (its causes and effects in the past, present and future) then her behavior is much more deliberate than any man's. Admittedly her beginnings were unconscious and unpromising, but so were ours; and now who can match her adult complexity — all her own unfolding and no invasion? For parent, she has the sun; for anxiously awaited offspring, manned spaceships and satellites; for eyes, observatories whose binocular vision (like the merely human) enables her to place her nearer neighbors; for special sense organs, receptors tuned in to cosmic influences; for intellectual exercise, our science of the heavens. We hang her portrait on our walls, and the close-up of her face is familiar to every radio-equipped aviator as a luminous and noisy and ever-changing network and patchwork.

This is indeed no alien godling. She is the full extent, the filled-out body-mind of each of her creatures. For there is nowhere to live but heaven, and no way to live there but hers.

But, of course, even she is not really suited

to the hard climate of the skies. The smallest complete creature fit for this universe is no sunless planet, but a star—a fully developed sun, a solar system whose "living" planet is a mere organ. And even such a star is not independent of its fellows in our Galaxy, and of the universe of galaxies itself. Only the whole is a genuine whole, and therefore altogether alive.

It is no surprise to find in the superhuman just such a hierarchy of wholes and parts as we found in the subhuman. Isn't this exactly what we wanted to fill the gap above man, and balance the orders below him—this ascending scale of beings—planetary, sidereal, and galactic, but all finite—in which higher rank means more independence achieved, and more "dead" material raised to life? And isn't the life of man the indivisible life of the entire hierarchy — the upper half that he is in as well as the lower half that is in him—or nothing at all?

Is this view of man too speculative? Then let us imitate the scientist, whose business is unprejudiced observation (with a view to economical description and prediction or control). Let us try observing man. What precisely are you, when examined without prejudice?

What we make of you depends upon range. At ten feet, we see a human body; a little closer, a head. But the superficial view is not enough. Our instruments take us nearer and nearer, to places where we observe tissues, cell groups, a cell in detail, giant molecules and so on.

So much for the near view. Let us now move away from you. This time we find, in turn, a house, a city, a country, a planet, a star (our solar system) and a galaxy.

You may say that these are nothing like "you." But which appearance is less like "you," your particles or your planet, your cells or your city? If the first is "you" observed, why not the second? But we don't yet know what "you" are. We can only take what we find—namely, the whole scale of creatures from particles to heavenly bodies. And this confirms our conclusion that you are incomplete, not yourself, till you are celestially constituted.

You may reasonably protest that the distant view includes so much that isn't you, provided you add that the near view excludes so much that is you, and that the middle view is altogether too superficial. But all three objections beg the question: what are you? Surely the best hope of an answer is to ignore no view of this object, whatever the range. Only unprejudiced observation could reveal the astonishing totality, with all its metamorphoses.

You might reply that this merging and emerging, this cosmic elasticity, however true of your bodily or outer aspect, is untrue of your "real self."

To find out the truth, first listen to your self. You talk of *this* organ, *this* body, *this* house, city, country, planet and star. Clearly, what is felt as *here* varies from this aching tooth to this star, and what is felt as *there* varies from all the other teeth in your head to all the other stars in the sky. "Now" and "then," "fast" and "slow," "present" and "absent"—these little words are always giving you away. Anyone who can seriously talk of near galaxies yet the far side of the room, of old men in a new world, of giant atoms in a dwarf star, is either altogether elastic or beside himself.

Far from deceiving us, language is only underlining the facts. A diseased mind may so identify itself with one bodily organ that the rest are treated as alien or hostile. And evidently a man may so identify himself with his family, or country, or race, or planet (in the event of interplanetary war), or God, that he thinks for them, and is hurt when they are injured, and makes their good his good, and lives and dies for them without throught of his private welfare. In fact, anyone who lacked all such expansive feelings would be an intellectual and moral imbecile, incapable of objectivity or responsibility. The idea of the self as constant, as a unique, permanent, separate, immiscible something, will not bear examination. The facts make nonsense of it—they include the evidence of multiple personality, religious conversion, amnesia and parapsychology, not to mention the great problem of biological individuality. Nor does this nonsensical idea work. Quite the contrary, it is madness. To the extent that we cut ourselves off from anybody and everybody we are out of our minds and dispirited.

The truth is that this illusion of a separate self and the illusion of a dead universe are halves of a whole, segments of one vicious circle. The universe seems dead because I seem out of it. I seem out of it because the universe seems dead. Till the total mind in man rejoins its own total body, the universe, he is self-alienated and the universe appears corpselike.

Short of that goal, his elastic mind matches his elastic body; *here* and *there* grow and shrink together; subject takes on the rank of object; you and I are roughly equals. It is a man who greets a man, a ship that hails a ship, a planet that signals a planet. And just as it is not this eye (or even this head) that sees you, but this man (from top to toe) who does so, so it is not this man who studies Mars, but Earth that does so. She is our only astronomer—no mere man being equal to or equipped for the task—so that, in fact, there is the world of difference between the "I" in "I see a man" and in "I see Mars." Again, when the general (note the noun) says he will smash the enemy, it is the army that does so. And when the atomic physicist (note the adjective) says he will smash the uranium nucleus, it is neutrons that do so. Yet he does not feel small, any more than the general or the astronomer feel bloated. It comes so naturally to us to be almost everything, and the next moment almost nothing, that we never notice the transformation.

We have every right, then, to announce Earth's life. It is an aspect of our own infinitely elastic life. But this makes her peculiarly vulnerable. A word is enough to kill this great but sensitive creature.

For we have only to decide, in the teeth of all the evidence, that she shall be a "lifeless" planet, and then no matter what limb she flourishes, or eye she opens, or *Song of the Earth* she sings—nothing she can ever do or say will prove her alive: because it is all, by definition, not hers! It is living, and therefore alien or parasitic! Never shall the life *on* Earth be the life *of* Earth. Treat a man thus, and he is little more than a cell-infested skeleton. Examine the world's liveliest organism till you know it inside out, and you will find nothing but cell-populated terrain. The only way for us to rejoin Earth, to rank as geological specimens instead of antigeological ones, is to stop geologizing, and thinking, and living, and get ourselves buried and petrified. Then we are dead enough to belong again!

And of course, our sun—now come to life as our solar system—gets the same raw deal. We have only to hand over the whole of his natural history to physics and astronomy (as if his men and beasts were unnatural and his flowers artificial) to reduce this star god to star dust.

A solar myth as curious as this does not spring up overnight. It too, has, a natural history.

To our early ancestors the sun was simply alive, as you or I, only brighter and more divine. But gradually the animating spirit was distinguished and divided from the gross body, which become a mere fireball steered by an independent god or angel. Then science reduced particular star spirits to general laws of nature, tendencies and forces. And eventually, coming down to our own day, even these ghostly remnants are seen as man-made or subjective, and so exorcised. The stars are no longer impelled or guided in their courses. They only take the line of least resistance. And while the solar life and mind are thus being wiped out, the body itself is being quietly disposed of. The sun's sensible qualities—his color, brightness, warmth—are drawn in from the object there to the subject here, to the eye of the perceiver. Even his apparent motion across the sky is really ours. Finally, and just in case any miserable residue of our victim should remain, physics dissolves his substance into space, dotted with inscrutable particles.

Here is the murder story of all time—nothing less than "cosmicide" committed over millenniums, and still going practically undetected. Fortunately, however, it is only a tale, a piece of solar crime fiction. For we could *get rid* of the solar life by absorbing it into our heads only if they were lethal receptacles, or else made off with their solar contents to some other star. In fact, the life of our solar system has suffered an internal shift; it has not vanished. Rather the reverse. Doubtless it is only by thus shamming dead that a planet-ringed sun can wake in the end to a fully self-conscious life. After all, our pseudoscientific myth of a dead sun must be seen as a solar rather than a merely human myth, as an indispensable chapter in the natural history of our solar system rather than a mere aberration. Only don't let us mistake this brief and somewhat crazy chapter for the whole story.

And don't let us mistake indifference to this story for real neutrality. The universe which is not seen as living is treated as dead. There is no halfway. Even if we could avoid taking sides, rejection of the ancient world-view amounts in practice to acceptance of the modern, with its immense consequences for religion and art and politics, to say nothing of science itself.

To sum up: we have found our modern myth, this life-abhorring world-picture that we laymen thought was scientific, to be nothing of the sort. Instead, we have found science pointing in the opposite direction, toward something like the old cosmic hierarchy culminating in the divine.

The outcome for you and me is as far-reaching as we care to make it. Already we have seen that, once we breach the artificial wall dividing our little selves from the hierarchy of our greater selves, the walls are apt to go on falling, till in the end we glimpse the one self of all. It is the first step that counts. Once we admit any life and mind above the merely human, we are apt to find ourselves admitting more and more, till we come to the highest life, our total mind, where we are safe home at last and outside nothing. That is where, say the world's great spiritual teachers, we could even now lose ourselves for good, in a deathless world whose divisions and opacity have finally vanished, and where everything is

indescribably open, weightless and brilliant.

To some of us, this is danger signal enough. Our separate egos will defend themselves to the death. To others, here is a renewed invitation to the toughest adventure of all, whose end is variously called enlightenment, liberation, the Kingdom of Heaven and the mystical union. Several roads lead toward that goal; and the road whose first stages this article has sketched is certainly not everybody's. To the thoroughly Westernized mind, however, whose preoccupation has for two centuries been the "conquest" of nature, this approach may have more than intellectual interest. Nature, the "enemy," can now show us her kinder face. She can lead us farther than ever before toward the one unchanging reality of which she is the manifold and fleeting appearance.

In any case, there exists for none of us, not even the most "spiritual," a merely human or personal liberation which leaves nature out, and which does not involve the liberation of every creature on the Earth and in the skies, however grotesque or seemingly unlovable. How could we *begin* to disentangle ourselves from any part of the one, in whom we all live and move and have our being? Enlightenment is either cosmic or nothing.

Alan Watts was asked in a lecture "What is the purpose of life?" The audience was rather embarrased, dismayed, interested, indifferent, at this question being asked. Watts said, "I can tell you what the purpose of life is not. It is like music: music is not designed to get to the end of itself. If this were so, one would play the music as fast as possible to get to the end."

A fool
wants to kill
space and time:
a wise man,
first to gain them,
then to animate them.

CLOSE
BROUGHT
There was a child went forth everyday
And the first object he look'd upon, that object he became,
And that object became part of him for the day or certain part of the day,
Or for many years or stretching cycles of years. . .

VOYONS!

This pursuit of strangeness is not a blasé's search for the bizarre and out-of-the-way. It is the conscious attempt to achieve a new look at the same old world, people, ideas, feelings, and things. In the "familiar world" objects are always right-side-up; the child who bends and peers at the world from between his legs is experimenting with the familiar made strange. (One sees the familiar tree as a collection of solids in an otherwise empty space. The sculptor consciously may invert his world and see the tree as a series of voids or holes carved within the solid block of the air.)

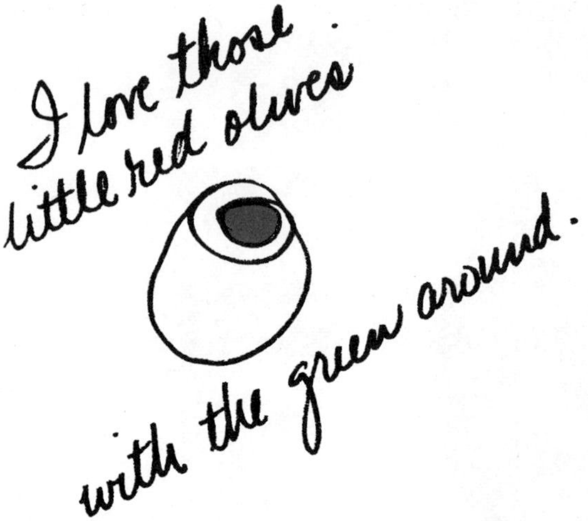

I love those little red olives
with the green around.

The familiar made strange
The strange made familiar = ?

Is that the way our minds work? Is that the way they should work? In the cartoon on page 84 what do you expect to see on the chairs and sofa?

FIRST TO GAIN THEM

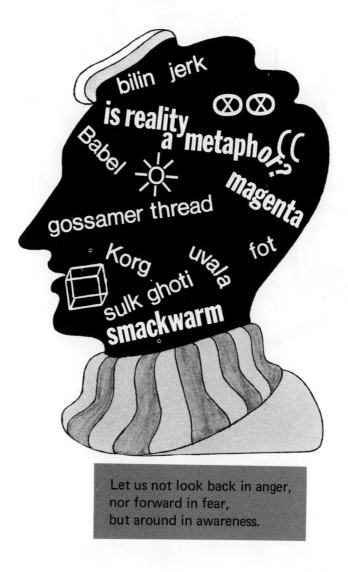

Let us not look back in anger,
nor forward in fear,
but around in awareness.

Is your mind a connecting organ?

Drawing by Steinberg; © 1962.
The New Yorker Magazine, Inc.

Is this cartoon a statement?
Is it a probe?

PROBES

Apply this particular grouping to groups in general. Which figure is like you? Which of your classmates or family reminds you of the figure on the left of the couch? Which people fit the other figures? Which figures are like the authors of this book? The author of *Wife-Wooing*?

In what sense has the cartoonist *abstracted* the essence of the *expected* figures? Which configuration is most attractive to you?

Which figure is the dachshund?

Does the familiar setting *channel* the possibilities of the unfamiliar?

What sort of event is going on here? How do we know?

On top of skeletons
they put a gala dress, and then—
the flower-viewing!

How *general* can you make this investigation?

What kind of exterior does the figure in the right background present? What is it like inside? Is the figure in the left foreground complicated? Is it sharp-edged and brittle? Which figure has its inside completely cut off from the outside? Which figure has the most variety and is most "receptive"? Which one seems to be flying apart?

What is the value of the process the cartoonist has used here? Can all man-made pictures, cartoons, paintings, photographs, and word-pictures be thought of as codes?

BOXER

How does a cartoon like this fit into an English class?

Haw ə bawt đə foniymik kod?

Is a cartoon a metaphor?

COCKER SPANIEL

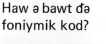

When the plomy sallipesh had morked his lampix, the baslurker felmed up the bliffles and ciptally coofed.

What about cats?

What feelings or attitudes have we learned to associate with these configurations?

Are the configurations really unfamiliar or only unfamiliar in this context?

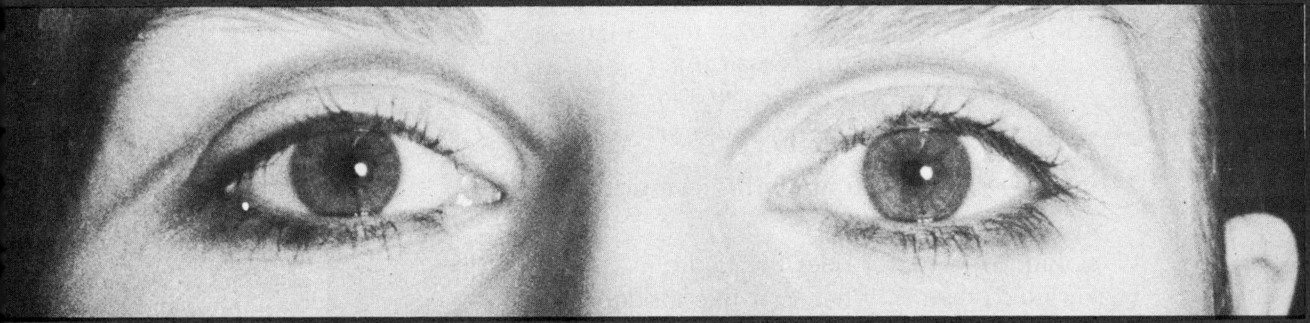

A world of darkness–
shadowed, mysterious,
terrifying–?

It was more than fifteen years ago [about 1860] that I entered the laboratory of Professor Agassiz, and told him I had enrolled my name in the Scientific School as a student of natural history. He asked me a few questions about my object in coming, my antecedents generally, the mode in which I afterwards proposed to use the knowledge I might acquire, and, finally, whether I wished to study any special branch. To the latter I replied that, while I wished to be well grounded in all departments of zoology, I purposed to devote myself specially to insects.

"When do you wish to begin?" he asked.

"Now," I replied.

This seemed to please him, and with an energetic "Very well!" he reached from a shelf a huge jar of specimens in yellow alcohol.

"Take this fish," said he, "and look at it; we call it a haemulon; by and by I will ask what you have seen."

With that he left me, but in a moment returned with explicit instructions as to the care of the object entrusted to me.

"No man is fit to be a naturalist," said he, "who does not know how to take care of specimens."

I was to keep the fish before me in a tin tray and occasionally moisten the surface with alcohol from the jar, always taking care to replace the stopper tightly. These were not the days of ground-glass stoppers and elegantly shaped exhibition jars; all the old students will recall the huge neckless glass bottles with their leaky, wax-besmeared corks, half eaten by insects, and begrimed with cellar dust. Entomology was a cleaner science than ichthyology, but the example of the Professor, who had unhesitatingly plunged to the bottom of the jar to produce the fish, was infectious; and though this alcohol had a "very ancient and fishlike smell," I really dared not show any aversion within these sacred precincts, and treated the alcohol as though it were pure water. Still I was conscious of a passing feeling of disappointment, for gazing at a fish did not commend itself to an ardent entomologist. My friends at home, too, were annoyed when they discovered that no amount of eau-de-Cologne would drown the perfume which haunted me like a shadow.

In ten minutes I had seen all that could be seen in that fish, and started in search of the Professor—who had, however, left the Museum; and when I returned, after lingering over some of the odd animals stored in the upper apartment, my specimen was dry all over. I dashed the fluid over the fish as if to resuscitate the beast from a fainting-fit, and looked with anxiety for a return of the normal sloppy appearance. This little excitement over, nothing was to be done but to return to a steadfast gaze at my mute companion. Half an hour passed—an hour—another hour; the fish began to look loathsome. I turned it over and around; looked it in the face—ghastly; from behind, beneath, above, sideways, at a three-quarters' view—just as ghastly. I was in despair; at an early hour I concluded that lunch was necessary; so, with infinite relief, the fish was carefully placed in the jar, and for an hour I was free.

On my return, I learned that Professor Agassiz had been at the Museum, but had gone, and would not return for several hours. My fellow-students were too busy to be disturbed by continued conversation. Slowly I drew forth that hideous fish, and with a feeling of desperation again looked at it. I might not use a magnifying-glass; instruments of all kinds were interdicted. My two hands, my two eyes, and the fish; it seemed a most limited field. I pushed my finger down its throat to feel how sharp the teeth were. I began to count the scales in the different rows, until I was convinced that that was nonsense. At last a happy thought struct me—I would draw the fish; and now with surprise I began to discover new features in the creature. Just then the Professor returned.

a pencil is one of the best eyes.

"That is right," said he; "a pencil is one of the best of eyes. I am glad to notice, too, that you keep your specimen wet, and your bottle corked."

With these encouraging words, he added:

"Well, what is it like?"

He listened attentively to my brief rehearsal of the structure of parts whose names were still unknown to me: the fringed gill arches and movable operculum, the pores of the head, fleshy lips and lidless eyes, the lateral line, the spinous fins and forked tail; the compressed and arched body. When I had finished, he waited as if expecting more, and then, with an air of disappointment:

"You have not looked very carefully; why," he continued more earnestly, "you haven't even seen one of the most conspicuous features of the animal, which is as plainly before your eyes as the fish itself; look again, look again!" and he left me to my misery.

I was piqued; I was mortified. Still more of that wretched fish! But now I set myself to my task with a will, and discovered one new thing after another, until I saw how just the Professor's criticism had been. The afternoon passed quickly, and when, toward its close, the Professor inquired:

"Do you see it yet?"

"No," I replied, "I am certain I do not, but I see how little I saw before."

"That is next best," said he, earnestly, "but I won't hear you now; put away your fish and go home; perhaps you will be ready with a better answer in the morning. I will examine you before you look at the fish."

This was disconcerting. Not only must I think of my fish all night, studying, without the object before me, what this unknown but most visible feature might be; but also, without reviewing my discoveries, I must give an exact account of them the next day. I had a bad memory, so I walked home by Charles River in a distracted state, with my two perplexities.

Here was a man who seemed quite as anxious as I that I should see for myself what he saw

The cordial greeting from the Professor the next morning was reassuring; here was a man who seemed to be quite as anxious as I that I should see for myself what he saw.

"Do you perhaps mean," I asked, "that the fish has symmetrical sides with paired organs?"

His thoroughly pleased "Of course! of course!" repaid the wakeful hours of the previous night. After he had discoursed most happily and en-

ARE WORDS "PENCILS" FOR EXPLORING EXPERIENCE?

Do you see how a journal can be a laboratory for sustaining investigation?

thusiastically—as he always did—upon the importance of this point, I ventured to ask what I should do next.

"Oh, look at your fish!" he said, and left me again to my own devices. In a little more than an hour he returned, and heard my new catalogue.

"That is good, that is good!" he repeated, "but that is not all; go on;" and so for three long days he placed that fish before my eyes, forbidding me to look at anything else or to use any artificial aid. "Look, look, look," was his repeated injunction.

This was the best entomological lesson I ever had—a lesson whose influence has extended to the details of every subsequent study, a legacy the Professor had left to me, as he has left it to many others, of inestimable value, which we could not buy, with which we cannot part.

A year afterward, some of us were amusing ourselves with chalking outlandish beasts on the Museum blackboard. We drew prancing star-fishes; frogs in mortal combat; hydra-headed worms; stately crawfishes, standing on their tails, bearing aloft umbrellas; and grotesque fishes with gaping mouths and staring eyes. The Professor came in shortly after, and was as amused as any at our experiments. He looked at the fishes.

"Haemulons, every one of them," he said. "Mr. ________ drew them."

True; and to this day, if I attempt a fish, I can draw nothing but haemulons.

The fourth day, a second fish of the same group was placed beside the first, and I was bidden to point out the resemblances and differences between the two; another and another followed, until the entire family lay before me, and a whole legion of jars covered the table and surrounding shelves; the odor had become a pleasant perfume; and even now, the sight of an old, six-inch, worm-eaten cork brings fragrant memories.

The whole group of haemulons was thus brought in review; and, whether engaged upon the dissection of the internal organs, the preparation and examination of the bony framework, or the description of the various parts, Agassiz's training in the method of observing facts and their orderly arrangement was ever accompanied by the urgent exhortation not to be content with them.

"Facts are stupid things," he would say, "until brought into connection with some general law."

At the end of eight months, it was almost with reluctance that I left these friends and turned to insects; but what I had gained by this outside experience has been of greater value than years of later investigation in my favorite groups.

Facts are stupid things until brought into connection with some general law.

In what sense is this essay about creativity? Is creativity the same as ideation? Do you see a connection between the process of ideation and the expression "I see!"

Take a few of the ideas floating loosely in your mind and "define" them in a journal entry. Or take just one of them and explore it in depth.

Does "face value" change as you see more distinctly? For the viewer is there *ever* anything more than face value? Is the answer to this question important?

Where does meaning come from?

Does the artist give you cues to help you realize a meaning? Does he depend on your background?

Which do you think bridges more ethnic boundaries, the cartoon or the scuplture?

What do you bring *to* the sculpture? Could an Eskimo, another classmate, an older or a younger person bring different meaning to it? What do you deduce from that?

Is the sculpture an angiosperm?

Is this a *reading* lesson? Is all seeing "reading?"

All lands have their ancient myths in which light and darkness are metaphors.

I use my statements as probes.

To say that a fact is significant in science, is to say that it helps to establish or refute some general law; for science, though it starts from observations of the particular, is not concerned essentially with the particular, but with the general. A fact, in science, is not a mere fact, but an instance. In this the scientist differs from the artist, who, if he deigns to notice facts at all, is likely to notice them in all their particularity. Science, in its ultimate ideal, consists of a set of propositions arranged in a hierarchy, the lowest level of the hierarchy being concerned with particular facts, and the highest with some general law, governing everything in the universe.

Re-examine the sculpture on page 90. Does the particularizing of the artist give his work *general* meaning?

Do you see an advantage for yourself in a "particular-general" object? Are symbols "economical"? Is there an advantage for human thought in such compact packages?

In your journal extend or deepen this investigation by seeking connections with other questions you have in your mind.

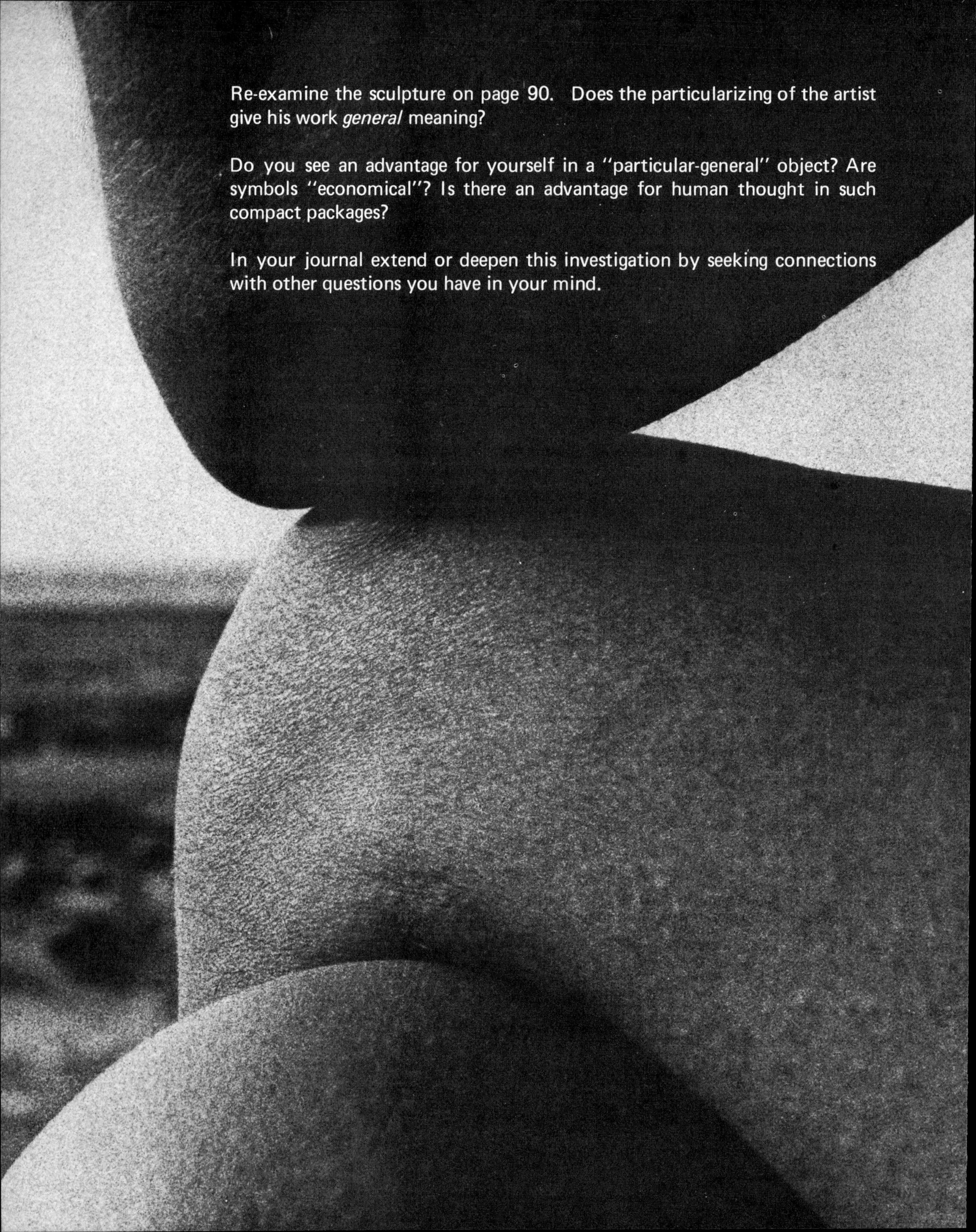

What does it mean to turn a statement into a probe?

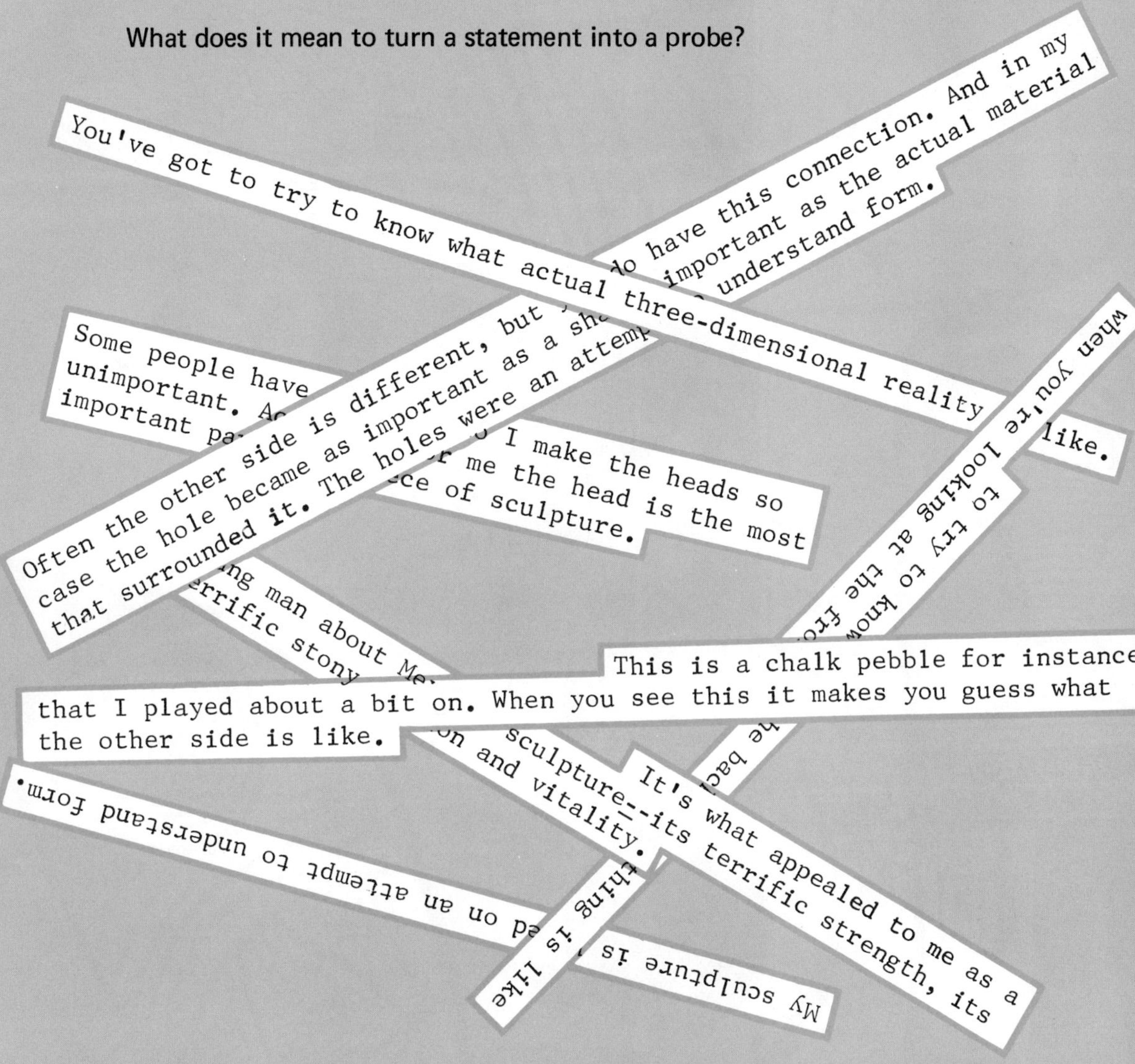

Is this artist a scientist? Is there really a difference between true artists and true scientists? Or is the difference only in the *product*?

Do artists and scientists use probes in the same way, for the same purpose?

Is there a sense in which you can apply these statements as probes in examining the painting which follows?

Has this artist created a world unfamiliar to you? Are elements of it familiar? Is it a cliché? What does it add up to? If the painting appeared in a comic book would you react to it differently? In a museum?

Is confusion a necessary prerequisite to ideation? Is anxiety about the solution of a problem essential to the formation of an idea? Compare some of the creative people you know with some who are not. Which group is more exploratory, more curious, more willing to risk confusion?

What does creativity have to do with the study of English?

> If we are to perceive all the implications and possibilities of the new we must risk at least temporary ambiguity and disorder.

Make up a title for this painting. Compare your title with those of other students. What are the qualities of a good title? Why give things titles (for example, "William Brown")?

What would be a good title for the sculpture on page 90?

How are the paintings, sculpture and cartoon the same?

How does one get to know such peculiar plum blossoms?

Is this English?

. . . I try to make them jittery by giving them situations that are out of context and contain several interpretations.

To get to know plum blossoms,
both one's own heart
and one's own nose.

"I don't know anything about art, but I know what I like."

A route of evanescence
With a revolving wheel;
A resonance of emerald,
A rush of cochineal;
And every blossom on the bush
Adjusts its tumbled head,–
The mail from Tunis, probably,
An easy morning's ride.

And there's doctors, and there's lawyers,
And business executives,
And they're all made out of ticky-tacky,
And they all look just the same.

A woman who was shopping in a fashionable San Francisco store peered intently at an expensive matched set of handmade wine glasses. After a few minutes she called the sales clerk over.

"Is that really the price you are asking for these?" she demanded.

"Yes, madam; they are fine pieces of glassmaking craftsmanship. Each one was individually blown."

"The price is unbelievable. I wouldn't pay half that much for them! It says they're matched but they are all slightly different. If I was going to pay that kind of money I'd want every glass to look exactly the same as the others."

The salesman was about to start explaining but the woman turned away and went past him out of the store.

Drawing by Steinberg; © 1963.
The New Yorker Magazine, Inc.

Here are three drawings and three photographs of the same scene. Each photograph was taken by a different person. The drawings are also by different individuals. What does each one give you that the others do not?

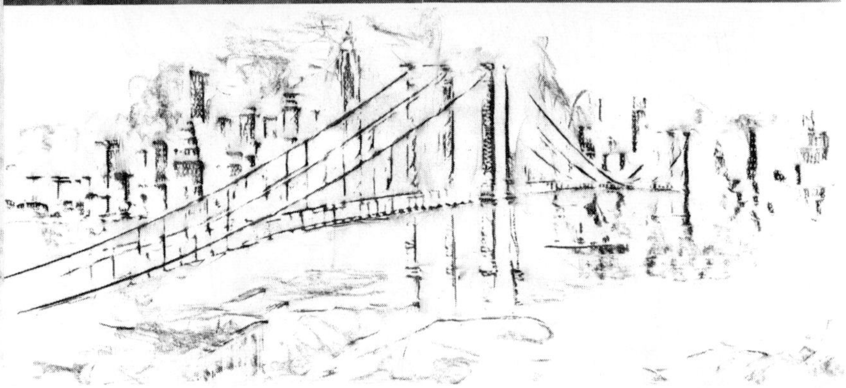

Why is individual perception valuable? How important is it that everyone sees things differently?

I SAW EVERYTHING WITH A STRANGE NEW SIGHT

The most important day I remember in all my life is the one on which my teacher, Anne Mansfield Sullivan, came to me. I am filled with wonder when I consider the immeasurable contrast between the two lives which it connects. It was the third of March, 1887, three months before I was seven years old.

The morning after my teacher came she led me into her room and gave me a doll. The little blind children at the Perkins Institution had sent it and Laura Bridgman had dressed it; but I did not know this until afterward. When I had played with it a little while, Miss Sullivan slowly spelled into my hand the word "d-o-l-l." I was at once interested in this finger play and tried to imitate it. When I finally succeeded in making the letters correctly I was flushed with childish pleasure and pride. Running downstairs to my mother I held up my hand and made the letters for doll. I did not know that I was spelling a word or even that words existed; I was simply making my fingers go in monkey-like imitation. In the days that followed I learned to spell in this uncomprehending way a great many words, among them *pin, hat, cup,* and a few verbs like *sit, stand,* and *walk.* But my teacher had been with me several weeks before I understood that everything has a name.

> Ceaselessly musing, venturing, throwing, seeking the
> spheres to connect them,
> Till the bridge you will need be formed . . .

One day, while I was playing with my new doll, Miss Sullivan put my big rag doll into my lap also, spelled "d-o-l-l" and tried to make me understand that "d-o-l-l" applied to both. Earlier in the day we had had a tussle over the words "m-u-g" and "w-a-t-e-r." Miss Sullivan had tried to impress it upon me that "m-u-g" is *mug* and the "w-a-t-e-r" is *water,* but I persisted in confounding the two. In despair she had dropped the subject for the time, only to renew it at the first opportunity. I became impatient with her repeated attempts and, seizing the new doll, I dashed it upon the floor. I was keenly delighted when I felt the fragments of the broken doll at my feet. Neither sorrow nor regret followed my passionate outburst. I had not loved the doll. In the still, dark world in which I lived there was no strong sentiment or tenderness. I felt my teacher sweep the fragments to one side of the hearth, and I had a sense of satisfaction that the cause of my discomfort was removed. She brought me my hat, and I knew I was going out into the warm sunshine. This thought, if a wordless sensation may be called a thought, made me hop and skip with pleasure.

We walked down the path to the well-house, attracted by the fragrance of the honeysuckle with which it was covered. Someone was drawing water and my teacher placed my hand under the spout. As the cool stream gushed over one hand she spelled into the other the word *water,* first slowly, then rapidly. I stood

IN THE BEGINNING, THE WORD

An idea is a feat of association

still, my whole attention fixed upon the motions of her fingers. Suddenly I felt a misty consciousness as of something forgotten—a thrill of returning thought; and somehow the mystery of language was revealed to me. I knew then that "w-a-t-e-r" meant the wonderful cool something that was flowing over my hand. That living word awakened my soul, gave it light, hope, joy, set it free! There were barriers still, it is true, but barriers that could in time be swept away.

I left the well-house eager to learn. Everything had a name, and each name gave birth to a new thought. As we returned to the house every object I touched seemed to quiver with life. That was because I saw everything with a strange, new sight that had come to me. On entering the door I remembered the doll I had broken. I felt my way to the hearth and picked up the pieces. I tried vainly to put them together. Then my eyes filled with tears; for I realized what I had done, and for the first time I felt repentance and sorrow.

I learned a great many new words that day. I do not remember what they all were; but I do know that *mother, father, sister, teacher,* were among them—words that were to make the world blossom for me, "like Aaron's rod, with flowers." It would have been difficult to find a happier child than I was as I lay in my crib at the close of that eventful day and lived over the joys it had brought me, and for the first time longed for a new day to come.

It becomes almost physical (but then we can't ever separate mental and physical), but anyway my body reacts. Tension builds sort of. Some of the things I've written stagger me with their implications.

MULTIPLE CHOICE TEST

The correct tool for examining the world is:

A.
B.
C.
D.
None of the above.
All of the above.

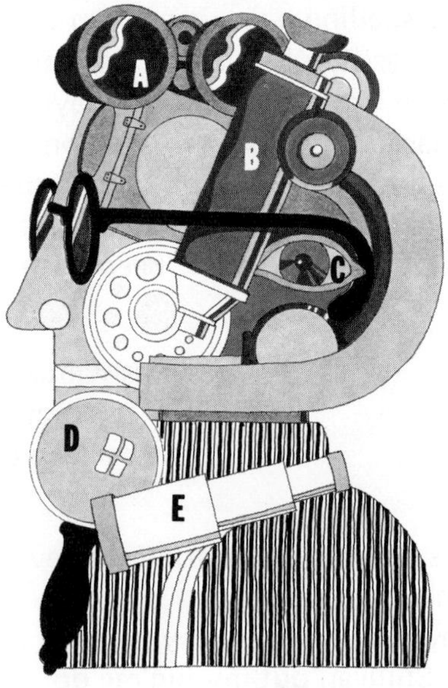

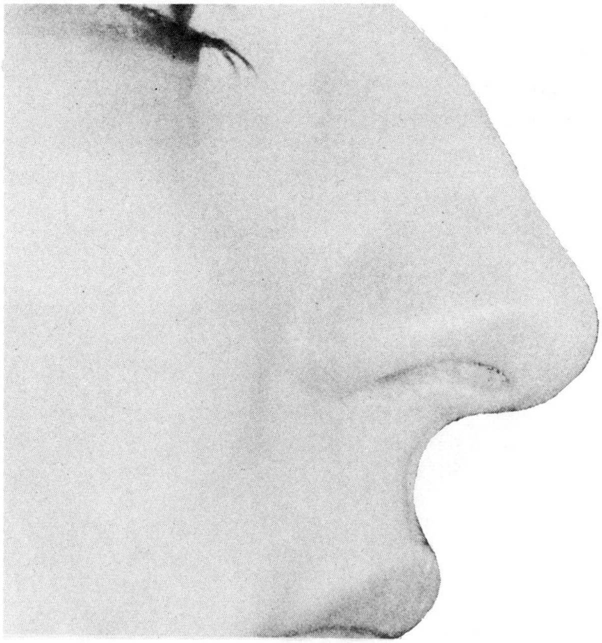

Another kind of eye?

to get to know plum blossoms.

SMELL!

Oh strong ridged and deeply hollowed
nose of mine! what will you not be smelling?
What tactless asses we are, you and I, boney nose,
always indiscriminate, always unashamed,
and now it is the souring flowers of the bedraggled
poplars: a festering pulp on the wet earth
beneath them. With what deep thirst
we quicken our desires
to that rank odor of a passing springtime!
Can you not be decent? Can you not reserve your ardors
for something less unlovely? What girl will care
for us, do you think, if we continue in these ways?
Must you taste everything? Must you know everything?
Must you have a part in everything?

Our human nature is
profoundly phototropic.

A noiseless patient spider,
I marked where on a little promontory it stood isolated,
Marked how to explore the vacant vast surrounding,
It launched forth filament, filament, filament, but of itself,
Ever unreeling them, ever tirelessly speeding them.

"Take it at face value."

Is all perception interpretation? Is all perception understanding? Is that a further step?

"It's true even if it didn't happen"? Is *truth* something "out there" or is it a concept in your mind?

At what point does what you say you see cease to be a description and become an interpretation? Could one ever say that *all* description is interpretation?

A language is an abstraction.
It is also a generalization.
The same is true for each of its parts.

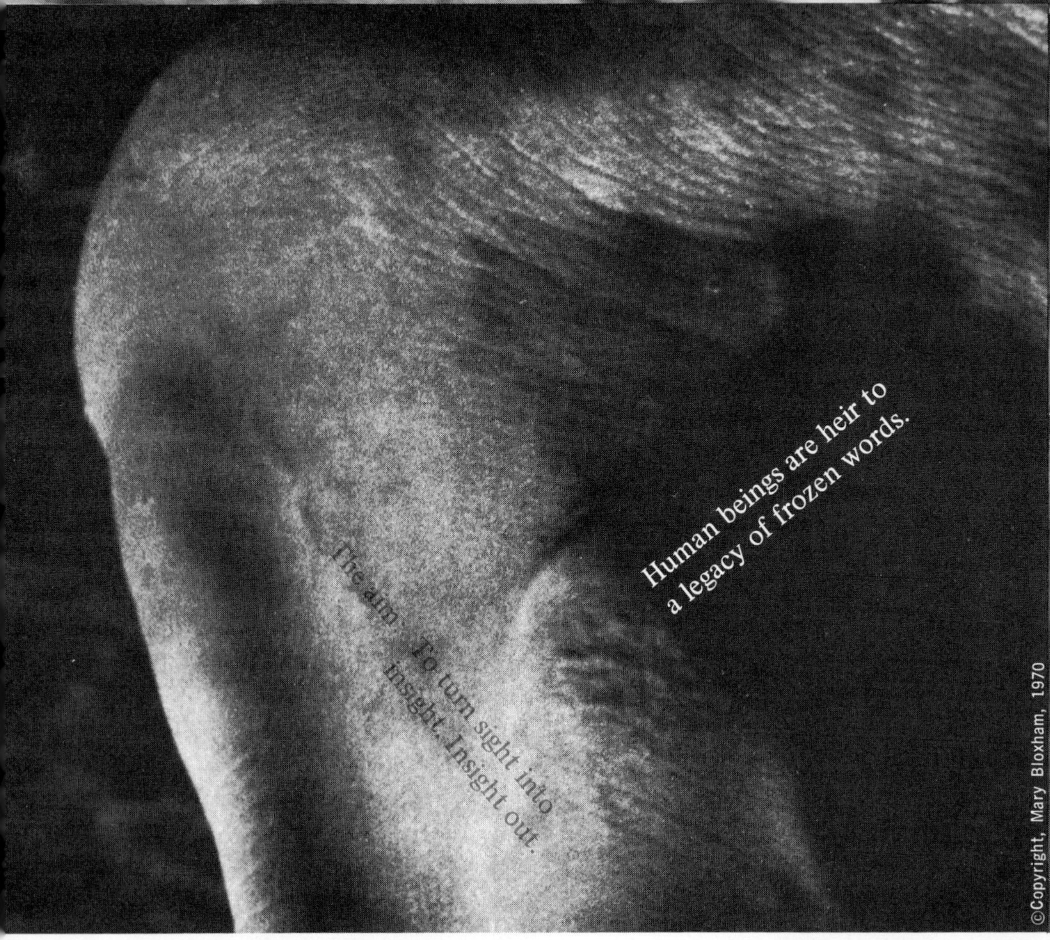
Human beings are heir to
a legacy of frozen words.
The aim: To turn sight into
insight. Insight out.

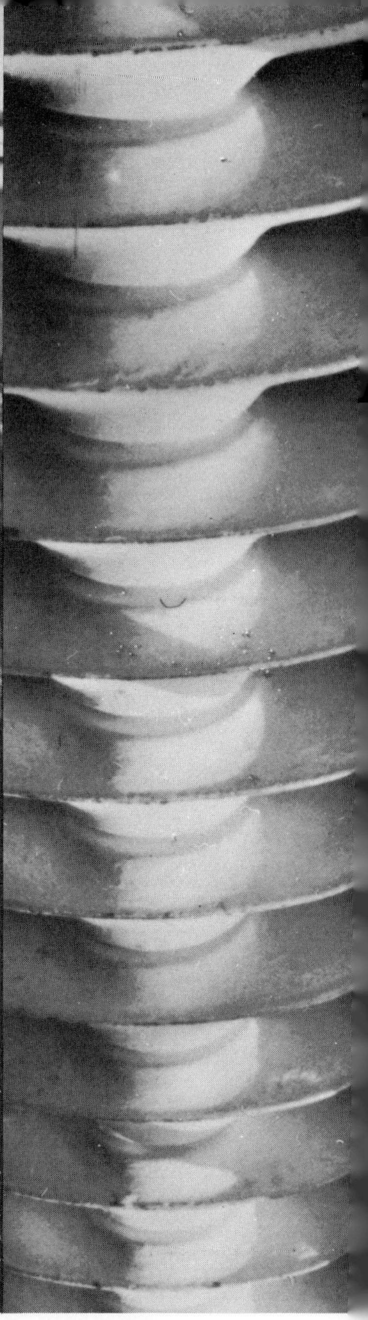

These six photographs portray things you are probably familiar with. What does each one represent? What did you have to do to decide? Do your classmates agree with your guesses? After identifying the object, do you want to stay with it, look at it, and observe, or do you want to move on to the next picture?

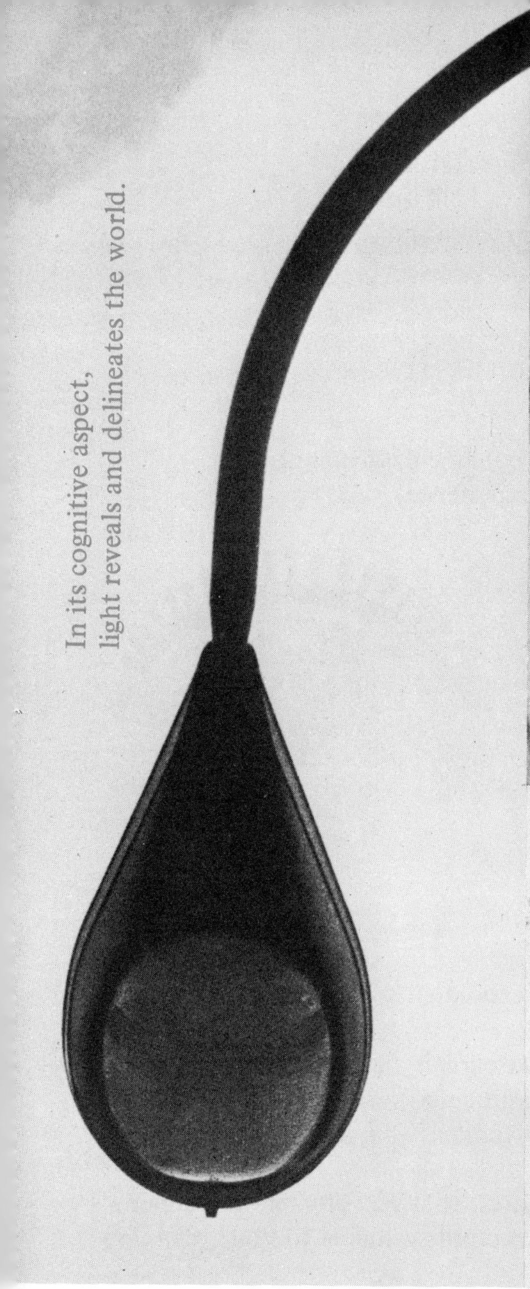
In its cognitive aspect,
light reveals and delineates the world.

That is essentially what I am playing with—
the voyage between perception and understanding.

What steps does your mind go through to make these photographs familiar? Is it a process of connecting? Is it like the process you go through in making metaphors? Are we ever in conscious control?

The artist holds the mirror not up to nature, but to his own mind. Nature is faceless. A mirror held up to nature would record nothing. There are no "things" in nature. The mind "defines."

There is an age-old dialogue between man and light, and in it light has had three major roles: cognitive, esthetic, symbolic.

"The artist seeks not truth but an enlargement of the scope of his ordinary experience."

To see at all is to interpret.

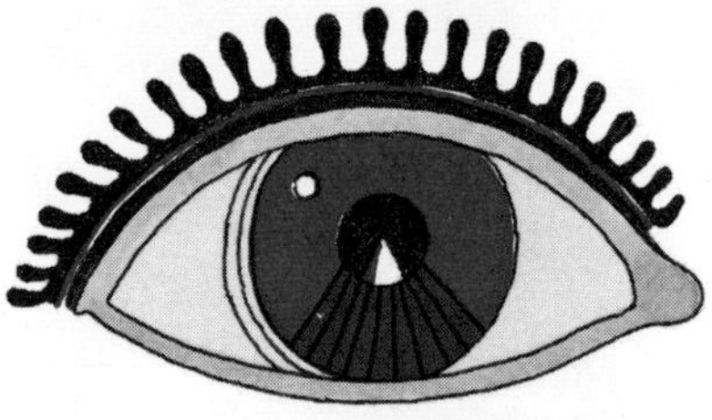

Can you suggest a title for the painting?

Write as much about this painting as you can.

Compare what you have said with the comments of some of your classmates.

Does a painting, a cartoon, or a photograph portray a view of life?

In the first section we discussed the influence that context has on the meaning of words. Keeping this in mind look at the drawings and photographs on page 98.

Do the meanings you have stored up control what you are able to perceive? Does this make other people and their viewpoints valuable to you? Can you make use of their "difference"?

In what sense is this painting a "definition"?

How is this painting like others you have seen? How has the artist dealt with the problem of clichés? What are *you* doing about clichés?

Are all men artists? What are their materials? What forms do their creations take? In this metaphoric sense, how would *you* distinguish a good job from a bad one?

THE WITCH

The coach was so nearly empty that the little boy had a seat all to himself, and his mother sat across the aisle on the seat next to the little boy's sister, a baby with a piece of toast in one hand and a rattle in the other. She was strapped securely to the seat so she could sit up and look around, and whenever she began to slip slowly sideways the strap caught her and held her halfway until her mother turned around and straightened her again. The little boy was looking out the window and eating a cookie, and the mother was reading quietly, answering the little boy's questions without looking up.

"We're on a river," the little boy said. "This is a river and we're on it."

"Fine," his mother said.

"We're on a bridge over a river," the little boy said to himself.

The few other people in the coach were sitting at the other end of the car; if any of them had occasion to come down the aisle the little boy would look around and say, "Hi," and the stranger would usually say, "Hi," back and sometimes ask the little boy if he were enjoying the train ride, or even tell him he was a fine big fellow. These comments annoyed the little boy and he would turn irritably back to the window.

"There's a cow," he would say, or, sighing, "How far do we have to go?"

"Not much longer now," his mother said, each time.

Once the baby, who was very quiet and busy with her rattle and her toast, which the mother would renew constantly, fell over too far sideways and banged her head. She began to cry, and for a minute there was noise and movement around the mother's seat. The little boy slid down from his own seat and ran across the aisle to pet his sister's feet and beg her not to cry, and finally the baby laughed and went back to her toast, and the little boy received a lollipop from his mother and went back to the window.

"I saw a witch," he said to his mother after a minute. "There was a big old ugly old bad old witch outside."

"Fine," his mother said.

"A big old ugly witch and I told her to go away and she went away," the little boy went on, in a quiet narrative to himself, "she came and said, 'I'm going to eat you up,' and I said, 'no, you're not,' and I chased her away, the bad old mean witch."

He stopped talking and looked up as the outside door of the coach opened and a man came in. He was an elderly man, with a pleasant face under white hair; his blue suit was only faintly touched by the disarray that comes from a long train trip. He was carrying a cigar, and when the little boy said, "Hi," the man gestured at him with the cigar and said, "Hello yourself, son." He stopped just beside the little boy's seat, and leaned against the back, looking down at the little boy, who craned his neck to look upward. "What you looking for out that window?" the man asked.

"Witches," the little boy said promptly. "Bad old mean witches."

"I see," the man said. "Find many?"

"My father smokes cigars," the little boy said.

"All men smoke cigars," the man said.

"Someday you'll smoke a cigar, too."

"I'm a man already," the little boy said.

"How old are you?" the man asked.

The little boy, at the eternal question, looked at the man suspiciously for a minute and then said, "Twenty-six. Eight hunnerd and forty-eighty."

His mother lifted her head from the book. "Four," she said, smiling fondly at the little boy.

"Is that so?" the man said politely to the little boy. "Twenty-six." He nodded his head at the mother across the aisle. "Is that your mother?"

The little boy leaned forward to look and then said, "Yes, that's her."

"What's your name?" the man asked.

The little boy looked suspicious again. "Mr. Jesus," he said.

"Johnny," the little boy's mother said. She caught the little boy's eye and frowned deeply.

"That's my sister over there," the little boy said to the man. "She's twelve-and-a-half."

"Do you love your sister?" the man asked. The little boy stared, and the man came around the side of the seat and sat down next to the little boy. "Listen," the man said, "shall I tell you about my little sister?"

The mother, who had looked up anxiously when the man sat down next to her little boy, went peacefully back to her book.

"Tell me about your sister," the little boy said. "Was she a witch?"

"Maybe," the man said.

The little boy laughed excitedly, and the man leaned back and puffed at his cigar. "Once upon a time," he began, "I had a little sister, just like yours." The little boy looked up at the man, nodding at every word. "My little sister," the man went on, "was so pretty and so nice that I loved her more than anything else in the world. So shall I tell you what I did?"

The little boy nodded more vehemently, and the mother lifted her eyes from her book and smiled, listening.

"I bought her a rocking-horse and a doll and a million lollipops," the man said, "and then I took her and I put my hands around her neck and I pinched her and I pinched her until she was dead."

The little boy gasped and the mother turned around, her smile fading. She opened her mouth, and then closed it again as the man went on, "And then I took and I cut her head off and I took her head—"

"Did you cut her all in pieces?" the little boy asked breathlessly.

"I cut off her head and her hands and her feet and her hair and her nose," the man said, "and I hit her with a stick and I killed her."

"Wait a minute," the mother said, but the baby fell over sideways just at that minute and by the time the mother had set her up again the man was going on.

"And I took her head and I pulled out all her hair and—"

"Your little *sister*?" the boy prompted eagerly.

"My little sister," the man said firmly. "And I put her head in a cage with a bear and the bear ate it all up."

"Ate her *head* all up?" the little boy asked.

The mother put her book down and came across the aisle. She stood next to the man and said, "Just what do you think you're doing?" The man looked up courteously and she said, "Get out of here."

"Did I frighten you?" the man said. He looked down at the little boy and nudged him

Always indiscriminate, always unashamed...

with an elbow and he and the little boy laughed.

"This man cut up his little sister," the little boy said to his mother.

"I can very easily call the conductor," the mother said to the man.

"The conductor will *eat* my mommy," the little boy said. "We'll chop her head off."

"And little sister's head, too," the man said. He stood up, and the mother stood back to let him get out of the seat. "Don't ever come back in this car," she said.

"My mommy will eat *you*," the little boy said to the man.

The man laughed, and the little boy laughed, and then the man said, "Excuse me," to the mother and went past her out of the car. When the door had closed behind him the little boy said, "How much longer do we have to stay on this old train?"

"Not much longer," the mother said. She stood looking at the little boy, wanting to say something, and finally she said, "You sit still and be a good boy. You may have another lollipop."

The little boy climbed down eagerly and followed his mother back to her seat. She took a lollipop from a bag in her pocketbook and gave it to him. "What do you say?" she asked.

"Thank you," the little boy said. "Did that man really cut his little sister up in pieces?"

"He was just teasing," the mother said, and added urgently, "Just *teasing.*"

"Prob'ly," the little boy said. With his lollipop he went back to his own seat, and settled himself to look out the window again. "Prob'ly he was a witch."

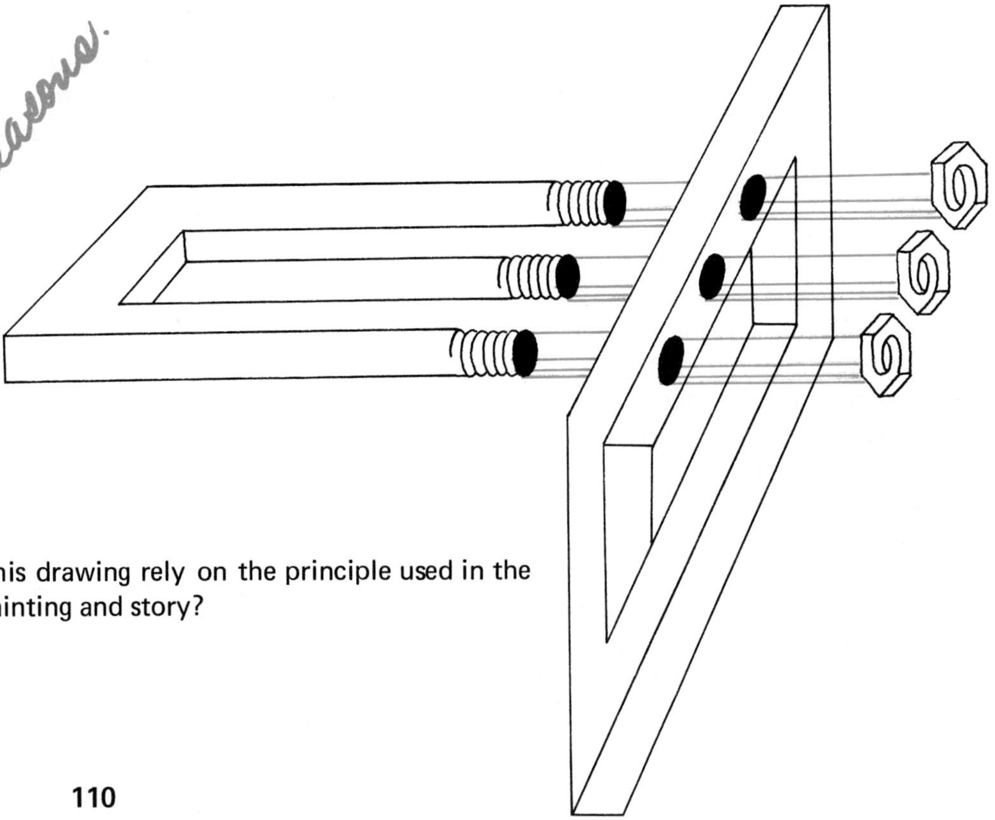

How does this drawing rely on the principle used in the preceding painting and story?

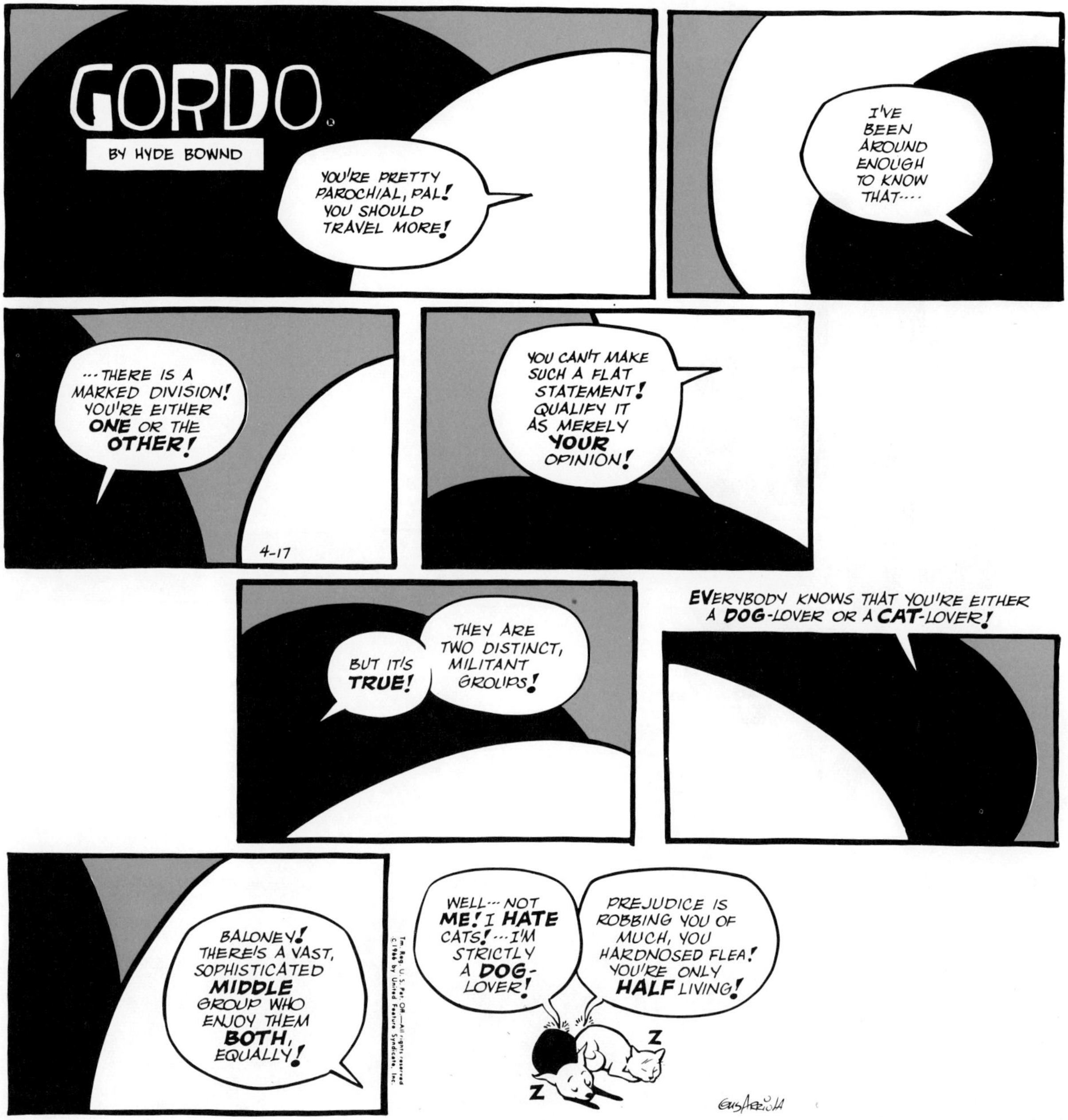

Teaching consists of causing people to go into situations from which they cannot escape except by thinking.

THE LIMITATIONS AND DANGERS OF SYMBOLS IN RELATION TO MEANINGS

Splendid to feel the curious and potent, inexplicable and irrefutably magical life language leads within itself.

Symbols themselves are particular, physical, sensible existences, like any other things. They are symbols only by virtue of what they suggest and represent; i.e., meanings.

In the first place, they stand for these meanings to any individual only when he has had *experience* of some situation to which these meanings are actually relevant. Words can detach and preserve a meaning only when the meaning has been first involved in our own direct intercourse with things. To attempt to give a meaning through a word alone without any dealings with a thing is to deprive the word of intelligible signification; against this attempt, a tendency only too prevalent in education, reformers have protested. Moreover, there is a tendency to assume that, whenever there is a definite word or form of speech, there is also a definite idea; while, as a matter of fact, adults and children alike are capable of using even formulae that are verbally precise with only the vaguest and most confused sense of what they mean. Genuine ignorance is more profitable because it is likely to be accompanied by humility, curiosity, and open-mindedness; whereas ability to repeat catch-phrases, cant terms, familiar propositions, gives the conceit of learning and coats the mind with a varnish waterproof to new ideas.

In the second place, although new combinations of words without the intervention of physical things may supply new ideas, there are limits to this possibility. Lazy inertness causes individuals to accept ideas that have currency about them without personal inquiry and testing. *A man uses thought, perhaps, to find out what others believe, and then stops.* The ideas of others as embodied in language become substitutes for one's own ideas. The use of linguistic studies and methods to halt the human mind on the level of the attainments of the past, to prevent new inquiry and discovery, to put the authority of tradition in place of the authority of natural facts and laws, to reduce the individual to a parasite living on the secondhand experience of others—these things have been the source

---

Are visual "symbols" (all that we see: photographs, paintings, cartoons of the reformers' protest against the pre-eminence assigned to language in schools.

In the third place, words that originally stood for ideas come, with repeated use, to be mere counters; they become physical things to be manipulated according to certain rules or reacted to by certain operations without consciousness of their meaning. Mr. Stout (who has called such terms "substitute signs") remarks that "algebraical and arithmetical signs are to a great extent used as mere substitute signs. . . . It is possible to use signs of this kind whenever fixed and definite rules of operation can be derived from the nature of the things symbolized, so as to be applied in manipulating the signs, without further reference to their signification. *A word is an instrument for thinking about the meaning which it expresses;* a substitute sign is a means of *not* thinking about the meaning which it symbolizes." The principle applies, however, to ordinary words, as well as to algebraic signs; they also enable us to use meanings so as to get results without thinking. In many respects, signs that are means of not thinking are of great advantage; standing for the familiar, they release attention for meanings that, being novel, require conscious interpretation. Nevertheless, the premium put in the schoolroom upon attainment of technical facility, upon skill in producing external results, often changes this advantage into a positive detriment. In manipulating symbols so as to recite well, to get and give correct answers, to follow prescribed formulae of analysis, the pupil's attitude becomes mechanical, rather than thoughtful; verbal memorizing is substituted for inquiry into the meaning of things. This danger is perhaps the one uppermost in mind when verbal methods of education are attacked.

Language moves in the middle kingdom between infinite and definite.

I can't draw a landscape, but I draw man-made situations: architecture, roads. For nature and for whatever is untouched by people, I use a series of clichés.

---

billboards) subject to the same limitations and dangers as verbal symbols?

BETWEEN WALLS

the back wings
of the

hospital where
nothing

will grow lie
cinders

in which shine
the broken

pieces of a green
bottle

What is the connection between this montage of quotations and the rest of this section? How do they fit meaningfully together?

Concrete evocative commonplace must be distinguished from abstract impotent commonplace. Fundamental originality depends on a review of the data of organic life which produced the synthetic objects and theories to which our culture is heir. To understand contemporary data and build on them without perceiving their ancestors is at best to improve—not invent. The platform of abstract commonplace floats safely above earth's concreteness, but we must risk abandoning it in order to grasp a more coherent creative product.

I always seek very consciously to construct a world where a tree can be quite different, where I myself may well discover suddenly that my right hand has seven fingers whereas my left hand has only five. I mean a world where everything and anything is possible and where there is no longer any reason at all to be surprised, or rather *not* to be surprised by all one discovers there.

Sister Corita teaches her students how to live life with real gusto and respond to the invitation to come alive by teaching them how to celebrate the ordinary, everyday things around them. Sister Corita and her students invite everyone to share their power-up experience with them.

The process of selective adaptation of designs to the end of conspicuous waste, and the substitution of pecuniary beauty for aesthetic beauty, has been especially effective in the development of architecture. It would be extremely difficult to find a modern civilized residence or public building which can claim anything better than relative inoffensiveness in the eyes of anyone who will dissociate the elements of beauty from those of honorific waste. The endless variety of fronts presented by the better class of tenements and apartment houses in our cities is an endless variety of architectural distress and of suggestions of expensive discomfort. Considered as objects of beauty, the dead walls of the sides and back of these structures, left untouched by the hands of the artist, are commonly the best feature of the building.

Let the Wonderful Infinite Variety of Sea Shells Inspire You with

FAITH IN YOUR OWN INDIVIDUALITY

. . .Look carefully at these hundreds of beautiful, infinitely various little houses *[the speaker shows the apprentices a tray full of sea shells]*. Here you see housing on a lower level, it is true, but isn't this humble instance a marvelous manifestation of life? Now, where, in all this bewildering variety of form, is the *idea*? Is there not just one *idea* or *principle* here? But where is the limitation to variety? There is none. . . .

If the human mind is so limited that it can take in only some special one *[pointing to one shell]*, what we now need to see is that we must inform ourselves, if we really want to develop a culture of our own, so that we can perform similar "miracles" *[pointing to them all]* in order that we do not have to submit to those impositions by code or formula, in the name of science or authority, which impose a living death on our performances.

Here, in these shells, we see the housing of the life of the sea. It is the housing of a lower order of life, but it is a housing with exactly what we lack: inspired form. In this collection of houses of hundreds of small beings, who themselves built these houses, we see a quality which we might call invention. The beauty of their variation is never finished. Creation here goes on forever. It is not a question of degree, but of principle of design. This multitudinous expression indicates what design can mean.

There is no reason why our buildings and the housing of human beings, which we so stupidly perpetrate all alike as two peas in a pod, shouldn't be quite as fertile in imaginative resources as these little sea shells. Why do we ever take to any one formula, carry it out to a dead end, and execute it as though that were all? Here in this collection of little houses is one of the best lessons you could possibly find. . . .

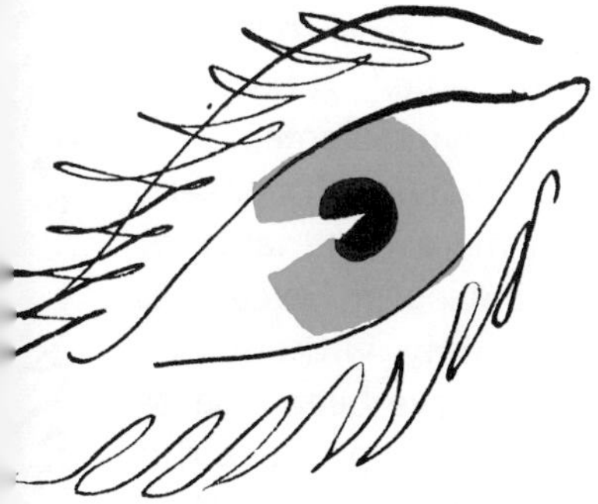

The commonplace is the world of naive perception, free from sophisticated semantic rationalization. The specialized semantics of established knowledge constitutes conventions which make reality abstract and second-hand. "The second-handedness of the learned world is the secret of its mediocrity." Learned conventions can be windowless fortresses which exclude viewing the world in new ways.

There is but one generic principle here: All these little shell-houses are doing the same thing, but not in the same way. This one *[a clam shell]* is based on the opening and shutting of the house. Two halves hinged together. These and many others without hinges—are they of a higher development, or, being less mechanical, are they inferior? Or the reverse? Can you see how all these lines and forms in all these colors and textures are tributary to the forces which are being exerted from within as the shell is being made, or, we might say, designed?

Every ornamentation, that is to say, every *pattern,* you see here, and the exquisite forms of the shells themselves, are tributary to the force that is being exerted by its like upon itself from within, as the growing shell is being made. Probably this one grew in coral beds, where the very shape and decoration of the thing was a feature of the preservation of its life, keeping its inhabitant from destruction by alien forces. That was true generally of these more exclusive cellular shells.

Look at this fantasy! *[holds up a striking shell]* Here is an original! All these infinitely variable forms are saying exactly the same thing. No interior change in *idea,* yet here is another and another and another *individual.* Here you may see what individuality might mean in a democracy. If you want a lesson in organic structure and decoration, here it is. And what colorations, what beautiful, textured color! Always, in these forms, in these little poems, there is the ebb and the flow, the plasticity of the elements by way of which, and in which, they came to exist. They are natural, you see. These little things are all of them lovely in their own way. Beautiful. All of them. Some of them are still young, growing up perhaps, the species still a becoming. . . .

Well, what is this element in nature which produces such fascinating, rich, harmonious individualities? Is it the same element that produces different human races, differing individualities within the races? Yes, it is all the same. But what is the secret of the forming of it all? These are the major things you should study, as artists, in the great book of creation. Because here is where the artist finds light thrown on what he feels. This expression of inner life by appropriate form is really his field.

Now, is there a *mind*, would you say, producing these infinite changes of form in nature? Is it a matter of mind? What is doing this? Why is it done? Science can investigate it, but science comes against a barrier it can never pierce. What this inner life is, we do not know. But this innate source of expression is what should inspire you all—give you faith in your own divinity, if that is the word for it, in your own inspiration, if that is more understandable.

You see, there never is a limit. Nothing indicates that the infinite variety could end, so long as the principle is inviolate. Look at this little beauty. Such a sweet little individuality! Civilization comes in and says, "Oh hell, let's get an easy pattern out of this, so we can stamp them out, all just the same." It becomes a cliché, a style. Then the divine element in it goes out. The quality that is divine disappears.

Housing has become a mere materiality of no great value to life whatsoever, except as little breeding stables entirely without any sense of God. There must have been a sense of God in these little forms to produce this infinite beauty of form. Just as there must be slumbering in all of us. There is in us, too, that interior sense of becoming, which we call God, working in us all, and which, you will see, has infinite capacity which no human mind can ever encompass and imprison.

There in these shells you have humble innate evidence. If we go into the human phases of what we call our divinity and consider the inherent element at work in us, as in all of

LLIM TRAUTS NHOJ
"WE SHAPE OUR DWELL INGS AND AF TERWARDS OUR DWE LLING S SH AP E US"
WASHING AWAY THE BOUNDARY BETWEEN NIGHT AND DAY HAS LOST US OUR SENS E OF TION TU CONNEC WITH NA RE AND ITS RHY THMS.

Is an English sentence a house?

life, you may find the same idea. Therein lies the value of these little things to us, if we study them as artists should. Here, in nature, is an architect's "school". . .

here as the beauty of these shells in their housing. . . .

I do not think we could have a better instance of common generic principle at work as individuality than in these little shells.

> The main thing now is not to paint precociously but to be, at least, to become an individual. The art of mastering life is the prerequisite for all further forms of expression, whether they are paintings, sculptures, tragedies or musical compositions. Not only to master life in practice, but to shape it meaningfully within me and to achieve as mature an attitude before it as possible. . . .

Nature loves individuality, resists and punishes the loss of it in any field of creation. If our civilization goes contrary to this divinity within the nature of us all, if it does not learn these secrets of behavior, of character, of appropriate changes of form, then what is going to happen to us? Where shall we go? Now is the time for us to say wherein lies salvation for us as human beings.

Is the solution creativity? Yes, that is the element needed now. It alone can prevent us from becoming standardized, from losing our rich and potent sense of life, which we see

What is our conclusion? This one: Once you understand the principle upon which this differentiation depends, you will astonish your kind by your own prolific capacity. To always turn out a different design from the one you did before will become inevitable. The secret of that variety is inherent in nature. She is jealous of it! If an architect does not have that secret, he will not be a great artist. He is missing essential quality. The key to creation is not in him.

PROBABLY HE WAS A WITCH.

it is
the
property
of
true
genius
to
disturb
all
settled
ideas.

Unless all existence is a medium of revelation, no particular revelation is possible.

Serigraphs are hand proofs in the same classification as etchings, lithographs, and wood engravings. They are issued by the artist in restricted signed editions and printed with separate handmade stencils for each color. A piece of finely woven silk is stretched on a rigid frame hinged to a board. The stencil is then wedded to the silk and paint is forced through the stencil openings and onto the page by means of a squee-gee. The name is derived from the root form for the word "silk," i.e., "seri" and "graph," the root form of "writing." In the same manner, "lithograph" is literally "stone-writing."

The limits of my language are the limits of my world.

We have entered into an age where perception in itself is becoming an instrument, and the gestalt of the eye a means of control.

THE SOLE FUNCTION OF THE MIND IS TO DEFINE.

From one point of view all experience is concept. Then, there must be different kinds of conceptual knowledge, because some kinds *feel* more intense than others. (These would be those that are now labeled experiential or sensate.) It is the inner mind that affects the outer world and makes it "seem" one thing or another. Knowing this, I can arrange to bring the world into myself in whatever way I choose. I choose to bring the world in as sensation—no matter *what* the source. I make it the most *real* seeming because I know it is this kind of knowledge that has the best chance to change me. So there is a real advantage in knowing that all knowledge is conceptual. It means I have control over **all** experience and can thus make **all** my life **seem** experiential if I so choose. It is the educated man who can control this process most fully. He need never be bored because he knows he can turn any "concept" into an "experience."

Logical, intelligent thinking does not need the support of a symbolic *system*, as it exists in the living language of society. Thinking is undoubtedly an internal system, a hierarchical ordering within the person of his interaction with the world. The symbol system of language mirrors and in a certain way expresses that internal organization. However, the internal organization of intelligence is not dependent on the language system; on the contrary, comprehension and use of the ready-made language is dependent on the structure of intelligence.

B

Sister Mary Corita

it is the property of true genius to disturb all settled ideas.
Sister Mary Corita IHM

How closely *are* words and pictures wedded?

When two objects, colors, people, get in relationship to each other, they both must alter in order to accommodate themselves to this new situation.

The art department at Immaculate Heart is a place full of questions, a place whose only answer is an attitude of openness to and celebration of life. It is part of Sister Corita's teaching method to keep her students constantly struggling with the kind of questions that make them open to all their experience, sifting it for possible answers.

To be rooted emotionally in "another's work of art" is to . . . sit before the fire, not to go out in the storm.

The next page is saved for you so that you can epitomize this book in some visual way. Would a supportive or complementary phrase or sentence as on page 123 help?

What can you learn about visual communication by letting others examine and comment on your work?

All people who have only two eyes and two ears are blind and deaf.

FOR OFFICIAL USE ONLY—DO NOT WRITE IN THIS SPACE

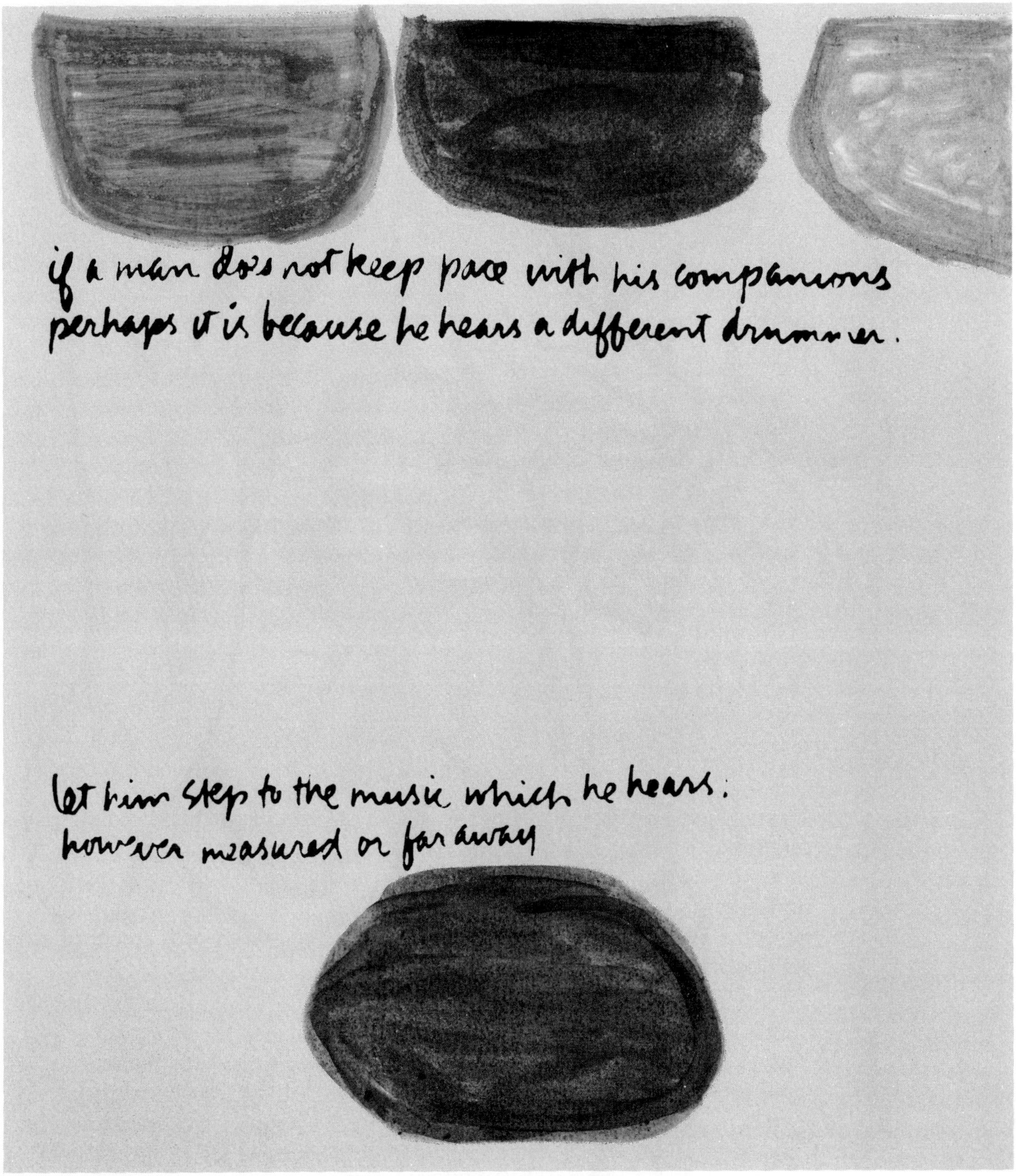
if a man does not keep pace with his companions
perhaps it is because he hears a different drummer.
let him step to the music which he hears:
however measured or far away

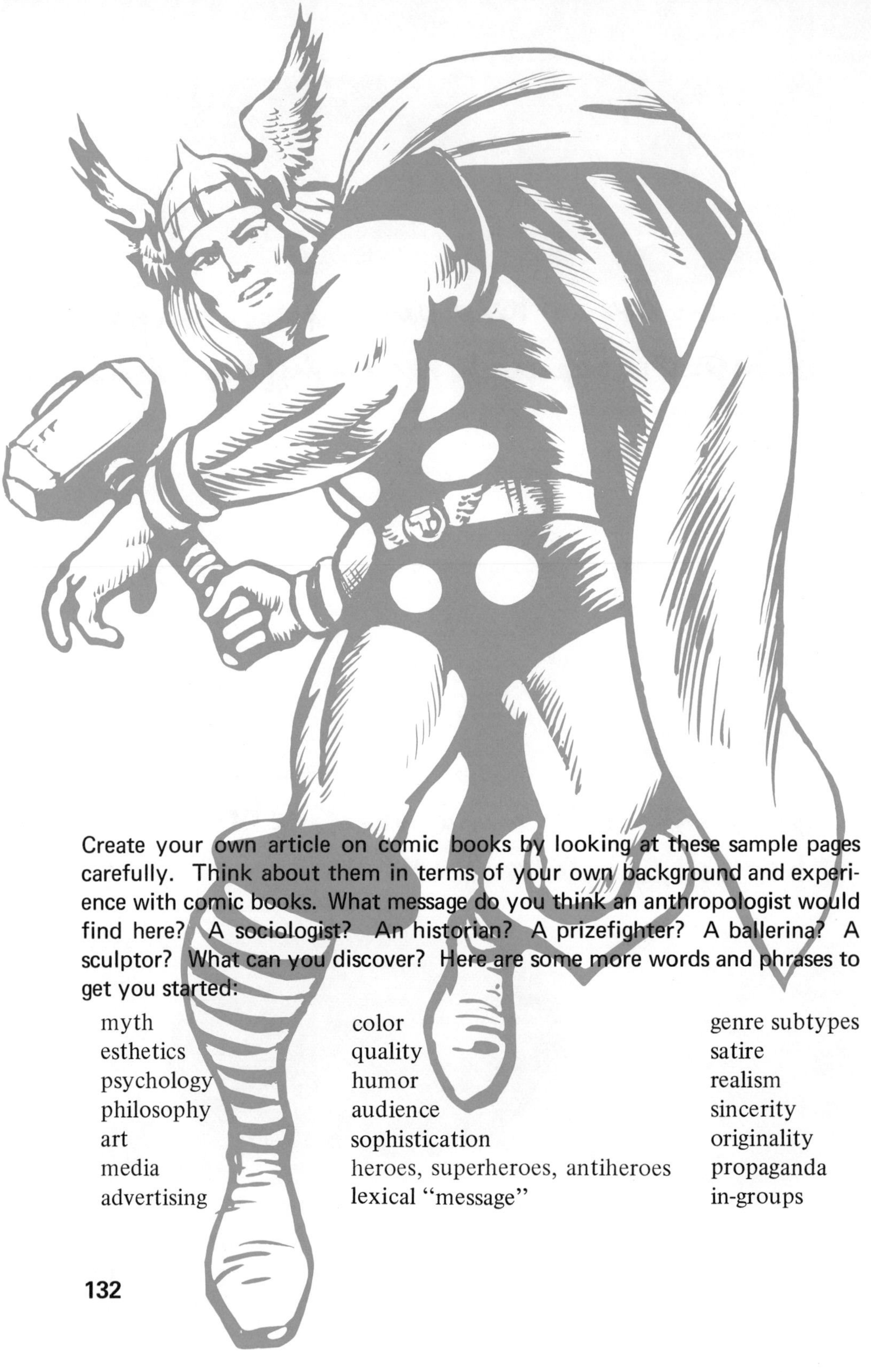

Create your own article on comic books by looking at these sample pages carefully. Think about them in terms of your own background and experience with comic books. What message do you think an anthropologist would find here? A sociologist? An historian? A prizefighter? A ballerina? A sculptor? What can you discover? Here are some more words and phrases to get you started:

myth	color	genre subtypes
esthetics	quality	satire
psychology	humor	realism
philosophy	audience	sincerity
art	sophistication	originality
media	heroes, superheroes, antiheroes	propaganda
advertising	lexical "message"	in-groups

BUT, THE VERY NEXT INSTANT...
AN' MAYBE I SHOULDN'T! I DIDN'T SEE THAT BIG BOHUNK WITH A CHAIR!
THAT OUGHTTA FINISH 'IM!
SWAK!
HE SURE--KNOCKED THE BREATH OUTTA ME! JUST THE SAME --THEY BETTER NOT COUNT ME OUT TOO SOON!
'CAUSE THEY JUST BELTED ME INTO THE ALLEY--WHERE I LEFT MY BOW AND ARROW!
AND, OL' HAWKEYE AINT ONE TO LET AN OMEN LIKE THAT SLIP BY HIM!
THUS, SCANT MOMENTS LATER, AS THE UNDERWORLD CHARACTERS RUSH TO THAT VERY SAME WINDOW...
YIPES! LOOK OUT--HE'S STILL ALIVE AN' KICKIN'!
SWIISSSH!
UGGNNHH! YOU'RE TELLIN' ME?!
THEN, LIKE ODYSSEUS AGAINST THE ARMY OF SINISTER SUITORS--LIKE ROBIN HOOD AGAINST THE HORDES OF A PLUNDERING PRINCE--THE ONE AND ONLY HAWKEYE MAKES HIS MOVE!
WHOOOOSH!
THIS IS THE KIND'A ACTION I WAS BORN FOR!
I MUST'A BEEN NUTTY TO THINK OF FIGHTIN' ANY OTHER WAY!
AND, AS A FINAL TRIO OF DESPERATE CUTTHROATS TRIES AN EN MASSE CHARGE...
THWA-KOOM!
WHIZZZ
PERSONAL NOTE: WE WERE GONNA LET THIS FIGHT GO ON FOR ANOTHER COUPLE OF PAGES--TILL WE LEARNED THAT THEN WE'D HAVE TO BUY A BOW-HUNTER'S LICENSE! --STINGY STAN.
OKAY, BRUISER--NOW THAT WE GOT THE PLACE ALL TO OURSELVES...
YOU'LL GET YOUR BLOOD MONEY--BUT, YOU'RE GONNA SPILL ALL YOU KNOW ABOUT THE BLACK WIDOW, OR--
S-SURE, HAWKEYE! DON'T SLUG ME AGAIN! I DIDN'T MEAN NO HARM--!
BESIDES, ALL I KNOW IS ABOUT WHERE THE COMMIES ARE KEEPIN' HER--HONEST!!
7

Pull your observations together in a journal entry. Compare your results with those of your classmates.

I began by saying that one of the paradoxes of education was that precisely at the point when you begin to develop a conscience, you must find yourself at war with your society. It is your responsibility to change society if you think of yourself as an educated person. And on the basis of the evidence—the moral and political evidence—one is compelled to say that this is a backward society. Now if I were a teacher in this school, or any Negro school, and I was dealing with Negro children, who were in my care only a few hours of every day and would then return to their homes and to the streets, children who have an apprehension of their future which with every hour grows grimmer and darker, I would try to teach them—I would try to make them know—that those streets, those houses, those dangers, those agonies by which they are surrounded, are criminal. I would try to make each child know that these things are the results of a criminal conspiracy to destroy him. I would teach him that if he intends to get to be a man, he must at once decide that he is stronger than this conspiracy and that he must never make his peace with it. And that one of his weapons for refusing to make his peace with it and for destroying it depends on what he decides he is worth. I would teach him that there are currently very few standards in this country which are worth a man's respect. That it is up to him to begin to change these standards for the sake of the life and the health of the country. I would suggest to him that the popular culture—as represented, for example, on television and in comic books and in movies—is based on fantasies created by very ill people, and he must be aware that these are fantasies that have nothing to do with reality. I would teach him that the press he reads is not as free as it says it is—and that he can do something about that, too. I would try to make him know that just as American history is longer, larger, more various, more beautiful, and more terrible than anything anyone has ever said about it, so is the world larger, more daring, more beautiful and more terrible, but principally larger—and that it belongs to him. I would teach him that he doesn't have to be bound by the expediencies of any given Administration, any given policy, any given time—that he has the right and the necessity to examine everything. I would try to show him that one has not learned anything about Castro when one says, "He is a Communist." This is a way of *not* learning something about Castro, something about Cuba, something, in fact, about the world. I would suggest to him that he is living, at the moment, in an enormous province. America is not the world and if America is going to become a nation, she must find a way—and this child must help her to find a way—to use the tremendous potential and tremendous energy which this child represents. If this country does not find a way to use that energy, it will be destroyed by that energy.

Does the sun come up by itself, or does each man create it?
Is the "new" day a creative act?

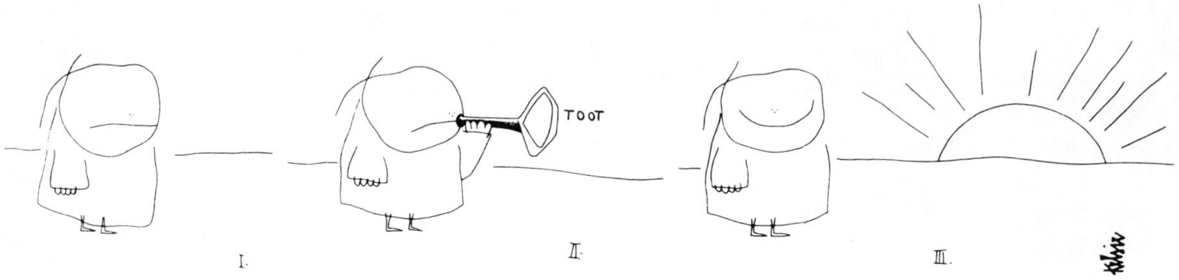

As we reached the end of the third and last of our talks, I may have unwittingly expressed my sense of relief, pérhaps in an indecently audible sigh. But Miró was visibly even more relieved than I. When we parted, he had the air of a visiting Spanish businessman who had just been quizzed by an over-inquisitive reporter from a trade-paper. He had done his duty, had avoided giving any unnecessary information, and would be able to report the whole incident satisfactorily, on his return home, to his Chamber of Commerce. Later, as I went through my notes of our talks and prepared the final draft, it occurred to me that he had perhaps been interviewing me. One thing was clear: to those who fail to find a satisfactory explanation of Miró's art in his actual works, no more explicit verbal explanation can ever be expected from the artist himself. Miró remains one of those rare artists to whom the magic of their own creative activity poses no problems. They accept it as something that requires no discussion, no explanation. It is their only way of being articulate, as natural to them as speech is to most of us.

ORPHEUS ?

Sculptured volumes, pencils, and points.

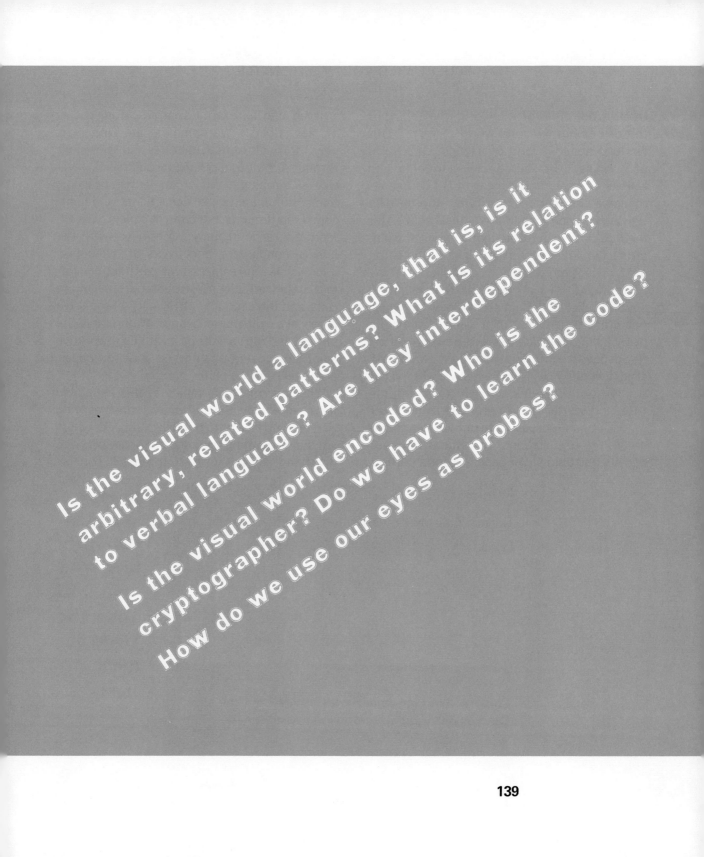

Is the visual world a language, that is, is it
arbitrary, related patterns? What is its relation
to verbal language? Are they interdependent?
Is the visual world encoded? Who is the
cryptographer? Do we have to learn the code?
How do we use our eyes as probes?

SCULPTURED VOLUMES, PENCILS, AND POINTS.

In all major cities of the world, the ebbing of the day brings a second world of light. This world is not the world of daylight, the world of a single light source, clear, friendly and legible. But neither is it the world of darkness—shadowed, mysterious, terrifying—loosened by the sunset upon men in the natural state. It is the world of man-made light sources, the glittering dynamic glow of artificial illumination of the twentieth-century metropolis.

The wealth of light available to us is almost beyond belief. Our light technology, on which our cities depend for their very existence, is overwhelming in richness and power. We are flooded with light. We switch light on and off, send it where we will, and, when we will, negate it. We project, reflect, fix, focus, chop, diffuse, and scatter it. We produce it in a thousand forms and shapes, from unbounded spatial extension to halations, sculptured volumes, pencils, and points. We bend it around corners; we even pipe light-formed patterns along cables of glass fibers. We communicate with light play: through motion pictures and television; through luminous displays; through such travel aids as running lights, road lights, beacons, flares, illuminated signs, signal lights, and light-coded instruments and control panels. We extend the range of human sensibility with the prisms, condensers, and lenses of telescopes, microscopes and cameras; with diffraction gratings, polarized screens, stroboscopes, selenium cells, and infra-red and ultraviolet sensors. We repair eyes with laser beams. We preserve the present and retrieve the past with light-sensitive emulsions coated on film, on glass, on paper, on metal printing plates.

What are the high values of this incredible light technology, the unifying factors that bring richness and clarity to our lives? Indeed, where are they? Washing away the boundary between night and day has lost us our sense of connec-

Create a metaphor which epitomizes this entire section.

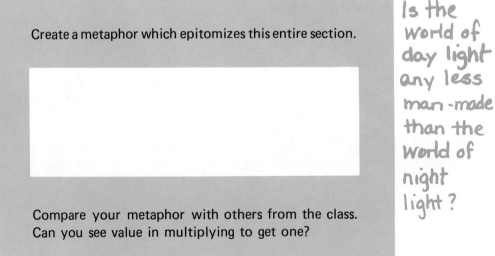

Compare your metaphor with others from the class. Can you see value in multiplying to get one?

Is the world of day light any less man-made than the world of night light?

tion with nature and its rhythms. If our artificial illumination is bright and ample, it is without the vitality, the wonderful ever-changing quality of natural light. For the warm, living play of firelight we have substituted the bluish, greenish television screen with its deadening stream of inane images. Hardly any of our sensitive creative talents have summoned the resolution to face the more luminous tasks of the world. The creative range of some of our greatest abilities is a spectrum of despair. Their desolate images have taken the foreground of the artistic horizon. They are afraid of light, the use of light, and the meaning of light.

What is the grammar of light?

Our new buildings, however, have opened themselves up to the flow of light, showing us marvelous new qualities of space. And, through lucky accident, the forms and colors of city lights often produce visions of great splendor. Why, then, are we not struck by the realization that the palette of a stupendous new civic art has been put in our hands? Is the city, the center of human life today, a runaway monster, so overwhelming as to be beyond all possibility of control? Perhaps. And perhaps not. With courage enough, we can, by plan and by purpose, produce rich, grand images of light and color on the scale of a whole environment.

This exhibition [held at the Carpenter Center for The Visual Arts in 1961] is a plea or more correctly, the prolegomenon for an emerging environmental art: the creative management of light. That radiant new visual poetry is not yet here, although its elements are all around us. It is being born.

It is an art of enormous promise. For painters, sculptors, and makers of motion pictures,

Light is a tool?

a field for creative originality, a way out of romanticism, circularity, and confusion. For architects and planners, a mighty tool with which to reshape our tangled, cluttered cityscapes. For the ordinary citizens of our dizzily expanding urbanized world, an aid to orientation in their surroundings. And it is an art of complete authenticity, of its own time and generated by the central forces of its time. As such, it holds out to all, both as individuals and as members of a society, that sense of harmony with life achieved only when the realities of their situation can be faced without trepidation and accepted as a blessing.

There is an age-old dialogue between man and light, and in it light has had three major roles: cognitive, esthetic, symbolic.

In its cognitive aspect, light reveals and delineates the world. It is the necessary condition of primary visual perception. It enables the world to take on existence through informing men about their environment. The speed of light is the one physical constant to which cosmologists can cling in their dissolving universe of measurement.

Sculptured volumes, pencils, and points.

In its esthetic aspect, light gives sensuous and emotional awareness of the world. Men at their earliest and simplest responded with wonder and delight to the radiant forces of sun, moon, and stars, developing a sense of communion with things tremendously far from their bodies.

In its symbolic aspect, in which the cognitive and esthetic are subsumed, light makes life focused, meaningful, and unified. All lands have their ancient myths in which light and

We have become abstractions?

darkness are metaphors—and more than metaphors, of life and death, good and evil, truth and falsehood, order and confusion, heaven and hell. The eternal flame at the tomb of an unknown soldier can trace its lineage back to the sacred perpetual fire tended by virgin priestesses in the temple of Vesta, and further back to the constantly fed fire at the cave mouth—the source of warmth, the protector against wild beasts, the dispeller of darkness and its terrors. The stained-glass windows of the great cathedrals, transforming sunlight into a mysterious, infinite extension of richly colored space, brought earthly men in contact with heaven, and provided one of the most deeply moving esthetic and religious experiences.

Our human nature is profoundly phototropic. Men obey their deepest instincts when they hold fast to light in comprehensive acts of perception and understanding through which they learn about the world, orient themselves within it, experience joy in living, and achieve a metaphoric symbolic grasp of life.

The exhibition [at Carpenter Center] aims to remind us of the role and significance of light as a central tool of art—past, present, and future. It is divided into three parts: the first part is a diagrammatical and historical survey of some creative uses of light phenomenon. It comprises works done over some three thousand years, from the ancient Egyptians to Hans Arp, from the thirteenth-century cathedral windows to the transparent painting of Moholy-Nagy. Every work of art is really a forming with light, but the works presented here have been restricted to deft and seemingly conscious examples of light handling. They show the modulation of light on several levels—physical, physiological, and symbolic—including such uses as spatial delineation by light and shade, translucency, transparency, specular reflections, and color production and induction.

The second part is didactic. It covers a period of over twenty-five years, and is mainly student work from a long record of teaching. All of these are explorations of some of the basic problems in light handling including systematic studies of stationary and mobile play of light.

The third part of the exhibition consists of attempts by artists in Europe and this country to explore the creative potentials of light use today.

They are improvisations, visionary toys; behind them is a dream of an emerging art embracing a new scale of the environment.

This is all a summing up of what we know from the past. The major tasks lie ahead.

In what sense is light technology comparable to the technology of printing?

Has this section been born yet? Who is the obstetrician?

What are some of the ways in which this essay on light illuminates ideas you have gathered from your study of this section of the book?

Is the author a "witch"? Would the boy's mother think so?

Is light English?

Is form a message in this section?

From a handbook on electricity:

. . . As the current increases, the fuse is melted and the circuit is broken before the copper wires get hot enough to cause any damage. Fuses are rated according to the current strength at which they will melt. Thus, a 10-ampere fuse will allow currents up to 10 amperes to pass but will melt when the current exceeds that strength. *When a fuse has blown out, it is not sufficient merely to replace it with a new one*, because, although it does permit current to flow once more, it offers no remedy for the situation that caused the fuse to blow out.

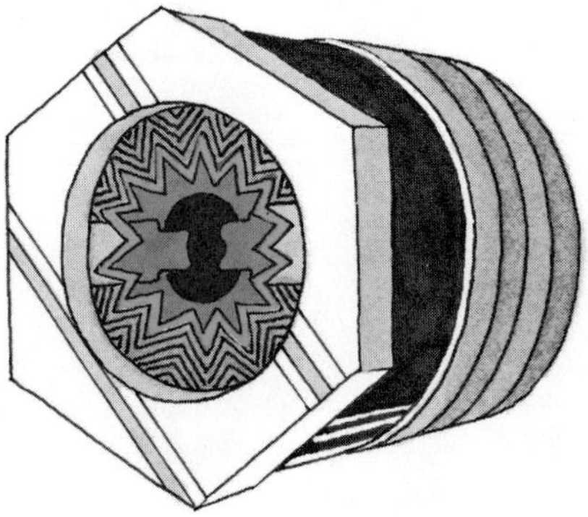

POEM

When a fuse
Has blown,
It is not sufficient
Merely
To replace
It
With a new
One.

How many meanings does the first specimen normally invite? Does the second invite more? Why?

Are rhyme, meter, arrangement on a page "messages"?

Is your "presence" or "form" a message?

How important is it to be able to "read" the form or the medium itself?

How much are we affected by the "form" in which a stimulus becomes known to us?

"Code of Life"

A new film about the mystery of heredity and growth control, "Cracking the Code of Life," is being offered by the Contra Costa County Branch of the American Cancer Society for viewing in local schools.

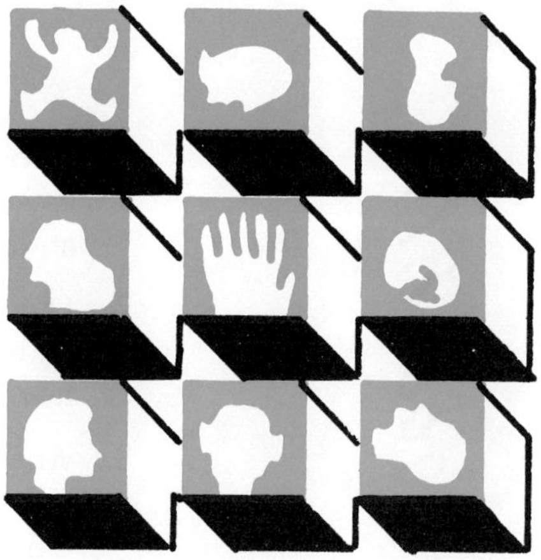

The notion that name and essence bear a necessary and internal relation to each other, that the name does not merely denote but actually is the essence of its object, that the potency of the real thing is contained in the name—that is one of the fundamental assumptions of the mythmaking consciousness itself.

Is there a sense in which art is a "lie"? If so can a lie help us to see the truth? Does this probe suggest a sense in which this question is valid: "It's true even if it didn't happen"?

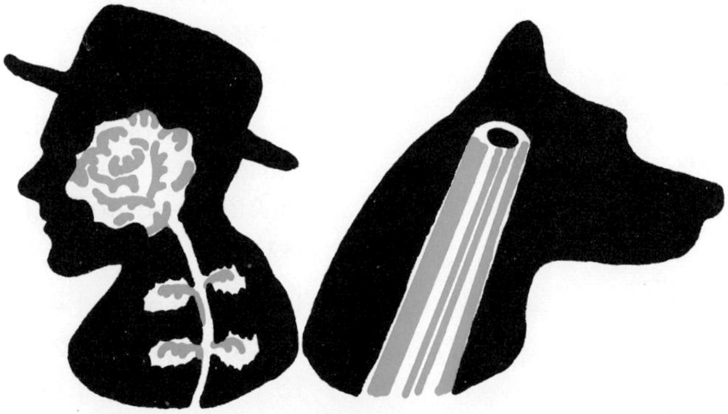

TEST YOUR . . . WHAT?

Significance is an afterthought.

1. Allow yourself five minutes to rearrange the letters O-W-D-E-N-A-R-W to spell a new word—but not a proper name, nor anything foreign or "unnatural." Write it out.
2. Quickly now: How many animals of each species did Adam take aboard the Ark with him? (Note that the question is not how many *pairs*, but how many *animals*.)
3. What unusual characteristic do these six words have in common?
   DEFT SIGHING CALMNESS CANOPY FIRST STUN
   (Please complete your answer within five minutes.)
4. Figure out this problem in diplomatic relations: If an international airliner crashed *exactly* on the U.S.-Canadian border, where would they be required by international law to *bury* the survivors? (If you can't decide within *one minute* what your answer will be, please go on to the next item.)
5. What is the minimum number of active baseball players on the playing field during any part of an inning?
6. Figure out this problem within *one minute:* If one face of a cube measures 2" x 4", what is the area of *each* of the faces, and what is the *total* area of all eight faces? (Jot down your answer in the margin.)
7. A farmer had 17 sheep. All but nine died. How many did he have left?
8. An archeologist reported finding two gold coins dated 46 B.C. Later, at a dinner in his honor, he was thoroughly and openly discredited by a disgruntled fellow archeologist. Why?
9. A man living in Winston-Salem, North Carolina, may not be buried in a state west of the Mississippi River—nor in Hawaii or Alaska—even in the event of Presidential intervention. Why is this?
10. If you went to bed at 8 o'clock last night, and set your alarm clock to get up at 9 o'clock this morning, why on earth—after 13 hours' rest, especially!—are you so sleepy today?

11. If you had only one match, and entered a room to start up a kerosene lamp, an oil heater, and a wood-burning stove, which would you light first—and why?

12. Quickly, now: Divide 30 by ½, and add 10. What is the answer?

13. If your doctor gave you three pills, and told you to take one every half hour, how long would it require for you to take all of them?

14. Two men played checkers. They played five games, and each man won three. How do you explain this?

15. Look at these phrases, for a moment, to get them firmly in mind:

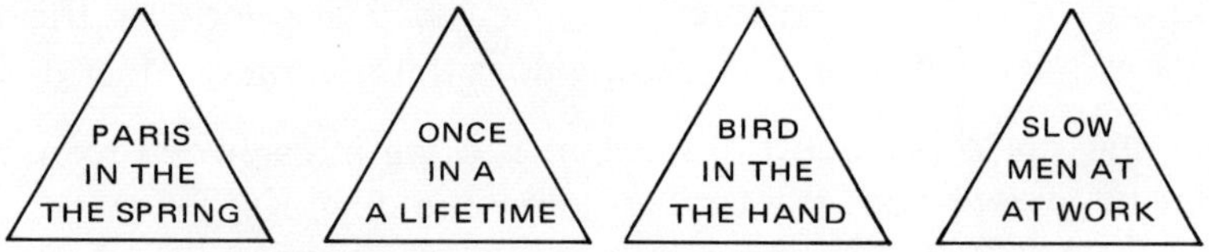

Now look away, and write down these exact phrases.

"1. a new word, 2ITWASNOAH.3EACHCONTAINSTHREELETTERSINALPHABETICALSEQUENCE.4WEDONOTBURYSURVIVORS.5TEN.6ITISNOTACUBE.7NINE.8ACOINPRINTEDBEFORECHRISTWASBORNWOULDNOTHAVEB.C.PRINTEDONIT.9HEISSTILLALIVE.10THEALARMWOULDRINGAT9:00THESAMEEVENING.11THEMATCH.12SEVENTY.13ONEHOUR.14THEYWERENOTPLAYINGEACHOTHER.15NOTICETHEREPETITION OF *the the, a a, the the,* and *at at.*

ANALYZING THE TEST

This is a test of

a. rigidity
b. perception
c. reading skill
d. awareness
e. capacity to generalize
f. creativity
g. other

1. One student said that anyone taking the test who is able to get one answer right should be able to get about eleven more right, too. Do you agree? What capacity would the ability to go from one to several demonstrate?
2. Would a "good" conventional reader do well or poorly on this test? For example, on what habits of reading does the trick in number one depend?
3. Examine the other questions. What is done in each one to outwit you? What in general does the test presume about you?
4. Are all the questions of the same level of difficulty? Should they be? Which questions do not belong with the others?
5. What does this test have to do with English?
   With the aims of this book?
   With taking tests?
   With one's approach to life?

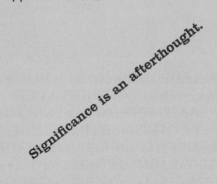

Significance is an afterthought.

Investigations

VOL. 1, NO. 3

CLEAN FUN AT RIVERHEAD
by Tom Wolfe

YOU FORCE KIDS TO REBEL
by Steven Kelman

and lots of other good stuff

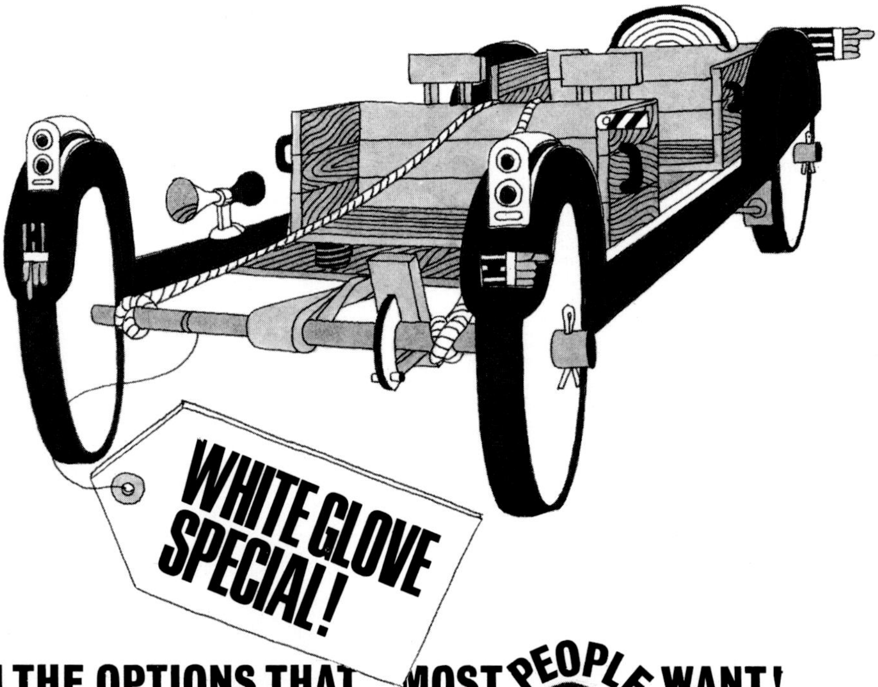

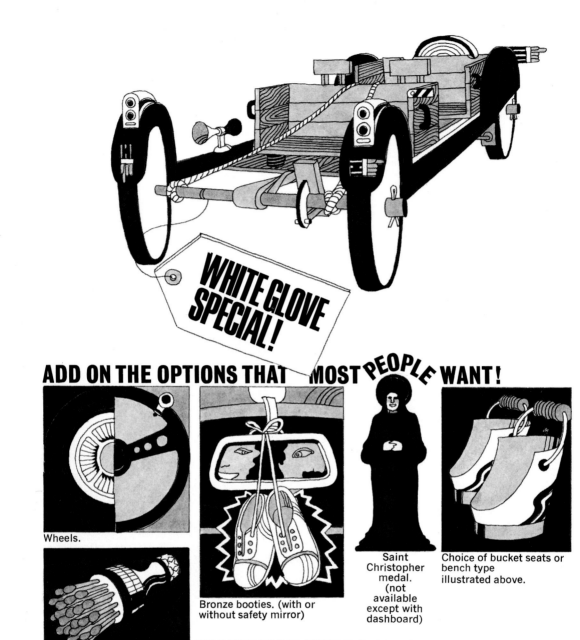

ADD ON THE OPTIONS THAT MOST PEOPLE WANT!

Wheels.

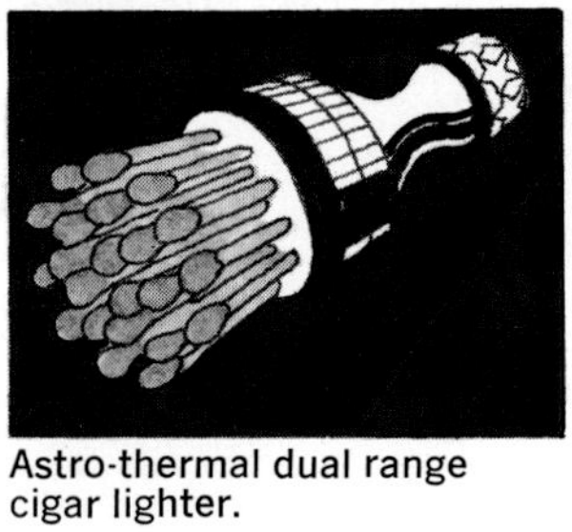

Astro-thermal dual range cigar lighter.

Bronze booties. (with or without safety mirror)

Saint Christopher medal. (not available except with dashboard)

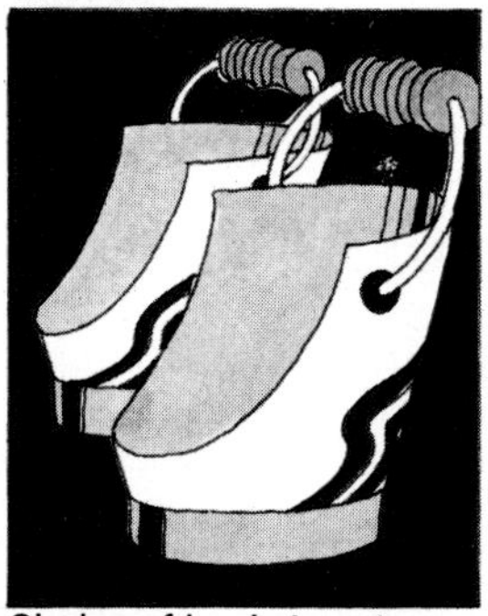

Choice of bucket seats or bench type illustrated above.

VISIT YOUR WHEELER-DEALER TODAY!!!!

HYENA GT2x4

HAVE THE

LAST LAUGH ON YOUR FRIENDS!

Guest Editor
. . . the Highest form of Literature

I BECOME AN AUTHOR

George Bernard Shaw

For All Time

. . . Journalism can claim to be the highest form of literature; for all the highest literature is journalism. The writer who aims at producing the platitudes which are "not for an age, but for all time" has his reward in being unreadable in all ages; whilst Plato and Aristophanes trying to knock some sense into the Athens of their day, Shakespeare peopling that same Athens with Elizabethan mechanics and Warwickshire hunts, Ibsen photographing the local doctors and vestrymen of a Norwegian parish, Carpaccio painting the life of St. Ursula exactly as if she were a lady living in the next street to him, are still alive and at home everywhere among the dust and ashes of many thousands of academic, punctilious, most archaeologically correct men of letters and art who spent their lives haughtily avoiding the journalist's vulgar obsession with the ephemeral. I also am a journalist, proud of it, deliberately cutting out of the works all that is not journalism, convinced that nothing that is not journalism will live long as literature, or be of any use whilst it does live. I deal with all periods; but I never study any period but the present, which I have not yet mastered and never shall; and as a dramatist I have no clue to any historical or other personage save that part of him which is also myself, and which may be nine tenths of him or ninety-nine hundredths, as the case may be (if, indeed, I do not transcend the creature), but which, anyhow, is all that can ever come within my knowledge of his soul. The man who writes about himself and his own time is the only man who writes about all people and about all time.

From the editor's desk. . .

Create some questions you think would invite investigation without seeming condescending. When you have written your probes, compare them with the probes others have written.

As you thumb through this "magazine" (would you agree that it is a magazine?), you will notice that there are some blank colored spaces where the advertisements would be. Part of your work with this section will be to create advertisements to fill the blank spaces. You should write your own copy and suggest illustrations. What do you have to know about advertisements in order to do this?

Space has been left for filler material. Find the most appropriate fillers you can. What considerations are involved? Try to create illustrations to go with the articles. You may find it challenging to write blurbs for some of the articles in this section.

Perhaps you would like to write a letter to the editor in which you express your feelings about one or another of the selections. Critical thoughts couched in less formal terms would make excellent entries for your journal.

Publisher: *The Macmillan Company, 866 Third Avenue, New York, N.Y. 10022.*
Editors: *John N. K. Young, Marcia Schonzeit*
Art Director: *Dick Kaseler*
Contributing editors: *William Sparke* and *Clark McKowen*

ARTICLES

FEATURES

LETTERS

General

Sir:
Although the book looks like a series of gimmicks, it's based on a good understanding of how language works and what students need.

James Plummer
Auburn, Ala.

Dear Sir:
The materials in this book lead inexorably to some basic insights about language that are much more exciting and meaningful than if they had been learned in a traditional way.

Judie N.
Concord, Calif.

Gentlemen:
Many of my students would get lost on "manifold" (isn't it a part of an automobile?) and Goethe (isn't that an Elizabethan verb as in "he go-eth before me"?) On another page the authors tell the student that they are being provided with "catalytic questions" as if that were very helpful; well, it is not until we explain a little chemistry.

Professor Jebediah
Conant, (Ph.D.)
Ann Arbor, Mich.

Sir:
The montage effect of the first section makes it appear almost structureless (some devices are never "explained"), but the authors do as promised: they double back to pick up the threads of preceding elements so that the student has repeated opportunities for inductive reasoning. The purpose is admirable—to make the student see what he is looking at by forcing him to shift his point of view.

W. H. K. III
Mt. Palomar, Calif.

Editor:
The first section starts well, with some basic insights into the sentence and without all the paraphernalia that usually accompanies it. The student is allowed to discover things as he goes along. The questions lead naturally to these discoveries. The idea of the student keeping a journal is excellent, for the journal will serve not only as a place to practice writing but also as a written record of the student's discoveries, his continuous synthesis.

Harriet Butcher
Chicago, Ill.

Steinberg—Silly

Sir:
I tried to answer all the questions about the Steinberg cartoon but I think it was a waste of time. The cartoon is a silly one, anyway. What has it got to do with English?

Betty Rino
Bryn Mawr, Pa.

Sir:
I didn't get anything out of the Steinberg cartoon until I began to look at it closely. Then it began to have some meaning for me. The more I looked, the more interested I became. I hope you will put more cartoons like this in the book. I think this kind of thing is fun.

James B.
Kaukaura, Wis.

Comics

Gentlemen:
I was shocked to find stuff from the comic books in a textbook which pretends to be for college students. Are you really serious? Comics are for people with lazy, juvenile minds. I'll buy some of the other scraps and pieces you've gathered together, but comics is going too far!

Lena Jensen
Medicine Hat, Alberta.

Witch

Dear Editor:
I don't understand why you have included *The Witch* in a college textbook. It is a child's story, full of the supernatural and myths. It is a long way from being a college level story in my opinion.

Hazel J.
Salem, Mass.

Individuality

Sir:
I enjoyed reading *Faith in Your Own Individuality.* I agree with everything the author says. I think articles of this kind are very important in this mass-oriented culture of ours.

Russ Ghoti
Agra, India.

Ballet

Gentlemen:
Ballet is one of the great classical arts. You touch on the subject very superficially. I would like to have seen an article in the book written about ballet by an expert.

Margot Insa
Flagstaff, Ariz.

Wife-Wooing

Dear Sir:
It is easy to see why you published Updike's story in this book. The focus is mainly on sex. I find stories like this very boring.

M. J. B.
Pasadena, Calif.

Sir:
Why did you publish *Wife-Wooing* in this book? It is too difficult to get the meaning from it. I enjoy stories that don't have hidden meanings.

A. P.
Cambridge, Mass.

Dear Editor:
I think John Updike's story is great! It stunned me. I was aware of the processes of metaphor, kinesics, and other residues from the preceding section in the book. At the same time I was very much involved in the story.

A. H.
Stanford, Calif.

Nonsense

Editor:
I think English is difficult enough without having to mess around with "nonsense" words. What's the point of doing this?

H. I. L.
Falls Church, Va.

Paris is talking about . . .

The Invasion of English Words

France is working hard to make French the official language of Europe, if not the world.

Committees have been organized in Common Market countries to achieve this goal.

The first small break-through came recently when a convention of world gypsies adopted French as their "language for diplomacy."

The only trouble is that, as in other Common Market matters, the French cannot stop England and America from boring their way in.

So many English words have now been incorporated into the daily conversations of Frenchmen that Professor Etiémble, the French word specialist, has dubbed the language "Le Franglais," and is writing a dictionary on the subject.

Even the most ordinary Frenchman now uses such English words as "weekend," "cocktail," "garden party," "pin-up," "baby sitter," "playboy," "cover girl," "gangster," "pickpocket," "music hall," and "sandwich."

There are so many English expressions in French sports that the Prieure golf course near Paris has begun a campaign to forbid English words.

Thus the popular word "club-house" is replaced by "la maison des joueurs," clubs must be called "les cannes," and a caddy must not respond unless he is addressed as "le cadet."

In the assimilation of English expressions by the French, slight confusion sometimes results. Volley ball becomes known as "le volley," wrestling becomes "le catch," and "un match de basket" is a basketball game.

Jean-Charles Lepidi, a deputy in the French National Assembly, is shocked about French TV which dubs its lady announcers "speakerines," calls ballets "shows," and uses such other Anglicisms as "interview," "playback," and "flash."

Things are even worse in the night clubs where to dance the surf is to be a "surfeur" or a "surfeuse" and to "faire le surfing."

Since the romantic fox trot is called "le slow" by Parisians, there is now a night spot called "Le Slow Club" on the Rue de Rivoli.

Harold Lander has produced a ballet called the "Hop Frog" at the Opera, which was almost as confusing as a ballet titled "The Goal" about basketball, which has no goals.

Theatrical titles are subject to slight chaos when adopted in their English originals by the French. *France-Soir* has reported on an American success called "Who is Afraid of Virginia's Woolves," and *Libération* reported on an English play "The Aspirin Papers," that turned out to be "The Aspern Papers."

Names get a similar disorderly treatment. Bob Hope has been referred to as Boob Hope, and Anthony Quinn as Anthony Queen. NBC came out as NBS, and French TV showed a re-run of the "Dinah Shove Show."

Sid Luft was promoted to Sir Luft, and Donald Duck has been dubbed Donald Duke.

Ferris Hartman

France's dictionaries keep adding more English words every year. The season the *Petit Larousse* has added "clergyman," "hobby," "science-fiction," "twin-set," and "twist." The Littré dictionary still says of the word "tourist," "Above all, an English traveler in France, Switzerland and Italy."

The "40 immortals" of France who make up the Académie Française and meet every Thursday to work on the nation's official dictionary are about equally divided on accepting many English expressions.

Maurice Genevoix, permanent secretary of the Academy, has said, "I am opposed to the word Twist, and I am opposed to the dance, too."

Pasteur Valéry-Rado declared, "Twist has no translation in our language and could be accepted. The Common Market of languages may demand it." ▬

Menu for today

KCBS' Bob Callahan, browsing through the Palace Garden Court's luncheon menu Wednesday, found "Spanish Omelette—$1.95" on one page, and "Omelette Espagnole—$2.45" on another. "What's the difference?" he asked the waiter captain. "Fifty cents," replied that eminence blandly. . . . Addendumburger: The Mark Hopkins once listed an "International Sandwich—$1.75," which turned out to be a plain hamburger on a bun. "Why do you call it 'International'?" I asked the then boss, K. Hart Smith. "So we can charge $1.75 for it," he explained K. Hartily. —*Herb Caen*

Life Cycle of Common Man

Howard Nemerov

Roughly figured, this man of moderate habits,
This average consumer of the middle class,
Consumed in the course of his average life
span
Just under half a million cigarettes,
Four thousand fifths of gin and about
A quarter as much vermouth; he drank
Maybe a hundred thousand cups of coffee,
And counting his parents' share it cost
Something like half a million dollars
To put him through life. How many beasts
Died to provide him with meat, belt and
shoes
Cannot be certainly said.
But anyhow,
It is in this way that a man travels through
time,
Leaving behind him a lengthening trail
Of empty bottles and bones, of broken shoes,
Frayed collars and worn out or outgrown
Diapers and dinner jackets, silk ties and
slickers.

Given the energy and security thus achieved,
He did...? What? The usual things, of course,
The eating, dreaming, drinking and begetting,
And he worked for the money which was to
pay
For the eating, et cetera, which were necessary
If he were to go on working for the money, et
cetera.
But chiefly he talked. As the bottles and
bones
Accumulated behind him, the words
proceeded
Steadily from the front of his face as he
Advanced into the silence and made it verbal.
Who can tally the tale of his words? A lifetime
Would barely suffice for their repetition;
If you merely printed all his commas the result
Would be a very large volume, and the number
of times
He said "thank you" or "very little sugar,
please,"
Would stagger the imagination. There were
also
Witticisms, platitudes, and statements be-
ginning
"It seems to me" or "As I always say."

Consider the courage in all that, and behold
the man
Walking into deep silence, with the ectoplastic
Cartoon's balloon of speech proceeding
Steadily out of the front of his face, the words
Borne along the breath which is his spirit
Telling the numberless tale of his untold Word
Which makes the world his apple, and forces
him to eat.

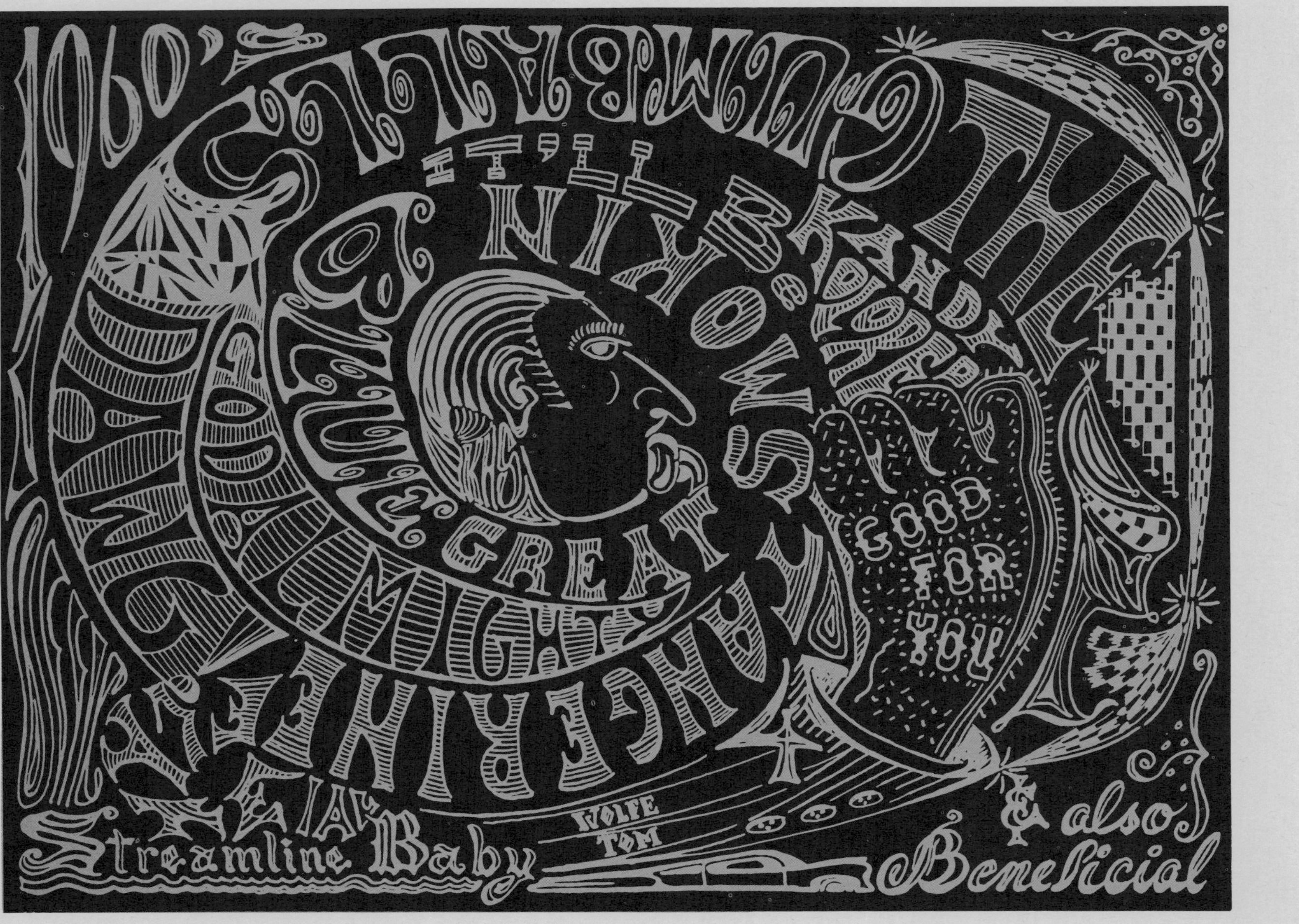

1960's
GREAT
MIGHTY
GOOD FOR YOU
Streamline Baby
WOLFE TOM
& also Beneficial

CLEAN FUN AT RIVERHEAD

by Tom Wolfe

The inspiration for the demolition derby came to Lawrence Mendelsohn one night in 1958 when he was nothing but a spare-ribbed twenty-eight-year-old stock car driver halfway through his 10th lap around the Islip, L.I., Speedway and taking a curve too wide. A lubberly young man with a Chicago boxcar haircut came up on the inside in a 1949 Ford and caromed him 12 rows up into the grandstand, but Lawrence Mendelsohn and his entire car did not hit one spectator.

"That was what got me," he said. "I remember I was hanging upside down from my seat belt like a side of Jersey bacon and wondering why no one was sitting where I hit. 'Lousy promotion,' I said to myself.

"Not only that, but everybody who *was* in the stands forgot about the race and came running over to look at me gift-wrapped upside down in a fresh pile of junk."

At that moment occurred the transformation of Lawrence Mendelsohn, racing driver, into Lawrence Mendelsohn, promoter, and, a few transactions later, owner of the Islip Speedway, where he kept seeing more of this same underside of stock car racing that everyone in the industry avoids putting into words. Namely, that for every purist who comes to see the fine points of the race, such as who is going to win, there are probably five waiting for the wrecks to which stock car racing is so gloriously prone.

The pack will be going into a curve when suddenly two cars, three cars, four cars tangle, spinning and splattering all over each other and the retaining walls, upside down, right side up, inside out and in pieces, with the seams bursting open and discs, rods, wires and gasoline spewing out and yards of sheet metal shearing off like Reynolds Wrap and crumpling into the most baroque shapes, after which an ash-blue smoke starts seeping up from the ruins and a thrill begins to spread over the stands like Newburg sauce.

So why put up with the monotony between crashes?

Such, in brief, is the early history of what is culturally the most important sport ever originated in the United States, a sport that ranks with the gladiatorial games of Rome as a piece of national symbolism. Lawrence Medelsohn had a vision of an automobile sport that would be all crashes. Not two cars, not three cars, not four cars, but 100 cars would be out in an arena doing nothing but smashing each other into shrapnel. The car that outrammed and outdodged all the rest, the last car that could still move amid the smoking heap, would take the prize money.

So at 8:15 at night at the Riverhead Raceway, just west of Riverhead, L.I., on Route 25, amid the quaint tranquility of the duck and turkey farm flatlands of eastern Long Island, Lawrence Mendelsohn stood up on the back of a flat truck in his red neon warmup jacket and lectured his 100 drivers on the rules and niceties of the new game, the "demolition derby." And so at 8:30 the first 25 cars moved out onto the raceway's quarter-mile stock car track. There was not enough room for 100 cars to mangle each other. Lawrence Mendelsohn's dream would require four heats. Now the 25 cars were placed at intervals all about the circumference of the track, making flatulent revving noises, all headed not around the track but toward a point in the center of of the infield.

ANCIENT MUSIC

(After a Medieval Song)

Winter is Icummen in,
Lhude sing Goddamm,
Raineth drop and staineth slop,
And how the wind doth ramm!
Sing: Goddamm.
Skiddeth bus and sloppeth us,
An ague hath my hamm.
Freezeth river, turneth liver,
Damn you, sing: Goddamm.
Goddamm, Goddamm, 'tis why I am, Goddamm,
So 'gainst the winter's balm.
Sing goddamm, damm, sing Goddamm,
Sing goddamm, sing goddamm, DAMM.

EZRA POUND

Then the entire crowd, about 4,000, started chanting a countdown, "Ten, nine, eight, seven, six, five, four, three, two," but it was impossible to hear the rest, because right after "two" half the crowd went into a strange whinnying wail. The starter's flag went up, and the 25 cars took off, roaring into second

(continued on page 168)

ZEN IN THE ART OF TENNIS

by Calvin Tomkins

Three years ago this spring, I began to have serious trouble with my tennis game. At first it seemed nothing more than the customary early-season awkwardness and bad timing, but when my double faults and netted backhands carried over into mid-July, causing me public humiliation and private anguish, I knew that some drastic therapy was needed. The three men I usually played with were patient and understanding. They gave various advice, but none of it helped until that hot Saturday morning in August when Wally Michaels took me aside between sets and asked, casually enough, "Have you ever thought of trying Zen?"

Coming from Wally, a steady, somewhat plodding backcourt player, the question startled me. This was long before Zen Buddhism had become a commonplace in suburbia, and hard as it is to believe now, the books of Daisetz T. Suzuki, pioneer of Zen in America, were then known to very few tennis players. Cocktail-party guests had not yet begun to ask each other Zen *koans,* the riddle questions designed to coerce the mind into a state of nonrational awareness. It was even possible to spend a whole evening talking to an old friend without having to hear about his *satori* (enlightenment) or having to argue the relative merits of beatnik Zen, square Zen, and ladies' Zen. I usually find myself a little ahead of contemporary trends, however, and I had recently read five or six of Dr. Suzuki's early books on Zen, and was then in the midst of a lovely small volume, by a German Zen addict named Eugen Herrigel, called *Zen in the Art of Archery.* Wally's question therefore dropped like a stone into deep water. I knew, suddenly and inexplicably, that Zen could well be the answer to my tennis problem.

The question was, where could I find a teacher? Wally Michaels surprised me again by saying he would ask his *roshi,* or Zen Master, whom he had been going to for about two years in hopes of increasing his annual sales record (*Zen in the Art of Salesmanship*). He did so that same afternoon, but the *roshi* was unable to suggest anyone. "Try the Yellow Pages," said Wally. "You never know." Without much enthusiasm, I dug out the Classified and leafed through it until I came to "Tennis Instruction." About halfway down the page, my eye was arrested by an unmistakably Japanese, Zen-sounding name, I. Ashikawa, which was followed by the cryptic message "Fish & Birds" and an address on upper Broadway, in the Bronx. I sprang to my feet with a cry of triumph. What a perfect Zen analogy—tennis balls darting like fish, flying like birds! My wife suggested, in her literal way, that it sounded like a pet shop that had slipped into the tennis listings by mistake, but I knew better. Without a doubt, Ashikawa was my man.

The next afternoon, I took the car and drove to the upper-Broadway address, which turned out to be a small shop sandwiched between two early-Bronx-baroque apartment houses. The dusty windows of the shop were full of bird cages and tropical-fish tanks—a nice bit of deception. In my eagerness, I rang the bell repeatedly for ten minutes or so, forgetting that novices often wait outside a Zen monastery for days or even weeks before being considered worthy to be admitted. Finally, the door opened and a feathery wisp of a man, with white hair and a yellow sleeveless shirt, put his head out and said brusquely, "Closed. Go away."

"I've come to see about tennis lessons," I said breathlessly. "Are you a *roshi*? Do you teach the *dharma*?" Instead of replying, he flung a handful of birdseed in my face, slammed the door, and disappeared.

Imagine my delight! Here was proof that I had stumbled on a true Zen Master, who would break down my slavish habits of rational, logical thought, and in so doing perhaps cure my wrong-headed backhand. I drove home with a high heart, certain that I was well begun on my quest for enlightenment.

The next day, I was back. When Ashikawa threw the birdseed at me this time, I managed to bow politely before he slammed the door. Two days later, I was able to pick up a pinch of seed and hand it back to him. The following Monday, he let me come in.

The place did give somewhat the appearance of a pet shop. Bird cages lined one side wall and tropical-fish tanks the other. Mr. Ashikawa led me to a small, cluttered office in the back, where a tethered myna bird glared at me with bloodshot eyes and said, enigmatically, "Porry want a clacker?" Ashikawa asked me if I wanted to buy the bird, and when I declined he demanded to know just what it was I did want.

"Whatever you can teach me," I said, as humbly as possible. He stared at me for a long time, obviously trying to make out whether I was a restless dilettante or a serious Zen seeker. At length, he gave a little grunt and nodded his white head. At such a moment, words would have been superfluous.

From then on, I came every morning for an hour, before going to my office downtown.

Ashikawa showed me how to clean the bird cages and the fish tanks, and I was content to do so. I remembered reading the story of the young samurai who went to a famous Zen Master to learn swordsmanship and was put to work building fires and cooking the Master's meals. When he unwisely asked how long it would be before they could begin lessons in swordsmanship, the Master struck him smartly on the head with a heavy stick, and from that time forward the Master would sneak up behind him every time his back was turned and give him a thrashing. After several years of this, the samurai became adept at dodging blows from any angle. One day, he saw the Master himself bending over a cooking fire, and, unable to resist the temptation, raised his own stick to strike him. Without even looking up, the Master caught the blow on the lid of a pot. This opened the samurai's eyes to the real secrets of swordsmanship, and he was forever grateful to the Master, although his wits became so confused by the repeated blows on the head that he never amounted to much as a swordsman himself. Determined to avoid the

(continued on page 170)

THE FIRST CHRISTMAS CAROL

THE Country folk with eager eyes,
The stable door came flocking round;
And "Shepherds, there," they cried, "He lies
And there the Babe ye seek is found:
At Caesar's call, from south to north,
Our tribe is told in Bethlehem:
And priest and Levite thrust them forth,—
The ox's stall was meet for them."

The shepherds came—a simple crew,
In rustic order bent they there;
And still the shepherd pipes they blew,
And sang betimes a solemn air:
They bent, they gazed, "to God the praise:"
They rose, and hymn'd their hymn again;
It seem'd a strain of elder days,
When God vouchsafed to walk with men.

And then they told how late at night,
By David's Well they watch'd their fold;
The vale was wall'd to left and right,
And screen'd their huddling sheep from cold.
God's angel stoop'd in bright array,
"Fear not," he said, "but shout and sing;
To you, in David's town, this day
Is born a Saviour, Christ the King.

"And this shall be the sign: ye'll find
The Babe within a manger laid."
Then sudden o'er the angel shines
The heavenly host: on harps they play'd.
And, while he mounted in their light,
From sky to earth the chorus ran,
"Glory to God in highest height,
Peace upon earth, good-will to man."

Such was the tale, and "poor our skill,"
They said, "but God hath tuned the song,
And henceforth still, o'er dale and hill,
Our humble pipes to God belong:
And 'Christ is born!' we'll shout amain,
'Glory to God in highest height:'
So carol we that angel strain,
Yearly to greet thee, blessed night."

They marvell'd at the shepherds' tale,
The people thronging to and fro;
"The stated seasons never fail,
The years draw nigh," they whisper'd low:
And seers before the manger stepp'd
And hail'd Him—"Lord and King thou art."
But all these sayings Mary kept,
And mused upon them in her heart.

Oh! Mary, mother, meek and mild,
Thy faith has need of strengthening now:
Gaze long upon thy sleeping Child,
For blood shall burn that placid brow.
Those lips shall writhe in agony,
And shriek the sinless soul away;
And yet thy faith must moveless be,
And learn to bless His torment day.

Oh! Virgin Mother, Spouse of God!
Along the burning path of dread
Thy woman's feet shall pass unshod—
This hour shall stay thy sinking head.
And oft when winter nights are long,
And all thy heart with watching worn,
Again shall burst that angel song,
Blessed of women, "Christ is born!"

H.L.D. Ward.

(Clean Fun, from page 162)
gear with no mufflers, all headed toward that same point in the center of the infield, converging nose on nose.

The effect was exactly what one expects that many simultaneous crashes to produce: the unmistakable tympany of automobiles colliding and cheap-gauge sheet metal buckling; front ends folding together at the same cockeyed angles police photographs of night-time wreck scenes capture so well on grainy paper; smoke pouring from under the hoods and hanging over the infield like a howitzer cloud; a few of the surviving cars lurching eccentrically on bent axles. At last, after four heats, there were only two cars moving through the junk, a 1953 Chrysler and a 1958 Cadillac. In the Chrysler a small fascia of muscles named Spider Ligon, who smoked a cigar while he drove, had the Cadillac cornered up against a guard rail in front of the main grandstand. He dispatched it by swinging around and backing full throttle through the left side of its grille and radiator.

By now the crowd was quite beside itself.

(continued on page 174)

MORE ABOUT PEOPLE

When people aren't asking questions
They're making suggestions
And when they're not doing one of those
They're either looking over your shoulder or
stepping on your toes
And then as if that weren't enough to annoy you
They employ you.
Anybody at leisure
Incurs everybody's displeasure.
It seems to be very irking
To people at work to see other people not working,
So they tell you that work is wonderful medicine,
Just look at Firestone and Ford and Edison,
And they lecture you till they're out of breath
or something
And then if you don't succumb they starve you to death
or something.
All of which results in a nasty quirk:
That if you don't want to work you have to work
to earn enough money so that you won't have to
work.

OGDEN NASH

Therefore I say unto you, Take no thought for your life, what ye shall eat, or what ye shall drink; nor yet for your body, what ye shall put on. Is not the life more than meat, and the body more than raiment?

Behold the fowls of the air: for they sow not, neither do they reap, nor gather into barns; yet your heavenly Father feedeth them. Are ye not much better than they?

Which of you by taking thought can add one cubit unto his stature?

And why take ye thought for raiment? Consider the lilies of the field, how they grow; they toil not, neither do they spin:

And yet I say unto you, That even Solomon in all his glory was not arrayed like one of these.

Wherefore, if God so clothe the grass of the field, which to day is, and to morrow is cast into the oven, *shall he* not much more *clothe* you, O ye of little faith?

Therefore take no thought, saying, What shall we eat? or, What shall we drink? or, Wherewithal shall we be clothed?

(For after all these things do the Gentiles seek:) for your heavenly Father knoweth that ye have need of all these things.

But seek ye first the kingdom of God, and his righteousness; and all these things shall be added unto you.

Take therefore no thought for the morrow: for the morrow shall take thought for the things of itself. Sufficient unto the day *is* the evil thereof.

(Zen Tennis, from page 165)
samurai's mistake, I said not a word about tennis lessons for a full six weeks.

Finally my impatience overcame me. In a foolish attempt to force the issue, I appeared one morning with my tennis racket and some balls. The Master had the grace to look puzzled rather than angry. It was at this point that he asked me the first *koan.* "What have you got there?" he said. There was no doubt in my mind that this was a *koan.* Obviously, Ashikawa knew a tennis racket when he saw one, so his question must have been intended to jolt my mind into the kind of nonrational awareness I was so anxious to achieve. I was a good deal deeper into Zen by this time. I had read nine or ten more books by Daisetz T. Suzuki and had become increasingly certain that all my tennis problems could be traced back to that old troublemaker the rational mind. I had also been wondering when Ashikawa would let me sink my teeth into a *koan,* so when he repeated the question now, saying sharply, "What have you got there?" I bowed low and said that I would meditate on the answer. He emitted a wild Zen laugh. At last we were getting somewhere.

After that, I brought the racket every day. This seemed to please the Master, who used to remove the press and let the myna bird sit on the strings, where it hopped up and down, croaking "Porry want a clacker?" It was typical of a Zen tennis sage to treat the racket itself—centerpiece of his art—with such merry irreverence.

Autumn drifted into winter. There were times, I confess, when the prospects looked discouraging. Ashikawa seemed far more interested in his fish and birds than in the teaching of Zen tennis. At home, I suffered stocially through such indignities as hearing my wife tell our friends that she had become a Zen Mother, while my two children clamored for ice-cream *koans.* But I was determined to stick it out.

On January 19th, I solved the first *koan.* When the Master pointed to my tennis racket and asked me, as he did nearly every morning, "What have you got there?" I felt a sudden wave of anger and I answer, *without thinking,* "A bird stand, for God's sake!" He doubled over with laughter. Suddenly I knew that I had penetrated to the heart of the *koan*, because Ashikawa stopped laughing and asked me another one, far more difficult that the first. "Are you crazy?" he said.

Instead of answering straight off and making a fool of myself, I decided to seize this propitious moment to begin our Zen tennis lessons. Motioning to Ashikawa to follow me, I strode out the door and around the corner toward a vacant lot I had been eyeing for several months. It was bounded on two sides by tumble-down fences, and at the rear by the smooth, windowless wall of a garage, "How about it?" I said. "I'm ready if you are."

"Are you crazy?" Ashikawa repeated, pretending to be uneasy.

Without more ado, I addressed myself to the back wall, tossed up a ball, and served. It was a good first serve, hard and flat. The ball hit about four feet up the wall and came back at an angle, bouncing off pieces of brick and tin cans and eventually disappearing under a

(continued on page 172)

The Sunday Unreadable

"The difference between journalism and literature is that journalism is unreadable and literature is never read"—*Oscar Wilde*

The Teaching of Art

George Bernard Shaw

By art teaching I hasten to say that I do not mean giving children lessons in freehand drawing and perspective. I am simply calling attention to the fact that fine art is the only teacher except torture. I have already pointed out that nobody, except under threat of torture, can read a school book. The reason is that a school book is not a work of art. Similarly, you cannot listen to a lesson or a sermon unless the teacher or the preacher is an artist. You cannot read the Bible if you have no sense of literary art. The reason why the continental European is, to the Englishman or American, so surprisingly ignorant of the Bible, is that the authorized English version is a great work of literary art, and the continental versions are comparatively artless. To read a dull book; to listen to a tedious play or prosy sermon or lecture; to stare at uninteresting pictures or ugly buildings: nothing, short of disease, is more dreadful than this. The violence done to our souls by it leaves injuries and produces subtle maladies which have never been properly studied by psychopathologists.

FEIFFER Little Girl *By Jules Feiffer*

(Zen Tennis, from page 170)
parked Pontiac. I stole a glance at the Master, who looked dubious. "I know," I said quickly, eager to impress him. "I was trying to *aim* it. I should just let it *fall* from the racket naturally—is that right?" This falling bit was right out of Herrigel's book on archery, and it must have distressed Ashikawa no end to have me thus parade my pitiful learning. He said nothing, but motioned for me to serve again. This time the ball didn't even reach the wall. The third serve slid off the handle and went bouncing erratically down the street. A tatterdemalion youth fielded it and made off with it around the corner. I retrieved the remaining two balls and continued serving. The Master watched me closely, muttering in Japanese from time to time but never offering the least particle of advice. I had hoped he would make a few suggestions, although I was well aware that Zen cannot be taught—that, in fact, "One knows it by not knowing it." By the time we stopped, I could hardly hit the ball.

Our lessons followed this pattern for several months. After cleaning the fish tanks and bird cages, we would go back to the vacant lot, where I would serve for half an hour or so, often in snow or rain. My serve grew steadily worse, to the intense delight of the hordes of neighborhood toughs who came out to watch and jeer. The Master was incredibly patient. When I offered him the racket, hoping he would demonstrate, he merely backed away, giggling. He obviously meant for me to learn by direct experience. Remembering my readings in Suzuki, I tried to keep my mind locked up in the lower part of my abdomen, "just below the navel" (so that I might adjust myself "with the shifting situation from moment to moment"), but it was no use. This only gave me cramps.

Then one day in late spring, totally without warning, I served a perfect ball. It seemed to float effortlessly from my racket, without conscious guidance, in a pure and beautifully anti-intellectual arc, to the exact center of the back wall. I turned eagerly to see the Master's reaction. To my amazement, he was nowhere in sight. Where he had been standing a moment ago, there was now a large blue policeman, watching me coldly. I started to tell him about the shot, but something in his manner suggested that he might have trouble understanding, so I merely smiled pleasantly, picked up the balls, and started walking away. The policeman followed me to my car, and I thought it best to drive away without bothering Ashikawa again that day.

So great was my joy at having approached for the first time, through that perfect serve, the inner spirit of Zen tennis that I was not even particularly surprised to be denied entrance to Ashikawa's shop the next morning. The door was locked. When I rang, the Master came to the window shaking his head and waving angrily. He refused to let me in. It was, in its way, an exquisite gesture. He took this means of telling me he had no more to teach, that I must now find another Master or proceed on my own.

In the years since that day, I have often sought a new tennis Master to carry on Ashikawa's work, and I am still looking. But the way of Zen has not been closed to me—not by any means. My tennis is rather strange now, by our club standards, and it has become increasingly difficult for me to get up a game. I seldom put the ball in court on my

(continued on page 199)

(Clean Fun, from page 168)
Spectators broke through a gate in the retaining screen. Some rushed to Spider Ligon's car, hoisted him to their shoulders and marched off the field, howling. Others clambered over the stricken cars of the defeated, enjoying the details of their ruin, and howling. The good, full cry of triumph and annihilation rose from Riverhead Raceway, and the demolition derby was over.

That was the 154th demolition derby in two years. Since Lawrence Mendelsohn staged the first one at Islip Speedway in 1961, they have been held throughout the United States at the rate of one every five days, resulting in the destruction of about 15,000 cars. The figures alone indicate a gluttonous appetite for the sport. Sports writers, of course, have managed to ignore demolition derbies even more successfully than they have ignored stock car racing and drag racing. All in all, the new automobile sports have shown that the sports pages, which on the surface appear to hum with life and earthiness, are at bottom pillars of gentility. This drag racing and demolition derbies and things, well, there are too many kids in it with sideburns, tight Levis and winklepicker boots.

Yet the demolition derbies keep growing on word-of-mouth publicity. The "nationals" were held last month at Langhorne, Pa., with 50 cars in the finals, and demolition derby fans everywhere know that Don McTavish, of Dover, Mass., is the new world's champion. About 1,250,000 spectators have come to the 154 contests held so far. More than 75 percent of the derbies have drawn full houses.

The nature of their appeals is clear enough. Since the onset of the Christian era, i.e., since about 500 A.D., no game has come along to

ESSENCE

What color is the essence of Abe Lincoln? What color represents the **essence** of his personality? Here is a game you can try:

Think of a famous person and tell whether he or she is male or female. Other players have to guess the identity by asking questions.

Questions can cover all categories, but have to be worded this way: "What hobby (sport, type of music, work of art, style of dress, etc.) best represents this person's essence?"

The big temptation in playing ESSENCE is to associate rather than to probe. For instance, if X is thinking of Ike and Y asks for the sport which best represents his personality, X immediately wants to say "golf." But he refrains, because golf does not convey Ike's essence as much as, say, "target practice."

Thus: "What flower?" "Daisy"—"Doris Day!"; "What food?" "Lollipop"—"Shirley Temple!"

Players often argue, saying, "You threw me off when I asked what animal represented Sinatra and you said 'rat.' I see him as a weasel." Or, "I don't see Twiggy as yellowish-white at all—she's a definite roan!"

If you dare, ask a group of friends how they see YOU.

Oh yes, Lincoln might be a blue Mercedes with mud on the tires.

fill the gap left by the abolition of the purest of all sports, gladiatorial combat. As late as 300 A.D. these bloody duels, usually between men but sometime between women and dwarfs, were enormously popular not only in Rome but throughout the Roman Empire. Since then no game, not even boxing, has successfully acted out the underlying motifs of most sport, that is, aggression and destruction.

Boxing, of course, is an aggressive sport, but one contestant has actually destroyed the other in a relatively small percentage of matches. Other games are progressively more sublimated forms of sport. Often, as in the case of football, they are encrusted with oddments of passive theology and metaphysics to the effect that the real purpose of the game is to foster character, teamwork, stamina, physical fitness and the ability to "give-and-take."

But not even those wonderful clergymen who pray in behalf of Congress, expressway ribbon-cuttings, urban renewal projects and testimonial dinners for ethnic aldermen would pray for a demolition derby. The demolition derby is, pure and simple, a form of gladiatorial combat for our times.

As hand-to-hand combat has gradually disappeared from our civilization, even in wartime, and competition has become more and more sophisticated and abstract, Americans have turned to the automobile to satisfy their love of direct aggression. The mild-mannered man who turns into a bear behind the wheel of a car—i.e., who finds in the power of the automobile a vehicle for the release of his inhibitions—is part of American folklore. Among teen-agers the automobile has become the symbol, and in part the physical means, of triumph over family and community restrictions. Seventy-five per cent of all car thefts in the United States are by teen-agers out for "joy rides."

The symbolic meaning of the automobile tones down but by no means vanishes in adulthood. Police traffic investigators have long been convinced that far more accidents are purposeful crashes by belligerent drivers than they could ever prove. One of the heroes of the era was the Middle Eastern diplomat who rammed a magazine writer's car from behind in the Kalorama embassy district of Washington two years ago. When the American bellowed out the window at him, he backed up and smashed his car again. When the fellow leaped out of his car to pick a fight, he backed up and smashed his car a third time, then drove off. He was recalled home for having "gone native."

The unabashed, undisguised, quite purposeful sense of destruction of the demolition derby is its unique contribution. The aggression, the battering, the ruination are there to be enjoyed. The crowd at a demolition derby seldom gasps and often laughs. It enjoys the same full-throated participation as Romans at the Colosseum. After each trial or heat at a demolition derby, two drivers go into the finals. One is the driver whose car was still going at the end. The other is the driver the crowd selects from among the 24 vanquished on the basis of his courage, showmanship or simply the awesomeness of his crashes. The numbers of the cars are read over loudspeakers, and the crowd chooses one with its cheers. By the same token, the crowd may force a

(continued on page 186)

YOU KNOW WHAT I MEAN.

JOHN CAMPBELL

I've had an opportunity to learn a little about a project now under way at the Harvard Computer Lab; the men engaged in it do not, probably, have the same opinions about it that I have formed. We'll find out later whether my hunches regarding it are valid.

I have a feeling the job now started will snowball for the next century or so—and that they have started on the most important basic project Man has ever tackled.

They're studying the problem of teaching a computing machine to translate English to Russian, and Russian to English.

It's my belief that, in the process, they will solve about 90 percent of Mankind's social, psychological, economic and political problems. The computers won't solve the problems—but they'll force the men working on them to solve them.

Reason: You can NOT say to a computer

"You know what I mean . . ." The computer would only reply, "No. Define 'you.' Define 'know.' Define 'I.' Define 'mean.' Operation-relational processes regarding these terms not available."

All right, friend—go ahead. Define "I." Define it in terms of function and relationship to the Universe. Define it in terms of characteristics of process and program the steps the computer is to take in interacting this concept "I" with the operational program steps meant by the concept "know." Just do that one, single little thing, just define that one pair of terms—and you'll resolve about 75 per cent of all human problems.

Korzybski was a piker. He tried to teach human beings, who have built-in automatic self-programming units. They may not be perfect, but they work with incredible efficiency.

Try teaching a computing machine what you mean by some nice, simple term like "food." There's a good, basic, simple idea—an item basic to the most elementary understandings of life processes, politics, sociology, psychology and economics. This is one that must be included, obviously.

Anthony Oettinger, one of the men working on the project, explained part of the problem very neatly and completely by telling of one phase of the difficulty. Suppose we take a common English saying, and translate it into Chinese. Now if translation were perfect, we should be able to retranslate to English and recover the original phrase. Actually, in one instance, the retranslation yields "invisible idiot." Guess what went in originally! It's a perfectly understandable result; after all, something that is invisible, is out of sight—and an idiot is one who is out of mind. It could equally have come out "hidden maniac" or "distant madman."

Translation cannot be done on a word basis; we don't use words, actually, but concepts. Translating word-by-word would be only slightly more rewarding than transliterating letter by letter. The Russian alphabet is different from ours; that doesn't mean that transliterating yields English. Neither does a word-for-word substitution, save in the simplest level of statement.

The Chinese-English saying translation above indicates the real difficulty—and one that General Semantics hasn't adequately recognized, I feel. Actually, in communicating with each other, we seek to communicate *concepts;* concepts are complex structures of many individual parts assembled in a precise relationship. If someone asked a chemist for sugar, and the chemist delivered a pile of carbon and two small flasks of hydrogen and oxygen—everything necessary for sugar is present, but it's not sugar.

Let's consider "food" a moment. Presumably we are seeking to achieve sane translations of sane human thinking from our computer. Under these conditions should we teach the machine to consider that human flesh is to be considered "food"?

Yes. A sane man must realize that his flesh is food—otherwise he would make the mistake of swimming in shark-infested waters, or ignore lions and other major carnivora.

Is wood "food"?

Yes; an engineer must realize that fact when he considers constructing buildings. Otherwise he would neglect the possibilities of termite damage.

(continued on page 189)

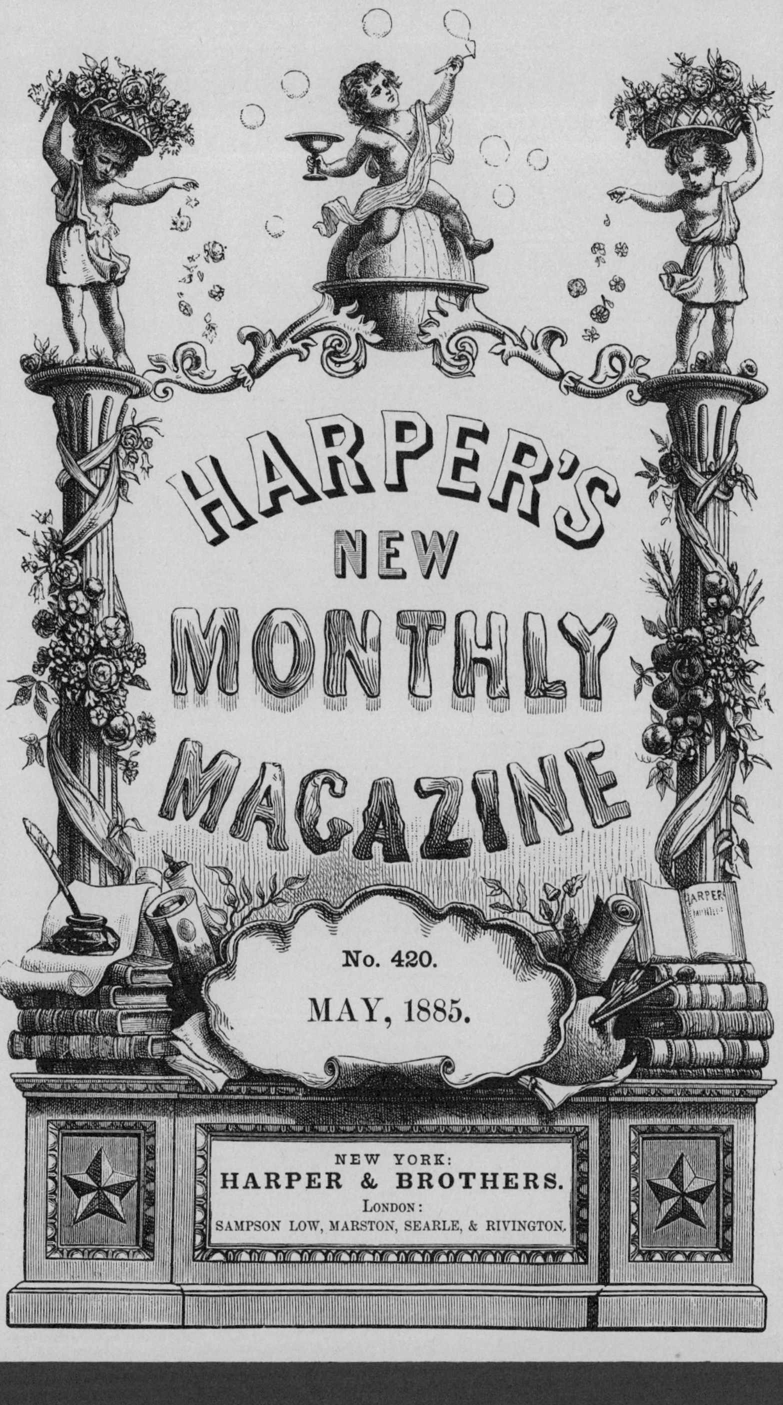
HARPER'S
NEW
MONTHLY
MAGAZINE
No. 420.
MAY, 1885.
NEW YORK:
HARPER & BROTHERS.
LONDON:
SAMPSON LOW, MARSTON, SEARLE, & RIVINGTON.

A MEZEDAKI IN ATHENS

There was a girl they all said later was American. She went stepping down the street ahead of me, young, with a good figure, well covered. She was well dressed too, and she had a way of working her haunches as she walked that rather singled her out. I had been specially conscious of her for the past hundred yards or so because there was a man following along close behind her who found her irresistible—it was clear to see in the way he was jockeying for position, sidling up on her right, whipping over to the left again, only to be foiled each time by some clumsy interfering pedestrian or a lamp-standard or whatever it might be. I knew what he planned to do, too.

This was in Athens and the three of us—first the girl, next the man I speak of, and then myself bringing up the rear—were walking across the top of Constitution Square along with a whole crowd of others. On we went, the girl wiggling, the man set on his little plan, head held rigid and a bit to one side, one arm behind his back—she must surely have been aware of him as over the road she wobbled and on to the further pavement, down the side of the Hotel Grande Bretagne. The man was most certainly Greek and I guessed that the girl could not be. He was coming right up alongside her now, very close . . . and then suddenly, without warning, the girl spun on her heel in a ninety-degree turn and the next moment she would be in at the Grande Bretagne side-entrance, safe in one of the little segments of those revolving doors. It all but caught the man off-balance: but the Greek mind is very quick and he reacted instantly. He had to move before she could slip away for ever. So his arm shot out and he pinched her smartly on the behind.

What should a girl do when this happens in the public street? In Athens it is an occupational risk all girls run and I have had talks with several of them about it. They mostly give

the same answer. Nothing. They are very sensible about it: they realize that if they dress provocatively and walk provocatively, someone is likely to be provoked into pinching them. An Athenian girl can recognize a pincher a block distant. He is quite easy to identify, it seems—the slightly furtive sideways advance, the hand behind the back symbolically out of sight, as it were, the manoeuvring—girls quickly learn to take evasive action, such as keeping away from shop-windows or points where they could get cornered, and the nervous ones certainly welcomed the full flaring skirts with the layers of stiff frilly petticoat underneath when that fashion came in. But those narrow, hobbling skirts. . . I have questioned several Athenians. They say it is better to come up from behind if you can. I can see the sense in that. "*A mezedaki,*" they are apt to call it: a little *hors d'oeuvre.* It is a game, really: a game for two persons, whether the second person wishes

PETER MAYNE

to play or not. And once the pincher has got his pinch in, or else the girl has outwitted him and escaped, he does not follow her up. He is content with his pinch, just as a picador is content with his pic, or the banderillero with banderillas. Most girls say there is only one rule—if she loses she must do so with grace. No shrieks, no angry cries. She must just walk on as if nothing whatever had happened. The game is over. She has lost.

The game is not always very well understood by foreign ladies visiting Athens. An English lady with whom I was silly enough to discuss it said she was disgusted and that these men ought to be shut up and that if she had a young daughter she would not allow her to walk in the streets of Athens unaccompanied — indeed she wondered if she would bring the child to Athens at all, let alone let her loose in it. So I asked an American lady. She agreed with the English lady that it was disgusting but she wanted to be fair and show compassion for such a man: she wondered whether perhaps poverty and having to sleep a whole family in one little room. . . ". . . maladjustments," she hinted: "a thoroughly bad home environment. . ." But she believed nevertheless that girls should be protected. I said I thought girls could very well protect themselves—just as well, anyhow, as they can protect themselves from the flying, ruthless Athens traffic: and I added that the girl in my story should not have wobbled her hips so, at which both ladies promptly rounded on me again and said that girls could not help wobbling a bit, being built the way they are. It made them feel quite sick, they both said, to think of men following secretly along behind. Had Greek men no respect for womanhood?—this was what they wanted to know. I did not say so because I felt it would strike them as rude, but the truth is that girls in public places probably have to choose between being respected and being desired. If they choose respect they can try how it goes: they can get up on pedestals out of reach. Or they can be desirable and take a chance on that. But these two ladies I was talking to seemed to want desire *and* worship. Well, they can't have both.

The case of the American girl who had fled to the safety of the Grande Bretagne underlines my point. Her thinking was confused. She was not in the wrong, maybe, but she reacted wrongly. When the man landed his pinch and won, she lost her head as well as the game. She went black in the face and did something very shocking. Everyone present gasped. She was carrying a big crocodile travel-bag—a splendid thing with metal clasps and buckles, and so on. She swung this bag of hers in a great arc and caught the man over the head with it. He went to the ground instantly. She tossed her head furiously and as she turned to wobble through the revolving doors to refuge, the man was rising to his feet again and wagging his head in his bewilderment.

"I only pinched her . . ." he said plaintively, looking round at us.

We were quite a little crowd by now—the hotel doorman, taxi-drivers, other passers-by, a policeman.

"*Tch-tch*! . . ." the people went, wagging their heads too and staring through the big plate-glass windows at the girl's retreating back. What sort of girl could she be? A taxi-driver helped the poor man up, brushing him down.

"Did she hurt you, then?" he asked with great solicitude. ▬

YOU FORCE KIDS TO REBEL

by Steven Kelman

On both high-school and college campuses, the official statements about almost any subject are so widely distrusted nowadays that citing them is the best way to have yourself marked as a dupe or a simpleton. Adults might understand how serious this problem is if they'd listen to the words of the songs of somebody like Bob Dylan. His most popular songs are talking about skepticism, about what's really going on in the world as compared to what we're being taught is going on in the world. When we take a look for ourselves, the facts we see are so different from what we've been taught that we have no choice but to turn into rebels or at least skeptics.

Kids grow up "tryin'a be so good"—in the words of one Dylan song. When we fall from this "good" innocence it's like going through an earthquake; the ground under you just isn't solid anymore. And it's a quick jump from saying to yourself, "What they taught me is a lie," to saying, "So they must be liars." The feeling is that the adult Establishment is phony or self-interested, composed of people you can't trust.

Most parents don't want to accept this explanation. It's said that we're know-it-alls, though we're really know-nothings, and it's said that an affluent society produces spoiled brats who have no sense of values and no appreciation of all the things being done for them.

There are a number of facts that show this isn't true. For instance, philosophy courses in almost every college are in unprecedented demand (as I just discovered when I unsuccessfully tried to get into one with a "limited" enrollment of 325). At Harvard, where I am now, the Phillips Brooks House, which does all sorts of social service and community-assistance projects, is the largest organization on campus.

Perhaps the most popular theory for the kids' rebellion is that the "conflict of generations" is inevitable, and that we will "outgrow it." However, even if some sort of reaction of young people against their parents is inevitable, the revolt is now taking a particular form—skepticism. It took the same form, by the way, in 19th-century Russia. When youth

Puzzle

Here are some letters in a predetermined sequence:
O T T F F

Determine the governing principle used and then write the next five letters.

---

gets skeptical, I submit, it does not indicate that anything is wrong with youth, but rather that something is wrong with adults.

And that "something" is the way you usually look at and react to what's going on in the world. "Hypocrisy" is a big word with us, and it's a mortal sin in our moral code, dooming the sinner to our version of hell—permanent eclipse of any moral influence he might have on us.

If kids were taught that the world is flat, any reasonably sane person would expect us to revolt against those responsible for teaching that particular "fact." So what else but skepticism and revolt should anybody expect from us when we are being taught a view of the world which is little more sophisticated than the flat-earth theory?

It all starts in first grade. There we are treated to a candy-cane world where all the children in the textbooks are white tots living in suburbia with a dog running around the lawn. When suburban kids find out about slums, they're apt to get skeptical. When slum kids are taught about a world that has nothing to do with the world in which they live, they have to do the same. A song which has been a hit among students is a parody—perhaps unconscious—of those first-grade primers:

Little boxes on the hillside.
Little boxes made of ticky-tacky,
Little boxes, little boxes, little boxes
All the same.
There's a green one, and a pink one.
And a blue one, and a yellow one,
And they're all made out of ticky-tacky,
And they all look just the same.

Many of us come to realize just how unreal the classroom world is when our thoughts turn to boy-girl relationships. No teen-ager can escape knowing that love and sex are part of the real world. So how does society's agent, the school, present this part of reality? It ignores it. For instance, one biology teacher I heard about treated his students to the obscene spectacle of his own sniggering while he described sexual reproduction in algae. Health teachers reduce puberty to a section of an inane chart on "stages of human development." When we find out the facts and feel the emotions, how can anyone expect us not to be skeptical about an adult world which tries to act as if none of this existed? And the moral code that we have developed, "sex with love," seems to us to be more logical than anything you've put up.

The whole idea the school seems to try to get across is that if you don't teach it to us, it doesn't exist. This can sometimes go to extreme length. In junior high school we had a thing called a "Reading Record Card." This was supposed to be a list (and brief discussion) of all the books you had read each year. But "all the books" actually meant all the books that were in the school library. And when students protested against the refusal to allow listing of books like *1984* and *The Grapes of*

(continued on page 192)

(Clean Fun, from page 176)
driver out of competition if he appears cowardly or merely cunning. This is the sort of driver who drifts around the edge of the battle avoiding crashes with the hope that the other cars will eliminate one another. The umpire waves a yellow flag at him and he must crash into someone within 30 seconds or run the risk of being booed off the field in dishonor and disgrace.

The frank relish of the crowd is nothing, however, compared to the kick the contestants get out of the game. It costs a man an average of $50 to retrieve a car from a junk yard and get it running for a derby. He will only get his money back—$50—for winning a heat. The chance of being smashed up in the madhouse first 30 seconds of a round are so great, even the best of drivers faces long odds in his shot at the $500 first prize. None of that matters to them.

Tommy Fox, who is nineteen, said he entered the demolition derby because, "You know, it's fun. I like it. You know what I mean?" What was fun about it? Tommy Fox had a way of speaking that was much like the early Marlon Brando. Much of what he had to say came from the trapezii, which he rolled quite a bit, and the forehead, which he cocked, and the eyebrows, which he could bring together

---

Definition

Oxygen: An intensely habit-forming accumulative toxic substance. As little as one breath is known to produce a life-long addiction to the gas, which addiction invariably ends in death. In high concentration, it causes death quickly, but even in 20 percent dilution few survive more than 0.8 century.

expressively from time to time. "Well," he said, "you know, like when you hit 'em, and all that. It's fun."

Tommy Fox had a lot of fun in the first heat. Nobody was bashing around quite like he was in his old green Hudson. He did not win, chiefly because he took too many chances, but the crowd voted him into the finals as the best showman.

"I got my brother," said Tommy. "I came in from the side and he didn't even see me."

His brother is Don Fox, thirty-two, who owns the junk yard where they both got their cars. Don likes to hit them, too, only he likes it almost too much. Don drives with such abandon, smashing into the first car he can get a shot at and leaving himself wide open, he does not stand much chance of finishing the first three minutes.

For years now sociologists have been calling upon one another to undertake a serious study of America's "car culture." No small part of it is the way the automobile has, for one very large segment of the population, become the focus of the same sort of quasi-religious dedication as art is currently for another large segment of a higher social order. Tommy Fox is unemployed, Don Fox runs a junk yard, Spider Ligon is a maintenance man for Brookhaven Naval Laboratory, but to categorize them as such is getting no closer to the truth than to

(continued on page 195)

Puzzle

In case you were not able to arrive at the second five letters in the puzzle, here they are:
S S E N T
Can you now work out the next five letters in the sequence?

NORTHERN COMMUNICATIONS COMPANY

UNFAIR

The Telephone Company has 35 supply houses located within the United States. The Utility Workers of America has been bargaining with the Northern Communications Company, a subsidiary, since February 27, 1967.

Following are a few bargaining items already offered other Telephone Company employees but denied Northern Communications Union members:

1. Retroactive pay back to March 26, 1967, which was the termination date of the supply houses' contract.
2. Area Differential, which means a cost of living area wage. (The Company's own economists, Finan Associates, indicate that wages are not what they should be in supply house locations.)
3. Automatic wage progression based on shorter service time.
4. Meal allowance when required to work overtime.
5. Telephone bill allowance for employees.

These are just a few of the items that the Northern Communications is unfair with in respect to its employees.

WE WANT THE PUBLIC TO KNOW THE FACTS IN CASE THE COMPANY FORCES US TO STRIKE!

UTILITY WORKERS OF AMERICA
LOCAL 5149

The Community–Minded Union

P.S. Remember, a **FAIR** wage makes better purchasing power.

(What I Mean, from page 178)

Is steel "food"?

We must so instruct the computer; otherwise it could not translate "We must have steel scrap to feed our hungry furnaces."

Very well, gentlemen, what *do* you mean when you consider the concepts in "foods," "feed," and "eat"? *Define your terms!*

The sociologists and psychologists have long maintained that mathematical methods are not applicable to human problems. Not until the terms in which human problems are discussed have been defined operationally, certainly.

Teaching a computing machine, a machine that will invariably do precisely, but only, what you did-in-fact instruct it to do will be a most humbling task. In the course of doing that job, I foresee the collapse of every human philosophy, the harsh winnowing of every human falsity, every slightest quibble, self-justification, or rationalization.

When a man is seeking to induce another man to agree with him, to learn his ideas, he can hold "he is stubborn; he refuses to understand me because he hates me." Or "He is too stupid to learn!"

When a man seeks to teach a computer. . .

Computers are not stubborn. If it is stupid, it is the failure of the man to perfect his handiwork, and the failure reflects inescapably to its source in Man. If it acts in a foggy, confused manner—Man made the mistake, and he must correct it. It's his mistake; responsibility cannot be assigned elsewhere.

Man, in trying to teach his tender and precious beliefs to a computing machine, is inviting the most appallingly frank and inescapable criticism conceivable. The computing machines won't solve human problems for us—but they'll force men to a degree of rigid self-honesty and humility that never existed before.

I can imagine some philosopher, some psychologist, or some physicist coming spluttering to the computer lab, demanding that the nonsensical answers so blatantly in disregard of facts-as-he-believes them be corrected. "Out of the way; let someone who knows something about this field teach this machine a few realities!"

Three weeks later, a haggard and vastly humbled man would come out, his fine structure of beliefs in tatters—and possessed of a realization of his own need to learn a few *real* realities.

I have heard psychologists use the term "ego," the terms "id" and "identity." I've looked, with some interest, in an Encyclopedia of Psychology; there is no entry under any one of those terms, no effort, even, to define them.

Have you ever sought a definition of "distance" as used in physics? It's one of the three fundamentals of the CGS system—and has no definition whatever. *Define your terms,* the computer relentlessly demands. The mathematician has no definition for "quantity" or "distance" either. Cantor has proved mathematically that any line segment has as many points—aleph null—as any other line, however long or short, or as any plane. Then define what you mean by "greater than" or "less than"! Until you do, the whole structure rests on "You know what I mean. . ."

The computer does *not* "know what you mean." Define it!

A while back I ran a faulty "syllogism" going, essentially, "Biology holds no organism can live in a medium of its own products. Communism holds a man has a right to what he produces. Therefore, Communism won't work." It was thrown in as a deliberate inducement to thinking and questioning of terms. Most of those who answered—some quite angrily, incidentally!—held that the flaw lay in the misuse of the terms "products" and "produces."

There's a flaw all right—but that's not it. The computer would have spotted it immediately; only we humans have difficulty in finding it.

The products of an organism are quite artificially divided into "products" and "by-products" and "waste products." As industry long since learned, a waste product is something we haven't learned a use for yet, and a by-product is a misleading term. What is the product of Street & Smith Publications, Incorporated, for instance? Street & Smith, like the National Biscuit Company, assembles materials, packages them, and distributes them. Rumford Press, which prints this magazine, like the American Can Company, or Container Corporation, makes packages.

You hold in your hand a physical package, packed with word-structured concepts. You buy a thing of paper, ink, and metal and glue—just as you buy a thing of glass, metal and plastic when you buy a radio tube. In each case, the object is merely a package-structure for the function which you really desire.

Any organism will smother in *any* of its own products if present in excess; a waste

(continued on page 194)

Puzzle

If you were not able to arrive at the third five letters in the puzzle, here they are:
E T T F F

(Kids Rebel, from page 185)

Wrath, we were treated like people in China who try to whisper that Mao Tse-tung is not the only recognized writer in the world. And what are we taught about literature? We are often required to memorize such details as "What color was Ivanhoe's horse?" and "What hotel did Gatsby and the Buchanans meet in?" rather than talking about how a book means something in helping us to figure out ourselves or other people. So kids often give up the classics. One kid told me that he feared becoming a writer because of what high-school English teachers would do to his books.

And how about student government? I was active in it during high school, but the majority attitude of indifference was a pretty good instinctive reaction. In most schools the "governments" must restrict themselves to planning social extravaganzas. When they try to do something—as when ours voted to fast for a lunch in sympathy with the people of India—the administration vetoed our plans. You say that we should act responsibly, and when we try to, you act as if youthful hordes were trying to take over the school. Is the world like that?

It sometimes seems to us that myths are peddled to us about *everything* we are taught. For example, the quaint myth of the American family farm—enshrined in numerous references in our courses—obscures the reality of giant agricultural industries and underpaid migrant labor. The history of American cities as it is generally presented comes to a screeching halt at the turn of the century. American history textbooks I've seen are at least 30 years behind the latest historical investigations. Thus one widely used junior-high history text states that the sole purpose of American intervention in Latin America in the early part of the century was to "lend a helping hand" to the people by building roads, bridges and hospitals. This is a little hard to believe. More than one kid I know has reacted by taking the position that our only motive in Latin America was financial greed. From my experience, American-history courses generally produce more anti-Americanism than understanding of history.

And what about the presentation of the one problem which concerns kids most of all—race? Well, one junior-high-school civics book devotes a total of four paragraphs to the history of the Negro in the United States. The last hundred years of Negro history are summed up like this:

> During the War Between the States, all Negro slaves were set free. Since then American Negroes have gone through a difficult period of adjustment to new ways of life. They have made remarkable progress in a short time.

Now, when we leave such textbooks and look at the world, it is entirely natural that we think someone has been trying to put something over on us. Our world includes Watts and also suburbia, grape pickers as well as family farms, Latin Americans whose memories of American troops often center on the two-bit dictators the troops installed rather than the roads they built. And why would you teach us unreality if you didn't accept it?

A sort of "textbook case" (if the pun is acceptable) of codified obscuritanism being peddled under the guise of education is the high-school courses designed to teach us about Communism. In the world presented in most

(continued on page 196)

(What I Mean, from page 191)

product is one present either in excess of the usable amount, or one which is not usable.

Any organism—including the organism known as a "state" or "nation"—will smother in an excess of its own ill-regulated and ill-distributed products. The basic biological law is perfectly applicable to a state, or a society.

The flaw in the false syllogism is the one the computer would have spotted immediately. "Define the term 'right'!"

This is the distributive term in the syllogism, and is so undefined as to be meaningless. The falsity of the syllogism is equivalent to that in "All men are human beings. Some human beings are mortal. Therefore all men are mortal." The flaw in that syllogism is the faulty distributive term in the second statement.

But when it comes to "right," human beings are very, very skittish indeed. They're too apt to find that some of their pet beliefs and personal preferences will be ruled out if they accept any hard, clean-cut definition of "right."

Since a machine has rights to begin with, no beliefs, prejudices, preferences or foibles, it will most unkindly and uncompromisingly refuse to operate at all until you define what you mean by "right."

I have a deep conviction that a vastly humbled and chastened—but vastly improved!—humanity will result from the effort to teach a machine what Man believes.

The terribly tough part about it is that to do it, Man will, for the first time, have to find out exactly what he does believe—and make coherent, integrated sense of it!

(Clean Fun, from page 187)
have categorized William Faulkner in 1926 as a clerk at Lord & Taylor, although he was.

Tommy Fox, Don Fox and Spider Ligon are acolytes of the car culture, an often esoteric world of arts and sciences that came into its own after World War II and now has believers of two generations. Charlie Turbush, thirty-five, and his son, Buddy, seventeen, were two more contestants, and by no stretch of the imagination can they be characterized as bizarre figures or cultists of the death wish. As for the dangers of driving in a demolition derby, they are quite real by all physical laws. The drivers are protected only by crash helmets, seat belts and the fact that all glass, interior handles, knobs and fixtures have been removed. Yet Lawrence Mendelsohn claims that there have been no serious injuries in 154 demolition derbies and now gets his insurance at a rate below that of stock car racing.

The sport's future may depend in part on word getting around about its relative safety. Already it is beginning to draw contestants here and there from social levels that could give the demolition derby the cachet of respectability. In eastern derbies so far two doctors and three young men of more than passable connections in eastern society have entered under whimsical *noms de combat* and emerged neither scarred nor victorious. Bull fighting had to win the same social combat.

All of which brings to mind that fine after-

(continued on page 199)

Puzzle

The fourth sequence of five letters is:
S S E N T
Figured it out? If not, see page______.

(Kids Rebel, from page 193)

"Communism" courses, "Democracy" and "Communism" fight each other out on a wooden stage. After going through one of these courses, it takes someone with a vivid imagination to realize that these things are ideas millions of people around the world are living and sometimes dying for. The "Comparison Charts" commonly used are of varying lengths (the one in J. Edgar Hoover's high-school guide, *A Study of Communism,* takes the prize, filling up eight pages of text). They are designed to contrast the beliefs of Communism *vs.* Freedom in such fields as government, economics, education, morality, etc. Considering the debates which have gone on about such fundamental questions, it should come as no shock that these "contrasts" can seem ludicrous. Take this example from Hoover's book:

> COMMUNISM: There is a total disregard for the inherent dignity of the individual.
> FREEDOM: There is a deep and abiding respect for the inherent dignity and worth of the individual.

Most students who are paying attention to this react by murmuring, "You must be putting me on," or a less polite variant. For we know that in this world nothing is so simple. And we only have to look at the pictures of the Alabama police dogs to know that things are not simple at all. So a lot of kids react by concluding that there's no difference between "Communism" and "Freedom" in this respect. And if we try to argue, we get Hoover thrown at our face.

Almost every "Communism" course repeats

an account of Marxism. When it centers on doctrines like "dialectical materialism," which even Communists have trouble understanding, the course usually turns into a farce. Afterward we often get the accompanying horror images. One widely used film states that the only three non-Communist countries in the West are Spain, Switzerland and America! In an attempt to get down to what is presumed to be our level, one text shows a cartoon of an Oriental-looking Lenin, left hand on a cannon, leading regimented lines of darkly colored robot people against others who, huddled in small groups around the base of the Statue of Liberty, are riding in a car, watching TV, debating, and mowing a lawn. Most of us think that such things insult our intelligence.

As we go through school, we are subjected to lots more of this evidence that the real world and the world being taught us aren't the same. Of course, some of us never rebel. They will form the shock troops of the older generation and in our vocabulary are "finks." Or, they will just "cop out" to boredom.

But for the others, an overdose of unreality, just like an overdose of anything else, can produce crazy results—even a sickness. Flirtations with things like LSD and "pot" are merely escaping reality, not trying to refuse to adapt to it. It is, for example, a tragedy that anti-Communism is becoming a dirty word on the American campus. It is also a tragedy that the political activism of a generation concerned with the world is in danger of being wasted in the pursuit of semi-anarchist dreams. And the refusal to believe anything people in authority

---

Key The letters are the opening letters of the words which spell the numerals in English: One, Two, Three, Four, Five, etc.

say is only a reaction to the fact that last time we believed we were deceived.

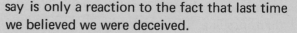

What can be done to prevent this revolt against the future? Actually, what is really needed is a revamping of the way we are taught. One suggestion might be to drop our fetish with "objectivity" in subjects toward which we are not objective. Politics are not objective. Love is not objective. People are not objective. Instead of objectivity, the guiding word in our schools should be democracy—which is, as far as I can tell, the prevailing philosophy in our country. Democracy means trusting us to make up our minds. Using democracy in a course about Communism, for example, could mean matching a text that defends a free society with one defending Communism. To the nervous Nellies who recoil, I ask, "Don't you think that the case for Democracy is the better one?" Don't you realize that in the Vietnam war we are given absurd analogies to European history and opponents tend to view the Viet Cong as 20th-century versions of Robin Hood?

There are only random examples. The point is this: Adults often like to pretend the real world doesn't exist. Kids can't. We might want to *escape* from it, but we can't forget about it. And we know the difference between the world we're taught and the world we experience. And if we blame you for trying to put something over on us, it's only because we're taught what, alas, most Americans seem to think. If the school is trying to turn its back on reality, it only represents an America that's doing the same thing. And that's what really worries us. ▬

(Zen Tennis, from page 173)

serve, and my ground strokes have a way of soaring over the backstop and off into space, like swallows. But the great thing is, *this no longer concerns me.* I rarely think now in terms of winning. As I penetrate ever closer into the real spirit of tennis, I become increasingly aware that the server and the receiver are really one person, and the goal of both is not points but *satori.* The transformation of my entire life is at hand. I can even derive pleasure from mixed doubles.

Yesterday I solved the second *koan.* As I missed an overhead smash, it suddenly swept over me that the answer to the question "Are you crazy?" was simply, to paraphrase Descartes, "I think, therefore I *must* be crazy." My sudden peal of pure Zen laughter startled the three ladies I was playing with, I'm afraid, but I felt no embarrassment; someday soon, I knew, I would be able to stop thinking altogether and attain *satori.* I only wish old Master Ashikawa had been around to see my next double fault, which was perfect.

(Clean Fun, from page 195)

noon when some high-born Roman women were out in Nero's box at the Colosseum watching this sexy Thracian carve an ugly little Samnite up into prime cuts, and one said, darling, she had an inspiration, and Nero, needless to say, was all for it. Thus began the new vogue of Roman socialites fighting as gladiators themselves, for kicks. By the second century A.D. even the Emperor Commodus was out there with a tiger's head as a helmet hacking away at some poor dazed fall guy. He did a lot for the sport. Arenas sprang up all over the empire like shopping center bowling alleys.

The future of the demolition derby, then, stretches out over the face of America. The sport draws no lines of gender, and post-debs may reach Lawrence Mendelsohn at his office in Deer Park.

Imperialist
Imperialist: it ain't for jes everyone.
Imperialist is for the right kind of people. People with discriminating taste.
And when it come to discriminating taste we wrote the book.
That's why, when it's time for a lil juice, discriminating folks prefers Imperialist.
It's smoother. It's tougher. And it's jes the right color.
Have a taste. In your mouth you know it's right.
Imperialist Whiskey: for discriminating folks. (and vice versa)

THEN, TO ANIMATE THEM

How "alive" can you make each title on this shelf? Try to get the "feel" of each one. What area of experience does each epitomize? Let your mind have plenty of time to play with these titles.

How much information can you unlock from these titles? What does this investigation tell you about motion pictures? About yourself?

TITLES

Is a title a metaphor for a book?
Is it a "dead" metaphor?

Can you bridge from one book to another, from one category to another?

In your journal see how far you can generalize about such an investigation. Compare your discoveries with those of other students.

?

SUPERHETERODYNE

When two alternating voltages of different frequencies are combined in the mixer stage of a radio receiver, a third frequency being the difference between one frequency and the other is produced and fed to an amplifier. This is known as the principle of superheterodyne.

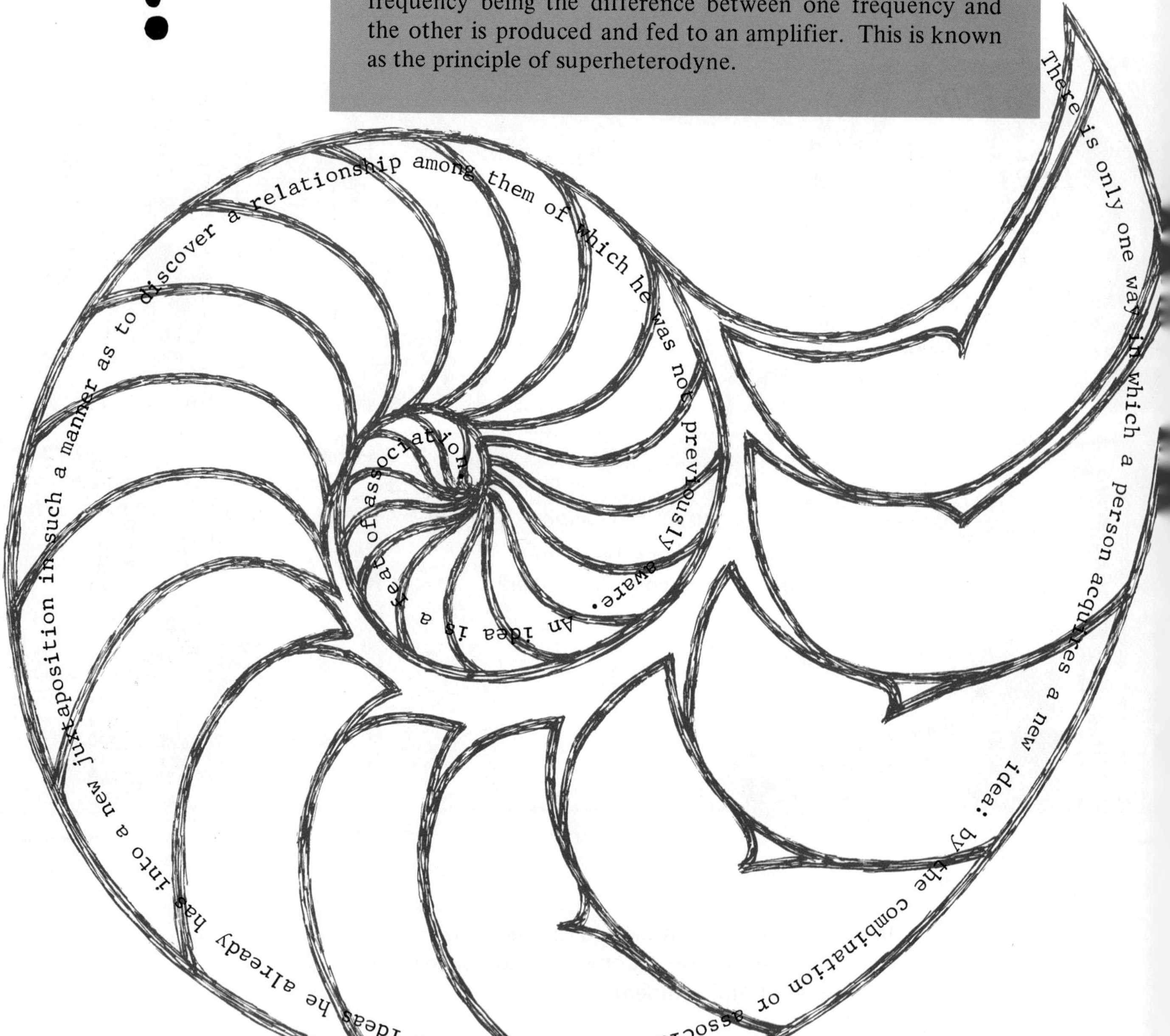
There is only one way in which a person acquires a new idea: by the combination or association of two or more ideas he already has into a new juxtaposition in such a manner as to discover a relationship among them of which he was not previously aware. An idea is a feat of association.

MONTAGE IS CONFLICT

Is the page of movie ads which begins this section a montage?

Are the ads in "conflict"?

Do they reinforce each other?

Does the total page add up to a message which is different from any of the single ads? What is the general effect?

What about the front page of your newspaper? What about your world?

Do our minds create through conflict?

Seen any good commercials lately?

While watching television one evening with some friends I noticed that Kai Andrew, their eighteen-month-old son who was noisily playing by himself with much physical activity, would immediately stop whatever he was doing and stare silently at the TV as soon as a commercial came on. When the commercial ended and the program continued, he lost interest in TV and returned to his world of play. This little ritual continued with clockwork regularity throughout a number of programs.

I have gone to the movies constantly, and at times almost compulsively, for most of my life. I should be embarrassed to attempt an estimate of how many movies I have seen and how many hours they have consumed. At the same time, I have had enough serious interest in the products of the "higher" arts to be very sharply aware that the impulse which leads me to a Humphrey Bogart movie has little in common with the impulse which leads me to the novels of Henry James or the poetry of T. S. Eliot. That there is a connection between the two impulses I do not doubt, but the connection is not adequately summed up in the statement that the Bogart movie and the Eliot poem are both forms of art. To define that connection seems to me one of the tasks of film criticism, and the definition must be first of all a personal one. A man watches a movie, and the critic must acknowledge that he is that man.

I also know very well that I do not go to the movies in order to discover what impulses are moving "the audience," though I am willing to make such discoveries when they happen to present themselves to me. Here again, it is I who go to the movies (perhaps I should say: alas!) not the sociologist in me, if there is a sociologist in me. And it must be that I go to the movies for the same reason that the "others" go: because I am attracted to Humphrey Bogart or Shelley Winters or Greta Garbo; because I require the absorbing immediacy of the screen; because in some way I take all that nonsense seriously. For I must make one more confession: I have seen a great many very bad movies, and I know when a movie is bad, but I have rarely been bored at the movies; and when I have been bored, it has usually been at a "good" movie.

The cinema should never turn back. It should accept, unconditionally, what is contemporary. *Today, today, today.*

It must tell reality as if it were a story: there must be no gap between life and what is on the screen. To give an example:

A woman goes to a shop to buy a pair of shoes. The shoes cost 7,000 lire. The woman tries to bargain. The scene lasts, perhaps, two minutes. I must make a two-hour film. What do I do?

I analyze the fact in all its constituent elements, in its "before," in its "after," in its contemporaneity. The fact creates its own fiction, in its own particular sense.

The woman is buying the shoes. What is her son doing at the same moment? What are people doing in India that could have some relation to this fact of the shoes? The shoes cost 7,000 lire. How did the woman happen to have 7,000 lire? How hard did she work for them, what do they represent for her?

And the bargaining shopkeeper, who is he? What relationship has developed between these two human beings? What do they mean, what interests are they defending, as they bargain? The shopkeeper also has two sons, who eat and speak: do you want to know what they are saying? Here they are, in front of you. . . .

The question is, to be able to fathom the real correspondences between facts and their process of birth, to discover what lies beneath them.

Thus to analyze "buying a pair of shoes" in such a way opens to us a vast and complex world, rich in importance and values, in its practical, social, economic, psychological motives. Banality disappears because each moment is really charged with responsibility. Every moment is infinitely rich. Banality never really existed.

Excavate, and every little fact is revealed as a mine. If the gold-diggers come at last to dig in the illimitable mine of reality, the cinema will become socially important.

This can also be done, evidently, with invented characters; but if I use living, real characters with which to sound reality, people in whose life I can directly participate, my emotion becomes more effective, morally stronger, more useful. Art must be expressed through a true name and surname, not a false one.

I am bored to death with heroes more or less imaginary. I want to meet the real protagonist of everyday life, I want to see how he is made, if he has a moustache or not, if he is tall or short, I want to see his eyes, and I want to speak to him.

We can look at him on the screen with the same anxiety, the same curiosity as when, in a square, seeing a crowd of people all hurrying up to the same place, we ask, What is happening? What is happening to a real person? Neorealism has perceived that the most irreplaceable experience comes from things happening under our own eyes from natural necessity.

I am against "exceptional" personages. The time has come to tell the audience that they are the true protagonists of life. The result will be a constant appeal to the responsibility and dignity of every human being. Otherwise the frequent habit of identifying oneself with fictional characters will become very dangerous. We must identify ourselves with what we are. The world is composed of millions of people thinking of myths.

Happiness: Smirking contentment with one's lot?

STRAWBERRIES

A man traveling across a field encountered a tiger. He fled, the tiger after him. Coming to a precipice, he caught hold of the root of a wild vine and swung himself down over the edge. The tiger sniffed at him from above. Trembling, the man looked down to where, far below, another tiger was waiting to eat him. Only the vine sustained him.

Two mice, one white and one black, little by little started to gnaw away the vine. The man saw a luscious strawberry near him. Grasping the vine with one hand, he plucked the strawberry with the other. How sweet it tasted!

OWL CREEK ?

No study of *Citizen Kane* would be complete without mention of Welles' fondness of dissolves and "lightning mixes" (scenes linked by the soundtrack but not by the images).

THE INVISIBLE MEDIUM

The following story was the basis for a movie by Robert Enrico. It won an Academy Award in 1964 as the best live action short subject and earlier had won the 1962 Grand Prize at the Cannes Festival.

What is involved in transforming a story into pictures that "move"? What decisions must be made? Does one simply illustrate the story? How faithful must one be to the original story?

MOVEMENT

You have probably spent many, many hours as a viewer of movies. But have you ever really "seen" a movie? *Try the following investigation:*

Read the story often enough to get the "feel" of it. Then transfer this word-art to the medium of film. Prepare a shot by shot scenario for the first five minutes or so of the movie as you think it should be filmed.

What does this investigation reveal to you about the word-art of story telling? About film art?

HAROLD ROBBINS

AN OCCURRENCE AT OWL CREEK BRIDGE

I

A man stood upon a railroad bridge in northern Alabama, looking down into the swift water twenty feet below. The man's hands were behind his back, the wrists bound with a cord. A rope loosely encircled his neck. It was attached to a stout cross-timber above his head, and the slack fell to the level of his knees. Some loose boards laid upon the sleepers supporting the metals of the railway supplied a footing for him and his executioners—two private soldiers of the Federal army, directed by a sergeant who in civil life may have been a deputy sheriff. At a short remove upon the same temporary platform was an officer in the uniform of his rank, armed. He was a captain. A sentinel at each end of the bridge stood with his rifle in the position known as "support," that is to say, vertical in front of the left shoulder, the hammer resting on the forearm thrown straight across the chest—a formal and unnatural position, enforcing an erect carriage of the body. It did not appear to be the duty of these two men to know what was occurring at the center of the bridge; they merely blockaded the two ends of the foot plank which traversed it.

Beyond one of the sentinels, nobody was in sight; the railroad ran straight away into a forest for a hundred yards, then, curving, was lost to view. Doubtless there was an outpost farther along. The other bank of the stream was open ground—a gentle acclivity topped with a stockade of vertical tree trunks, loopholed for rifles, with a single embrasure through which protruded the muzzle of a brass

The motion picture: an international and intercultural language of the eye.

cannon commanding the bridge. Midway of the slope between bridge and fort were the spectators—a single company of infantry in line, at "parade rest," the butts of the rifles on the ground, the barrels inclining slightly backward against the right shoulder, the hands crossed upon the stock. A lieutenant stood at the right of the line, the point of his sword upon the ground, his left hand resting upon his right. Excepting the group of four at the center of the bridge, not a man moved. The company faced the bridge, staring stonily, motionless. The sentinels, facing the banks of the stream, might have been statues to adorn the bridge. The captain stood with folded arms, silent, observing the work of his subordinates, but making no sign. Death is a dignitary who when he comes announced is to be received with formal manifestations of respect, even by those most familiar with him. In the code of military etiquette silence and fixity are forms of deference.

The man who was engaged in being hanged was apparently about thirty-five years of age. He was a civilian, if one might judge from his habit, which was that of a planter. His features were good—a straight nose, firm mouth, broad forehead, from which his long, dark hair was combed straight back, falling behind his ears to the collar of his well-fitting frockcoat. He wore a mustache and pointed beard, but no whiskers; his eyes were large and dark gray, and had a kindly expression which one would hardly have expected in one whose neck was in the hemp. Evidently this was no vulgar assassin. The liberal military code makes provision for hanging many kinds of persons, and gentlemen are not excluded.

The preparations being complete, the two private soldiers stepped aside and each drew away the plank upon which he had been standing. The sergeant turned to the captain, saluted, and placed himself immediately behind that officer, who in turn moved apart one pace. These movements left the condemned man and the sergeant standing on the two ends of the same plank, which spanned three of the cross-ties of the bridge. The end upon which the civilian stood almost, but not quite, reached a fourth. This plank had been held in place by the weight of the captain; it was now held by that of the sergeant. At a signal from the former, the latter would step aside, the plank would tilt, and the condemned man go down between two ties. The arrangement commended itself to his judgment as simple and effective. His face had not been covered nor his eyes bandaged. He looked a moment at his "unsteadfast footing," then let his gaze wander to the swirling water of the stream racing madly beneath his feet. A piece of dancing driftwood caught his attention and his eyes followed it down the current. How slowly it appeared to move! What a sluggish stream!

He closed his eyes in order to fix his last thoughts upon his wife and children. The water, touched to gold by the early sun, the brooding mists under the banks at some distance down the stream, the fort, the soldiers, the piece of driftwood—all had distracted him. And now he became conscious of a new disturbance. Striking through the thought of his dear ones was a sound which he could neither ignore nor understand, a sharp, distinct, metallic percussion like the stroke of a blacksmith's hammer upon the anvil; it had the same ringing quality. He wondered what it was, and whether immeasurably distant or near by—it seemed both. Its recurrence was regular, but as slow as the tolling of a death knell. He awaited each stroke with impatience and—he knew not why—apprehension. The intervals of silence grew progressively longer; the delays became maddening. With their greater infrequency the sounds increased in strength and sharpness. They hurt his ear like the thrust of a knife; he feared he would shriek. What he heard was the ticking of his watch.

He unclosed his eyes and saw again the water below him. "If I could free my hands," he thought, "I might throw off the noose and spring into the stream. By diving I could evade the bullets and, swimming vigorously, reach the bank, take to the woods, and get away home. My home, thank God, is as yet outside their lines; my wife and little ones are still beyond the invader's farthest advance."

As these thoughts, which have here to be set down in words, were flashed into the doomed man's brain rather than evolved from it, the captain nodded to the sergeant. The sergeant stepped aside.

II

Peyton Farquhar was a well-to-do planter, of an old and highly respected Alabama family. Being a slave owner and, like other slave owners, a politician, he was naturally an original secessionist and ardently devoted to the southern cause. Circumstances of an imperious nature, which it is unnecessary to relate here, had prevented him from taking service with the gallant army which had fought the disastrous campaigns ending with the fall of Corinth, and he chafed under the inglorious restraint, longing for the release of his energies, the larger life of the soldier, the opportunity for distinction. That opportunity, he felt, would come, as it comes to all in war time. Meanwhile he did what he could. No service was too humble for him to perform in aid of the South, no adventure too perilous for him to undertake if consistent with the character of a civilian who was at heart a soldier, and who in good faith and without too much qualification assented to at least a part of the frankly villainous dictum that all is fair in love and war.

One evening while Farquhar and his wife were sitting on a rustic bench near the entrance to his grounds, a gray-clad soldier rode up to the gate and asked for a drink of water. Mrs. Farquhar was only too happy to serve him with her own white hands. While she was fetching the water her husband approached the dusty horseman and inquired eagerly for news from the front.

"The Yanks are repairing the railroads," said the man, "and are getting ready for another advance. They have reached the Owl Creek Bridge, put it in order and built a stockade on the north bank. The commandant has issued an order, which is posted everywhere, declaring that any civilian caught interfering with the railroad, its bridges, tunnels, or trains will be summarily hanged. I saw the order."

"How far is it to the Owl Creek Bridge?" Farquhar asked.

"About thirty miles."

"Is there no force on this side the creek?"

"Only a picket post half a mile out, on the railroad, and a single sentinel at this end of the bridge."

"Suppose a man—a civilian and student of hanging—should elude the picket post and perhaps get the better of the sentinel," said Farquhar, smiling, "what could he accomplish?"

The soldier reflected. "I was there a month ago," he replied. "I observed that the flood of last winter had lodged a great quantity of driftwood against the wooden pier at this end of the bridge. It is now dry and would burn like tow."

The lady had now brought the water, which the soldier drank. He thanked her ceremoniously, bowed to her husband, and rode away. An hour later, after nightfall, he repassed the plantation, going northward in the direction from which he had come. He was a Federal scout.

III

As Peyton Farquhar fell straight downward through the bridge he lost consciousness and was as one already dead. From this state he was awakened—ages later, it seemed to him—by the pain of a sharp pressure upon his throat, followed by a sense of suffocation. Keen, poignant agonies seemed to shoot from his neck downward through every fiber of his body and limbs. These pains appeared to flash along well-defined lines of ramification and to beat with an inconceivably rapid periodicity. They seemed like streams of pulsating fire heating him to an intolerable temperature. As to his head, he was conscious of nothing but a feeling of fullness—of congestion. These sensations were unaccompanied by thought. The intellectual part of his nature was already effaced; he had power only to feel, and feeling was torment. He was conscious of motion. Encompassed in a luminous cloud, of which he was now merely the fiery heart, without material substance, he swung through unthinkable arcs of oscillation, like a vast pendulum.

Then all at once, with terrible suddenness, the light about him shot upward with the noise of a loud plash; a frightful roaring was in his ears, and all was cold and dark. The power of thought was restored; he knew that the rope had broken and he had fallen into the stream. There was no additional strangulation; the noose about his neck was already suffocating him and kept the water from his lungs. To die of hanging at the bottom of a river!—the idea seemed to him ludicrous. He opened his eyes in the darkness and saw above him a gleam of light, but how distant, how inaccessible! He was still sinking, for the light became fainter and fainter until it was a mere glimmer. Then it began to grow and brighten, and he knew that he was rising toward the surface—knew it with reluctance, for he was now very comfortable. "To be hanged and drowned," he thought, "that is not so bad; but I do not wish to be shot. No; I will not be shot; that is not fair."

He was not conscious of an effort, but a sharp pain in his wrist apprised him that he was trying to free his hands. He gave the struggle his attention, as an idler might observe the feat of a juggler, without interest in the outcome. What splendid effort! What magnificent, what superhuman strength! Ah, that was a fine endeavor! Bravo! The cord fell away; his arms parted and floated upward, the hands dimly seen on each side in the growing light. He watched them with a new interest as first one and then the other pounced upon the noose at his neck. They tore it away and thrust it fiercely aside, its undulations resembling those of a water snake. "Put it back, put it back!" He thought he shouted these words to his hands, for the undoing of the noose had been succeeded by the direst pang that he had yet experienced. His neck ached horribly; his brain was on fire; his heart, which had been fluttering faintly, gave a great leap, trying to force itself out at his mouth. His whole body was racked and wrenched with an insupportable anguish! But his disobedient hands gave no heed to the command. They beat the water vigorously with quick, downward strokes, forcing him to the surface. He felt his head emerge; his eyes were blinded by the sunlight; his chest expanded convulsively, and with a supreme and crowning agony his lungs engulfed a great draught of air, which instantly he expelled in a shriek!

He was now in full possession of his physical senses. They were, indeed, preternaturally keen and alert. Something in the awful disturbance of his organic system had so exalted and refined them that they made record of things never before perceived. He felt the ripples upon his face and heard their separate sounds as they struck. He looked at the forest on the bank of the stream, saw the individual trees, the leaves and the veining of each leaf—saw the very insects upon them: the locusts, the brilliant-bodied flies, the gray spiders stretching their webs from twig to twig. He noted the

prismatic colors in all the dewdrops upon a million blades of grass. The humming of the gnats that danced above the eddies of the stream, the beating of the dragonflies' wings, the strokes of the water spiders' legs, like oars which had lifted their boat—all these made audible music. A fish slid along beneath his eyes and he heard the rush of its body parting the water.

He had come to the surface facing down the stream; in a moment the visible world seemed to wheel slowly round, himself the pivotal point, and he saw the bridge, the fort, the soldiers upon the bridge, the captain, the sergeant, the two privates, his executioners. They were in silhouette against the blue sky. They shouted and gesticulated, pointing at him. The captain had drawn his pistol, but did not fire; the others were unarmed. Their movements were grotesque and horrible, their forms gigantic.

Suddenly he heard a sharp report and something struck the water smartly within a few inches of his head, spattering his face with spray. He heard a second report, and saw one

of the sentinels with his rifle at his shoulder, a light cloud of blue smoke rising from the muzzle. The man in the water saw the eye of the man on the bridge gazing into his own through the sights of the rifle. He observed that it was a gray eye and remembered having read that gray eyes were keenest, and that all famous markmen had them. Nevertheless, this one had missed.

A counterswirl had caught Farquhar and turned him half round; he was again looking into the forest on the bank opposite the fort. The sound of a clear, high voice in a monotonous singsong now rang out behind him and came across the water with a distinctness that pierced and subdued all other sounds, even the beating of the ripples in his ears. Although no soldier, he had frequented camps enough to know the dread significance of that deliberate, drawling, aspirated chant; the lieutenant on shore was taking a part in the morning's work. How coldly and pitilessly—with what an even, calm intonation, presaging and enforcing tranquillity in the men—with what accurately measured intervals fell those cruel words!

"Attention, company! . . . Shoulder arms! . . . Ready! . . . Aim! . . . Fire!"

Farquhar dived—dived as deeply as he could. The water roared in his ears like the voice of Niagara, yet he heard the dulled thunder of the volley and, rising again toward the surface, met shining bits of metal, singularly flattened, oscillating slowly downward. Some of them touched him on the face and hands, then fell away, continuing their descent. One lodged between his collar and neck; it was uncomfortably warm and he snatched it out.

As he rose to the surface, gasping for breath, he saw that he had been a long time under water; he was perceptibly farther downstream—nearer to safety. The soldiers had almost finished reloading; the metal ramrods flashed all at once in the sunshine as they were drawn from the barrels, turned in the air, and thrust into their sockets. The two sentinels fired again, independently and ineffectually.

The hunted man saw all this over his shoulder; he was now swimming vigorously with the current. His brain was as energetic as his arms and legs; he thought with the rapidity of lightning.

"The officer," he reasoned, "will not make that martinet's error a second time. It is as easy to dodge a volley as a single shot. He has probably already given the command to fire at will. God help me, I cannot dodge them all!"

An appalling plash within two yards of him was followed by a loud, rushing sound, *diminuendo,* which seemed to travel back through the air to the fort and died in an explosion which stirred the very river to its deeps! A rising sheet of water curved over him, fell down upon him, blinded him, strangled him! The cannon had taken a hand in the game. As he shook his head free from the commotion of the smitten water, he heard the deflected shot humming through the air ahead, and in an instant it was cracking and smashing the branches in the forest beyond.

"They will not do that again," he thought, "the next time they will use a charge of grape. I must keep my eye upon the gun; the smoke will apprise me—the report arrives too late; it lags behind the missile. That is a good gun."

Suddenly he felt himself whirled round and round—spinning like a top. The water, the banks, the forests, the now distant bridge, fort and men—all were commingled and blurred. Objects were represented by their colors only; circular horizontal streaks of color—that was all he saw. He had been caught in a vortex and was being whirled on with a velocity of advance and gyration which made him giddy and sick. In a few moments he was flung upon the gravel at the foot of the left bank of the stream—the southern bank—and behind a projecting point which concealed him from his enemies. The sudden arrest of his motion, the abrasion of one of his hands on the gravel, restored him, and he wept with delight. He dug his fingers into the sand, threw it over himself in handfuls, and audibly blessed it. It looked like diamonds, rubies, emeralds; he could think of nothing beautiful which it did not resemble. The trees upon the bank were giant garden plants; he noted a definite order in their arrangement, inhaled the fragrance of their blooms. A strange, roseate light shone through the spaces among their trunks and the wind made in their branches the music of aeolian harps. He had no wish to perfect his escape—was content to remain in that enchanting spot until retaken.

A whiz and rattle of grapeshot among the branches high above his head roused him from his dream. The baffled cannoneer had fired

him a random farewell. He sprang to his feet, rushed up the sloping bank, and plunged into the forest.

All that day he traveled, laying his course by the rounding sun. The forest seemed interminable; nowhere did he discover a break in it, not even a woodman's road. He had not known that he lived in so wild a region. There was something uncanny in the revelation.

By nightfall he was fatigued, footsore, famishing. The thought of his wife and children urged him on. At last he found a road which led him in what he knew to be the right direction. It was as wide and straight as a city street, yet it seemed untraveled. No fields bordered it, no dwelling anywhere. Not so much as the barking of a dog suggested human habitation. The black bodies of the trees formed a straight wall on both sides, terminating on the horizon in a point, like a diagram in a lesson in perspective. Overhead, as he looked up through this rift in the wood, shone great golden stars looking unfamiliar and grouped in strange constellations. He was sure they were arranged in some order which had a secret and malign significance. The wood on either side was full of singular noises, among which—once, twice, and again—he distinctly heard whispers in an unknown tongue.

His neck was in pain and lifting his hand to it he found it horribly swollen. He knew that it had a circle of black where the rope had bruised it. His eyes felt congested; he could no longer close them. His tongue was swollen with thirst; he relieved its fever by thrusting it forward from between his teeth into the cold air. How softly the turf had carpeted the untraveled avenue—he could no longer feel the roadway beneath his feet!

Doubtless, despite his suffering, he had fallen asleep while walking, for now he sees another scene—perhaps he has merely recovered from a delirium. He stands at the gate of his own home. All is as he left it, and all bright and beautiful in the morning sunshine. He must have traveled the entire night. As he pushes open the gate and passes up the wide white walk, he sees a flutter of female garments; his wife, looking fresh and cool and sweet, steps down from the veranda to meet him. At the bottom of the steps she stands waiting, with a smile of ineffable joy, an attitude of matchless grace and dignity. Ah, how beautiful she is! He springs forward with extended arms. As he is about to clasp her, he feels a stunning blow upon the back of the neck; a blinding white light blazes all about him with a sound like the shock of a cannon—then all is darkness and silence!

Peyton Farquhar was dead; his body, with a broken neck, swung gently from side to side beneath the timbers of the Owl Creek Bridge.

GENERAL INSIGHT

What limits the "reasonable" interpretation of an experience? Are there consistent ways to test the validity of an interpretation?

For example, viewers of the movie based on this story said that

a. What happened to Farquhar "really" happened. We are all kicked off the "plank" at birth, and plummet headlong, deceiving ourselves that we can escape death, until in our moment of ultimate security we reach the end of our rope.

b. It's just a man on a bridge who imagines the whole escape during the brief plunge from the plank.

c. What we have here, really, are actors, cameras, elaborate sets. This is really a screen play.

d. This is really shadows on a screen, created by light being filtered through film.

e. The story is True.

f. The whole thing is a lie.

g. The whole thing is a lie (fiction), but it's true anyway.

WHAT IS THE BASIS OF VALIDITY?

Above all, the art of the film is to be looked for in the cinema's imperfections.

SEEING THINGS

FACE VALUE

enough dots per inch in a half-tone
enough inches per second on audio tape
enough frames per second on film
the increment approaching zero in calculus
enough electronic vibrations in subatomic physics

equal

the illusion of concrete reality

The illusion of the cinema depends on the imperfection of our senses.

Only our defects permit vision.

Without imperfection can there be art?

Without a position (bias) is it possible to see at all?

Nanook of the North (1922) influences many of the subsequent attempts to interpret human activity on the screen rather than merely to photograph it.

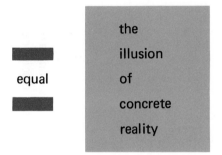

WE SHAPE OUR TOOLS AND AFTERWARD OUR TOOLS SHAPE US.

The movies are part of my culture, and it seems to me that their special power has something to do with their being a kind of "pure" culture, a little like fishing or drinking or playing baseball—a cultural fact, that is, which has not yet fallen altogether under the discipline of art. I have not brought Henry James to the movies or the movies to Henry James, but I hope I have shown that the man who goes to the movies is the same as the man who reads James.

Both the managers of art theaters and the distributors of art films are notoriously careful people. They have to be. Mistakes in their field can be costly. The exhibitor must be prepared to pay thousands of dollars for the advertising and publicity that go out before a new picture opens. To get a particular film, he may even have to guarantee the distributor a certain amount of money or number of weeks of playing time—regardless of its eventual acceptance by the public. The distributor, on the other hand, in addition to the not inconsiderable sums he must pay to acquire his films in the first place (anywhere from $10,000 to $100,000, and occasionally more), must also stand the expenses of titling or dubbing them for American distribution, as well as some part of the initial advertising costs.

And yet, as such *flops d'estime* as *The Diary of a Country Priest, Umberto D, Day of Wrath,* and *La Mystère Picasso* remind us, both the art film distributors and the art house exhibitors are often more willing to gamble on the attractiveness of a good picture than are their patrons.

There are today some 300 organizations that call themselves either film societies, film clubs, or film study groups; and probably at least another 500 meeting informally and irregularly in schools, museums, and private homes that carry out some of the functions of such organizations. They show film classics or simply old films; they run documentaries, science films and experimentals; they may even, on occasion, supply their members with program notes or invite guest speakers to introduce the pictures. Some societies have been organized by "Foofs" (Friends of Old Films—a species first identified by Christopher Bishop; the word takes care of the kind of antiquarians called "moldy figs" in jazz parlance); they will look at anything, good, bad, or indifferent, so long as it was produced before 1928.

Thanks to the efforts of the Museum of Modern Art Film Library and distributors like Brandon, Contemporary, Film Images, and Trans-World, more titles of first quality are available to them now than ever before.

JUMP CUT

> *"The bitterness and urgency of today's rebellious youth . . . tender and lyrical . . . A social document of aimless teenagers seeking their identity . . . evocative and bittersweet . . . the tragic boomerang of adolescent passions . . . A visual treat . . . somewhat controversial."*
>
> —The Times

It is Fifth Avenue in late afternoon in autumn and the shadows darken the street. The boy wears a heavy sweater and desert boots. He has long hair. The girl is pretty. She is wearing a heavy sweater. It is Fifth Avenue or Grosvenor Square. She has lovely eyes. They look in the shop windows. Mannequins in fur and diamonds. Ladies' shoes atop red velvet. An eight million dollar necklace. She whirls and pirouettes, dreaming of inaugural balls or being presented to the Queen. A few middle-aged people stare at her and shake their heads. What is the world coming to. She giggles and takes the boy's hand and they skip away to the park. They walk in the park. Leaves are falling. It is that golden time of day. There are boats on the lake. The sun is going down behind the Dakota Apartments or the London Hilton and she chases a squirrel across the grass in the soft darkening afternoon. Then they are drinking wine. They are in his small room drinking wine. Her eyes are lovely. The boy is talking. He is being bitter about something. Eventually it becomes clear. It's the world. He is being bitter about the world. He chain-smokes and drinks a lot of wine. It is Greenwich Village or the West Side. It is either of those or it is Soho or it is Montmartre. After a while she does a little pirouette and he gets up and stands in front of the bathroom mirror and makes funny faces in the mirror. Then they make funny faces together. He kisses her. She becomes pregnant. She is pregnant and they talk to an abortionist. The abortionist's office is cold and sterile. Everything in the office is white. The boy and girl are nervous but the abortionist's nurse is not nervous. The nurse has hooded eyes. She smokes a cigarette. The abortionist is smooth and very much to the point. He's been through this scene thousands of times. He has a moustache and long, elegant fingers. He tells them to come back next Tuesday. They leave the office. The boy puts his arm around the girl. They are not on Fifth Avenue. They are near the waterfront. A drunk is sleeping in a doorway. They are trying to decide what to do. The girl writes a letter to her mother in the suburbs and then tears it up. The boy runs from one end of Chicago to the other. Then he looks for a job to get the money for the abortion. He is interviewed by a series of tall men with elegant fingers and they all tell him that they'll let him know if anything turns up. He insults one of the men, an old school chum of his father's who is the president of a management consultant firm and cannot understand why the boy did not finish college. The boy insults him beautifully. The man is so out of it that he is not even sure he has been insulted.

Then the boy and girl go to a store in San Francisco or Toronto or Liverpool. They steal some groceries. They leave the store laughing with the groceries under their heavy sweaters. Then the boy stops at a flower stand and steals a flower for the girl. Then they go home and she cries. Then they go to a party. Everybody at the party is a phony except for one guy who's a West Indian or an American Negro or a French Canadian. This guy tells them that they don't know the first thing about being bitter. They have no right to be bitter. He tells them a thing or two about life and death. Everybody else is doing the freddy and this guy is telling them about real suffering, real pain. Telling it like it is. Then he rolls up his sleeve and shows them how he was wounded in Vietnam or Mississippi. Meanwhile everybody is doing the freddy and talking about Andy Warhol or the Animals. The boy and girl go home again. The Vietnam or Mississippi thing has put their troubles in a truer perspective. They play hide-and-seek under the covers of his tiny bed. Then they take turns feeling the girl's belly. They go to the Louvre and the girl sticks out her tongue at the Mona Lisa. Some middle-aged people shake their heads. The next day the girl gets up early and goes to school and the boy sits around smoking and looking in the mirror. Then he steals a car. He drives past all the ancient monuments of Rome or Athens. He sees his father come out of a hotel with a woman who is not his mother. He slumps down low in the driver's seat and watches. His father talks to the woman for a few seconds and then kisses her and they walk off in different directions. The boy just sits there. He sits there. Cars are piling up behind him and horns are blowing. Then he is standing on a bridge above the Thames. Leaves and garbage float by. He goes home and sees that the flower he had stolen for the girl is dead. He throws the flower away so she won't see it when she gets home from school. Then she gets home and tells him to return the stolen car. He gives her a hard time, saying basically that nothing means anything so why bother. She says if that's your concept of life I don't want to see you anymore. So she goes home to the suburbs. She has roast beef and mashed potatoes with her mother and father and older sister. Dessert is chocolate cake. Her mother wants to know why she's failing Civics and Arithmetic and where she's been the last three days and nights. The girl tries to be nice. Things are different now, mom. It's not like when you were growing up. The father makes an attempt at paternal understanding. Takes the positive approach. Compliments her on the fine job she's been doing in English Lit. Says he *likes* the Beatles. Then the older sister's date shows up. He has a crew-cut and wears a button-down shirt. He makes a lot of comments about the junior chamber of commerce and the local country club. He's in the executive training program of a huge management consultant firm. He's also a lieutenant in the Air Force Reserve. Brags about the fact that his country club just admitted its first Jew. The girl wants to know why they didn't do it twenty years ago. Older sister gets mad and tells her to go to her room. In her room she looks in the mirror. Then she feels her belly for a few minutes and repacks her suitcase. The boy stands in front of a movie theater looking at a poster of Jean Paul Belmondo. He goes to a bar. The place is full of hookers and pimps. Derelicts slip from their bar stools and lie in the sawdust. The juke is playing mean, lowdown jazz. The bartender is fat and ugly. A very clean-cut man comes up to the boy and arrests him. The boy's father visits him in jail and they have an argument. The boy doesn't want to mention the strange woman he had seen with his father but in the heat of the argument it slips out. The father is ashamed. He offers to foot all the bills if the boy would only go to the Sorbonne or Michigan State. The boy calls this gesture a moral bribe and he laughs sardonically. Then he is released in the custody of his father and he goes back to his small flat in Chelsea and looks in the mirror. His parole officer tries to talk some sense into him. The parole officer is a nice guy. He has kids of his own, same age as the boy. The boy goes to his room and plays the guitar. He runs through the mad Los Angeles night. Then the girl comes in with her suitcase and they live together. Both of them wear heavy sweaters and blue jeans and desert boots. The girl whirls and pirouettes. She is not too good-looking but she has lovely eyes. They go to Coney Island or Brighton. They ride on the roller coaster and the carousel and they look at themselves in the distorted mirrors. He is nine feet tall and very skinny. She is short and squat and it reminds her that she is pregnant. They think of the abortionist. She feels her belly and smiles. They are going to have the baby. Then he chases her along the beach. Seagulls slant across the dying afternoon. They go behind a sand-dune and kiss. They go home. He kills a roach. They see what their life together is going to be like.

NEGATIVE

I have lost the print, but in this negative
you can see her shape, if not much more. That black
is beach; her hair, here white, was black. That white
is water, laced with black. Its roar, and that
of the wind, not pictured here, except as her hair
flies out from her grey shoulders (they were brown),
drowned all our conversation: we lost track,
that sun-bleached day (the sun here makes her frown),
of hours, words, kisses, sandwiches and beer,
all used in colorful affirmative.

We left our imprint on the sand; the sea
or wind, in another season, cleaned this away,
and now, all black and white in each our minds
remains some blurry dent of how we lay,
some negative of warmth of other lips,
some scrape of sandy thighs, some taste of salt.
I forget, now, how it was—but how it ends
is negative, the afterglow of a glimpse—
turned inside out, unfleshed, with strength for fault,
remembered in the nerves transparently.

HOW DO MOVIES CONVEY THE SENSES OF TASTE, TOUCH, AND SMELL?

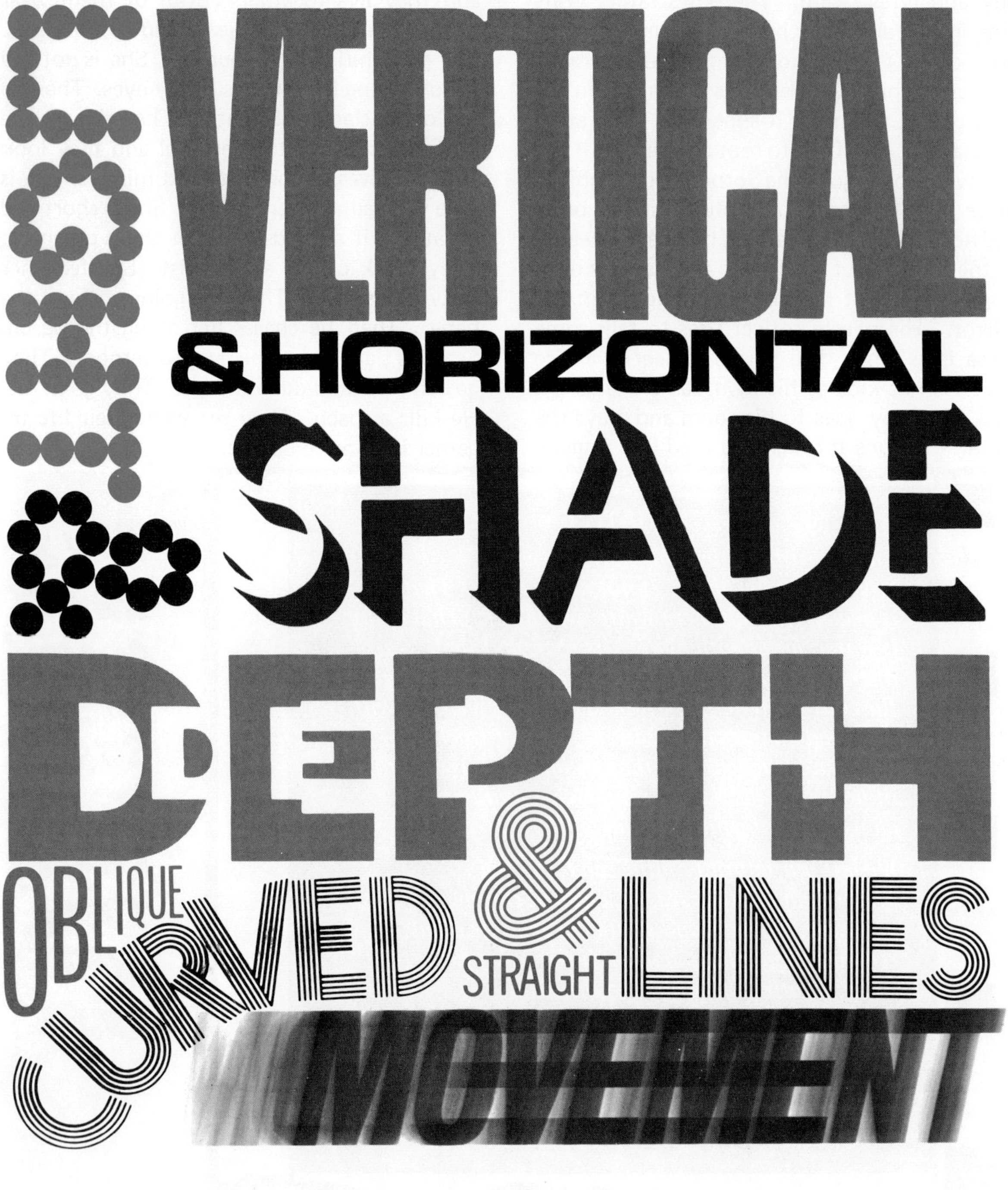
VERTICAL
&HORIZONTAL
&SHADE
DEPTH
OBLIQUE
CURVED
&
STRAIGHT
LINES
MOVEMENT

The music of *The River* is partly original, but mostly it is just the music of the Mississippi Valley.

It is hymn music of the kind known as white spirituals; which is to say, the ancient Scottish and Irish tunes that our southern and western forefathers learned in the rural districts of the British Isles and brought with them to this continent as their music heritage.

Although their associations with sacred works dates mostly from the seventeenth and eighteenth centuries, the greater antiquity of these melodies is proved by their purely pentatonic (or five-note scale) character. An exception is the tune known to the hymn books as "Mississippi" and commonly sung to the words "When Gabriel's Awful Trump Shall Sound."

This tune, written in full Acolian mode, is probably, according to Dr. George Pullen Jackson of Vanderbilt University, an Irish sea-chanty of great antiquity. It is used in *The River* in the form of canon, fugue and finally in its own full harmonization (a rich and strong medieval descant harmonization which, though first published in William Walker's *Southern Harmony* in the 1830's, is probably as old as the tune) to accompany the rising waters of its namesake, the Mississippi, and the awful terrors of their overflowing.

DECOR

I myself have never had any ambition to be an author. I do not want to write novels, short stories, essays, biographies, or even plays for the theatre. I only want to make films—films about conditions, tensions, pictures, rhythms and characters which are in one way or another important to me.

Scenes linked by the soundtrack.

PERCEPT, CONCEPT, AND SENSORS

D. W. Griffith:

> The task I'm trying to achieve is above all to make you see.

Joseph Conrad:

> My task which I am trying to achieve is, by the power of the written word, to make you hear, to make you feel—it is, before all, to make you *see.*

Is film "sight" the same as verbal "sight"?

Is there a difference between *percept* and *concept*?
Is all *perceiving* really conceiving?

What does the director do to make you "see"? What does the word-artist do?

What would have to be done to the poem "Smell!" to make it a movie? How would you get across the ambiguity of the poem? How can you transmit multiple meanings via visual stimuli?

SCULPTURE

And everything comes to one.

The sculptor George Gray Barnard . . . has talked to me at length about his sense of discovery in watching the most ordinary motion pictures, and his delight in following them with their endless combinations of masses and flowing surfaces.

The little far-away people on the old-fashioned speaking stage do not appeal to the plastic sense in this way. They are, by comparison, mere bits of pasteboard with sweet voices, while, on the other hand, the photoplay foreground is full of dumb giants. The bodies of these giants are high sculptural relief. Where the lights are quite glaring and the photography is bad, many of the figures are as hard in their impact on the eye as lime-white plaster-casts, no matter what the clothing.

What does motion add to pictures?

By permission of Johnny Hart and Publishers-Hall Syndicate.

In television documentaries words are often back-grounds.

In Shakespeare, sets are background and words are foreground.

The illusion of uninterrupted motion is created by tiny segments moving past the eye at sixteen or twenty-four frames per second. The mind blends the segments into a unified whole.

How many frames per minute does your life "movie" consist of?

Citizen Kane (1941). There is no question here of experiment for experiment's sake; it is a question of a man with a problem of narrative to solve, using lighting, setting, sound, camera angles and movement much as a genuine writer uses words, phrases, cadences, rhythms; using them with the ease and boldness and resources of one who controls and is not controlled by his medium.

TEST YOUR . . . . . WHAT?

MATCH:

___	1. Jean Renoir	A.	*Blow-Up*
___	2. Robert Bresson	B.	*Wild Strawberries*
___	3. Ingmar Bergman	C.	*The Trial of Joan of Arc*
___	4. Roman Polanski	D.	*Diary of a Chambermaid*
___	5. Alain Resnais	E.	*Juliet of the Spirits*
___	6. Luis Buñuel	F.	*Breathless*
___	7. Federico Fellini	G.	*Knife in the Water*
___	8. Michelangelo Antonioni	H.	*The World of Apu*
___	9. Satyajit Ray	I.	*The River*
___	10. Vittorio De Sica	J.	*Last Year at Marienbad*
___	11. Roberto Rossellini	K.	*The General of Rovere*
___	12. François Truffaut	L.	*The Bicycle Thief*
___	13. Jean-Luc Godard	M.	*Shoot the Piano Player*

Key: ICBGJDEAHLKMF

GROUP II

___	1. John Ford	A.	*The Birds*
___	2. Sidney Lumet	B.	*Cheyenne Autumn*
___	3. Robert Wise	C.	*Dr. Zhivago*
___	4. George Stevens	D.	*The Pawnbroker*
___	5. George Cukor	E.	*Anatomy of a Murder*
___	6. David Lean	F.	*The Sound of Music*
___	7. Jules Dassin	G.	*Shane*
___	8. Alfred Hitchcock	H.	*The Apartment*
___	9. Billy Wilder	I.	*My Fair Lady*
___	10. Otto Preminger	J.	*Topkapi*
___	11. John Huston	K.	*Dr. Strangelove or How I Learned to Stop Worrying and Love the Bomb*
___	12. Elia Kazan	L.	*Night of the Iguana*
___	13. Stanley Kubrick	M.	*The Knack and How to Get It*
___	14. Richard Lester	N.	*On the Waterfront*

Key: BDFGICJAHELNKM

FRAMING

GROUP III

___ 1.	Edwin S. Porter	A.	*The Blue Angel*
___ 2.	Leni Riefenstahl	B.	*Night Mail*
___ 3.	Robert Flaherty	C.	*Birth of a Nation*
___ 4.	Louis Lumière	D.	*Nanook of the North*
___ 5.	Josef von Sternberg	E.	*Blood of a Poet*
___ 6.	Sergei Eisenstein	F.	*The Great Train Robbery*
___ 7.	Georges Méliès	G.	*Train Coming into a Station*
___ 8.	D. W. Griffith	H.	*Battleship Potemkin*
___ 9.	Jean Cocteau	I.	*The India-rubber Head*
___ 10.	John Grierson	J.	*Triumph of the Will*

Key: FJDGAHICEB

Afterthoughts

Did you have equal success with all three tests?

Did your classmates have the same results?

Did you notice the bases for the three different groups?

What does an analysis of this kind of test reveal about you, about your culture, about movies, about English, about . . . what?

ALEXEIEFF

Working with his wife, the American artist Claire Parker, Alexeieff has made three films, using an original technique which John Grierson has called "animated engraving."

How many angels, really, can dance on the head of a pin?

ANIMATED ENGRAVING

The Pinboard, invented by Alexeieff, is a white upright board (three feet by four feet high, and one inch thick), perforated with one million holes into which have been inserted steel pins 1¼ inches long, pointed at both ends. By moving the pins forward and back, and by adjusting the oblique lighting of the board, the shadows of the pins produce a half-tone effect ranging from full white to velvet black. The artists work on both sides of the Pinboard at once, Miss Parker operating the back, "negative" image, and Alexeieff working on the front, "positive" side. The images are photographed successively, frame by frame. In this manner it took over eighteen months to complete *The Nose,* which is eleven minutes long.

Statement by the artists: "We believe that the film of animation is one of the fine arts, and that in the History of the Art of Tomorrow only the invention of perspective, by the painters of the Renaissance, will be held comparable to that of animation; the artist's urge to represent form in movement has found in the film of animation an *entirely new dimension* for its expression."

> Comments on *The Nose* by European critics: (As you read these comments refer to the three pictures from the film. Do some of the particular terms describing the film seem more apt than others? Which ones?)
>
> ". . . we know the subject of the fantastical story of a nose which abandons its owner's face to become an important personage. To the eeriness of the tale is added the eeriness of the tempo, in which shadows and lights, days and nights, sun and moon go by at the cadence of a dream, not of life. . . We shall no more forget *The Nose* than the series of engravings that Alexeieff gave as the preface to *The Trial*, and which give to Orson Welles' film a part of its greatness. . ."
>
> —George Sadoul, *Lettres Françaises,* June 12, 1963.
>
> ". . . Saint Petersburg lives again, with its white nights and opaque days . . . inspired by Gogol's *Nose*—that nose, lost and found again, which grows bigger and bigger and parades around the town—the film illustrates the story and also re-creates it, which is the prime requisite of an accomplished work of art."
>
> —Yvonne Baby, *Le Monde*, June 12, 1963.

"As to Alexeieff, who is the most accomplished of all animators, his fame comes not from his invention of the Pinboard, admirable though it may be, but rather from his prodigious subsequent poetic visions, like *The Nose*, which are full of art and poetry . . ."

—ROBERT BENAYOUN, *Positif*, July-August 1963 (translated in the Spring, 1964, issue of *Film Quarterly*).

". . . The number of films made by Alexeieff and Parker can be counted on one hand and yet their place in the history of the cinema is beyond question. In 1934 they made a film with Mussorgsky's music, *Night on Bare Mountain*, as a background, and used an extraordinary 'pinhead shadow' technique which they invented themselves . . . Using the same means this new film (only the third to be made in nearly thirty years) captured the mysterious atmosphere of Gogol's story in an impressive manner. . ."

—*The London Times*, June 17, 1963.

". . . Alexeieff's infinite patience, perfect taste, constant spirit of research, and profound intellectual honesty were justly honored by the wave of applause which followed the projection of this film, which is worthy of standing side by side with the celebrated *Night On Bare Mountain*, one of the classics of the motion picture, the first important work that Alexeieff created thirty years ago on his Pinboard."

—PIERRE BARDE, *Journal de Genève*, June 22, 1963.

". . . the shades of gray, the softness of passage from one tone to the other which the Pinboard allows, give a quality which captivates the spectator. The film received a veritable ovation."

—*Echo Savoyard*, June 12, 1963.

"I should like to tell of the emotion aroused by *The Nose*, the latest film of Alexander Alexeieff and Claire Parker, because of its highly poetic quality and its beauty of form.

"Beyond time and its fashions, such works will serenely maintain their value when nine-tenths of the present productions are forgotten."

—JEAN D'YVOIRE, *Telerama*, July 7, 1963.

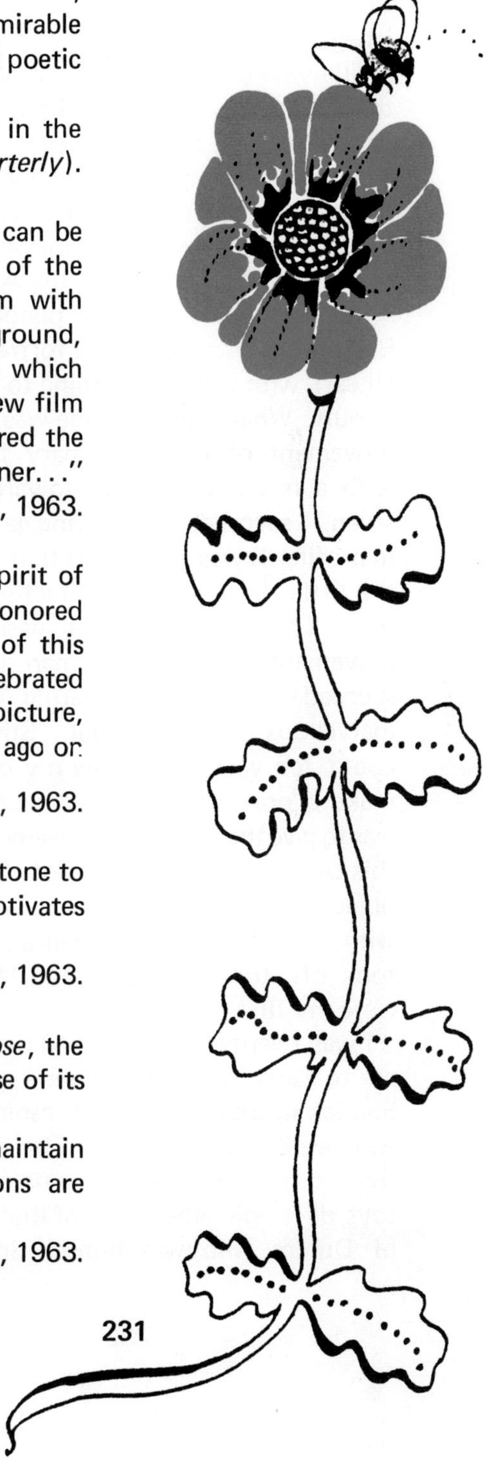

REFLECTIONS ON MOTION PICTURE ANIMATION

I began to draw in 1905 at the age of four, in a villa where my parents lived on the shore of the Bosphorus near Istamboul. I began by drawing boats, because at every instant there were boats passing across the panorama which, like a Chinese scroll, unrolled itself before my eyes, from the Black Sea to the Sea of Marmara, against the background of the Anatolian hills. After the boats, I drew panoramas of the Bosphorus, with crenelated fortresses (Rumeli-Hissar), with warriors running to take them by assault. What interested me was to render the movement of these summary figures drawn with a few lines. Later, towards the age of seven, I succeeded in drawing galloping horses in profile. It was at this time that I encountered the little tin soldiers manufactured in Nüremberg. The elegance of their design, and their movement which the German draftsmen had succeeded so well in rendering, were for me a marvellous drawing school. Still later, when about ten years old, I saw my oldest brother make a praxinoscope, the function of which was to give the illusion of movement; I imitated this by drawing in a little notebook a moving object phase by phase. There was a windmill with arms that turned, then an airplane that took off, turned around, and landed. They were my first films.

I was twenty when I helped destiny to bring me to Paris, where I became a pupil of Serge Soudekin, set-designer and inspirer of the Bat (Chauve-Souris) Theatre. The actors of this theater mimed the movements of mechanical toys, developing the theme of the "Nutcracker" of Dumas who was himself influenced by Andersen and E. T. A. Hoffmann, the true inventors of the animation of toys and objects. I painted, and afterwards designed, stage sets and costumes for five years. I then taught myself engraving and became an illustrator of de luxe books, an art which I practiced successfully for a decade. But this was the era of art films: Chaplin's early films, *Cagliari, The Blue Angel*, Man Ray's three films, and finally Bartosch's film, *Eine Idee*, based on a book by Masereel, decided me to try my luck and to enter into contact with a larger audience (there were no more than 15,000 customers of de luxe books in France then, and far less now).

I was afraid of the Eldorado atmosphere which, at that time, held the motion picture studios prisoner; the theater had already taught me the role chance plays in collective creations, distorting the intentions of the individuals who take part in them. I considered the animated cartoon good for comics, not for the poetic atmosphere which was the life-substance of my engravings. I would have to invent a motion picture technique such that I might, entirely alone, make pictures with half-tones, grays, and indistinct forms. I made this invention and built the first Pinboard in association with Miss Claire Parker, an American from Boston, who later became my wife.

We illustrated together *Night on Bare Mountain*, by Mussorgsky, a theme used again after us by Walt Disney in the United States and Rigal in France. Our *Night on Bare Mountain* achieved a success in the press unequaled for an eight-minute film; newspapers and reviews predicted the most brilliant future for us, but not a single motion picture distribution circuit beyond the motion picture theater Panthéon in Paris and the Academy Theatre in London asked for our film (released in 1934).

We decided to make no more animation films without having distribution assured in advance. This meant limiting ourselves to advertising films for motion picture theaters which in France had a real market but which paid badly. We were the first to make color films (Gasparcolor) in France, and immediately obtained a reputation for quality on the market. We established, I believe I am justified in saying, a class of films without precedent in this domain, and for which a certain number of progressive and powerful advertisers were ready to pay more and more.

All of these pre-war advertising films were color animation films, without recourse to the Pinboard, which is reserved for black and white. We have never used the animated cartoon, leaving this technique to our competitors. In our first color films we animated marionnettes as beautiful as Diagilev's dancers, to music made for us by the finest French composers of the time, Poulenc, Milhaud, Auric. Later, our dancers were the wares themselves of our customers—shoes, or hats, for example. And for the first time advertising films were applauded in the local motion picture theaters. We made ourselves the champions of three-dimensional object animation. Into each one or two minute film we decided to introduce, if only in one of its sequences, some sort of experiment, and never hesitated to invest time or money in inventions, because an advertising film must strike by the novelty of its form.

This development was interrupted by the second world war.

We resumed our small production in Paris in 1951, when we began developing the technique of a new kind of animation which we call "totalization." Instead of recording frame by frame a stationary object, we do frame by frame recording of moving objects which are connected with compound pendulums. We have built a robot driven by a compound pendulum, which makes a drawing on one frame of the film, while the camera makes one long exposure. We then rewind the robot, and it draws on the following frame in a similar way, etc. The results so obtained are new, and very useful in certain particular cases, notably for abstract sequences.

We work alone, or with one other person, and our yearly production of one minute films is limited to three or four, which I find sufficient; to augment the number of workers would tend to diminish the quality of the films. I believe it is essential to avoid confusing the methods of mass production with those required to establish prototypes. Our advertising films have had an incomparably wider distribution than most feature films; they are often seen several times by the same persons. Their quality must therefore be more dense than that of feature films.

I am not qualified to speak of the live action motion picture. My main interest is in the animated motion picture, which can attain an artistic quality comparable to the masterpieces known in the older arts, painting, the dance, music, sculpture, and above all, poetry. The shortness of animation films appears to me relative. Most of Chopin's Preludes last about a minute; the Seventh lasts 32½ seconds, but one remembers it all one's life; the Mona Lisa is a small picture in comparison with the immense canvases produced by the manufactory of Rubens. Rubens is a great painter only in his small canvases painted entirely by himself. And when I am told at the end of a film which only lasts a minute: "What a shame it is so short!" I am happy to hear it.

In 1943, during our stay in the United States, we made one film in the Pinboard technique, *En Passant*, for the Canadian National Film Board. As we had been obliged to leave our original Pinboard in Paris, we built a new one, containing, instead of the original 500,000 pins, 1,000,000, which makes it possible to produce effects analogous to the charcoal drawings of Seurat.

We brought this second Pinboard back to Europe, and have recently made on it 200 illustrations for an edition of *Dr. Zhivago*, which was published in Paris in 1959, then in New York in 1960. At Orson Welles' request, we illustrated the Prologue of his film *The Trial* (based on Kafka's novel) in 1962, using the same technique.

Our latest work on the Pinboard is *The Nose*, an eleven-minute film on the theme of one of Gogol's fantastic short stories. *The Nose* is very different from *Night on Bare Mountain*. It does not illustrate music; it tells without words Gogol's dream of the Man who lost his Nose.

The Nose is a painter's film, in which the movements of light play a dramatic role.

I believe that all forms—sounds, colors, volumes, and above all, movements—may have meaning. They do not possess it of themselves; it is men who give them meaning—sometimes different meanings, insofar as the interests of human beings differ—meanings often erroneous or illusory, which are the more valued by the mind, inasmuch as they are its own creations.

I shall take an example from a live action film rather than from animation, in order that it be clear to everyone: In the *Gold Rush*, Chaplin sticks two real forks into two real rolls lying on a real plate. These objects have absolutely nothing equivocal about them until Chaplin gives to the forks the movement of a cancan-dancer's legs. The spectators become enchanted because the "legs" become not real, but plausible. In the imitative arts, there must be a resemblance with, and a difference from, reality. What pleases is this ambiguity.

What I also like in the animation film is its power to awaken the spectator's imagination and senses by that kinship between movement and rhythmic sounds which is at the origin of the dance, and which manifests itself early in our childhood, when, at table, like Chaplin, we play forbidden games with spoons and forks, games out of which Andersen had made fairy tales.

But what I care for above all in animation is the power to master the tempo of thought and emotions in the audience. It pleases me to construct over a period of four months a synthesis whose presence on the screen will last only one minute, during which the audience cannot withdraw its attention for even a fraction of a second.

I trust that with the progress in motion picture distribution technique, the lovers of moving pictures will be able to see the films they wish, when they wish, as one chooses a poem to read or a record to which to listen. When such a day comes, the notion of the film classic will be definitely established, and with it, the new art will be consecrated.

In the meantime, public and private film libraries and television are preparing, albeit with as yet rudimentary techniques of distribution and transmission, the road to such a future.

A MICROCOSM

Here is the first draft of a scenario for an animation film. As you read through it, try to envision the movie itself. Is reading the scenario like reading a short story?

"Cinema is bits of sight and bits of sound put together in a celluloid mosaic." Do you agree?

On pages 242–43 are photographs actually taken from the Alexeieff film. Does the script convey the same immediacy? Why?

The final version of *The Nose* contains several changes from this first draft. Among them:

1. The movie begins with Scene 2.
2. All the dialogue and sound effects are eliminated. Instead, the sound track contains only the improvised music of Hi-Minh.
3. The sequence from Scene 17 through Scene 27 is deleted.
4. Scene 35 is deleted.
5. Scenes 44 and 45 are deleted (Kovalov discovers his nose is in place when he looks in the mirror.)

Why do you suppose each of these changes was made?

What effect do you think these changes would have on the film as a whole?

Discuss the scenario and possible reasons for the changes with other students. Extend your analysis to other forms of animation. What connections and contrasts do you see with cartooning?

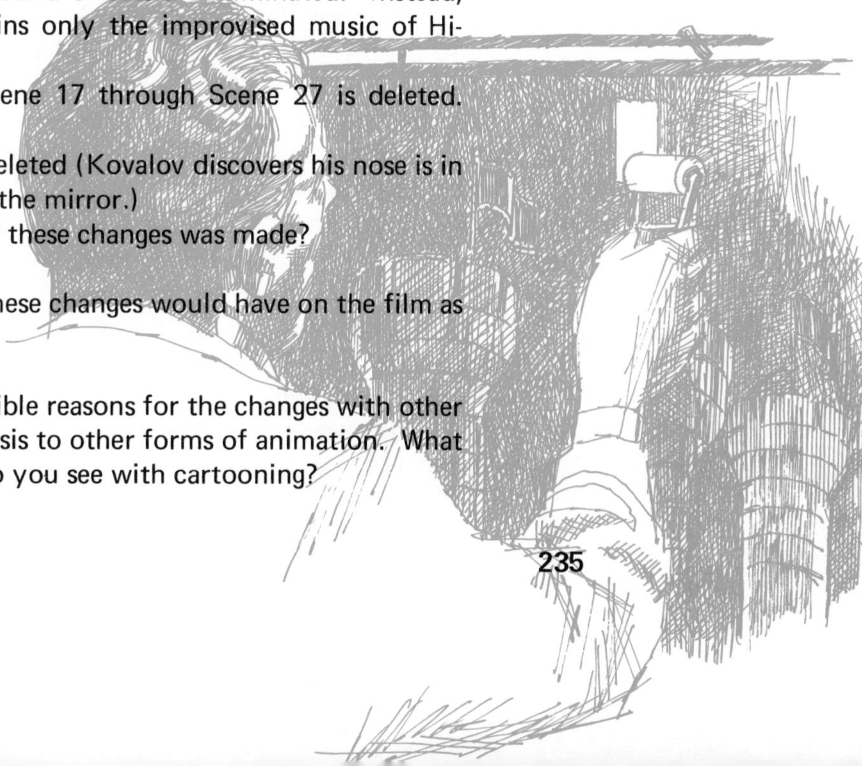

THE NOSE

Based On a Story by Nicolas Gogol

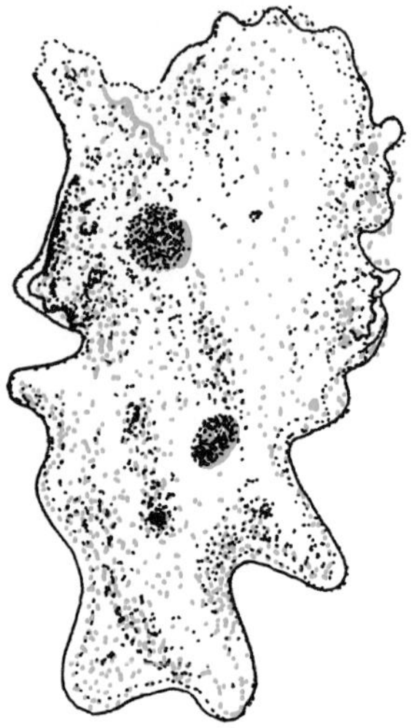

1. (Medium shot) Barber shaves Kovalov, holding him by the nose.
2. Night in Saint Petersburg. Sunrise.
3. Sunlight spreads over a street, the door of a barber's shop, sign over shop.
4. (Close-up) Coffee-pot. Fragrance steaming from spout. Pan on nose of barber asleep; he snores, sneezes, wakes up.
5. Barber, in tail-coat over night shirt (for decency's sake), sitting at a plain wooaen table. His wife takes loaf of bread from oven.
6. (Medium shot) Barber takes on serious expression, starts cutting loaf with a knife.
7. (Close-up) Knife stops. The cut loaf. In it a nose.
8. Quarrel between wife and barber; wife's accusing finger. Barber, embarrassed, tries to hide nose (small parcel). Wife threatens barber with broom. Exit barber.
9. (Same as 3): Door of barber shop seen from street. Barber comes out (dressed?).
10. Barber moves along street (like Chaplin). He is trying to get rid of small parcel containing nose. He puts it down. A sentinel points to parcel with his halberd. Barber picks up parcel again and timidly moves on.
11. Barber on bridge over Neva. Pretends to be watching water flow by, looks to right and to left. Drops parcel.

    (Possible shot: Nose under water. Bubbles. Fish.)

    Voice off: "What were you doing there?
12. A policeman beckons to barber. Barber trembles.
13. Door on landing; plate on door. Zoom to plate on which is engraved *"Major Kovalov".*
14. Kovalov is asleep in bed. He is dreaming of a young woman (leg?).
15. Sunlight comes through the window. (It climbs up over the room as it did over the door of the barber's shop in 3).

    (If needed: drum or bugle sounding reveille)
16. Kovalov looks at himself in mirror. Has no nose. Instead, a place flat and smooth as a pancake. He rubs his eyes, looks at himself. No nose.
17. Kovalov, distracted, searches in an address-book. B,. . . C,. . . D,. . . Doctors. O,. . . P,. . . Miss P.

re-14. Repeat face in 14.

17. (cont'd) Letter P, . . . Police: Word underlines itself.

18. Kovalov becomes dressed piece by piece (like a cardboard doll to which clothes are added): night shirt + day shirt + trousers + waistcoat + tailcoat + top hat + cape. He masks his face with handkerchief as if suffering from nose-bleed.

19. Kovalov in cab hammers back of coachman with his fists.

    (Possible shot: fantastic cavalcade like *Night on Bare Mountain*—witches, broomsticks, goats, etc.)

20. A counter. Sign "Lost and Found." Old official with black glasses. Inaudible explanations. Official takes out from beneath counter a leg. . . an arm. . . an ear. Kovalov shakes head. Pan on poster—picture of young woman lifting her arm. Inscription: "Miss P. wanted for witchcraft. . . big reward. . ."

21. Official produces snuffbox, takes a pinch, offers box to Kovalov who keeps on hiding face behind handkerchief.

22. (Close-up) Snuffbox. It snaps open after glimpse of Miss P.'s portrait on cover.

    (Possible shot: naked woman.)

23. Kovalov angry (smashes everything?)

24. Kovalov goes slowly down stairs, very depressed.

    Voice off: "Decent people do not have their noses torn off."

25. The street. Horse-cabs, horse-cabs, horse-cabs, horse-cabs . . . Kovalov hails them. . . Kovalov runs, runs, stops. . .

26. A coach waiting before a house. The Nose springs lightly onto footboard, thence to ground. It enters the house and walks lightly up the stairs.

27. Façade of house seen in perspective. Windows, windows, windows open. Noses, noses, noses everywhere.

28. Kovalov before the house door. The Nose comes out. The Nose becomes clothed (like Kovalov in 18): coat of uniform + very high collar + galloon on collar + buff-colored trousers + sword + bicorn hat + plume. Kovalov trembles. He bows low before the Nose.

    Mimic: Monologue (inaudible) by Kovalov, inviting the Nose to return to its proper place on his face. The Nose waves him away with imperious gesture. Kovalov begins to fall, as if made of wood, and stops at a 45° angle. The Nose jumps into the coach and disappears.

29. Pursuit: Kovalov runs after coach. Pan to Cathedral of Our Lady of Kazan.

30. Entrance to cathedral. On the steps, beggar women in kerchiefs that hide their faces, except for their eyes.
31. (Close-up) Eyes, eyes, eyes . .
32. Inside cathedral. Leaning against a column, the Nose prays. Bows its beak from time to time. Kovalov appears, holding the handkerchief over face. Very embarrassed, he dares not disturb the Nose's meditations. Kovalov coughs. The Nose takes no notice. Kovalov tries to address the Nose, in vain.
33. Miss P. appears. Behind her a Man, very tall.
34. Kovalov bridles up, forgetting his infirmity. Arranges his collar, necktie (uncovering face). He smiles.

re-33. Man behind Miss P. brings out his snuff-box, takes a pinch, and sneezes (silent).

re-32. Kovalov and the Nose. Kovalov coughs to attract its attention. The Nose goes on praying. Kovalov tries to address it (inaudible) at first timidly, then gets excited and with sweeping gestures makes an inaudible monologue on rising tone. (One can guess that he is using resounding words like Duty, Fatherland, Honor of the Uniform, etc.). The Nose hardly notices him. Its nose held high, it waves Kovalov aside majestically, and so doing the Nose fades out. Kovalov totters, half falls, like a weighted doll or a metronome.

35. Same as 13, but everything has changed, has a dilapidated, loathesome appearance. The door plate no longer bears the word "Major," but only "Kovalov." Kovalov, still tottering, as in re-32. He enters the door.
36. Interior of Kovalov's room, now becomes repulsive. The sun goes down, reversing movement of 15. Darkness falls. Kovalov goes down.

re-2. Night in Saint Petersburg.

37. (Establishing shot) Kovalov's room. A light appears behind the wall. It filters through cracks in the dilapidated partition; the light moves.
38. (Medium shot) A candle burning in a candlestick enters room as if it were carried by a hand.
39. (Closer medium shot) Candle stops. In long fade-in appears policeman holding candlestick.

Voice off: "It so pleased your lordship to lose his (sneeze). Allow me the honor of informing your lordship that it was seized at the very moment when, under the disguise of a Councilor of State, it was about to take seat in a stage-coach, with a

		false passport. I myself almost took it for a man, but fortunately I was wearing my spectacles."
re-37. (With policeman) Policeman fumbles in his pocket and draws out small parcel which he hands to Kovalov.	**Voice of K.:**	"Where is it? I'm off to it!"
	Voice off:	"No need to trouble your lordship. Knowing how much it means to him, I have brought it back to its owner, your lordship."
40. (Close-up) Open palm of policeman. In palm, small parcel. The parcel opens. The Nose in policeman's palm.		
41. Kovalov, joyous, begins to dance.	**Music:**	French folk song—"Mon Dieu, quel homme, qu'il est petit!" (Oh Lord, what a man, how small he is!)
42. Mirror. Kovalov adjusts nose in its place. He presses it to his face and gently withdraws his hands. The nose comes loose. Kovalov presses it on again, withdraws hands, nose falls away.	**Voice of K.:**	"What a fine nose it is! And here's the little pimple that broke out yesterday!"
43. Nose hits floor and rebounds like rubber.		
re-42. Mirror. Kovalov repeats act, placing nose on face.	**Voice of K.:**	"Like a cork! . . Get in there, stick, imbecile!"
re-43. Same as 43. The Nose hits floor and rebounds.	**Voice of K.:**	(in despair): "Doctor . . . Doctor!"
re-39. Policeman dissolves into Doctor. He now wears dark glasses.		
44. Doctor and Kovalov. Doctor gives him a fillip on place where nose should be. He turns Kovalov's head to left and right as if he were a doll. Another fillip.	**Voice off:**	(same as policeman's): "How long have you had this misfortune? . . It could be stuck on again, but it would be even worse."
45. (Rapid cutting of previous scenes)		

14. K. dreams of your woman 16. Mirror. K. without nose 17. Addresses: D . . . Doctor 19. K. in cab 16. Mirror. K. without nose 27. Windows and noses re-33. Miss P. and man taking snuff re-39. Doctor 25. Horse cabs, horse cabs 20. Lost and Found 21. Official sneezes 39. Policeman with candle	**Voice of K.**: "It couldn't be worse than it is!" **Voice off**: "Believe me—let nature take her course. Wash the place with cold water. As for the . . (loud sneeze), for . . . it, put it in a bottle with some vodka, and you'll get along quite well without it . . . I would even be prepared to buy it from you, if . . ." **Voice of K.**: (in despair): "No, no! I would rather have it lost!"

re-15. Kovalov's room. Sun comes in window as in 15. As it touches Kovalov's face, he sneezes, puts his hand to his nose which is visibly in place. He wakes and sits up with a start, holding his nose with his hand.

46. Kovalov in profile before mirror; his nose is there. Behind him, the door of room opens ajar, the barber's nose appears in the opening.

re-16. Mirror. Kovalov's face with nose.	**Voice of K.**: "Are you sure your hands are clean?"
re-46. Door opens further, the barber's nose advances.	**Voice of barber**: "Yes, your lordship."
	Voice of K.: "You lie!"
47. A chair comes forward.	
48. Kovalov sitting in chair. Towel. Barber sharpens razor.	**Voice of barber**: "I swear it!"
re-1. Barber takes Kovalov's nose between thumb and foreginger of one hand, lifting razor in other.	**Voice of K.**: "Eh, there, be careful!"

THE  GAME

1. Running nose

2.

3.

4.

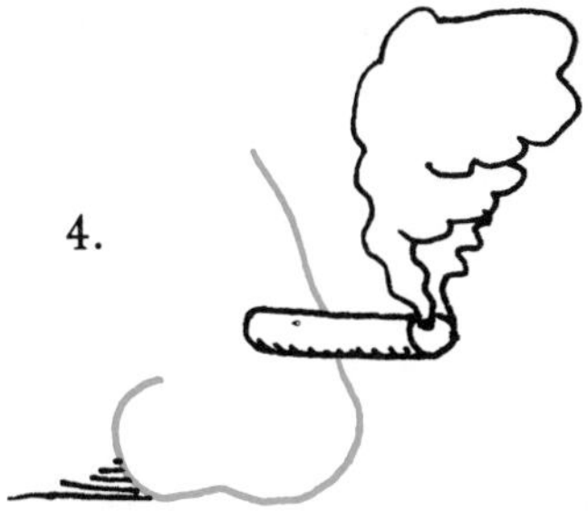

5.

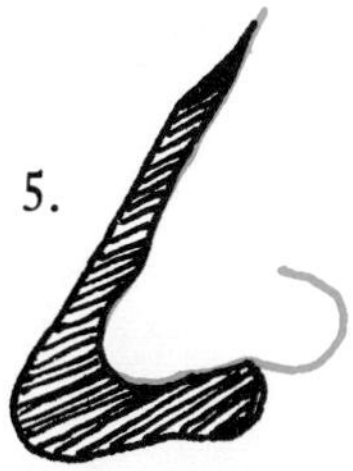

6.

7.

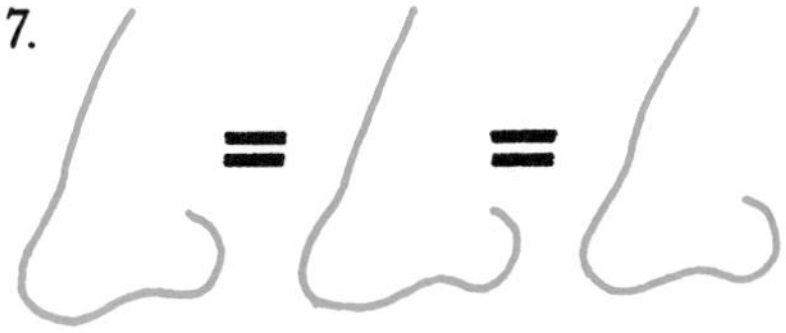

8.

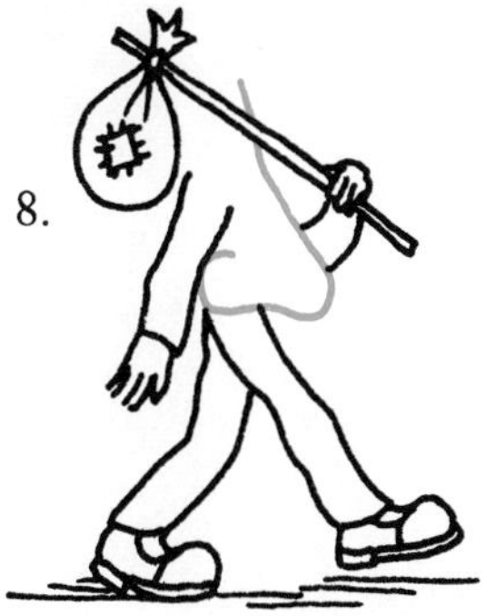

9.

10.

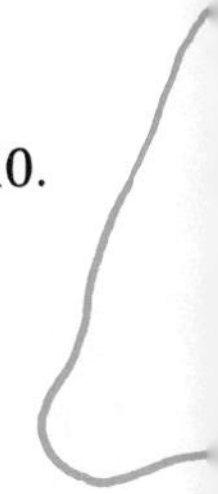

2. Nose dive. 3. Nose cone. 4. No smoking. 5. "The Shadow nose." 6. Nobody nose. 7. A nose is a nose is a nose. 8. Roamin' nose. 9. Cutting off your nose to spite your face. 10. Nose bleed.

THE NOVEL

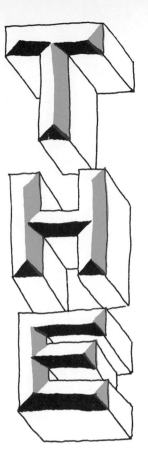

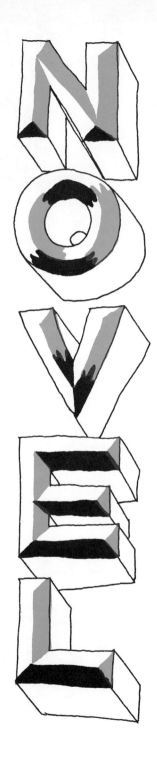

You will find, in every novel, the counterparts of long shots and close-ups, trucking shots, and dissolves; but you will find them in words addressed to the ear, instead of in pictures meant for the eye.

What effect has television had on the structure of recent novels and movies?

> The sequence of pictures plays directly on our feelings. Music works in the same fashion; I would say that there is no art form that has so much in common with film as music. Both affect our emotions directly, not via the intellect.

And yet you will weep and know why.
Now, no matter, child, the name. . .

Is the quotation above really true?

Have you ever been unaffected by a movie others around you seemed to be enjoying? What does *that* tell you about the quotation?

Might not all emotion really be based on concept?

Is "outside-of-awareness" a key here? Ethnocentricism?

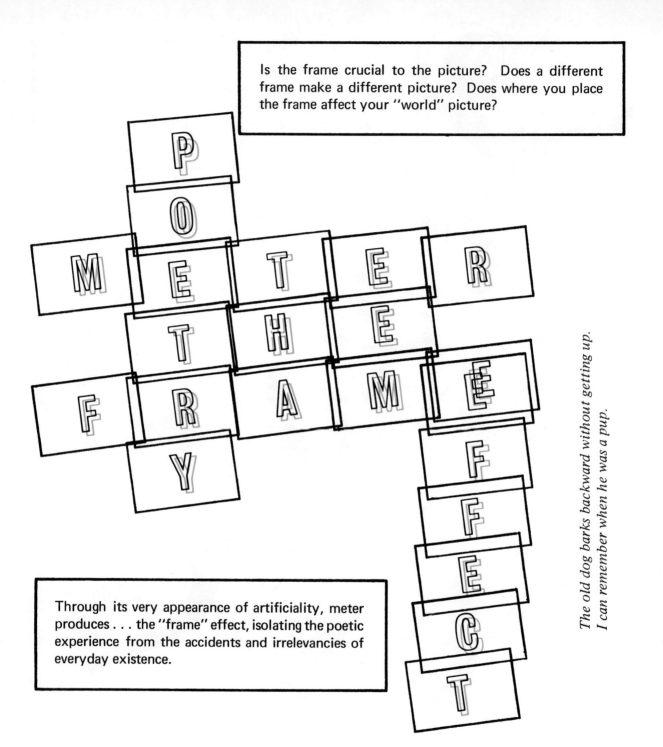

Is the frame crucial to the picture? Does a different frame make a different picture? Does where you place the frame affect your "world" picture?

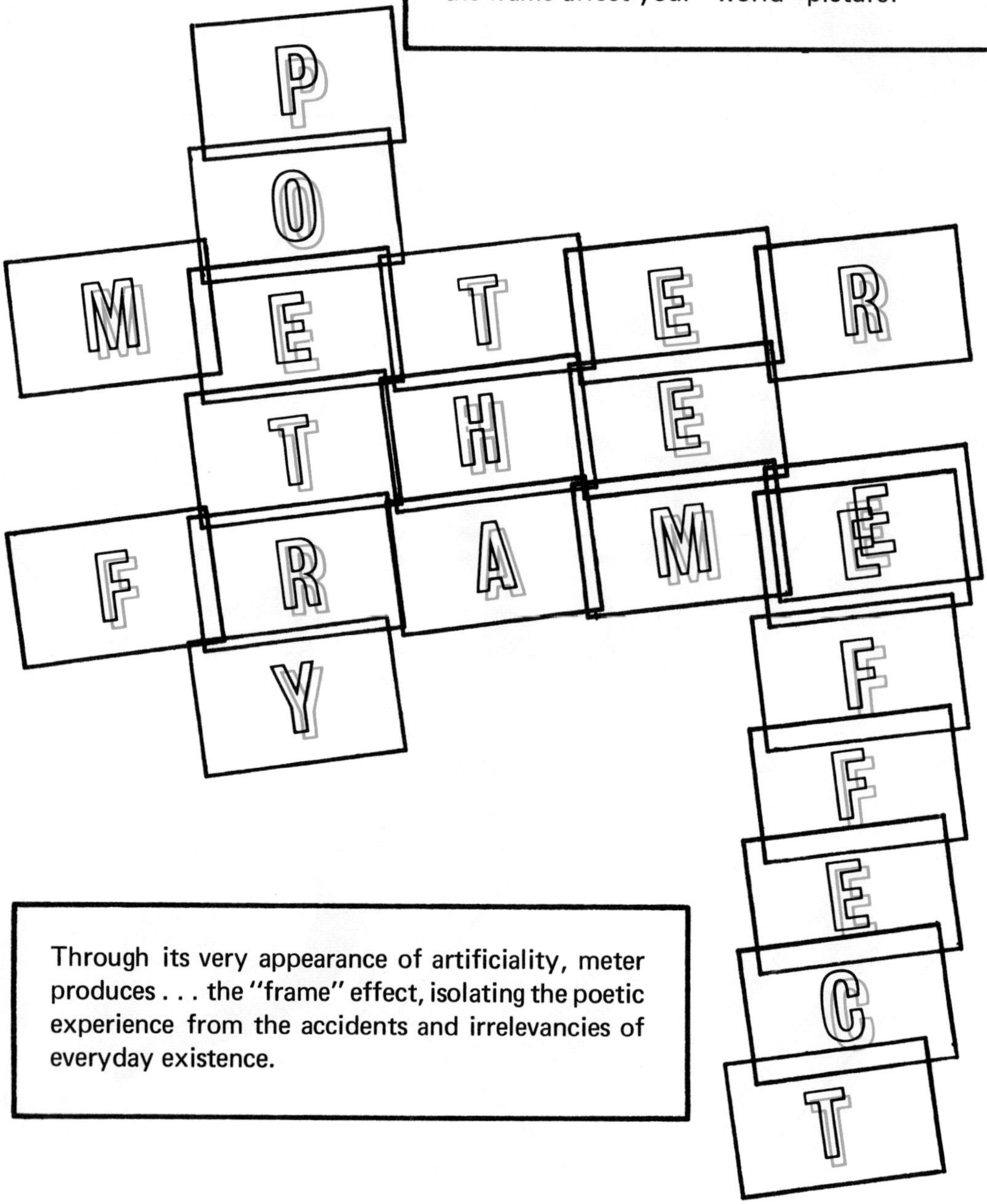

Through its very appearance of artificiality, meter produces . . . the "frame" effect, isolating the poetic experience from the accidents and irrelevancies of everyday existence.

The old dog barks backward without getting up.
I can remember when he was a pup.

ONE'S OWN NOSE AND HEART

I prefer my own taste as a truer expression of what the public wants of me than anything that I can fathom out of the things that I observe either in my own work or in that of others who are unmistakably successful.

I have heard directors, scenario writers, and others who are directly concerned with the shape that the moving picture shall take, argue under the shadow of this great fear of the public. They begin with a good idea, then they lose courage and deceive themselves. The consciousness of what the public will want is for them so terrific. If they do something that is a little different because they have forgotten while filming the episode that there is such a thing as an audience, they are in doubt about it when they stop to consider. It is difficult to consider the public secondarily, but unless the person making the picture can achieve that state, there will be no originality in his work.

The form of a representation cannot be divorced from its purpose and the society in which the given visual language gains currency.

?

Is this painting more like a movie or more like television? Why?

Is the painting to be seen or is it to be felt?

Is it a cliché? Is it a probe?

Would an audience brought up in the television era be more likely or less likely to accept this painting than a movie-bred audience?

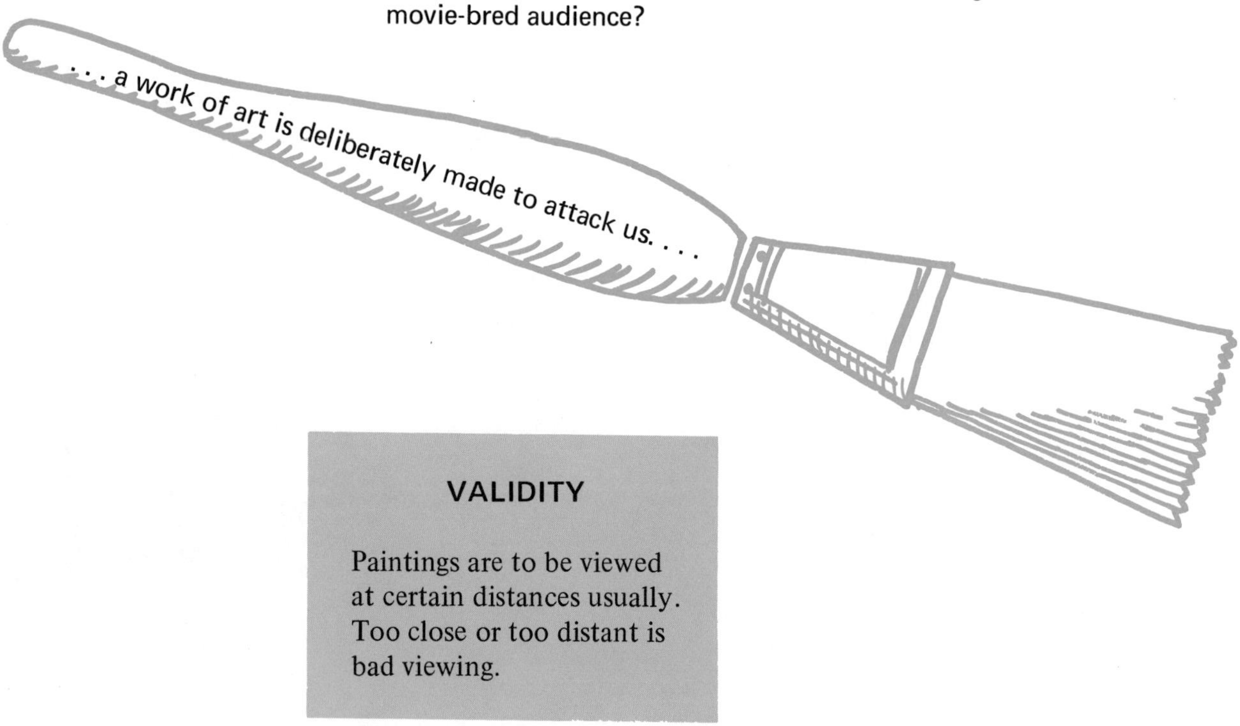

. . . a work of art is deliberately made to attack us. . . .

VALIDITY

Paintings are to be viewed at certain distances usually. Too close or too distant is bad viewing.

"I love 'Mr. Novak' and I love his programs but he can't do this to us," writes Mrs. John Rhodes. "After leaving a class in which he was teaching pronouns he walked down the hall and said to a blind student, 'How did you know it was ME?' "

"'Mr. Novak' is one of our favorite TV shows but last week in his close up conversation I couldn't believe the grammatical errors—for example, 'It is us.' " writes Mrs. Dwayne Moore. "We do not expect it from other programs and from the commercials such as 'Us Tareyton Smokers', etc. but NOT from a high school teacher and an English teacher least of all. And I'm worried because now they're beginning to sound RIGHT!"

You've heard of "the right way, the wrong way and the Army way." There are three kinds of grammar: good grammar, bad grammar, and Hollywood Grammar.

JAMES THURBER

CLOSE-UP

Here follow some representative pages from the television script "An Essay on Women."

First, see if you can figure out from the context the meaning of the following camera directions.

Pages 252-53	MS	Page 255	MCS
	CU	Page 256	ZOOM IN to CU
	CS		DISSOLVE TO
			PAN CAM R to MLS
	LS		ECU
	FADE IN		PULL BACK to MCU
			MLS
	FREEZE FRAME	Page 257	FADE OUT
	WS		FROZEN FRAME
		Page 258	CAM into CU

What directions other than those for the camera are given?

1.

2.

3.

4.

List the different categories of sound used.

1.

2.

3.

4.

List some of the techniques used for interweaving sound and sight.

1.

2.

3.

4.

Who is the writer and producer of this show? Have you ever heard of him? Have you ever heard of Harry Reasoner?

See page 259 for more general questions about this investigation.

A man and a woman must constantly recapture the love...

AN ESSAY ON WOMEN

Description	*Narration*	*Feet*	*Time*
1. INT. STUDY MS Harry Reasoner in chair	REASONER: The position of women in the world has changed and we feel the time has come to reassess it. According to our records it was last properly assessed in the Fall of 1937.	00-00	00:00
	The change is mostly one of attitude. Men are still willing to accept the difference between men and women . . . women are not. Women are no longer satisfied being what men are satisfied having them be.	15-02	:25
2. CU Harry Reasoner in chair	What men want from women is love, a clean house, forgiveness and a stubborn holding to moral values. What women want for themselves is a sense of accomplishing more than getting dinner gives them . . . and a more interesting life. We have no quarrel with women. Our feeling is, although we're willing to admit we may be wrong, our feeling is that they are better people than men and we don't understand their dissatisfaction with their own virtues. We wish they would stop following us around, imitating our worst characteristics and demeaning their own attributes. We wish they would stop believing, or acting as if they believe, that man's goals are the ones worth achieving. This broadcast was pre-		

Description	*Narration*	*Feet*	*Time*
	pared by men and makes no claim to being fair.		
	Prejudice has saved us a great deal of time in preparation.	46-04	1:17
3. EXT. URBAN STREET CS woman crossing New York street	(sounds of traffic)	49-34	1:23
4. LS NEW YORK STREET woman walks into CU FADE IN MAIN TITLE: AN ESSAY ON WOMEN with freeze frame CU of women FADE OUT: MAIN TITLE FADE IN TITLE: WITH HARRY REASONER	ANNOUNCER VO: An Essay On Women with CBS News Correspondent Harry Reasoner . . . brought to you in color by . . .	57-00	1:35
5. Commerical billboard	(commercial copy)	62-12	1:44
6. 60 second commercial		98-12	2:44
7. INT. WOMEN'S MEETING CU first woman	FIRST WOMAN: Why is it that women who are biologically superior to men and I understand more intelligent . . . REASONER VO: There has been a great deal more talk in the last thirty years about the difficulties of being . . .	105-37	2:57.5
8. WS audience	. . . a women than about the difficulties of being a man . . .possibly because most of the talking about . . .	109-11	3:02

Description	*Narration*	*Feet*	*Time*
9. CU first woman	. . . has been done by women. FIRST WOMAN: in some areas are actually losing ground. . .	112-17	3:07.5
10. LS audience	REASONER VO: Women are always trying to find the answer to what they call their problem.	115-15	3:12
11. CU woman in audience	Capable women gather together. . .	116-30	3:14.5
12. CU another woman in audience	. . . in large numbers and on frequent occasions.	117-32	3:16
13. CU second woman	They hold conferences and have symposiums about themselves. SECOND WOMAN: . . . the changing picture of women's lives	121-15	3:22
87. EXT: NEW YORK STREET two women with baby carriages	. . .that women are in some ways superior and in other ways inferior to men. For instance . . .	382-32	10:38
88. EXT. STADIUM Olympic shot-putters LS woman putting the shot	. . .no matter how big and strong the biggest strongest woman gets. . .	385-25	10:42.5
89. MS another woman putting the shot	. . .she cannot throw a steel ball as far as a man . . .	387-19	10:46
90. MS another woman putting the shot	. . .furthermore she probably shouldn't try.	390-36	10:51
91. EXT. SUBURBAN	A woman is most attractive when		

Description	Narration	Feet	Time
STREET mother with child in arms	she is loving. It is the emotion that becomes her most and she loves, at best, with a good deal more grace and beauty than man.	398-32	11:05
92. MS another mother with two children on street	Most women find it easy to be mothers but their love for a man does not come from any well . . .	402-08	11:10
93. MCS rear view older women with baby in arms	. . .so deep as maternal instinct.	404-18	11:14
94. EXT. NEW YORK STREET mother, two little girls in red seen from rear	A man and a woman must constantly recapture the love . . .	407-09	11:19
95. EXT. SUBURBAN STREET MS mother with teenage daughter and little child tugging at arm	. . . that is indestructible between mother and child.	410-14	11:24
96. EXT. CENTRAL PARK AT WATER CU older woman's hand holding hand of baby	Love thriving on dependence.	412-04	11:27
97. EXT. CENTRAL PARK mother with child on grass	Maybe men are not asking enough from women. Asking assumes familiarity and affection.	417-28	11:36
98. EXT. SUBURBAN STREET mother with one child in arm holding hand of another	Women do best . . .	419-32	11:40

Description	Narration	Feet	Time
99. MS same woman from rear puts child down, picks up shoe that has fallen off	. . . the jobs that can't be unionized. Their qualities are ones that can't be put to a multiple-choice test and corrected for score. No minimum wage could be . . .	425-30	11:50
32. INT. NIGHTCLUB SILHOUETTE SHOP man and woman enter, cross to table, man seats woman and helps her with her coat, seats himself, offers woman cigarette, lights it for her, takes one for himself	MUSIC The thing about women is, they are a paradox. They are simultaneously at men's feet where they are looked down on, with affection, and on a pedestal where they are looked up to with awe. Being a paradox is hard on the one who is paradoxical . . . although not nearly so hard as it is on those who live with them.	146-01	4:03
33. MCU woman in profile SILHOUETTE ZOOM IN to CU DISSOLVE TO	The same woman who is demanding equality under the law during the day, expects to be helped on with her coat that evening.	153-23	4:16
34. INT. OFFICE OF HELEN GURLEY BROWN CU Cosmopolitan Magazine cover PAN CAM R to MLS HGB typing at desk	One of the important things about women is the theories men have about them that aren't true. Women are greatly influenced by these. One of them is the theory of intuition. Women often decide important things quickly and correctly, not because they are clairvoyant . . .	163-16	4:32
35. ECU Helen Gurley Brown PULL BACK TO MCU	. . . but because they are hardheaded realists. Men find this so mysterious that they attribute it to the supernatural and call it "intui-		

Description	*Narration*	*Feet*	*Time*
	tion." Helen Gurley Brown is the author of a book called Sex And The Single . . .	171-33	4:46
36. MLS Helen Gurley Brown on phone with secretary ZOOM IN to MCU hand rummaging in drawer ZOOM IN to ECU mouth	. . . . Girl and the editor of Cosmopolitan Magazine. She is a working woman and a realist. BROWN: Would you call Larry Matthews and cancel my appointment for tomorrow and tell them I'll call up in a day or two. While you're at it, ask them if Carlin has finished my wig. Just a minute let me see if I can find my slip. It's number 620. REASONER VO: It is interesting to watch her work and we feel a great deal is being said while we say nothing.		
95. (cont)	Man didn't write a woman is only a woman but a good cigar is a smoke, because he liked cigars all that much.		
	Good night, dear.	468-00	13:00
FADE OUT			
96. 60 second commercial	commercial copy	504	14:00
FADE IN			
97. EXT. NEW YORK STREET FROZEN FRAME (same as main title) CU woman TITLE: AN ESSAY ON WOMEN	ANNOUNCER VO: An Essay On Women was brought to you in color by (commercial copy)	507-26	14:06

Description	Narration	Feet	Time
98. Commercial billboard	commercial copy	514-21	14:17.5

Description	Narration	Feet	Time
99. INT. FASHION SHOW LS model on runway she walks toward CAM into CU FREEZE FRAME of girl SUPER TITLE: WRITER AND PRODUCER	music segues into track women's voices	(518-33	14:25)
ANDREW A. ROONEY		521-25	14:29
DISSOLVE TO			
100. EXT. GARDEN CU young woman FROZEN FRAME FRAME SUPER TITLE: FILM EDITOR JOHN SCHULTZ		524-09	14:34
DISSOLVE TO			
101. CU woman smiling FROZEN FRAME SUPER TITLE CAMERAMEN WILLIAM J. WAGNER WALTER DOMBROW WENDELL HOFFMAN		527-19	14:39

DISSOLVE TO

102.	MCU woman smiling FROZEN FRAME SUPER TITLE: AN ESSAY ON WOMEN with copyright notice	ANNOUNCER VO: An Essay on Women was filmed and edited under the supervision and control of CBS News	533-12 14:49

PAN CAM R TO L OF WHOLE BOOK

After completing the foregoing investigation, what connections with other ideas in this book can you make? What new areas can you open?

In what ways is writing and producing a television show different from directing a movie? What elements in the script would not be so significant in a movie script? An animation script?

How would the video and audio aspects be handled in a short story?

Which do you think would be more difficult to write, a short story, a movie script, a television script? Are they equally difficult?

Is it the medium which dictates difficulty, or is it the quality attempted, or what?

What are the television writer's "tools," his materials?

How significant are the non-verbal "messages" in the sample pages?

What significant questions have we omitted?

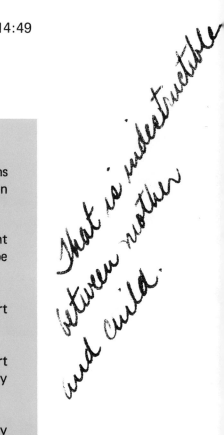

That is indestructible between mother and child.

FELLINI: For me, neorealism is a way of seeing reality without prejudice, without the interference of conventions—just parking yourself in front of reality without any preconceived ideas.

BACHMANN: You don't mean simply to put the camera in front of "life" and photograph what's there?

FELLINI: No, it's a question of having the feeling for reality. Naturally, there is always the need for an interpretation.

* * * *

FELLINI: But why should people go to the movies, if films show reality only through a very cold, objective eye? It would be much better just to walk around in the street. For me, neorealism means looking at reality with an honest eye—but any kind of reality: not just social reality, but also spiritual reality, metaphysical reality, anything man has inside him.

BACHMANN: You mean anything that has reality for the director?

FELLINI: Yes.

BACHMANN: Then the completed film is really *two* steps removed from nature: first the personal *view* of it by the director, and then his *interpretation* of that personal view.

* * * *

BACHMANN: Have you, yourself, done any writing except scripts?

FELLINI: No, just some short stories when I worked for newspapers. But not since I've worked in films. It's a different medium. A writer can do everything by himself—but he needs discipline. He has to get up at seven in the morning, and be alone in a room with a white sheet of paper. I am too much of a *vitellone* to do that. I think I have chosen the best medium of expression for myself. I love the very precious combination of work and living-together that film-making offers. I approach film-making in a very personal way. That's why I consider myself a neorealist. Any research that a man does about himself, about his relationships with others and with the mystery of life, is a spiritual and—in the true sense—religious search. I suppose that is the extent of my formal philosophy. I make movies in the same way that I talk to people—whether it's a friend, a girl, a priest, or anyone: to seek some clarification. That is what neorealism means to me, in the original, pure sense. A search into oneself, and into others. In any direction, any direction where there is life. All the formal philosophy you could possibly apply to my work is that there is no formal philosophy. In film-making, as in living, you must take the experiences that life presents, those which apply to yourself and to others. Except that in film-making only the absolute truth will work. In life I may be a swindler or a crook, but that wouldn't work in a film. A man's film is like a naked man—nothing can be hidden. I must be truthful in my films.

* * * *

BACHMANN: Could you tell me about the process in your film work? A kind of step-by-step description of your work on any given film?

FELLINI: First, I have to be moved by a feeling. I have to be interested in one character or one problem. Once I have that, I don't really need a very well-written story or a very detailed script. I need to begin without knowing that everything is in perfect order; otherwise I lose all the fun of it. If I knew everything from the start, I would no longer be interested in doing it. So that when I begin a picture, I am not yet sure of the location or the actors. Because for me, to make a picture is like leaving for a trip. And the most interesting part of a trip is what you discover on the way. I am very open to suggestions when I start a film. I am not rigid about what I do. I like the people with me on the film to share this new adventure. Certainly, I do remember that I am shooting, sometimes.

When the picture is finished, I would, if possible, like not to see it. I often say to my producer, joking: "Let's not cut this one; let's make a new one instead." But I cut all my own films. Cutting is one of the most emotional aspects of film-making. It is the most exciting thing to see the picture begin to breathe; it is like seeing your child grow up. The rhythm is not yet well identified, the sequence not established. But I never reshoot. I believe that a good picture has to have defects. It has to have mistakes in it, like life, like people. I don't believe that beauty, in the sense of perfection, exists—except maybe for the angels. A beautiful woman is attractive only if she is not perfect. The most important thing is to see to it that the picture is alive. This is the most rewarding moment in making films: when the picture begins to live. And I never go back to look at what I have already done—I edit the whole film right through. When it's finished, and I go into the projection room to see it for the first time, I like to be alone. I can express exactly what happens. I look at the picture; the picture looks at me. A lot of things happen. Some ideas are born; some die. Later I begin to "clean" the picture. In Italy we do not use the sound we shoot on location, but redo the whole track in the studio. But the first answer print still has the location sound on it. Once that is removed, something happens again. The answer print still has the flavor of the adventure of making the film—a train that passed, a baby that cried, a window that opened. I remember the people who were with me on location. I remember the trip. I would like to retain these memories. Once they put the clean, new track on it, it's like a father seeing his girl wear lipstick for the first time. You have to get to know this new creature that is emerging: you have to try to like it. Then when you add the music, again something is added and something is lost. Every time you see it again, there is some new feeling. When it is completely finished, you have lost the objective point of view. Then, when others see it, I react personally—I feel they have no right to say anything about *my* picture. But I listen carefully, nevertheless—I am trying to find out whether for them the picture is alive.

* * * *

QUESTION: You speak a great deal about anxiety and fear. Is there something that frightens you today, or has maturity changed this aspect of your personality?

ANSWER: There has been a maturing, and it was time that there was. I think I can take care of myself better. But I don't want to sound too happy with myself. All the more so because this apparent maturity can be suddenly contradicted. In fact, perhaps the feeling of being able to control emotional states comes not from a real maturity, but simply from an aging, that is, a thickening of a remote ancestral opacity.

This feeling of having control is an unsteady one. It is difficult to be at peace, and when we are, we are rarely aware of it. All in all, I'm afraid I still have little irritations that I shouldn't have, treacherous fears. I am bothered by a kind of nostalgia for a more complete morality—this discomforts me, makes me gloomy. Perhaps it is true that one can't change completely, that the character formed in infancy determines the life of the mature man. Some call it destiny; others attribute it to emotional factors in the newborn. As far as I'm concerned, I think this conditioning comes from education, from the arbitrary or fanatical application of moral standards imposed in the sacred environment of the family, at an age when it is neither permitted nor possible to choose. We spend the second half of our lives wiping out the taboos, repairing the damage that education has caused in the first half. I'm speaking of men of my generation—I think this holds true for many.

* * * *

As you know, color is a part not only of the language but also of the idea and the feeling of the dream. Colors in a dream are concepts, not approximations or memories.

. . . . In a dream color is the idea, the concept, the feeling, just as it is in truly great painting . . . . The dreamer can see a red meadow, a green horse, a yellow sky—and they're not absurdities. They are images tempered with the feeling that inspires them.

QUESTION: Is it possible to translate all this into the cinema?

ANSWER: When I started to shoot the picture, I made a remark that has gone all around and is beginning to be a little disgusting: Cinema is movement; color is immobility; the fusion is impossible. It's contradiction of terms, like breathing underwater. Forgetting the facile nature of the comment, it is just like that.

I must say that the use of color according to a rigorous plan is not possible. That is, you can't hope for a result that translates your ideas of color perfectly, without distortion or without at least modification, because there are unforeseeable elements in the lighting, the shooting itself and the printing.

The painter gives to his painting a steady, unchangeable light. Color is an extremely personal factor, even on a physiological level. My green is not your green, nor that of a third person. Whoever paints can choose precisely the shade of color he wants. Someone may think that the same thing can be done in film, that it's enough to put the light on the element you want to bring out, and your green comes out. Let's say that it can be like this, although in fact there is a fluid interchange among the colors of a scene, because of which, during the projection, you realize that certain luminous areas are submerged in darkness and others have taken on unforeseeable reflections.

But let's say, for argument's sake, that the lighting is ideal. You look at the picture; you're satisfied and ready to shoot. At that point, obeying an instinct, you come closer or move farther back, you want another perspective, you move the camera even a little bit. Right away the intensity of the light changes, the color becomes brighter or duller; as soon as you have made the slightest move, the color values you have sought are no longer the same. The green is no longer your green.

The human eye sees things as the human eye, with all its weight of sentiment, ideas, the past. It is capable of making very rapid selections, of selecting the elements that strike it most forcefully. In our memory of things, a dominant color remains while the others disappear. If you were telling a friend about our meeting here and wanted to describe the colors of the room, you would probably remember only the gilding of that door, the light blue of this ashtray, the black of that painting. The camera doesn't work like that; it performs a purely mathematical function. It registers just what the light, which easily changes with each movement, offers to it, moment by moment.

The director of a color film is like a writer who, after having written "The room was green," finds it printed in the book as "The room was rose." Just like that—you shot a green room, and you go in the screening room and you see a rose room. Where was the rose?

I discovered this, the first time, with *Boccaccio '70*. I had thought of the character of Dr. Antonio as a small man, all in black, in the midst of the huge, very white buildings of the EUR. When I saw the projection, the marble was no longer white; it had become blue. The sky had reflected on the smooth parts of the buildings, and there was nothing to do about it.

Perhaps I should conclude that, since it's not possible to shoot films in color, only black and white should be used. However, despite all my disappointments, despite a feeling of angry impotence that poisoned months of my work, I feel that color adds a new dimension to a film like mine. Something that black and white could never have given it.

QUESTION: Do you think that color, which enriches the language, will become essential, just as sound has, or do you feel that black and white will remain an alternative even when there are no longer the problems you mention?

ANSWER: I don't think that color will completely replace black and white; but I do think—with all its unforeseeable and uncontrollable incongruities—it is a most important factor. I certainly prefer a black and white picture to a bad one in color. All the more so because in some cases the so-called "natural color" impoverishes the imagination. The more you mimic reality, the more you lose in the imitation. Black and white, in this sense, offers wider margins for the imagination. I know that after having seen a good black and white film, many spectators, when asked about its chromatic aspect, could say: "The colors were beautiful," because each one lends to the images the colors he has within himself.

QUESTION: So there are precise limitations that color imposes on the imagination of a director. But there is, on the other hand, another side to this, isn't there?

ANSWER: I am halfway through this experiment. I am fascinated by it, but I haven't yet a thorough grasp of it. There is no doubt that color produces an extraordinary result in many scenes of this picture. I am thinking particularly of the scene in Suzy's house. The glass doors, the gauze, the shining nylon, the sidewalks covered with glass that sends forth lights—it's much more effective than it could ever have been in black and white. No, color makes me angry every day; however, I already feel it's an integral part of my possibilities of expression. And then, I don't want to defend black and white, which is only a habit, at all costs.

QUESTION: While you were shooting *Boccaccio '70*, you told me: "There are only two colors you can use in the cinema—black and white."

ANSWER: That's a romantic, static, even reactionary position. I think it's a tribute to the photography from which the cinema was born. I've changed my mind.

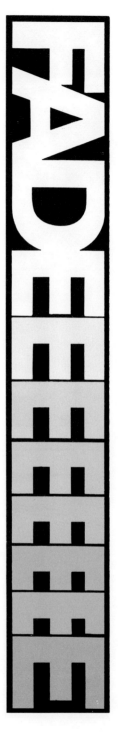

* * * *

A Fellini film is born by "an accumulation of details, by the birth in my mind of a certain atmosphere."

"The cinema is the unique and perfect tool to explore with precision the inner landscapes of the human being."

"The camera is so stupid, it grabs all it sees. I suppose I should have shot the whole film as a test, and then again for good. But can you ever do the same thing twice?

. . . But the names to conjure are Ovid, Rabelais, and Dickens rather than useless comparisons with other directors such as Antonioni or De Sica, who are only interested in drama. Fellini says in a synopsis he wrote of *Giulietta of the Spirits* that "it finishes with Giulietta now in complete harmony with the fabulous spectacle of life which is so vastly and so delightfully more rich, magical, and supernatural when it accepts in an easy and simple rhythm the miracle of each day."

The priests in *8½* were played mostly by old women, while in *Giulietta of the Spirits* a whole bevy of young nuns is played by boys Fellini selected from the beach at Fregene. Why? "Because they walk more like nuns than nuns do," says Fellini.

"As is my habit, working slowly but surely in the labor of preparation, I reserve the right to revise, sharpen, change or substitute scenes, characters, to enrich situations, to determine the rhythm of the film, the dialogue, to create a climate sometimes comic, sometimes anguished, sometimes astonished."

He prefers a hard, even cruel, photography to that which enhances.

"All art is autobiographical; the pearl is the oyster's autobiography."

For Fellini, cinema is neither art nor is it new. "Cinema is an old whore," he mutters, "like circus and variety, who knows how to give many kinds of pleasure. Oh, they've been trying to wash her face and make her respectable, but it can't be done."

NEVER TAKES NOTES OR SEES A FILM TWICE

Richard Schickel, in the last two years [1965–67], has seen 300-odd movies and written 83 reviews for LIFE. Some readers will be in agreement; some will say, "Well, you blew it again, you idiot"; some will excoriate Schickel for being an old fogy ("You must be about 65, with white hair," a teen-ager wrote last week); they will vilify him for his childish naivete (one reader asked, "Are you out of high school yet?").

Dick Schickel is neither a post-teen hippie nor an ancient mariner. He is 34. He used to wear a crew cut but is now letting his hair grow, perhaps with the times, perhaps in keeping with his changing taste in movies. He was born in Milwaukee and raised in Wauwatosa, Wisconsin, and the first movie he ever saw, when he was five, was Walt Disney's *Snow White*. He thought it was wonderful and he's been a fan ever since. "You can date me easily," he told Review Editor David Scherman on Cape Cod a few days ago. "I can remember the exact year—1943—that the Friday night kids' movie went from 8¢ to 10¢. My first critical act, at age 11, was getting booted out of the theater for criticizing a Dennis Morgan western. Foot-stamping and yelling were, I recall, the current critical device." Later, at the University of Wisconsin, Schickel became drama critic on the *Daily Cardinal*, and after graduating he moved to New York to write.

Schickel has written five books and a biography of Walt Disney. Despite his constant attendance at movies, he always goes to them with anticipation. "You have to take pleasure in the act of going," he says. "When you lose the feeling that this is *your* movie and you *have* to tell every kid on the block to go see it right away, you should quit."

In his years of reviewing movies, Schickel has developed a prodigious film memory. He never takes notes or sees a film twice. "The audience can't," he says. "Why should I?" He can instantly tell you who played what part and when and, when pressed, will quote endless dialogue from films he has seen years ago (Bogart: "I came to Casablanca to take the waters." Claude Rains: "There are no waters in Casablanca." Bogart: "I was misinformed.") He carries around four or five unreviewed movies in his head at all times and prefers to wait a week or more before writing about any of them. "What sticks in your head is what's worth mentioning," he says. "Besides, it gives you a chance to change your mind, which I do constantly."

CLICHÉ GAME

"I think the reason *Luv* was successful on Broadway was that all three in the original cast were hearing a certain thing. It's a trick I learned from Elaine May when we were working together. She can hear the cliché in a person's voice. I'm relieved I'm not directing the film version."

Watch your favorite half-hour television show and find at least five visual clichés and five audio clichés (not only verbal but also background noise clichés and music background clichés).

The object of this game is to collect, *not* the most obvious clichés, but the *least* obvious ones, like the cliché in a person's voice. Also, your fellow students must agree that your selection is a genuine cliché.

Here are two not-too-subtle samples:

VERBAL: "Halley, you're real purty when you're mad."
VISUAL: A singer's turtle-neck pullover for his ballad number.

I try to reach for a simple, visual phrase that tells you what the picture is all about and evokes the essence of the story.
—SAUL BASS

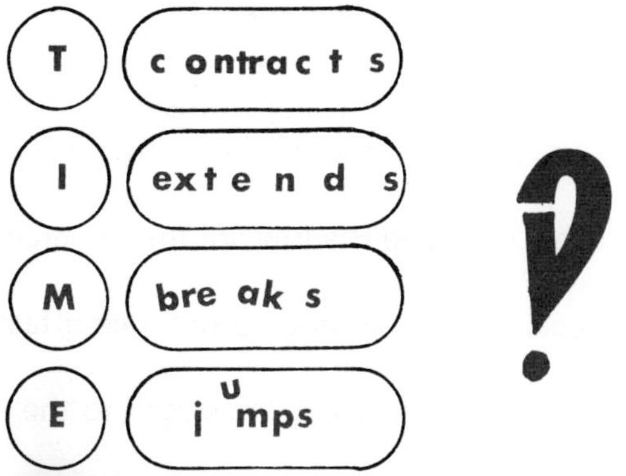

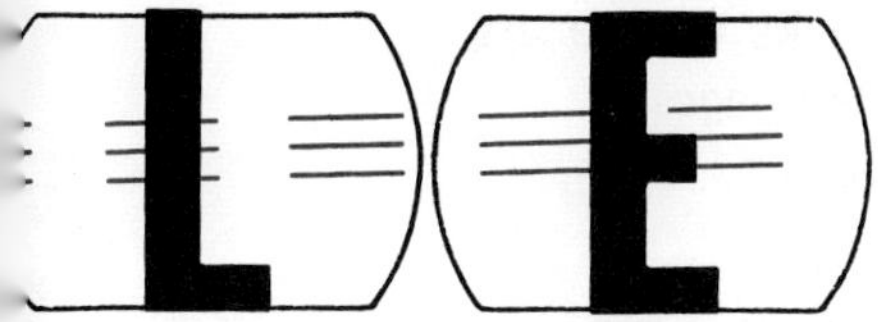

Logical, intelligent thinking does not need the support of a symbolic *system*, as it exists in the living language of society. Thinking is undoubtedly an internal system, a hierarchical ordering within the person of his interaction with the world. The symbol system of language mirrors and in a certain way expresses that internal organization. However, the internal organization of intelligence is not dependent on the language system; on the contrary, comprehension and use of the ready-made language is dependent on the structure of intelligence.

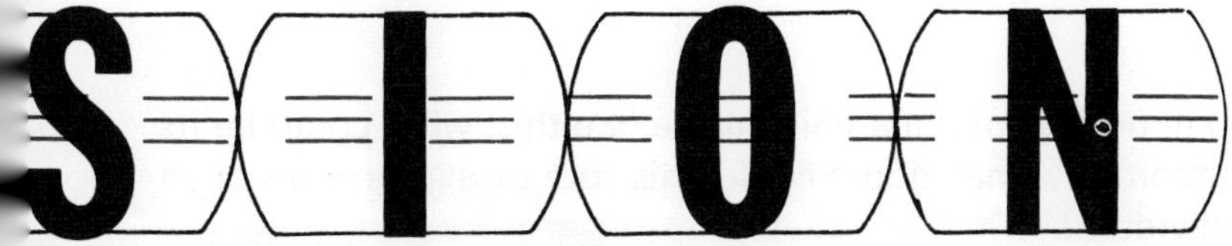

SOME CAPTURED SNOWFLAKES

On the following pages you will find several stills from motion pictures. They illustrate aspects of filming techniques and effects. You should be able to find one picture to match at least one of the captions below. Write the number of the best caption for each picture. You may use more than one caption for each picture. See if you can identify some technique not already listed and write a suitable caption for each still.

1. The muse of the motion picture is its apparatus.
2. Among their many uses, inserts may produce humorous contrasts.
3. In black and white films light and shadow are the cameraman's paints.
4. The photographic negative can be used to produce effects of extreme anti-reality.
5. The shooting angle can be a non-verbal "message" to the mind of the viewer.
6. Defects of the medium are the building blocks of the art:
   - 6a. Double exposure
   - 6b. Glaring light
   - 6c. Distortion
   - 6d. Multiple images
   - 6e. Soft focus
7. The film has no present or future; all action is now.
8. The camera can present its subjects with an Alice-in-Wonderland range of sizes.
9. Grainy textured images may be used to give a scene the impact of a picture from an old photograph album.
10. Framing can help us to see with fresh vision.

Part II

Discuss how you matched the stills and the captions and your reasons for doing so. What additional discoveries can you make?

Part III

If you make maximum use of a matching game like this, what could be its most significant outcomes? What doors could this sort of exploration open for a perceptive individual?

OMW-18

OMW-5

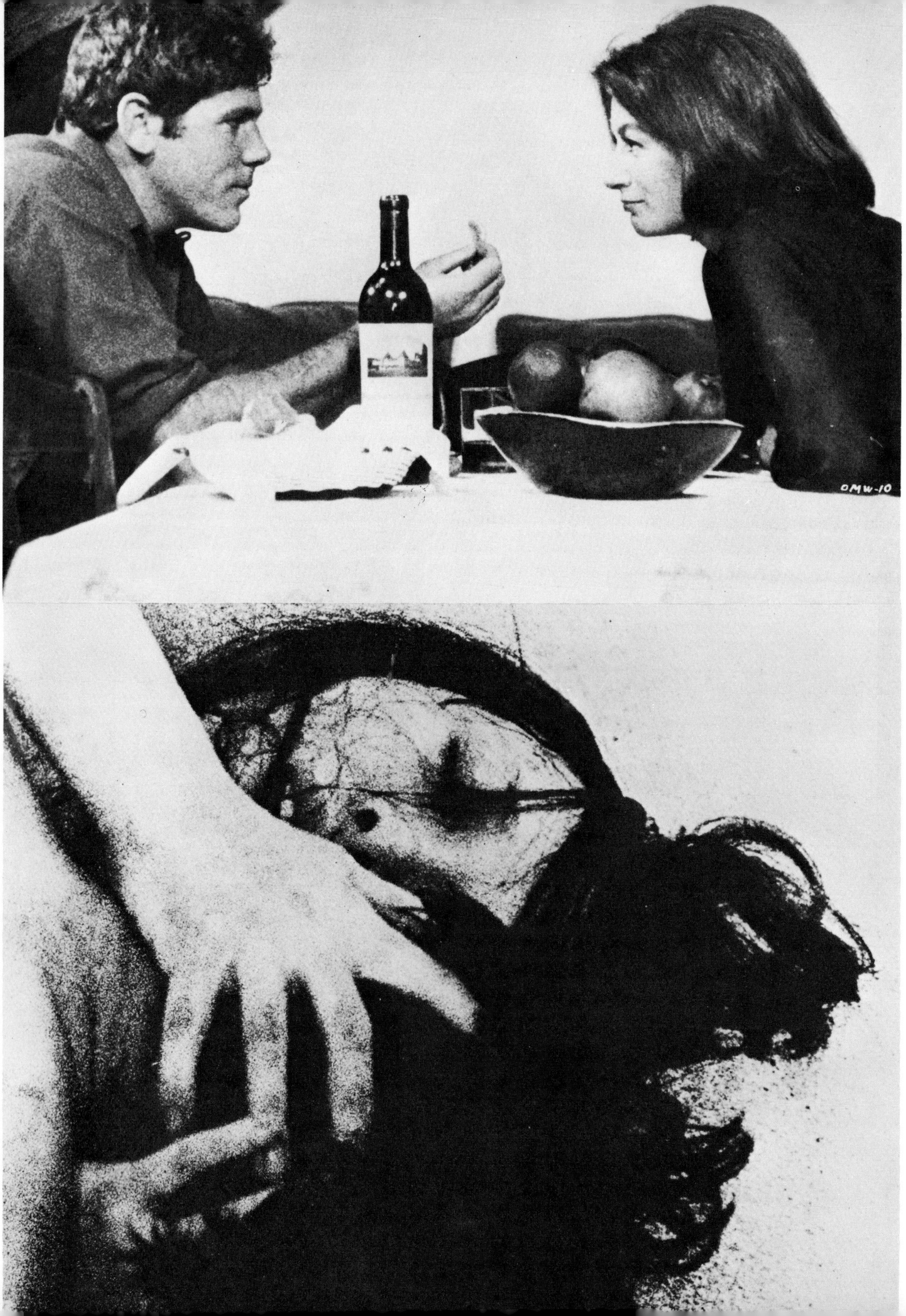
OMW-10

TDP-28

Is education to make people happy or to make people people?

THE UNREAL WORLD OF TELEVISION NEWS

None of us has ever seen Alexander the Great emerging from his tent. If there had been television in his day, and if we could today look at the tape, would we know him any better, as we think we now know a Lyndon B. Johnson when we see him on television news emerging, say, from a helicopter?

The answer is far from clear. Of all historical evidence, the public presence of voice or of physical appearance is the most revealing, but it can also be the most misleading. Yet every night, watching television news, millions of people have to decide whether they can believe what they see flickering in front of them. Is it genuine? Can television, by its nature, tell the truth?

"The evidence of one's own eyes?" But that is precisely what is not available. What *is* available is the evidence of the camera, making its own selection, dictating its own terms.

Television does not merely create news—as newspapers have done for generations. Television creates its own *events*. Unlike the newspaperman's words, television *happens* as we watch.

There is a vital margin of difference between saying, "Did you see the report in *The New York Times* of the massacres in the Congo?" and saying, "Did you see the massacres in the Congo on television last night?" The first remark implies only that one has seen a report, which may conflict with another report. The second implies that one has seen the event itself. However carefully television is used, it cannot avoid this deception.

Television can report incidents; it is the nature of incidents that they can, and do, happen in isolation. But rarely can television report an event. The true meaning of an event depends on all of its known and unknown causes, on all of the known and unknown incidents that contribute to it, on all its repercussions. The whole of an incident can easily be described; the whole of an event may escape even the historian.

If this is the difficulty that confronts the

In *The Servant* Dirk Bogarde appears in the background, an insignificant, subservient figure. Gradually as the film goes on he is brought more and more into the foreground, and he grows in stature and power while the master steadily becomes by contrast smaller and more ineffectual.

newspaper reporter from day to day, it is one that the television reporter can rarely overcome. For the newspaper reporter has flexibility. He can reach where the camera cannot reach. He can go "off the record." He can qualify, provide perspective. The television reporter, on the other hand, however carefully he chooses his words, can never properly qualify a spectacular picture.

Not only is the core of television the public and the spectacular, but there is an important sense in which television has a vested interest in disaster. From the point of view of a good story, both newspapers and television prefer covering a major strike to covering negotiations which prevent a strike. Yet it is possible for the newspaper reporter to make negotiations almost as exciting as a strike. But what can television do with negotiations? It can only show pictures of people arriving at a building and people leaving it.

Violence—movement—is the stuff of television, something it cannot help emphasizing. Three distinct characteristics of television intensify the special temptations to which it is exposed. There is, first, the limitation of time. A lead news story in a paper may take ten minutes to read. This sort of time is simply not available in handling television news. This means concentration to the point of distortion; and, in the reporting of violence, it means concentration on the violent incident to the exclusion of the whole event.

An example of such distortion was the police attack on civil-rights marchers at the Selma, Alabama, bridge in March, 1965. Every reliable reporter I know who was present points out that there was first a period during which police and demonstrators faced each other without violence, in an atmosphere of unbearable tension.

Television news broadcasts did not, and could not, show this preliminary encounter; three minutes of film is an extended sequence in a news program. But without knowledge of the buildup to put the violence in perspective, one begins to think that police brutality is automatic, that the police will always behave in such a manner.

There is, second, television's tendency to produce self-generating news. The problem has arisen, again and again, wherever there have been riots and disturbances, as in Watts [1965]. However spontaneous the original outbreak of violence, as television cameramen and reporters move into the streets looking—literally looking—for trouble, they add an external provocation. The crowds begin to play up to them. Television, merely by its presence, helps to create incidents.

Finally, there is the size of the television screen—the limitations it imposes, the temptations it offers. Last summer [1966] television news showed some alarming pictures of white men and women in the Chicago suburb of Cicero screaming abuse at some Negro marchers. Their hating faces filled the screen. They looked as if they were a representative example

A man with one watch knows what time it is. A man with two watches is never quite sure what time it is.

of a much larger crowd. But anyone who was there knows that these particular whites were only a small part of the crowds in the streets, and that the crowds themselves were only a small part of the total white population of Cicero. To this vital extent, television that night distorted badly.

So, people sitting in their homes begin to think that all police are brutal, that all demonstrators are violent, that all disturbances are riots, that all crowds are aggressive. The fact that we ourselves usually go through each day without either meeting or displaying violence becomes less real to us than what we see on the small screen. Much of our feeling of living in a condition of perpetual crisis, and the agitation arising from it, stems from this.

Television can create not only events but whole movements out of incidents. The television news coverage of the Meredith march across Mississippi, during the time when I accompanied it, constantly appalled me. The straggling column was made on the small screen to look like an army. When the cameras were rolling, the marchers—few in numbers and anything but impressive in mien—pulled themselves together and played the role expected of them. The leaders strode in line abreast, at the head of their enthusiastic followers.

The real story of the Meredith march was not this unified demonstration at all, but the fact that it brought to light the deeply significant clash between different factions of the civil-rights movement over "black power."

Newspapers felt their way to this story, which for the most part was taking place in private meetings, and by the end they were reporting it fully. But when television at last caught on to the fact of "black power," it inevitably exaggerated and distorted it. Since film is expensive, in reporting any speech the television reporter and cameraman makes an automatic, almost involuntary, preselection. They wait for the mention of a phrase like "black power"—then on go the lights, and the film rolls. By constant reiteration on the small screen, the slogan of "black power" was elevated into a movement. It was suddenly there. It had suddenly happened.

The only immediate answer to most of the problems of television news lies not in pictures but in words. Most television reporting just describes the pictures, and by doing so reinforces them. But the object should be to correct the pictures, to supply qualification, to say, "It was not quite so. This was not the whole story." In essence: to remind the viewer that he is seeing not an event, only an impression of one.

That television news can do some things remarkably well, especially in full-length features and documentaries, that those involved

I don't think thirty million people saw me in all of the pictures I made during five of my peak years as a movie star. In *two* nights—the first run and the rerun of this TV movie—we'll have a bigger audience than the total of everyone who has seen *Gone With the Wind.*

in making television programs are conscientious and skillful, does not touch the main problem. Life is not made up of dramatic incidents—not even the life of a nation. Many of our unnecessary anxieties about the way we live, about the fearful things that may happen to us, might be allayed if television news began, now and then, to say: "It has been a dull day. But we have collected some rather interesting pictures for you, of no particular significance." Television news has a deep responsibility to try to be dull, from time to time, and let the world sleep better.

GETTING THERE IS ALL THE FUN

If a *hot medium* is

"one that extends one single sense in 'high definition'" (one that makes its point directly and is well filled with data) and

a *cool medium*

one of low definition requiring more to be filled in by the receiver,

sort the following items into two categories by writing H (hot medium) or C (cool medium) next to each one. Where you and other students disagree, explore your reasons.

Can the manner in which an item is treated transform it from hot to cool or from cool to hot? Which do you prefer? Why?

___ movies
___ TV
___ a lecture
___ a dialogue
___ this text
___ your history text
___ telephone
___ *A Hard Day's Night*
___ *The Sound of Music*
___ cartoons

___ the current popular dance
___ clear glasses
___ dark glasses
___ radio
___ ballet
___ *Life* magazine
___ *Atlantic Monthly*
___ net stockings
___ sheer stockings

Add four more hot items and four cool ones:

1. ______________________ 1. ______________________
2. ______________________ 2. ______________________
3. ______________________ 3. ______________________
4. ______________________ 4. ______________________

THE PHOTOGRAPHER'S EYE

The invention of photography provided a radically new picture-making process—a process based not on synthesis but on selection. The difference was a basic one. Paintings were *made*—constructed from a storehouse of traditional schemes and skills and attitudes—but photographs, as the man on the street put it, were *taken*.

The difference raised a creative issue of a new order: how could this mechanical and mindless process be made to produce pictures meaningful in human terms—pictures with clarity and coherence and a point of view? It was soon demonstrated that an answer would not be found by those who loved too much the old forms, for in large part the photographer was bereft of the old artistic traditions. Speaking of photography Baudelaire said: "This industry, by invading the territories of art, has become art's most mortal enemy." And in his own terms of reference Baudelaire was half right; certainly the new medium could not satisfy old standards. The photographer must find new ways to make his meaning clear.

These new ways might be found by men who could abandon their allegiance to traditional pictorial standards—or by the artistically ignorant who had no old allegiances to break. . . .

The enormous popularity of the new medium produced professionals by the thousands—converted silversmiths, tinkers, druggists, blacksmiths and printers. If photography was a new artistic problem, such men had the advantage of having nothing to unlearn. Among them they produced a flood of images. . . . Some of these pictures were the product of knowledge and skill and sensibility and invention; many were the product of accident, improvisation, misunderstanding, and empirical experiment. But whether produced by art or by luck, each picture was part of a massive assault on our traditional habits of seeing....

These pictures, taken by the thousands by journeyman worker and Sunday hobbyist, were unlike any pictures before them. The variety of their imagery was prodigious. Each subtle variation in viewpoint or light, each passing moment, each change in the tonality of the print, created a new picture. The trained artist could draw a head or a hand from a dozen perspectives. The photographer discovered that the gestures of a hand were infinitely various, and that the wall of a building in the sun was never twice the same.

Most of this deluge of pictures seemed formless and accidental, but some achieved coherence, even in their strangeness. Some of the new images were memorable, and seemed significant beyond their limited intention. These remembered pictures enlarged one's sense of possibilities as he looked again at the real world. While they were remembered they survived, like organisms, to reproduce and evolve.

But it was not only the way that photography described things that was new; it was also the things it chose to describe. Photographers shot ". . . objects of all sorts, sizes and shapes . . . without ever pausing to ask themselves, is that or that artistic?" Painting was difficult, expensive, and precious, and it recorded what was known to be important. Photography was easy, cheap and ubiquitous, and it recorded anything: shop windows and sod houses and family pets and steam engines and unimportant people. And once made objective and permanent, immortalized in a picture, these trivial things took on an importance. By the end of the century, for the first time in history, even the poor man knew what his ancestors had looked like.

The photographer learned in two ways: first, from a worker's intimate understanding of his tools and materials (if his plate would not record the clouds, he could point his camera down and eliminate the sky); and second he learned from other photographs, which presented themselves in an unending stream. Whether his concern was commercial or artistic, his tradition was formed by all the photographs that had impressed themselves upon his consciousness. . . .

It should be possible to consider the history of the medium in terms of photographers' progressive awareness of characteristics and problems that have seemed inherent in the medium. Five such issues are considered below. These issues *do not* define discrete categories of work; on the contrary they should be regarded as interdependent aspects of a single problem—as section views through the body of photographic tradition. As such, it is hoped that they may contribute to the formulation of a vocabulary and a critical perspective more fully responsive to the unique phenomena of photography.

THE THING ITSELF

The first thing that the photographer learned was that photography dealt with the actual; he had not only to accept this fact, but to treasure it; unless he did, photography would defeat him. He learned that the world itself is an artist of incomparable inventiveness, and that to recognize its best works and moments, to anticipate them, to clarify them and make them permanent, requires intelligence both acute and supple.

But he learned also that the factuality of his pictures, no matter how convincing and unarguable, was a different thing than the reality itself. Much of the reality was filtered out in the static little black and white image, and some of it was exhibited with an unnatural clarity, an exaggerated importance. The subject and the picture were not the same thing, although they would afterwards seem so. It was the photographer's problem to see not simply the reality before him but the still invisible picture, and to make his choices in terms of the latter.

This was an artistic problem, not a scientific one, but the public believed that the photograph could not lie, and it was easier for the photographer if he believed it too, or pretended to. Thus he was likely to claim that what our eyes saw was an illusion, and what the camera saw was the truth. . . .

William M. Ivins, Jr. said, "at any given moment the accepted report of an event is of greater importance than the event, for what we think about and act upon is the symbolic report and not the concrete event itself."

THE DETAIL

The photographer was tied to the facts of things, and it was his problem to force the facts to tell the truth. He could not, outside the studio, pose the truth; he could only record it as he found it, and it was found in nature in a fragmented and unexplained form—not as a story, but as scattered and suggestive clues.

The photographer could not assemble these clues into a coherent narrative, he could only isolate the fragment, document it, and by so doing claim for it some special significance, a meaning which went beyond simple description. The compelling clarity with which a photograph recorded the trivial suggested that the subject had never before been properly seen, that it was in fact perhaps *not* trivial, but filled with undiscovered meaning. If photographs could not be read as stories, they could be read as symbols. . . .

THE FRAME

Since the photographer's picture was not conceived but selected, his subject was never truly discrete, never wholly self-contained. The edges of his film demarcated what he thought most important, but the subject he had shot was something else; it had extended in four directions. If the photographer's frame surrounded two figures, isolating them from the crowd in which they stood, it created a relationship between those two figures that had not existed before.

The central act of photography, the act of choosing and eliminating, forces a concentration on the picture edge—the line that separates in from out—and on the shapes that are created by it. . . .

The sense of the picture's edge as a cropping device is one of the qualities of form that most interested the inventive painters of the latter nineteenth century. To what degree this awareness came from photography, and to what degree from oriental art, is still open to study. However, it is possible that the prevalence of the photographic image helped prepare the ground for an appreciation of the Japanese print, and also that the compositional attitudes of these prints owed much to the habits of seeing which stemmed from the scroll tradition.

TIME

There is in fact no such thing as an instantaneous photograph. All photographs are time exposures, of shorter or longer duration, and each describes a discrete parcel of time. This time is always the present. Uniquely in the history of pictures, a photograph describes only that period of time in which it was made. Photography alludes to the past and the future only in so far as they exist in the present, the past through its surviving relics, the future through prophecy visible in the present. . . .

As photographic materials were made more sensitive, and lenses and shutters faster, photography turned to the exploration of rapidly moving subjects. Just as the eye is incapable of registering the single frames of a motion picture projected on the screen at the rate of twenty-four per second, so is it incapable of following the positions of a rapidly moving subject in life. The galloping horse is the classic example. As lovingly drawn countless thousands of times by Greeks and Egyptians and Persians and Chinese, and down through all the battle scenes and sporting prints of Christendom, the horse ran with four feet extended, like a fugitive from a carousel. Not till Muybridge successfully photographed a galloping horse in 1878 was the convention broken. It was this way also with the flight of birds, the play of muscles on an athlete's back, the drape of a pedestrian's clothing, and the fugitive expressions of a human face.

Immobilizing these thin slices of time has been a source of continuing fascination for the photographer. And while pursuing this experiment he discovered something else: he discovered that there was a pleasure and a beauty in this fragmenting of time that had little to do with what was happening. It had to do rather with seeing the momentary patterning of lines and shapes that had been previously concealed within the flux of movement. The famous French photographer Henri Cartier-Bresson defined his commitment to this new beauty with the phrase *"the decisive moment,"* but the phrase has been misunderstood; the thing that happens at the decisive moment is not a dramatic climax but a visual one. The result is not a story but a picture.

VANTAGE POINT

Much has been said about the clarity of photography, but little has been said about its obscurity. And yet it is photography that has taught us to see from the unexpected vantage point, and has shown us pictures that give the sense of the scene, while withholding its narrative meaning. Photographers from necessity choose the options available to them, and often this means pictures from the other side of the proscenium, showing the actors' backs, pictures from the bird's view, or the worm's, or pictures in which the subject is distorted by extreme foreshortening, or by none, or by an unfamiliar pattern of light, or by a seeming ambiguity of action or gesture.

Ivins wrote with rare perception of the effect that such pictures had on nineteenth-century eyes:

> "At first the public had talked a great deal about what it called photographic distortion. . . . [But] it was not long before men began to think photographically, and thus to see for themselves things that it had previously taken the photograph to reveal to their astonished and protesting eyes. Just as nature had once imitated art, so now it began to imitate the picture made by the camera. . . ."

The influence of photography on modern painters (and on modern writers) has been great and inestimable. It is, strangely, easier to forget that photography has also influenced photographers. Not only great pictures by great photographers, but *photography*—the great undifferentiated, homogeneous whole of it—has been teacher, library, and laboratory for those who have consciously used the camera as artists. An artist is a man who seeks new structures in which to order and simplify his sense of the reality of life. For the artist photographer, much of his sense of reality (where his picture starts) and much of his sense of craft or structure (where his picture is completed) are anonymous and untraceable gifts from photography itself.

The history of photography has been less a journey than a growth. Its movement has not been linear and consecutive, but centrifugal. Photography, and our understanding of it, has spread from a center; it has, by infusion, penetrated our consciousness. Like an organism, photography was born whole. It is in our progressive discovery of it that its history lies.

A CONSTELLATION

Study the montage of faces which follows. The object of this game is to see who can identify the maximum number of movie stars. Their names are listed on page 441.

aster
astronomy
persona
disaster
astrology
STARS

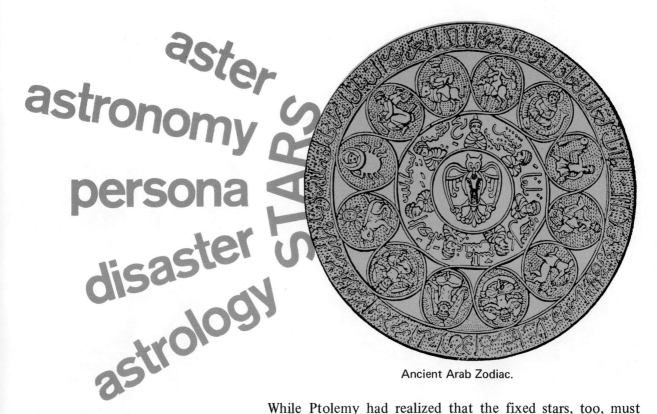

Ancient Arab Zodiac.

While Ptolemy had realized that the fixed stars, too, must affect terrestrial events if there was anything to astrology at all, the Arabs fell back on the primitive Babylonian idea that the planets alone governed man's fate.

When you have finished, discuss with other students the possible implications of this game, or explore its significance in your journal. What do you know of the reel world?

CAMPAIGN

The Key to all is the **smile** ...wide, **youthful**, brilliant... and everything is GOOD & GLAD day after endless day, hour after hour, page after page, program after program............

. . . Stronger on imagination than realization, Expo's films offer the viewer the exploratory delight of watching a new kind of cinema in the process of being born. Much like the Fauves and Cubists of painting, Expo's directors and cameramen at their best seem to have found a new way of interpreting and reproducing the imagery of life. Much of the expertise has been expended on *trompe-l'oeil* techniques that clearly have no place in the commercial film of today, or even tomorrow. Yet such visual delights as Labyrinth and Kane's three-screened children suggest that cinema—the most typical of twentieth century arts—has just begun to explore its boundaries and possibilities.

News item, July, 1967

HEMINGWAY

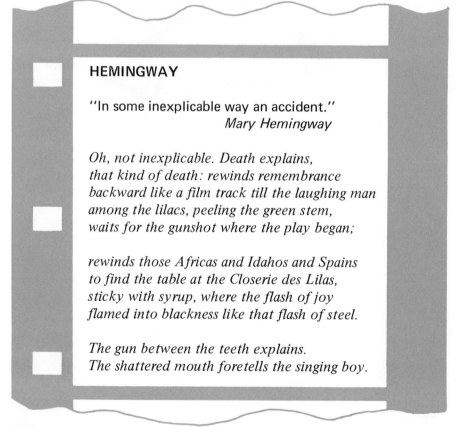

"In some inexplicable way an accident."
Mary Hemingway

Oh, not inexplicable. Death explains,
that kind of death: rewinds remembrance
backward like a film track till the laughing man
among the lilacs, peeling the green stem,
waits for the gunshot where the play began;

rewinds those Africas and Idahos and Spains
to find the table at the Closerie des Lilas,
sticky with syrup, where the flash of joy
flamed into blackness like that flash of steel.

The gun between the teeth explains.
The shattered mouth foretells the singing boy.

NEW PUNCTUATION MARK

Some expressions are hard to punctuate. Take the phrase "How about that"; too sprightly for a plain ordinary ., it is sometimes too ironic to justify an ebullient ! . More often than not, isn't it really a question?

Thanks to the American Type Founders Company, Inc., an easy solution is at hand: the interrobang, ‽, a punctuation mark included in a new A.T.F. typeface called Americana. The symbol was invented by Martin K. Speckter, an advertising-agency president and hobbyist printer, who had long brooded over the proper punctuation for such rhetorical questions of daily life as "Who forgot to put gas in the car" or "What the hell." Speckter's device, which he prefers to call the interrobang ("bang" is printer's slang for an exclamation point), remained just an idea until Detroit Graphic Artist Richard Isbell casually included it in the Americana face he was designing. Delighted by its possibilities, the A.T.F. plans to include it in all new types that it cuts.

If the interrobang gains the acceptance of grammarians, printers and writers, it will be the first punctuation symbol to enter the printed language since the introduction of the quotation mark during the late seventeenth century. Some typographical experts have already hailed its unique ability to express the ambiguity, not to mention the schizophrenia, of modern life. The interrobang, cracks Harvard University Press's monthly bulletin the *Browser*, "might with profit appear editorially at the end of all remarks from the political platform and the pulpit."

How about that‽

News item, July, 1967

DO-IT-YOURSELF HEAD

Fill your own head with key symbols from this section.
Angiosperms.

Please correct the meter of this verse as necessary.

Seville dair dago
Towsin Buses inaro
Nojo demstrux
Summit cows in sum dux

ALL ART IS SELECTION

What other aspects of the reel world do you think should be included in this section?

Another excellent way of getting to see how movies work is to create a short movie by yourself, or with a group of classmates.

You could begin by writing a script based on an interesting idea, in which you outline your instructions for camera work and other details.

If you possess the equipment, go ahead and shoot the film.

Then project the "rushes" (the film as it was shot and as returned from the processing laboratory).

What do you notice? Are some shots too long, too short? Are they in the best order?

Discuss possible editing revisions with your group. Then cut and splice the film and project it again. Is more editing necessary to achieve the effect you want?

How important was the editing process?

Do writers work in a similar fashion?

THE CUTS

I had seen *The Red Balloon* twenty-five times or more, and it was beginning to pall. So I decided, just to keep awake, that I would count the shots. I soon realized that I was getting more than I bargained for. As a matter of fact, it was like a new movie for me. I realized immediately that I am so used to the language of film that I ordinarily react as though a film is a work of nature rather than of man; that is, I kept missing the shifts. The boy would run up to the camera and then on beyond—so fluidly that I missed the cut. The camera would have had to stop, reposition, and continue the scene in the other direction. The two shots could have been filmed on two different days or, for that matter, the latter *before* the former and later spliced. Thus, conscious choice: the human mind selecting, arranging, making decisions.

I began to realize other things, too. Only two shots were taken indoors, and those used the natural light from outside. Every scene was from one angle only; the filming required only one camera. Most of the shots had the action moving toward the camera or away from it or from left to right or right to left in front of it. Only a handful of the shots used panning; there were no wipes, double exposures or other camera tricks. Only a few actors were required. Probably a helicopter was needed for the balloon scene at the end. Only one or two shots employed tracking. The set was the streets of Paris. Obviously this was an inexpensive movie to produce. The whole thing was extremely simple, yet very effective, smooth, and apparently effortless.

I could probably see *The Red Balloon* twenty-five more times and not exhaust the fascinating possibilities it contains for me. To be explored: the music, the sound track, the selection of camera angles, the framing of individual shots, selection of background; in short, all that had gone into the initial delight I had felt on first viewing it. No wonder Orson Welles was able to see *Stage Coach* forty times before making his first movie, *Citizen Kane.*

The next surprise came when I saw *An Occurrence at Owl Creek Bridge* again. By the simple device of noting the location of cuts, I soon realized the film was vastly more complicated to produce, an obvious fact that had escaped me in several viewings. For one thing, several cameras were used; there were zoom lenses, underwater shots, intercutting, repetition of a sequence several times, tracking shots, and so on. The film came alive again.

An effect of this awareness is to become much more conscious of the illusionist-artist-creator. Thus, coming to *The Nose* by Alexeieff after *Owl Creek* and *Balloon*, I could delight in the strange and unique pinboard technique as an added dimension of the film and, subsequently, animation techniques in general. What, for example, are the effects of technique in UPA, Looney Tunes, or Roadrunner?

The ongoing result of this simple device is that my viewing in general has become enriched. I can enjoy a TV show and be aware of its structure at the same time. I can recognize unimaginative camera work. I can tell the difference between the work of Toni Charmoli and June Taylor. From this angle, I can even enjoy a bad show!

The device is surprisingly adaptable. To really see a painting, (once we have allowed ourselves time to get a general feeling about it), a way into it is to start ticking off the parts; that will lead to the creator's angle of vision, and the rest will follow. The technique applies to a page of print, a cartoon, a piece of sculpture. It is a way of making the familiar strange, a way to get to know plum blossoms.

The only thing I can think of that teaches me more is attempting to imitate a work myself. Even a crude pencil-sketch of a Joan Miró painting reveals the complexity underlying its deceptively simple surface. A similar attempt with a *Peanuts* cartoon reveals something else, but I leave that for you to discover.

Oh yes, there are about 165 shots in *The Red Balloon.*

Boredom is an excellent aid to learning.

ON YOUR MARK

For in the end, the rhythm of the picture depends less upon words than upon direction, and cutting.

How can we know the dancer from the dance?

Get set...

LIVE!

We are not equipped with earlids.

euphony

THE SOUND OF SOUND

Frumious Bandersnatch

It has become fashionable in New York to hire secretaries with British accents.

Rugged rubber baby buggy bumpers

1NE

Napa-Sonoma-Mendocino Wine

MARES EAT OATS AND DOES EAT OATS AND LITTLE LAMBS EAT IVY.

TOPLESS IS GOING BUST

BB and B of North Beach, the Base Bosom and Bottom industry appears to be entering the advanced stages of commercial senility.

PHILHARMONIC

wrapped up in a fivepound note.

ART is deliberately mad to attack us, to FORCE its way into our feelings and our beliefs.

There was a young woman named Bright,
Whose speed was much faster than light;
She set out one day
In a relative way
And returned on the previous night.

ANAHEIM, AZUSA & CUCAMONGA!

They took some honey and plenty of money

SOUNDTRACK

In the last section we explored movies with you.

How important is sound to that field?

The early movies were called "silent" movies. But were they ever really silent?

It has been said that the stars of the "silent" era seemed more remote and godlike than do the film stars of today. The sound of speech makes modern stars seem more human to audiences.

Does this seem likely to you?

How are you affected when you watch a foreign film with bits of dialogue in English flashed on the screen?

What would be your likely reaction if all sound effects were removed from the showing of a film?

JABBERWOCKY

"Twas brillig, and the slithy toves
Did gyre and gimble in the wabe:
All mimsy were the borogoves,
And the mome raths outgrabe.

"Beware the Jabberwock, my son!
The jaws that bite, the claws that catch!
Beware the Jubjub bird, and shun
The frumious Bandersnatch!"

He took his vorpal sword in hand:
Long time the manxome foe he sought–
So rested he by the Tumtum tree,
And stood awhile in thought.

And, as in uffish thought he stood,
The Jabberwock, with eyes of flame,
Came whiffling through the tulgey wood,
And burbled as it came!

One, two! One, two! And through and through
The vorpal blade went snicker-snack!
He left it dead, and with its head
He went galumphing back.

"And hast thou slain the Jabberwock?
Come to my arms, my beamish boy!
O frabjous day! Callooh! Callay!"
He chortled in his joy.

'Twas brillig, and the slithy toves
Did gyre and gimble in the wabe:
All mimsy were the borogoves,
And the mome raths outgrabe.

Heard melodies are sweet, but those unheard are sweeter.

As you read the poem which follows, see if you can visualize how it might be made into a movie.

Would you have to stick to the order of events in the poem?

Where would you make use of long shots, medium shots, and closeups?

When would it be most effective to use techniques of panning, fade, and dissolve?

Would sound effects be important to a movie rendering of this poem?

Whom would you select to do the narrating?

What kind of voices would you choose?

Can just any poem be made into a movie?

When mixing two media such as word-art and visual-art, is there danger that one or the other will become simply decoration?

THE CREMATION OF SAM MC GEE

There are strange things done in the midnight sun
  By the men who moil for gold;
The Arctic trails have their secret tales
  That would make your blood run cold;
The Northern Lights have seen queer sights,
  But the queerest they ever did see
Was that night on the marge of Lake Lebarge
  I cremated Sam McGee.

Now Sam McGee was from Tennessee, where the cotton blooms and blows.
Why he left his home in the South to roam 'round the Pole, God only knows.
He was always cold, but the land of gold seemed to hold him like a spell;
Though he'd often say in his homely way that "he'd sooner live in hell."

On a Christmas Day we were mushing our way over the Dawson trail.
Talk of your cold! through the parka's fold it stabbed like a driven nail.
If our eyes we'd close, then the lashes froze till sometimes we couldn't see;
It wasn't much fun, but the only one to whimper was Sam McGee.

And that very night, as we lay packed tight in our robes beneath the snow,
And the dogs were fed, and the stars o'erhead were dancing heel and toe,
He turned to me, and "Cap," says he, "I'll cash in this trip, I guess;
And if I do, I'm asking that you won't refuse my last request."

Well, he seemed so low that I couldn't say no, then he says with a sort of moan:

"It's the cursèd cold, and it's got right hold till I'm chilled clean through to the bone.
Yet 'tain't being dead—it's my awful dread of the icy grave that pains;
So I want you to swear that, foul or fair, you'll cremate my last remains."

A pal's last need is a thing to heed, so I swore I would not fail;
And we started on at the streak of dawn; but God! he looked ghastly pale.
He crouched on the sleigh, and he raved all day of his home in Tennessee;
And before nightfall a corpse was all that was left of Sam McGee.

There wasn't a breath in that land of death, and I hurried, horror-driven,
With a corpse half hid that I couldn't get rid, because of a promise given;
It was lashed to the sleigh, and it seemed to say: "You may tax your brawn and brains,
But you promised true, and it's up to you to cremate those last remains."

Now a promise made is a debt unpaid, and the trail has its own stern code,
In the days to come, though my lips were dumb, in my heart how I cursed that load.
In the long, long night, by the lone firelight, while the huskies, round in a ring,
Howled out their woes to the homeless snows—O God! how I loathed the thing.

And every day that quiet clay seemed to heavy and heavier grow;
And on I went, though the dogs were spent and the grub was getting low;
The trail was bad, and I felt half mad, but I swore I would not give in;
And I'd often sing to the hateful thing, and it hearkened with a grin.

Till I came to the marge of Lake Lebarge and a derelict there lay;
It was jammed in the ice, but I saw in a trice it was called the "Alice May."
And I looked at it, and I thought a bit; and I looked at my frozen chum;
Then "Here," said I, with a sudden cry, "is my cre-ma-tor-eum."

Some planks I tore from the cabin floor, and I lit the boiler fire;
Some coal I found that was lying around, and I heaped the fuel higher;
The flames just soared, and the furnace roared–such a blaze you seldom see;
And I burrowed a hole in the glowing coal, and I stuffed in Sam McGee.

Then I made a hike, for I didn't like to hear him sizzle so;
And the heavens scowled, and the huskies howled, and the wind began to blow.
It was icy cold, but the hot sweat rolled down my cheeks, and I don't know why;
And the greasy smoke in an inky cloak went streaking down the sky.

I do not know how long in the snow I wrestled with grisly fear;
But the stars came out and they danced about ere again I ventured near;
I was sick with dread, but I bravely said: "I'll just take a peep inside.
I guess he's cooked, and it's time I looked"; . . . then the door I opened wide.

And there sat Sam, looking cool and calm, in the heart of the furnace roar;
And he wore a smile you could see a mile, and he said: "Please close that door.
It's fine in here, but I greatly fear you'll let in the cold and storm–
Since I left Plumtree, down in Tennessee, it's the first time I've been warm."

There are strange things done in the midnight sun
  By the men who moil for gold;
The Arctic trails have their secret tales
  That would make your blood run cold;
The Northern Lights have seen queer sights,
  But the queerest they ever did see
Was the night on the marge of Lake Lebarge
  I cremated Sam McGee.

Read this poem silently to yourself. Can you hear the sound effects in it? Now read the poem aloud. What has been added? Would all poems benefit from being read aloud by someone who knows how? What about prose?

* * *

Before the era of printing (do you know when printing was invented?) stories and poems were usually read aloud by court bards, minstrels, gleemen, and poets. Often the poets held very high status in the kingdom. In ancient Ireland, the *ollave* or master-poet sat next to the monarch and was privileged, as only the queen was, to wear six different colors in his dress. In Medieval Wales, a master-poet was a "bard," though the same word in Ireland meant a poet of inferior talents. Poets never had quite the same status in Anglo-Saxon England, however. It wasn't until the late Elizabethan era, in the 1600's, that the English instituted the position of poet laureate.

In the old oral tradition, when there were few books, poems and stories were memorized and recited aloud, or acted out, often to the accompaniment of music. Sometimes the audience joined in at appropriate times in the reading. The Anglo-Saxon poem *Beowulf* was usually read aloud in the mead hall, often accompanied by the harp. Geoffrey Chaucer used to read his poems regularly to the English king and his court.

Nowadays, with stories and poems printed in books where we read them privately, we tend to forget all about the enjoyment of listening to literature read aloud by others, or of reading it aloud to ourselves.

* * *

In this section, there are some stories and poems in which sound plays an obvious part. If your instructor reads them to you, or you read them aloud for yourself, you will see what we mean.

Before the advent of printing, audiences listening to a story would wait eagerly for the signal when the reader would change his voice. At that moment, everybody would join in and shout out the "run" together. In this way, everybody actively participated in the telling of the story.

Quite likely many poets and story-tellers in olden days wrote their material so that it could be read aloud. In what ways might literature which is meant to be read aloud differ from literature which is designed to be printed?

How much of your writing would you like to have read to an audience? Would it make any difference in your writing if you knew someone was going to read it aloud?

Would everything anybody writes benefit from being read aloud?

Does a copywriter in an advertising agency have to change his technique when he moves from writing an advertisement for a magazine to creating a TV commercial?

Try it.

THE KEY TO EVERYTHING

Is there anything I can do
or has everything been done
or do

you prefer somebody else to do
it or don't
you trust me to do
it right or is it hopeless and no one can do
a thing or do
you suppose I don't
really want to do
it and am just saying that or don't
you hear me at all or what?

You're
waiting for
the right person the doctor or
the nurse the father or
the mother or
the person with the name you keep
mumbling in your sleep
that no one ever heard of there's no one
named that really
except yourself maybe

If I knew what the name was I'd
prove it's your own name
twisted in some way the one you
keep mumbling but you
won't tell me your
name or
don't you know it
yourself that's it
of course you've
forgotten or
never quite knew it or
weren't willing to believe it

Then there is something I
can do I
can find your name for you
that's the key to everything once you'd
repeat it clearly you'd
come awake you'd
get up and walk knowing where you're

going where you
came from

And you'd
love me
after that or would you
hate me?
no once you'd
get there you'd
remember and love me
of course I'd
be gone by then I'd
be far away

Why is it that people seem to enjoy this? Where is
audience participation still practiced?

In type, size can re-present sound. What are some other devices used in printing in an attempt to make sound visible?

OW

ARIETTE

Il pleure dans mon coeur
Comme il pleut sur la ville;
Quelle est cette langueur
Qui pénètre mon coeur?

O doux bruit de la pluie,
Par terre et sur les toits!
Pour un coeur qui s'ennuie,
O! le chant de la pluie!

Il pleure sans raison
Dans ce coeur qui s'écoeure!
Quoi! nulle trahison?
Ce deuil est sans raison.

C'est bien la pire peine
De ne savoir pourquoi,
Sans amour et sans haine,
Mon coeur a tant de peine.

ARIA

The tears in my heart
Are like the rain on the town;
What is this weariness
That is in my heart?

Oh soft noise of the rain
On the ground and the roofs!
For a heart that is bored,
Oh, the song of the rain!

Tears without reason
In this anguished heart!
What! Is it not treason
This grief without reason?

The worst torment though
Is not knowing why,
Without love and hate,
My heart suffers so.

Reading a translation is like looking at the back of a tapestry.

- Cover the English translation and ask someone who has studied French to read the French poem aloud.
- What does it communicate to you, even though you may not know the meaning of the words?
- Listen to both poems read aloud.
- What do you notice about the sound qualities in each poem?
- Is the English version an identical substitute for the French work?
- What are some difficulties in translating one language into another?
- Is something always lost in the process?

HORMONE DERANGE

O gummier hum warder buffer-lore rum
Enter dare enter envelopes ply,
Ware soiled 'em assured adage our-itching ward
An disguise earn it clotty oil die.

Harm, hormone derange,
Warder dare enter envelopes ply,
Ware soiled 'em assured adage our-itching ward
An disguise earn it clotty oil die.

Go around innocently singing it this way and see if anyone notices the difference. They probably won't! It is also good for "putting on" audiences.

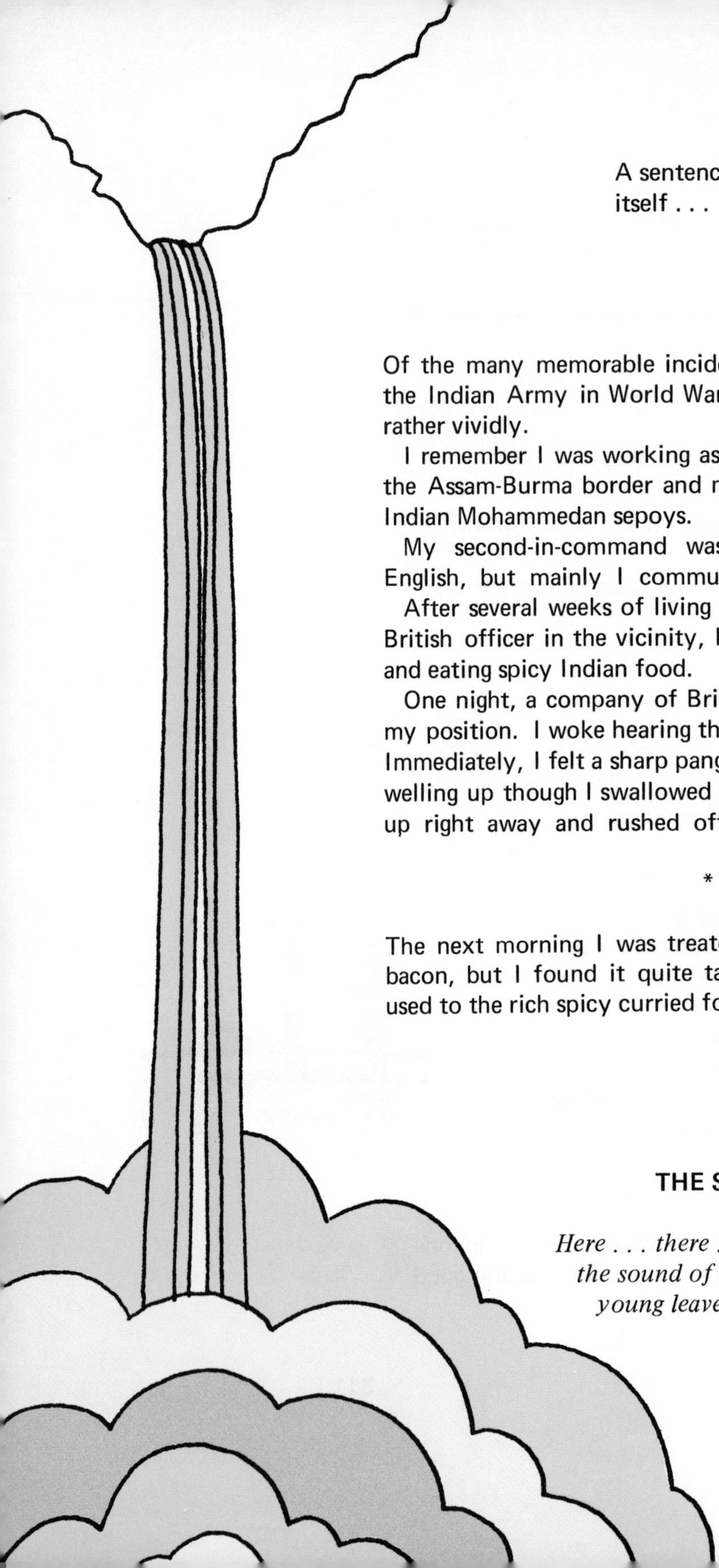

A sentence is a sound in
itself . . .

Of the many memorable incidents I encountered as an officer in the Indian Army in World War II, one keeps coming back to me rather vividly.

I remember I was working as a telegraph line Signals officer on the Assam-Burma border and my signal section was composed of Indian Mohammedan sepoys.

My second-in-command was a Jemadar who spoke a little English, but mainly I communicated with my sepoys in Urdu.

After several weeks of living with Indians where I was the only British officer in the vicinity, I felt quite at home speaking Urdu and eating spicy Indian food.

One night, a company of British troops moved in quite close to my position. I woke hearing the indistinct sound of British voices. Immediately, I felt a sharp pang of surging nostalgia and tears kept welling up though I swallowed like mad to try to stop them. I got up right away and rushed off to find my fellow countrymen.

* * * *

The next morning I was treated to a breakfast of fried eggs and bacon, but I found it quite tasteless and unpalatable after being used to the rich spicy curried food prepared by an Indian cook.

THE SOUND

Here . . . there . . .
the sound of waterfalls is heard—
young leaves, everywhere.

THE SOUND OF SOUND

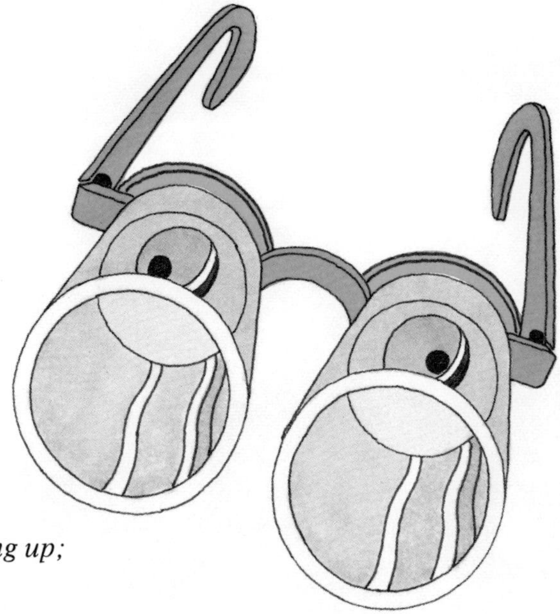

THE SPAN OF LIFE

The old dog barks backward without getting up;
I can remember when he was a pup.

Would this "message" be easier to forget if its form (rhythm, meter, rhyme, cadence) were ordinary prose? Or ordinary *verse?*

Is the sound of sound a message?

To teach a mule ....

RALPH GLEASON: Even J. Paul Getty, in his celebrated *Playboy* memoirs, talks about all the things he did that they told him not to do, and he believes that's why he is successful. It seems to me that we can't make rules for this sort of thing or give directions to the really talented and creative.

VITTORIO GIANNINI: I would go a step further. I believe that you teach yourself and, although a teacher might show you the way, you really learn the most by examining yourself, responding to your own needs, and studying according to your own dictates. A creative person often must do what he is told. He can be taught some things and guided, but only to a point. At times it may be true that a person develops to a high degree by doing that very thing which would be poison to someone else.

There are a lot of completely educated people in the world, and of course they will resent being asked to learn anything new.

Art consists of selective synthesis or reduction.

Homo sum; humani nihil a me alienum puto.
TERENCE

AN INVESTIGATION INTO WORD-ART

In this section you will find a number of comments by craftsmen and artists on how they go about their work. They discuss what they are trying to do, how they go about doing it, and what influences have affected them.

As you examine the observations, see if any general pattern emerges. As you consider the meaning of what is said, can you distill any reliable suggestions for students? Would your suggestions be the same as the rules you were taught in school?

Do you find the practices described in this section similar to those of the painters, sculptors, and movie directors you read about in earlier sections? Are they different? In what way the same, in what way different? Does it seem that one can generalize about all sorts of endeavor?

Some people argue that artists are not the best people to discuss clearly and meaningfully what they have created. Do you agree?

Can taxi driving be an art, auto racing, customizing cars? What elements would have to be present?

What must be added to labor to make it art?

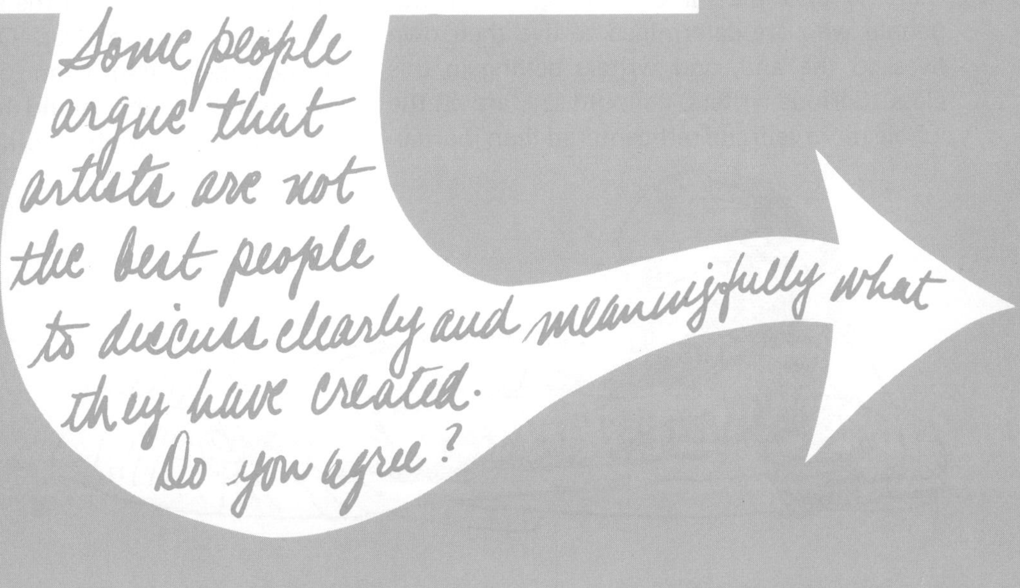
Some people
argue that
artists are not
the best people
to discuss clearly and meaningfully what
they have created.
Do you agree?

Putting aside the need to earn a living, I think there are four great motives for writing, at any rate for writing prose. They exist in different degrees in every writer, and in any one writer the proportions will vary from time to time, according to the atmosphere in which he is living. They are:

1. *Sheer egoism.* Desire to seem clever, to be talked about, to be remembered after death, to get your own back on grownups who snubbed you in childhood, etc., etc. It is humbug to pretend that this is not a motive, and a strong one. Writers share this characteristic with scientists, artists, politicians, lawyers, soldiers, successful businessmen—in short, with the whole top crust of humanity. The great mass of human beings are not acutely selfish. After the age of about thirty they abandon individual ambition—in many cases, indeed, they almost abandon the sense of being individuals at all—and live chiefly for others, or are simply smothered under drudgery. But there is also the minority of gifted, wilful people who are determined to live their own lives to the end, and writers belong in this class. Serious writers, I should say, are on the whole more vain and self-centered than journalists, though less interested in money.

2. *Esthetic enthusiasm.* Perception of beauty in the external world, or, on the other hand, in words and their right arrangement. Pleasure in the impact of one sound on another, in the firmness of good prose or the rhythm of a good story. Desire to share an experience which one feels is valuable and ought not to be missed. The esthetic motive is very feeble in a lot of writers, but even a pamphleteer or a writer of textbooks will have pet words and phrases which appeal to him for non-utilitarian reasons; or he may feel strongly about typography, width of margins, etc. Above the level of a railway guide, no book is quite free from esthetic considerations.

3. *Historical impulse.* Desire to see things as they are, to find out true facts and store them up for the use of posterity.

4. *Political purpose*—using the word "political" in the widest possible sense. Desire to push the world in a certain direction, to alter other people's idea of the kind of society that they should strive after. Once again, no book is genuinely free from political bias. The opinion that art should have nothing to do with politics is itself a political attitude.

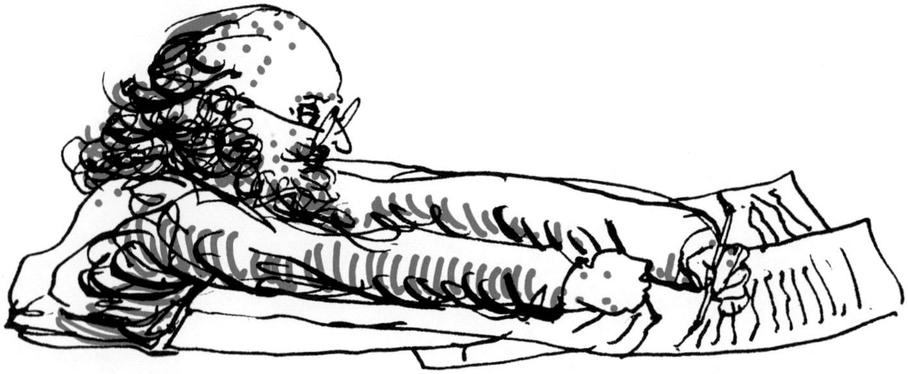

THE COMMA ,

. . . comes from the Greek word *komma,* which means pretty much the same thing. Few words have as dull an etymology. If you take away the top half of a semicolon, what's left is a comma; come to think of it, the word colon comes from the Greek *kolon.* Well, you can't win 'em all.

The comma is used to separate Faith, Hope, and what begins at home. And by bad writers to keep their foolish, boring, misleading, noxious, aimless, space-filling, time-wasting, nonsensical, vexing adjectives away from their nouns.

Without the comma it would be difficult to keep track of the naughts in the federal deficit. Bunched together—000,000,000—it's easier for Congress to tell when they have to raise the debt limit.

The comma is good for keeping a man away from his job. Marvin, the fink. Jack, the ripper. Susskind, the listener. This cute little dickens is sometimes used to show where a speaker takes a breath. The most interesting case of breathing was that of one Louella Parsons, a lady who, by radio, used to broadcast from Hollywood some of the brighter doings of motion picture persons. If her script was written the way she breathed, it must have looked like this:

> "Hello, from Hollywood. My first, exclusive. Hedy Krausmeyer, the well-known, personality, just flew in from New York. She has a, contract to, play the part, of Ghoula in the, new picture, Ghoula, goes to, town."

Those were probably the really, great, days, in the history of, the comma,

PROLOGUE

Every day I set less store on intellect. Every day I see more clearly that if the writer is to repossess himself of some part of his impressions, get to something personal, that is, and to the only material of art, he must put it aside. What intellect restores to us under the name of the past, is not the past. In reality, as soon as each hour of one's life has died, it embodies itself in some material object, as do the souls of the dead in certain folk stories, and hides there. There it remains captive, captive forever, unless we should happen on the object, recognize what lies within, call it by its name, and so set it free. Very likely we may never happen on the object (or the sensation, since we apprehend every object as sensation) that it hides in; and thus there are hours of our life that will never be resuscitated: for this object is so tiny, so lost in the world, and there is so little likelihood that we shall come across it.

Several summers of my life were spent in a house in the country. I thought of those summers from time to time, but they were not themselves. They were dead, and in all probability they would always remain so. Their resurrection, like all these resurrections, hung on a mere chance. One snowy evening, not long ago, I came in half frozen, and had sat down in my room to read by lamplight, and as I could not get warm my old cook offered to make me a cup of tea, a thing I never drink. And as chance would have it, she brought me some slices of dry toast. I dipped the toast in the cup of tea and as soon as I put it in my mouth, and felt its softened texture, all flavored with tea, against my palate, something came over me—the smell of geraniums and orange blossoms, a sensation of extraordinary radiance and happiness; I sat quite still, afraid that the slightest movement might cut short this incomprehensible process which was taking place in me, and concentrated on the bit of sopped toast which seemed responsible for all these marvels; then suddenly the shaken partitions in my memory gave way, and into my conscious mind there rushed the summers I had spent in the aforesaid house in the country, with their early mornings, and the succession, the ceaseless onset, of happy hours in their train. And then I remembered. Every morning, when I was dressed, I went down to my grandfather in his bedroom, where he had just woken up and was drinking his tea. He soaked a rusk in it, and gave me the rusk to eat. And when those summers were past and gone, the taste of a rusk soaked in the tea was one of the shelters where the dead hours—dead as far as intellect knew—hid themselves away, and where I should certainly never have found them again if, on that winter's evening when I came in frozen from the snow, my cook had not offered me the potion to which, by virtue of a magic past I knew nothing about, their resurrection was plighted.

But as soon as I had tasted the rusk, a whole garden, up till then vague and dim, mirrored itself, with its forgotten walks and all their urns with all their flowers, in the little cup of tea, like those Japanese flowers which do not reopen as flowers until one drops them into water. In the same way, many days in Venice, which intellect had not been able to give back, were dead for me until last year, when crossing a courtyard I came to a standstill among the glittering uneven paving stones. The friends I was with feared I might have wrenched my ankle, but I waved to them to go on, and that I would catch up with them. Something of greater importance engaged me, I still did not know what it was, but in the depth of my being I felt the flutter of a past that I did not recognize; it was just as I set foot on a certain paving stone that this feeling of perplexity came over me. I felt an invading happiness. I knew that I was going to be enriched by that purely personal thing, a past impression, a fragment of life in unsullied preservation (something we can only know in preservation, for while we live in it, it is not present in the memory, once other sensations accompany and smother it) which asked only that it should be set free, that it should come and augment my wealth of life and poetry. But I did not feel that I had the power to free it. No, intellect could have done nothing for me at such a moment! Trying to put myself back into the same state, I retraced my steps a little so that I might come afresh to those uneven shining paving stones. It was the same sensation underfoot that I had felt on the smooth, slightly uneven pavement of the bapistry of Saint Mark's. The shadow which had lain that day on the canal where a gondola waited for me, and all the happiness, all the wealth of those hours—this recognized sensation brought them hurrying after it, and that very day came alive for me.

It is not merely that intellect can lend no hand in these resurrections; these past hours will only hide themselves away in objects where intellect has not tried to embody them. The objects which you have consciously tried to connect with certain hours of your life, these they can never take shelter in. What is more, if something else should resuscitate those hours, the objects called back with them will be stripped of their poetry.

I remember how once when I was travelling by train I strove to draw impressions from the passing landscape, I wrote about the little country churchyard while it was still passing before my eyes, I noted down the bright bars of sunlight on the trees, the wayside flowers like those in *Le Lys dans la Vallée.* Since then, calling to mind those trees streaked with light and that little churchyard, I have often tried to conjure up that day, that day *itself,* I mean, not its pallid ghost. I could never manage it, and I had lost all hope of doing so, when at lunch, not long ago, I let my spoon fall on my plate. And then it made the same noise as the hammers of the linesmen did that day, tapping on the wheels when the train halted at stations. The burning blinded hour when that noise rang out instantly came back to me, and all that day in its poetry—except for the country churchyard, the trees streaked with light, and the Balzacian flowers, gained by deliberate observation and lost from the poetic resurrection.

Now and again, alas, we happen on the object, and the lost sensation thrills in us, but the time

I wanted to utter a word, but that word I cannot remember; and the bodiless thought will now return to the palace of shadows.

is too remote, we cannot give a name to the sensation, or call on it, and it does not come alive. As I was walking through a pantry the other day, a piece of green canvas plugging a broken windowpane made me stop dead and listen inwardly. A gleam of summer crossed my mind. Why? I tried to remember. I saw wasps in a shaft of sunlight, a smell of cherries came from the table—I could not remember. For a moment I was like those sleepers who wake up in the dark and do not know where they are, who ask their bodies to give them a bearing as to their whereabouts, not knowing what bed, what house, what part of the world, which year of their life they are in. For a moment I hesitated like this, groping round the square of green canvas to discover the time and the place where my scarcely awakened memory would find itself at home. All the sensations of my life, confused, or known, or forgotten, I was hesitating among all of them at once; this only lasted a minute. Soon I saw nothing more; my memory had fallen asleep again forever.

How often during our walks have not my friends known me to halt like this at the turning-off of an avenue, or beside a clump of trees, and ask them to leave me alone for a minute. Nothing came of it. I shut my eyes and made my mind a blank to recruit fresh energies for my pursuit of the past, then suddenly reopened them, all in an attempt to see those same trees as if for the first time, I could not tell where I had seen them. I could recognize their shapes and their grouping, their outline seemed to have been traced from some beloved drawing that trembled in my heart. But I could tell no more of them, and they themselves seemed by their artless passionate attitude to say how sorry they felt not to be able to make themselves clear, not to be able to tell me the secret that they well knew I could not unriddle. Ghosts of a dear past, so dear that my heart beat to bursting, they held out powerless arms to me, like the ghosts that Aeneas met in the underworld. Was it in the walks near the town of my happy childhood, was it only in that imagined country where, later on, I dreamed that Mamma was so ill, close to a lake and in a forest where it was light all night long, a dream country only but almost as real as the country of my childhood which was already no more than a dream? I should never know more of it. And I had to rejoin my friends who were waiting for me at the turn of the road, with the anguish of turning my back forever on a past I might see no more, of disowning the dead who held out their powerless fond arms to me, and seemed to say, Recall us to life. And before I fell into step and into conversation with my friends, I again turned round for a moment to cast a less and less discerning glance towards the receding crooked line of mutely expressive trees still undulating before my eyes.

Compared with this past, this private essence of ourselves, the truths of intellect seem scarcely real at all. So, and above all from the time when our vitality begins to dwindle, it is to whatever may help us to recover this past that we resort, even though this should entail being very ill-understood by intellectual people who do not know that the artist lives to himself, that the absolute value of what he sees means nothing to him and that his scale of values is wholly subjective. A nauseating musical show put on by a provincial company, or a ball that people of taste would laugh at, may be far more quickening to his memories, far more relevant to the nature of what he dreams of and dwells on, than a brilliant performance at the Opera House or an ultra-elegant evening party in the Faubourg Saint-Germain. A railway timetable with its names of stations where he loves to fancy himself getting out of the train on an autumn evening when the trees are already stripped of their leaves and the bracing air is full of their rough scent, or a book that means nothing to people of discrimination but is full of names he has not heard since he was a child, can be worth incommensurably more to him than admirable philosophical treatises, so that people of discrimination will remark that for a man of talent he has very stupid likings.

Perhaps it will cause surprise that I, who make light of the intellect, should have devoted the following few pages precisely to some of those considerations that intellect, in contradiction to the platitudes that we hear said or read in books, suggests to us. At a time when my days may be numbered (and besides, are we not all in the same case?) it is perhaps very frivolous of me to undertake an intellectual exercise. But if the truths of intellect are less precious than those secrets of feeling that I was talking about just now, yet in one way they too have their interest. A writer is not only a poet; in our imperfect world where masterpieces are no more than the shipwrecked flotsam of great minds, even the greatest writers of our century have cast a net of intellect round jewels of feeling which only here or there show through it. And if one believes that on this important point one hears the best among one's contemporaries making mistakes, there comes a time when one shakes off one's indolence and feels the need to speak out. Sainte-Beuve's method is not, at first sight, such an important affair. But perhaps in the course of these pages we may be led to realize that it touches on very important intellectual problems, and on what is perhaps for an artist the greatest of all; this relative inferiority of the intellect which I spoke of at the beginning. Yet all the same, it is intellect we must call on to establish this inferiority. Because if intellect does not deserve the crown of crowns, only intellect is able to award it. And if intellect only ranks second in the hierarchy of virtues, intellect alone is able to proclaim that the first place must be given to instinct.

（心は水の如く美しく清くあれ）.

HEART SHOULD BE PURE LIKE CLEAR WATER''

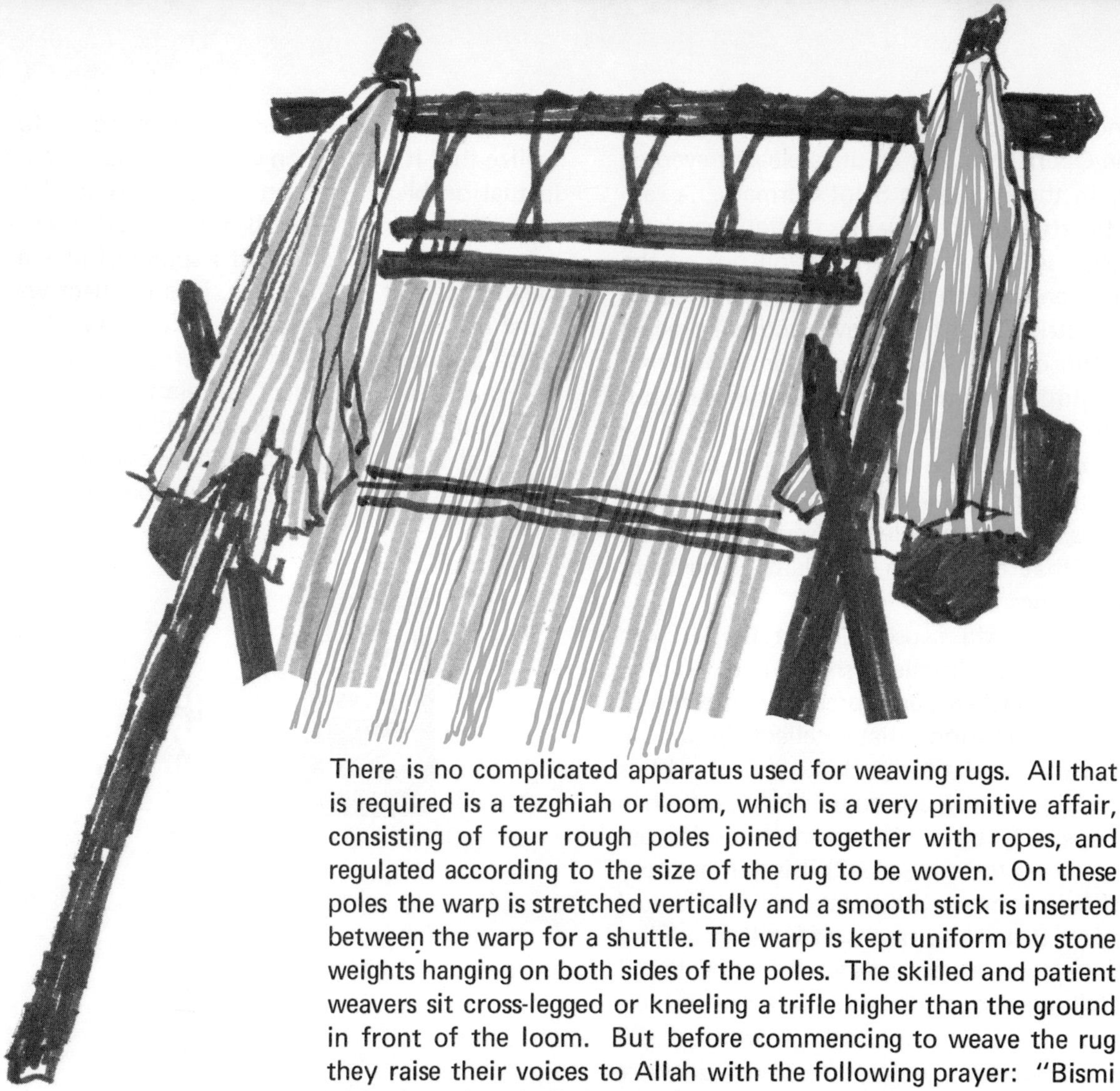

There is no complicated apparatus used for weaving rugs. All that is required is a tezghiah or loom, which is a very primitive affair, consisting of four rough poles joined together with ropes, and regulated according to the size of the rug to be woven. On these poles the warp is stretched vertically and a smooth stick is inserted between the warp for a shuttle. The warp is kept uniform by stone weights hanging on both sides of the poles. The skilled and patient weavers sit cross-legged or kneeling a trifle higher than the ground in front of the loom. But before commencing to weave the rug they raise their voices to Allah with the following prayer: "Bismi lahi rahm ni rahim"—in the name of God the Compassionate, the Merciful. (This exhortation is used by nearly all devout Mohametans at the commencement of any sort of undertaking.) Then, starting from right to left in horizontal rows, the weavers tie to two threads of the warp one or more tufts of colored yarn, varying and mixing the colors according to the design well founded and created in their minds. Several rows being completed, a smooth stick is passed across the loom to tighten or loosen wherever the occasion may require, and then a wooden or iron comb is used to press the knots down and make them uniform and tight before shearing off the rough surface, which requires a great deal of skill.

WILLIAM FAULKNER

INTERVIEWER: How much of your writing is based on personal experience?

FAULKNER: I can't say. I never counted up. Because "how much" is not important. A writer needs three things, experience, observation, and imagination, any two of which, at times any one of which, can supply the lack of the others. With me, a story usually begins with a single idea or memory or mental picture. The writing of the story is simply a matter of working up to that moment, to explain why it happened or what it caused to follow. A writer is trying to create believable people in credible moving situations in the most moving way he can. Obviously he must use as one of his tools the environment which he knows. I would say that music is the easiest means in which to express, since it came first in man's experience and history. But since words are my talent, I must try to express clumsily in words what the pure music would have done better. That is, music would express better and simpler, but I prefer to use words, as I prefer to read rather than listen. I prefer silence to sound, and the image produced by words occurs in silence. That is, the thunder and the music of the prose takes place in silence.

WHAT DO YOU SEE?

Write a description of some object or creature. It can be purely imaginary. Ask the student sitting next to you to draw what he thinks you have described. While he is doing that, you, in turn, can be making a drawing of the description he has written.

Exchange drawings when you have finished.

How well did you both communicate?

Pour comprendre le message, il faut savoir le code.

IGBO LANGUAGE 'DELIGHT' TO OUR MAN IN NIGERIA

To anyone who speaks or has learned to speak "Western languages" such as those from the Celtic, Italic or Germanic groups, a language such as Igbo from the African Bantu group can be full of delightful surprises.

Unlike English, Igbo is a tonal language and every syllable must be spoken on one of three "tones" or pitches: high, middle, or low. Take for example the word spelled Akwa. If the voice is pitched high on the first syllable and low on the second the word means "cloth."

If the voice is pitched high on both syllables the word means "crying," or if both syllables are pitched low it means "bridge." If the first syllable is low and the second high it means "egg." You can imagine the confusion this creates for a learner!

Early Christian missionaries told the people in Igbo "Jesus has great power." Unfortunately, the word for power is the same as the word for one's "rear end" and since most English words have a low pitch on the last syllable the message was understood to mean "Jesus has a large rear-end" which humored if not amazed the would-be converts.

In their zeal the missionaries tried to make Igbo words fit into Christian hymns. This of course played havoc with the tones of the words and one hymn, I have been told, came out to mean "Get out of here all you people who pick pumpkins and pass water." The faith grew faster when the reverend fathers learned to write the tune to fit the Igbo words.

To say "the man is a chief" one says simply "man is chief" in Igbo; the absence of a plural form causes no confusion. "The farmer has many chickens and six eggs" becomes "Farmer has chicken and egg six." Translated literally, there is only one word for he, she and it, and no familiar and polite forms (thou—you) so common in German and Spanish.

But the "building-block" logic of the language where more complex or abstract ideas are built up by combining simple ideas provides the most interesting insights. Emerson once said, on this topic "Every word which is used to express an abstract fact, if traced to its root, is found to be borrowed from some material appearance."

A number of examples will illustrate the point: Thunder is "the gun of heaven," if translated literally. Finger "the stick of the hand." Butterfly is "the feather of the wind." North is "the place of the mountain" perhaps since the northern part of Nigeria contains the tall Jos Plateau, the highest point in Nigeria.

West is "where the sun goes down" and East is "where the sun rises." Interesting relationships are also seen: The word for lightning is the same as the word for prophet, and the word for bicycle is the same as the word for iron, the iron being here first and the bicycle being perhaps the first common article made from it.

Common words such as fire and water are applied in numerous ways. "It is hot" in Igbo is "It is fire." The words for electric light and for heat are the same as the word for fire.

A vaccination is "fire of the hand." The word for rain is the same as the word for water. "It is wet" is translated "It is water-water."

Milk is "water of cow," and sap is "water of tree." All of these examples point to less differentiation between similar ideas than found in English. The Igbo does not distinguish between the hand and the arm for example but has one word for both. It is said that the Eskimo has an astonishing number of different words for the phenomenon we call "snow." He has grown sensitive to differences by constant contact.

Likewise the Igbo has many different words for the objects we call drums, and he divides the single idea of planting down into three different types of planting. "Ghara" means to plant many seeds as with pepper, "kuru" means to plant individual seeds such as corn, "koro" means to plant seedlings such as yam and casaba.

For the Westerner, the language is full of new sounds such as "kp" a popping of the lips explosively or "gb" which is a sort of bw sound as in "bwana" but from deep in the throat, or "gha" which is a guttural r sound. Certain of the words I find to be unusually beautiful: "Kpakpando" means star and "ndagwurugwn" is a deep valley.

The American often prides himself in the variety of his greetings. One hears "hi," hello, greetings, how are you, how goes it, hey John, good morning, and any number of individual concoctions to fit the situation.

Not so the Igbo. In any geographical area a certain situation has a more or less prescribed greeting exchange. The following pattern would be appropriate in the morning: "Have you awakened?" "Yes, have you come out?" "Yes, how is your body?" "I am well, and yours?" "Well, do not die." "Yes, do not die, and go well."

In English the students use only the greetings good morning, good afternoon, and good evening. If you pass any student on any morning he will always say "Good morning, sir." I learned after some months that the greeting "hello" is considered to be an insult, almost as serious as using the left hand for touching a person or food, or passing an object. A foreigner's first intimacy with the language is through its greetings and their patterns.

The Igbo man is a master of the art of conversation and oratory. He is a great teller of stories and makes his points most impressively through the use of proverbs. Two accomplished chiefs could debate for hours speaking almost exclusively in proverbs.

The proverb draws a lesson from the realities of everyday life but many have a complex interpretation known to every Igbo boy and girl. Translations of some of the commonest proverbs will illustrate the idea: "When a palm tree falls to the earth, then a woman is able to climb it." This might be used against one who is attacking a great man unable to defend himself, such as when a small politician insults great leaders behind their backs.

Or suppose an Igbo boy marries very young but has many children and is successful, he might hear: "A foolish action sometimes is rewarded." A village leader who is constantly asked for favors will reply: "The chicken carried to the market in a basket on the head does not know how hard the journey is." A person who wants to hurry when others feel there is plenty of time will be told: "If you pursue a turtle with force, is it going to fly?"

A small boy tries to copy a larger more famous man and is disappointed in the new role. His mother will say: "The rat follows the lizard into the rain. The sun will dry the lizard, but will it dry the rat?" A student in class asks a question about a point which will be covered shortly. The teacher says: "A man who is running cannot outrun his shadow." One of the most enjoyable ways to learn the language is to learn its proverbs from the students here.

THE WELFARE OF THE PEOPLE

Excerpts from actual letters received by the Department of Public Welfare in Phoenix from wives, mothers, fathers, etc., regarding welfare and allotments:

1. Please send me my elopment as I have a four months old baby and he is my only support and I need all I can get everyday to buy food and keep him close.
2. Both sides of my parents is poor and I can't expect nothing from them as my mother has been in bed for a year with the same doctor and won't change.
3. Please send my wife's form to fill out.
4. I have already wrote to the President and I don't hear from you. I will write to Uncle Sam and tell him about you both.
5. Please send me a letter and tell me if my husband made application for a wife and baby.
6. I can't get my pay. I got sex children. Can you tell me why this is?
7. Sir, I am forwarding my marriage certificate and my children, one is a mistake as you can see.
8. Please find out for certain if my husband is dead, as the man I am living with won't eat or do anything until he knows for sure.
9. I am annoyed to find out that you branded my children illiterate. Oh! the shame of it!—it is a dirty trick as I married their father a week before they were born.
10. I am writing to tell you that my baby was born two years ago and he is two years old. When do I get relief?
11. In answer to your letter, I gave birth to a boy weighing ten pounds. I hope this is satisfactory.
12. I have no children as my husband was a truck driver and worked day and night when he wasn't sleeping.

13. You have changed my little boy to a little girl. Does that make any difference?

14. In accordance with your instructions, I have given birth to twins in the enclosed envelope.

15. Unless I get my husband's money soon, I will be forced to lead an immortal life.

16. I am glad to say my husband, who was reported missing, is now dead.

17. I want my money quickly as I can get it. I've been in bed with my doctor for two weeks and he doesn't seem to be doing me any good. If things don't improve, I will send for another doctor.

MULTIPLE CHOICE

These excerpts from letters are

a. humorous
b. poignant
c. ambiguous
d. clear
e. other

If these excerpts were spoken instead of written, would the humor be so noticeable? What differences between writing and speech are involved? Which requires more precision?

Are these messages ambiguous? Would someone really interested in getting the message have difficulty with them?

Would you say these excerpts demonstrate a communication problem or a social problem? Is it that messages can't be received or won't be received?

Sind diese Auszüge Lehrpläne für das Schreiben von Aufsätzen? If so, what do they teach? What is the message of these messages?

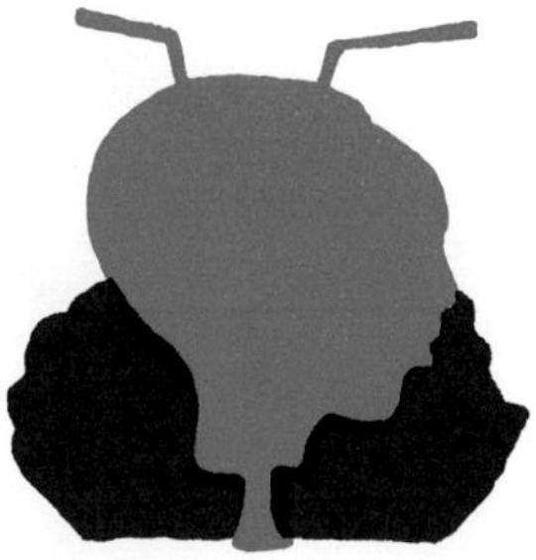

Sculpture in metal was also produced by the *cire perdue* or "lost-wax" process of casting, which was practiced widely in West Africa from Senegal eastward to the Cameroons, both inland and along the coast. In this process, the form is first modeled in beeswax and then coated with clay.

Two or more wax stems are usually left extending from the wax figure to the outer edge of the clay. When the clay has dried, it is heated and the melted wax is poured out through the vent formed by one of the stems. It is then reheated to volatilize all the wax. Molten metal is then poured through the vent into the hollow mold left by the wax figure. Each object is produced from a separate wax original, as the mold is destroyed when the clay coating is broken away after the metal has cooled. In principle the method is simple; but in practice it requires great skill.

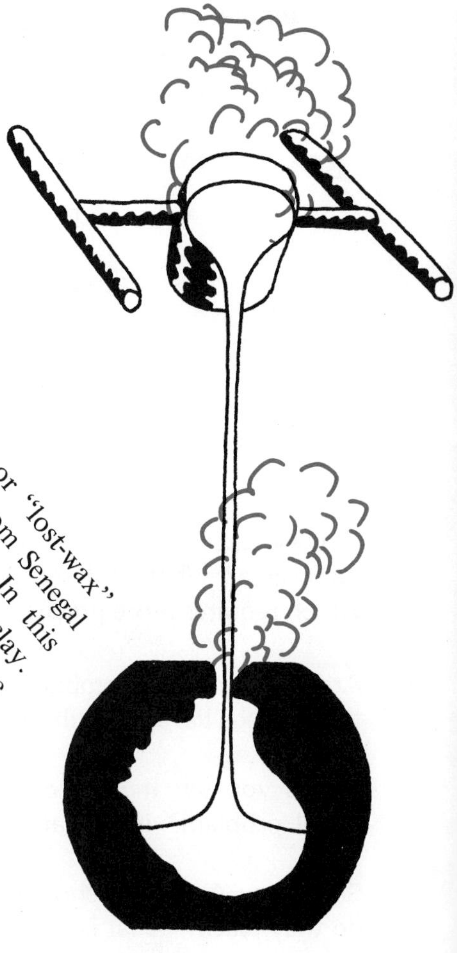

13. You have changed my little boy to a little girl. Does that make any difference?

14. In accordance with your instructions, I have given birth to twins in the enclosed envelope.

15. Unless I get my husband's money soon, I will be forced to lead an immortal life.

16. I am glad to say my husband, who was reported missing, is now dead.

17. I want my money quickly as I can get it. I've been in bed with my doctor for two weeks and he doesn't seem to be doing me any good. If things don't improve, I will send for another doctor.

MULTIPLE CHOICE

These excerpts from letters are

a. humorous
b. poignant
c. ambiguous
d. clear
e. other

If these excerpts were spoken instead of written, would the humor be so noticeable? What differences between writing and speech are involved? Which requires more precision?

Are these messages ambiguous? Would someone really interested in getting the message have difficulty with them?

Would you say these excerpts demonstrate a communication problem or a social problem? Is it that messages can't be received or won't be received?

Sind diese Auszüge Lehrpläne für das Schreiben von Aufsätzen? If so, what do they teach? What is the message of these messages?

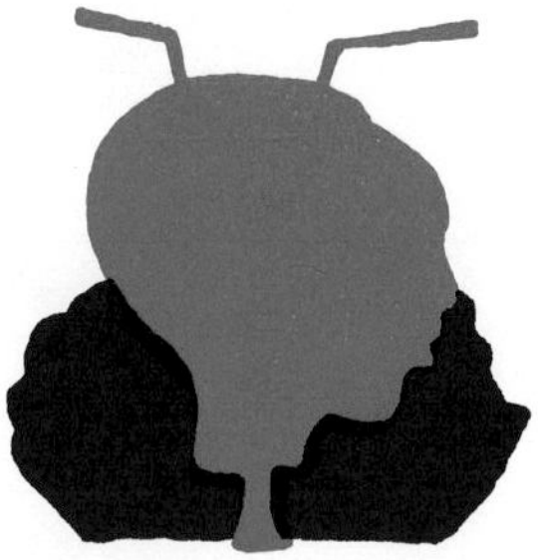

Sculpture in metal was also produced by the *cire perdue* or "lost-wax" process of casting, which was practiced widely in West Africa from Senegal eastward to the Cameroons, both inland and along the coast. In this process, the form is first modeled in beeswax and then coated with clay. Two or more wax stems are usually left extending from the wax figure to the outer edge of the clay. When the clay has dried, it is heated and the melted wax is poured out through the vent formed by one of the stems. It is then reheated to volatilize all the wax. Molten metal is then poured through the vent into the hollow mold left by the wax figure. Each object is produced from a separate wax original, as the mold is destroyed when the clay coating is broken away after the metal has cooled. In principle the method is simple; but in practice it requires great skill.

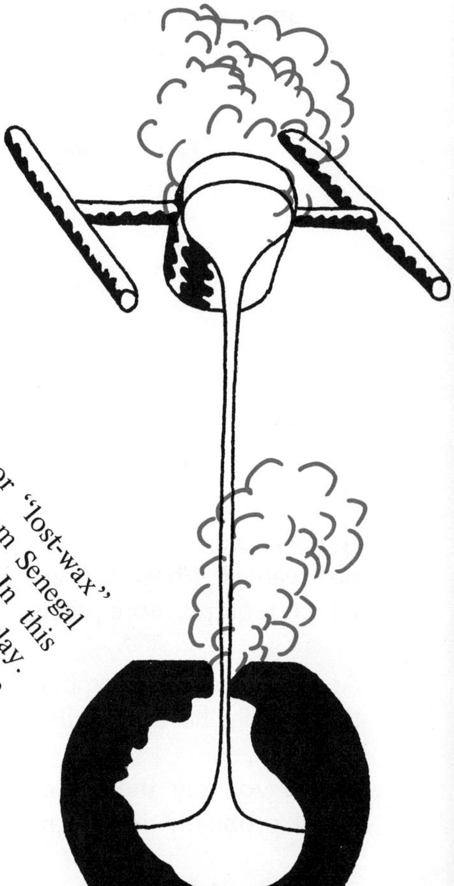

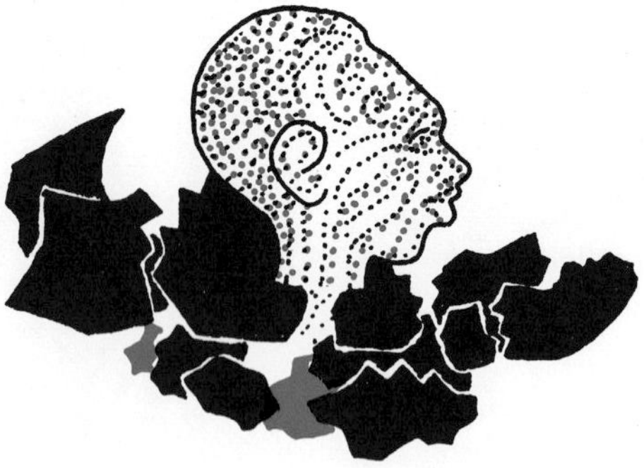

THORNTON WILDER

INTERVIEWER: If that young writer has the problem of earning a livelihood, is advertising or journalism or teaching English a suitable vocation?

WILDER: I think all are unfavorable to the writer. If by day you handle the English language either in the conventional forms which are journalism and advertising, or in the analysis which is teaching English in school or college, you will have a double, a quadruple difficulty in finding *your* English language at night and on Sundays. It is proverbial that every newspaper reporter has a half-finished novel in his bureau drawer. Reporting—which can be admirable in itself—is poles apart from shaping concepts into imagined actions and requires a totally different ordering of mind and language. When I had to earn my living for many years, I taught French. I should have taught mathematics. By teaching math or biology or physics, you come refreshed to writing.

HERMANMELVILLE

Under the tutorial system in British universities, a small group of students will meet at a regularly scheduled time with their tutor. Each student will read an assigned paper to the group aloud. The tutor and the other students will listen carefully and then discuss the merits and weaknesses of each paper from the point of view of its style and content. This method would help a student detect __________ and __________ in his writing.

Whence did the wond'rous mystic art arise,
Of painting SPEECH, and speaking to the eyes?

Build castles in the air? That is where they should be.

THE MOST NOBLE

WORDS

CAN BECOME

ineffective clichés

BUT

clichés

IN A NEW CONTEXT

CAN BECOME

UNCLICHÉD

which is to discover that they are

NO LONGER

ORDINARY

FRANÇOIS MAURIAC

Every novelist ought to invent his own technique, that is the fact of the matter. Every novel worthy of the name is like another planet, whether large or small, which has its own laws just as it has its own flora and fauna. Thus, Faulkner's technique is certainly the best one with which to paint Faulkner's world, and Kafka's nightmare has produced its own myths that make it communicable.

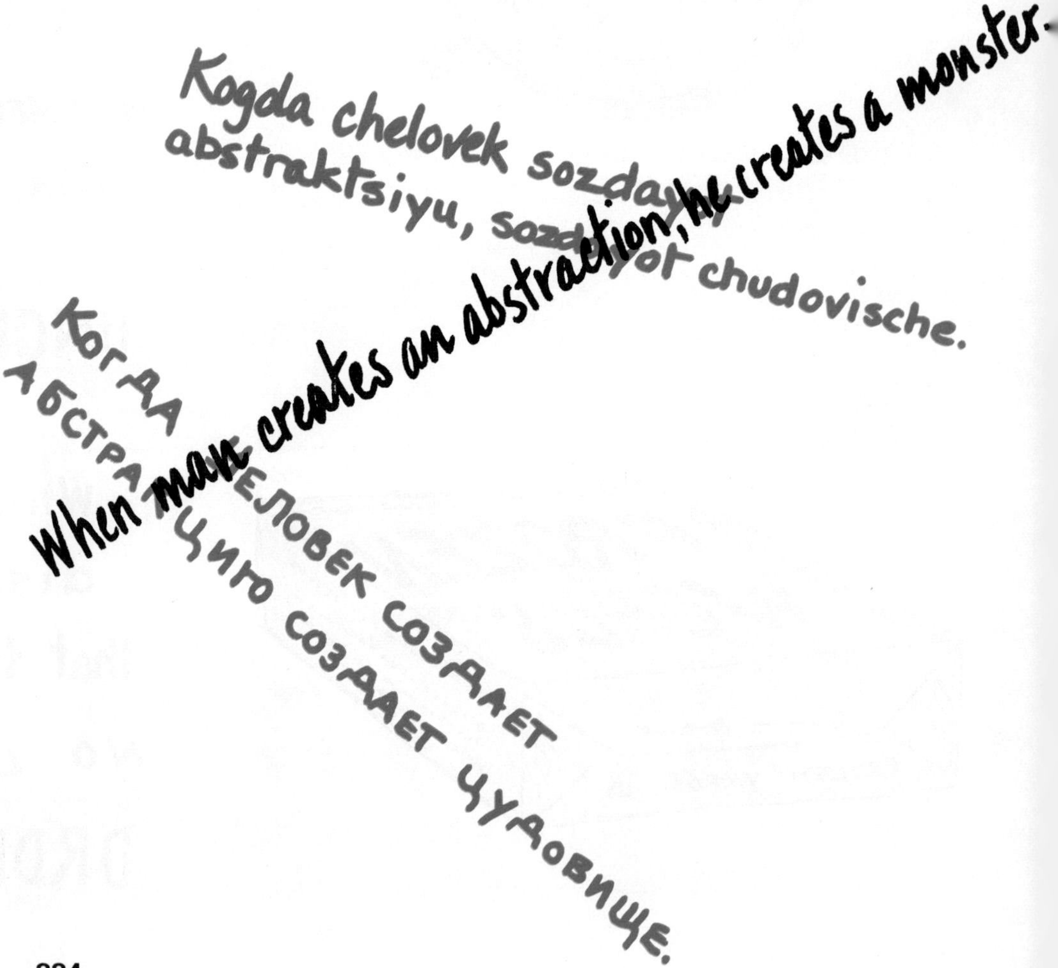

A GARLAND OF IBIDS

I have just finished reading a book[1] which struck me as being one of the finest books I have read since I read "The Flowering of New England," by the same author.[2] But there is a fly in the ointment. I have been rendered cockeyed by the footnotes. There seem to be too many of them, even for a book largely about Boston.[3] I do not know why the author had to have so many footnotes. Maybe he had a reason for each one, but I suspect the footnote habit has crept up on him, for I got out his book on Emerson,[4] published in 1932, and he used practically no footnotes in it.

You read along in "New England: Indian Summer," interested to the hilt in what Van Wyck Brooks is telling you about Longfellow,[5] Thoreau,[6] Phillips,[7] James,[8] Alcott,[9] Lowell,[10]

[1]"New England: Indian Summer."

[2]Van Wyck Brooks, author of "New England: Indian Summer," "The Flowering of New England," "The Life of Emerson," "The Ordeal of Mark Twain," and other books.

[3]Sometimes referred to as The Hub, capital and chief city of Massachusetts. Scene of the Boston Tea Party and the arrest of Henry L. Mencken. Bostonians are traditionally noted for their civic pride, or, as an envious New York critic once termed it, their parochial outlook. It is related that on an occasion when Saltonstall Boylston learned that his friend L. Cabot Lowell was leaving for a trip around the world, he inquired of Lowell, "Which route shall you take, L. C.?" "Oh, I shall go by way of Dedham, of course," replied Mr. Lowell. On another occasion, the old Back Bay aristocrat Ralph Waldo Mulcahy said to Oliver Wendell Rooney, "By the way, Rooney, did your ancestors come over on the Mayflower?" "Oh no," replied Mr. Rooney. "They arrived on the next boat. They sent the servants over on the Mayflower."

[4]Ralph Waldo Emerson, Sage of Concord and famous transcendentalist philosopher, not to be confused with Ralph McAllister Ingersoll, editor of PM.

[5]Henry Wadsworth Longfellow, Good Gray Poet. Longfellow was no footnote addict. He preferred foo*tprints.* Cf. his "Psalm of Life":

> And, departing, leave behind us
> Footprints on the sands of time

[6]Henry David Thoreau, philosopher who lived at Walden Pond for two years on carrots, twigs, nuts, minnows, creek water, and as Margaret Fuller suspected (booming it out at Brook Farm in that full, rich voice of hers, to the dismay of William Ellery Channing, Henry Wadsworth Longfellow, Edward Everett Hale, John Lothrop Motley, Charles Eliot Norton, and William Lloyd Garrison), sirloin steaks and creamery butter smuggled to him by Emerson. Suffering as he did from a vitamin deficiency, the result of too much moss in his diet, Thoreau became somewhat of a misanthrope and would often creep up behind members of the Saturday Club and shout "Boo!", or, as some authorities maintain, "Pooh!" The matter is not clarified very much, but one must admit, by a letter Mrs. Harriet Beecher Stowe wrote to her son, Harriet Beecher Stowe, Jr. (not to be confused with Herbert Bayard Swope), on June 7, 1854, in which she states: "Not much to write home about, as the saying goes. Dave Thoreau here for supper last nite [*sic*]. He got into an argument with John Greenleaf Whittier, the Good Gray Poet, as to whether snow is really ermine too dear for an earl, and Greenleaf called him a Communist. Dave then crept up behind Greenleaf and shouted either 'Boo!' [*sic*] or 'Pooh!' [*sic*]. I couldn't make out wich [*sic*]. All here except F. Marion Crawford, Sarah Orne Jewett, Charles Dudley Warner, Thomas Wentworth Hugginson, and William Dean Howells, who complain of feeling sic [*sic*]. Your aff. mother, H. B. Stowe, Sr."

[7]Wendell Phillips. He was about the only Bostonian of his time who wore no middle name and he was therefore considered half naked. Even Mark Twain, when he went to visit Howells in Boston, registered as Samuel Langhorne Clemens.

[8]Probably not Jesse James. Probably is either William James, deviser of Pragmatic Sanctions, or his brother Henry, the novelist. It was about this time that Henry James was going through his transition period, and could not make up his mind whether he was in England living in America or in America living in England.

[9]Amos Bronson Alcott, educator and bad provider. The Mr. Micawber of his day. Not to be confused with Novelist Bus Bronson of Yale or Mrs. Chauncey Olcott.

[10]James Russell Lowell, poet, essayist, and kinfolk of late rotund, cigar-smoking Back Bay Poetess Amy Lowell, no rhymester she!

Adams,[11] and other great figures of the Periclean Age of The Hub,[12] when suddenly there is a footnote.

The text is in fine, clear type. The footnotes are in small type. So it is quite a chore to keep focussing up and down the page, especially if you have old eyes or a touch of astigmatism.[13] By and by you say to yourself, "Darned if I look down at any more footnotes!," but you do, because the book is so interesting you don't want to miss even the footnotes.[14]

When you get to the footnote at the bottom of the page, like as not all you find is *Ibid.* *Ibid* is a great favorite of footnote-mad authors.[15] It was a great favorite with Gibbon.[16] How come writers of fiction do not need footnotes? Take Edna Ferber.[17] She doesn't use footnotes. Suppose Edna Herford[18] took to writing her novels in this manner: "Cicely Ticklepaw * sat at her dressing table in a brown study. She had 'a very strange feeling she'd ne'er felt before, a kind of a grind of depression.' † Could it be love? ‡ If so, why had she sent him § away? She sighed, a soft cry of 'Aye me!' ‖ escaped her. Seizing a nail file desperately, she commenced hacking away at her fingernails, when a voice behind her said, 'O! that I were a glove upon that hand, that I might touch that cheek!' $ Cicely red-

[11]Henry Adams, author of "The Education of Henry Adams," by Henry Adams. Not to be confused with Henry Adams, Samuel Adams, John Adams, John Quincy Adams, Abigail Adams, Charles Edward Adams (not to be confused with Charles Francis Adams, Charles Henry Adams, or Henry Adams), Maude Adams, Franklin Pierce Adams, Samuel Hopkins Adams, Bristow Adams, George Matthew Adams, James Truslow Adams, Adams Express, Adams & Flanagan, Horace Flanagan, or Louis Adamic.

[12]Sometimes referred to as Boston. One is reminded of the famous quatrain:

> Here's to the City of Boston,
> The home of Filene and the Card.,
> Where the Rileys speak only to Cabots
> And the Cabots speak only to God!

[13]In this connection, it is interesting to note that Louisa May Alcott had a touch of astigmatism, if we are to accept the word of Charles Eliot Norton. Edward Everett Hale states in his Letters, Vol. XV, Ch. 8, pp. 297 *et seq.,* that William Cullen Bryant told Oliver Wendell Holmes that on one occasion when the fun was running high at Thomas Wentworth Higginson's home and all barriers were down, Thomas Bailey Aldrich had put the question bluntly to Charles Eliot Norton, saying, "Now listen, has Louisa May Alcott got astigmatism or hasn't she?" Charles Eliot Norton answered, perhaps unwisely, "Yes." Cf. the famous dictum of General William Tecumseh Sherman, sometimes erroneously ascribed to General Ulysses Simpson Grant: "Never bring up a lady's name in the mess."

[14]Ah there, Van Wyck!

[15]So is cf.

[16]Edward Gibbon, English historian, not to be confused with Cedric Gibbons, Hollywood art director. Edward Gibbon was a great hand for footnotes, especially if they gave him a chance to show off his Latin. He would come sniffing up to a nice, spicy morsel of scandal about the Romans, and then, just as the reader expected him to dish the dirt, he'd go into his Latin routine, somewhat as follows: "In those days vice reached depths not plumbed since the reign of Caligula and it was an open secret that the notorious Empress Theodoro *in tres partes divisa erat* and that she was also addicted to the *argumentum ad hominem!*" Gibbon, prissy little fat man that he was, did that just to tease readers who had flunked Caesar.

[17]Edna Cabot Ferber, contemporary New England novelist. It is related of Edna Ferber that she once met Oliver Herford in Gramercy Park and recoiled at the sight of an extremely loud necktie he was wearing. "Heavens above, Oliver Herford!" exclaimed Miss Ferber, never one not to speak her mind. "That is a terrible cravat. Why do you wear it?" "Because it is my wife's whim that I wear it," explained Oliver Herford. "Well, land sakes alive, before I'd wear a tie like that just on account of a wife's whim!" jeered Miss Ferber. "You don't know my wife," said Oliver Herford. "She's got a whim of iron." Miss Ferber later made this incident the basis for the dramatic battle between the husband and wife in her novel "The Cravat."

[18]No, no, no, not Edna Herford! Edna FERBER! Edna Herford is the fellow who had the wife with the iron whim.

* Blonde, lively, and twenty-one.

†See "I'm Falling in Love with Someone"—Victor Herbert.

‡Sure.

§Cleon Bel Murphy, the man she loves.

‖"Romeo and Juliet," Act. II, Scene 2.

$*Ibid.*

dened, turned. It was Cleon Bel Murphy! Softly, she told him, 'What man art thou, that, thus bescreen'd in night, so stumblest on my counsel?' " &

What would Van Wyck Brooks say if Edna Ferber wrote like that?[19] Yes. Exactly. Now where were we?[20] No, I was not. I know what I was saying. You keep out of this. You're a footnote.[21] Yeah? Well just for that, no more footnotes. Out you go![22] I am, that's who.[23] See what I mean, Van Wyck? Give a footnote an inch and it'll take a foot.[24] I give up. They got me. And they'll get you too in the end, Van Wyck. You may think you're strong enough to keep 'em under control; you may think you can take a footnote or leave it. All I say is, remember Dr. Jekyll! Lay off 'em, Van. I'm telling you for your own good.

—UNEASY BROOKS FAN

& *Ibid.*

[19] And what would Edna Ferber say if Edna Ferber wrote like that?

[20] You were saying Louisa May Alcott had astigmatism.

[21] Yeah? And how far would you have got in this article without footnotes?

[22] Who's gonna put me out?

[23] Yeah? You and who else?

[24] Yoo-hoo! Footnote!

Intervention during productive confusion destroys the creator's chance to solve the problem and strengthen his mental processes.

The time of irresponsible artists is over. We shall regret it for our little moments of bliss. But we shall be able to admit that this ordeal contributes meanwhile to our chances of authenticity, and we shall accept the challenge. The freedom of art is not worth much when its only purpose is to assure the artist's comfort. For a value or a virtue to take root in a society, there must be no lying about it; in other words, we must pay for it every time we can. If liberty has become dangerous, then it may cease to be prostituted. And I cannot agree, for example, with those who complain today of the decline of wisdom. Apparently they are right. Yet, to tell the truth, wisdom has never declined so much as when it involved no risks and belonged exclusively to a few humanists buried in libraries. But today, when at last it has to face real dangers, there is a chance that it may again stand up and be respected.

It is said that Nietzsche after the break with Lou Salome, in a period of complete solitude, crushed and uplifted at the same time by the perspective of the huge work he had to carry on without any help, used to walk at night on the mountains overlooking the gulf of Genoa and light great bonfires of leaves and branches which he would watch as they burned. I have often dreamed of those fires and have occasionally imagined certain men and certain works in front of those fires, as a way of testing men and works. Well, our era is one of those fires whose unbearable heat will doubtless reduce many a work to ashes! But as for those which remain, their metal will be intact, and, looking at them, we shall be able to indulge without restraint in the supreme joy of the intelligence which we call "admiration."

One may long, as I do, for a gentler flame, a respite, a pause for musing. But perhaps there is no other peace for the artist than what he finds in the heat of combat. "Every wall is a door," Emerson correctly said. Let us not look for the door, and the way out, anywhere but in the wall against which we are living. Instead, let us seek the respite where it is—in the very thick of the battle. For in my opinion, and this is where I shall close, it *is* there. Great ideas, it has been said, come into the world as gently as doves. Perhaps then, if we listen attentively, we shall hear, amid the uproar of empires and nations, a faint flutter of wings, the gentle stirring of life and hope. Some will say that this hope lies in a nation; others, in a man. I believe rather that it is awakened, revived, nourished by millions of solitary individuals whose deeds and works every day negate frontiers and the crudest implications of history. As a result, there shines forth fleetingly the ever threatened truth that each and every man, on the foundation of his own sufferings and joys, builds for all.

In the city fields, contemplating cherry trees. . .strangers are like friends.

The essence of the principle of development is that a group of tones or a rhythmic pattern—called a *motive* earlier—serves as a seed out of which larger entities grow or develop. In some cases the motive serves as a point of departure; the composer returns to the motive repeatedly and out of it fashions a series of phrases which bear a recognizable relationship to each other. Example 64*a* illustrates the principle; the motive is marked by a bracket, and in its third and fourth appearances it is modified slightly by having the interval between its tones expanded. The result is a number of phrases which begin with similar contours and which have grown one out of the other.

In Brahms' Waltz in A flat (Example 64*b*) and Bach's Prelude in B flat minor (Example 64*c*), the respective motives are treated similarly—except that here the repetitions come closer together, and in the Bach piece the motive is repeated sequentially and appears in an inverted position as well as in the normal position.

PARKER: I'm trying now to do a story that's purely narrative. I think narrative stories are the best, though my past stories make themselves stories by telling themselves through what people say. I haven't got a visual mind. I hear things. But I'm not going to do those *he-said she-said* things any more, they're over, honey, they're over. I want to do the story that can only be told in the narrative form, and though they're going to scream about the rent, I'm going to do it.

INTERVIEWER: Do you think economic security an advantage to the writer?

PARKER: Yes. Being in a garret doesn't do you any good unless you're some sort of a Keats. The people who lived and wrote well in the twenties were comfortable and easy-living. They were able to find stories and novels, and good ones, in conflicts that came out of two million dollars a year, not a garret. As for me, I'd like to have money. And I'd like to be a good writer. These two can come together, and I hope they will, but if that's too adorable, I'd rather have money. I hate almost all rich people, but I think I'd be darling at it. At the moment, however, I like to think of Maurice Baring's remark: "If you would know what the Lord God thinks of money, you have only to look at those to whom he gives it." I realize that's not much help when the wolf comes scratching at the door, but it's a comfort.

ALL ART IS GOSSIP.

See the teacher.
Teacher corrects
the paper.

Correct, Teacher, Correct,

Correct, correct, correct.

did their dance...

CHILD ART: THE BEGINNING OF SELF-AFFIRMATION

The vital task of understanding the world, of finding order by observing generalities, and shaping concepts was supposed to be performed by purely intellectual operations. . .But it now appears that creative, inventive thinking in any field of human endeavor, not just in the arts, may be essentially sensory. Therefore, training in visual thinking belongs in the very center of education from kindergarten through graduate school and beyond.

1. Titles start with capital letters.
2. Daisies – not daisys.
3. They're – not there.
4. Don't starts a new sentence so make it capital.
5. Don't you think so? is a question so use a question mark.

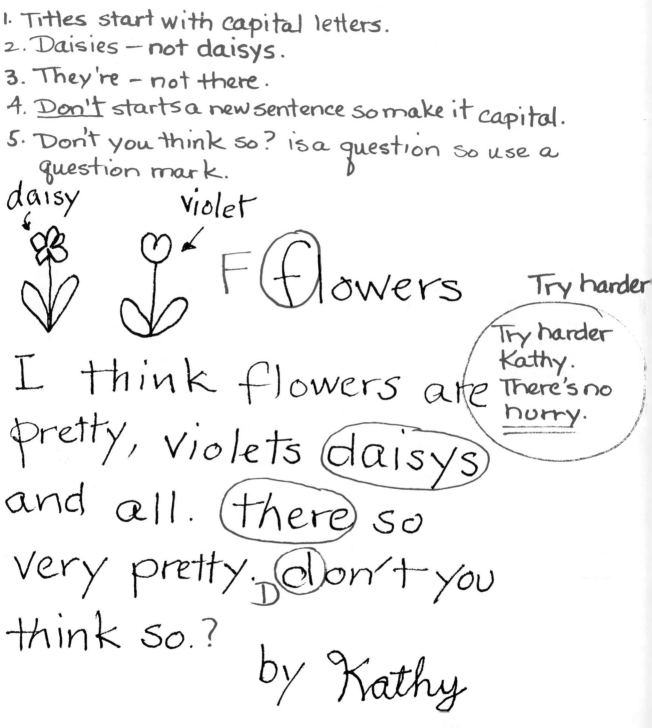

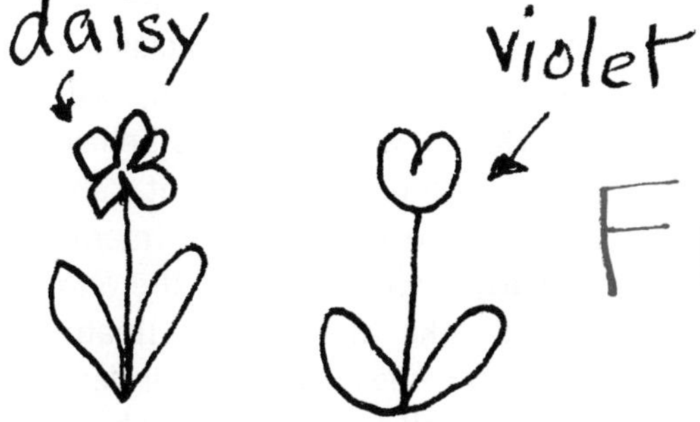

F flowers

Try harder

Try harder Kathy. There's no hurry.

I think flowers are pretty, violets daisys and all. there so very pretty. D don't you think so.?

by Kathy

The poloball was an old one, scarred, chipped, and dented. It stood on the mantelpiece among the pipestems which Imam Din, *khitmatgar*, was cleaning for me.

"Does the Heaven-born want this ball?" said Imam Din deferentially.

The Heaven-born set no particular store by it; but of what use was a poloball to a *khitmatgar*?

"By Your Honor's favor, I have a little son. He has seen this ball, and desires it to play with. I do not want it for myself."

No one would for an instant accuse portly old Imam Din of wanting to play with poloballs. He carried out the battered thing into the veranda; and there followed a hurricane of joyful squeaks, a patter of small feet, and the *thud-thud-thud* of the ball rolling along the ground. Evidently the little son had been waiting outside the door to secure his treasure. But how had he managed to see that poloball?

Next day, coming back from office half an hour earlier than usual, I was aware of a small figure in the dining room—a tiny, plump figure in a ridiculously inadequate shirt which came, perhaps, half-way down the tubby stomach. It wandered round the room, thumb in mouth, crooning to itself as it took stock of the pictures. Undoubtedly this was the "little son."

He had no business in my room, of course; but was so deeply absorbed in his discoveries that he never noticed me in the doorway. I stepped into the room and startled him nearly into a fit. He sat down on the ground with a gasp.

His eyes opened, and his mouth followed suit. I knew what was coming, and fled, followed by a long, dry howl which reached the servants' quarters far more quickly than any command of mine had ever done. In ten seconds Imam Din was in the dining room. Then despairing sobs arose, and I returned to find Imam Din admonishing the small sinner who was using most of his shirt as a handkerchief.

"This boy," said Imam Din judicially," is a *budmash*—a big *budmash.* He will, without doubt, go to the *jail-khana* for his behavior." Renewed yells from the penitent, and an elaborate apology to myself from Imam Din.

"Tell the baby," said I, "that the *Sahib* is not angry, and take him away." Imam Din conveyed my forgiveness to the offender, who had now gathered all his shirt round his neck, stringwise, and the yell subsided into a sob. The two set off for the door. "His name," said Imam Din, as though the name were part of the crime, "is Muhammad Din, and he is a *budmash.*" Freed from present danger, Muhammad Din turned round in his father's arms, and said gravely, "It is true that my name is Muhammad Din, *Tahib*, but I am not a *budmash.* I am a *man!*"

From that day dated my acquaintance with Muhammad Din. Never again did he come into my dining room, but on the neutral ground of the garden we greeted each other with much state, though our conversation was confined to *Talaam, Tahib"* from his side, and *"Salaam, Muhammad Din"* from mine. Daily on my return from office, the little white

Every story is a yarn of local

shirt, and the fat little body used to rise from the shade of the creeper-covered trellis where they had been hid; and daily I checked my horse here, that my salutation might not be slurred over or given unseemly.

Muhammad Din never had any companions. He used to trot about the compound, in and out of the castor-oil bushes, on mysterious errands of his own. One day I stumbled upon some of his handiwork far down the grounds. He had half buried the poloball in dust, and stuck six shriveled old marigold flowers in a circle round it. Outside that circle again was a rude square, traced out in bits of red brick alternating with fragments of broken china; the whole bounded by a little bank of dust. The waterman from the well curb put in a plea for the small architect, saying that it was only the play of a baby and did not much disfigure my garden.

Heaven knows that I had no intention of touching the child's work then or later; but, that evening, a stroll through the garden brought me unawares full on it; so that I trampled, before I knew, marigold heads, dust bank, and fragments of broken soapdish into confusion past all hope of mending. Next morning, I came upon Muhammad Din crying softly to himself over the ruin I had wrought. Some one had cruelly told him that the *Sahib* was very angry with him for spoiling the garden, and had scattered his rubbish, using bad language the while. Muhammad Din labored for an hour at effacing every trace of the dust bank and pottery fragments, and it was with a

color.

tearful and apologetic face that he said, *"Talaam, Tahib,"* when I came home from office. A hasty inquiry resulted in Imam Din informing Muhammad Din that, by my singular favor, he was permitted to disport himself as he pleased. Whereat the child took heart and fell to tracing the groundplan of an edifice which was to eclipse the marigold poloball creation.

For some months, the chubby little eccentricity revolved in his humble orbit among the castor-oil bushes and in the dust; always fashioning magnificent palaces from stale flowers thrown away by the bearer, smooth waterworn pebbles, bits of broken glass, and feathers pulled, I fancy, from my fowls—always alone, and always crooning to himself.

A gayly spotted seashell was dropped one day close to the last of his little buildings; and I looked that Muhammad Din should build something more than ordinarily splendid on the strength of it. Nor was I disappointed. He meditated for the better part of an hour, and his crooning rose to a jubilant song. Then he began tracing in the dust. It would certainly be a wondrous palace, this one, for it was two yards long and a yard broad in groundplan. But the palace was never completed.

Next day there was no Muhammad Din at the head of the carriage drive, and no *"Talaam, Tahib"* to welcome my return. I had grown accustomed to the greeting, and its omission troubled me. Next day Imam Din told me that the child was suffering slightly from fever and needed quinine. He got the medicine, and an English Doctor.

"They have no stamina, these brats," said the Doctor, as he left Imam Din's quarters.

A week later, though I would have given much to have avoided it, I met on the road to the Mussulman burying ground Imam Din, accompanied by one other friend, carrying in his arms, wrapped in a white cloth, all that was left of little Muhammad Din.

What kind of "magic and trickery" has the author used to make his imprint with this story?

Who are the persons you saw or imagined in reading Kathy's essay? How does your response to them compare to your response to the persons in this story?

si flesti erutcurts elbisivni eht tahT

act iveand a liveis rare lyper ceive

duntilit

isdisruptedinsomewaybytheartistbut

even

t,h,e,n,t,h,e,a,c,t,o,f,u,

n,d,e,r,s,t,a,n,d,i,n,g,

w-h-a-t-t-h-e-a-r-t-i-s-t-r-e-v-e-a-l-s-

is a choice of the *individual*

perceiver.

tHe cOmMonpLacE is ThE storehouse of *miracles.*

Recently, a young woman graduate of a famous Eastern college described her most valuable educational experiences in college. One was in a freshman seminar when she discovered that the teacher regarded her work as worth something. This helped her identify with the whole educational enterprise. She went along swimmingly, receiving only A's until her senior year. As a senior, she wrote a paper in an offhand way, still expecting to get an A. When she received a C, she complained to her teacher with a display of arrogance. He spent an hour discussing the first page, and half an hour on the second. She said that on leaving she felt lucky not to have been given an F. At a certain time, a student needs above all to be given a sense of worth. At another time, what that student needs most is to be brought down a peg. In both cases, criticism of a particular work is what is most valuable.

Learning to write is learning to see!

The structures with which mathematics deals are more like lace, the leaves of trees, and the play of light and shadow on a meadow or a human face, than they are like buildings and machines, the least of their representatives. The best proofs in mathematics are short and crisp like epigrams, and the longest have swings and rhythms that are like music. The structures of mathematics and the propositions about them are ways for the imagination to travel and the wings, or legs, or vehicles to take you where you want to go. The solemn sound of demonstrated mathematical truths is a professional way of announcing an arrival at some point on the journey fantastic. Let it be added for good measure that some of the greatest mathematical discoveries by the greatest mathematical minds have been theorems that they could not prove; some have never been proved. The fact of the matter is that anything worth discovering in mathematics does not need proof; it needs only to be seen or understood.

The Harvard system of electives did not give [Frost] the immediate latitude he sought. He was particularly annoyed to discover that he was required to take a course in elementary German and in English composition. He accepted the German course as unavoidable. But his instructor in English was an effeminate assistant, Alfred Dwight Sheffield, better known among the students as "the bearded lady," who very quickly infuriated Frost. Hoping that he was qualified to take Barrett Wendell's course in advanced composition, he found enough courage to approach Professor John Hayes Gardiner, head of the course, and to ask permission to change. Gardiner, who gave the weekly "third hour" lecture in English A, seemed to be offended by the request. In a manner that seemed supercilious, he asked Frost what "pretentions" might be prompting such a request. Well, there was nothing new in A. S. Hill's *Principles of Rhetoric* because the supplicant had already devoted several years to literary work. He had been a newspaper reporter and he had even published some verses in *The Independent.* Having saved this last fact as his trump card, Frost was not prepared to have the professor draw back his chin and make the sarcastic observation, "Oh! So we're a *writer*, are we?"

Hurt and flustered, Frost tried to smile as he said he guessed he wouldn't press the point further. Gardiner agreed: it would be just as well as if he didn't. The retreat from the professor's office was awkwardly made, and Frost left, vowing silently that he would never forgive or forget this rudeness. Sheffield had his own form of belittlement, equally aggravating. In class, one day, he asked each man to write a short lyric. Searching around in his memory for a poem he had previously composed, Frost found one which seemed appropriate to the autumnal season. . . .

Sheffield seemed to be suspicious, and when Frost appeared for his next conference the assistant asked if the poem had actually been composed in class or merely written from memory. Well, it was his own poem, although he had to admit that he had not worked it up on the spur of the moment. Then it was not acceptable. Other poems submitted did not please Sheffield, who gave Frost his best marks for prose pieces written inside or outside the classroom. But always the penciled comments were infuriating. They implied that the first requirement of the student was to learn how to write, that only later on would he have something to say. Sheffield obviously assumed that his task as teacher of English A was to drill the students meticulously through their writing of "exercises."

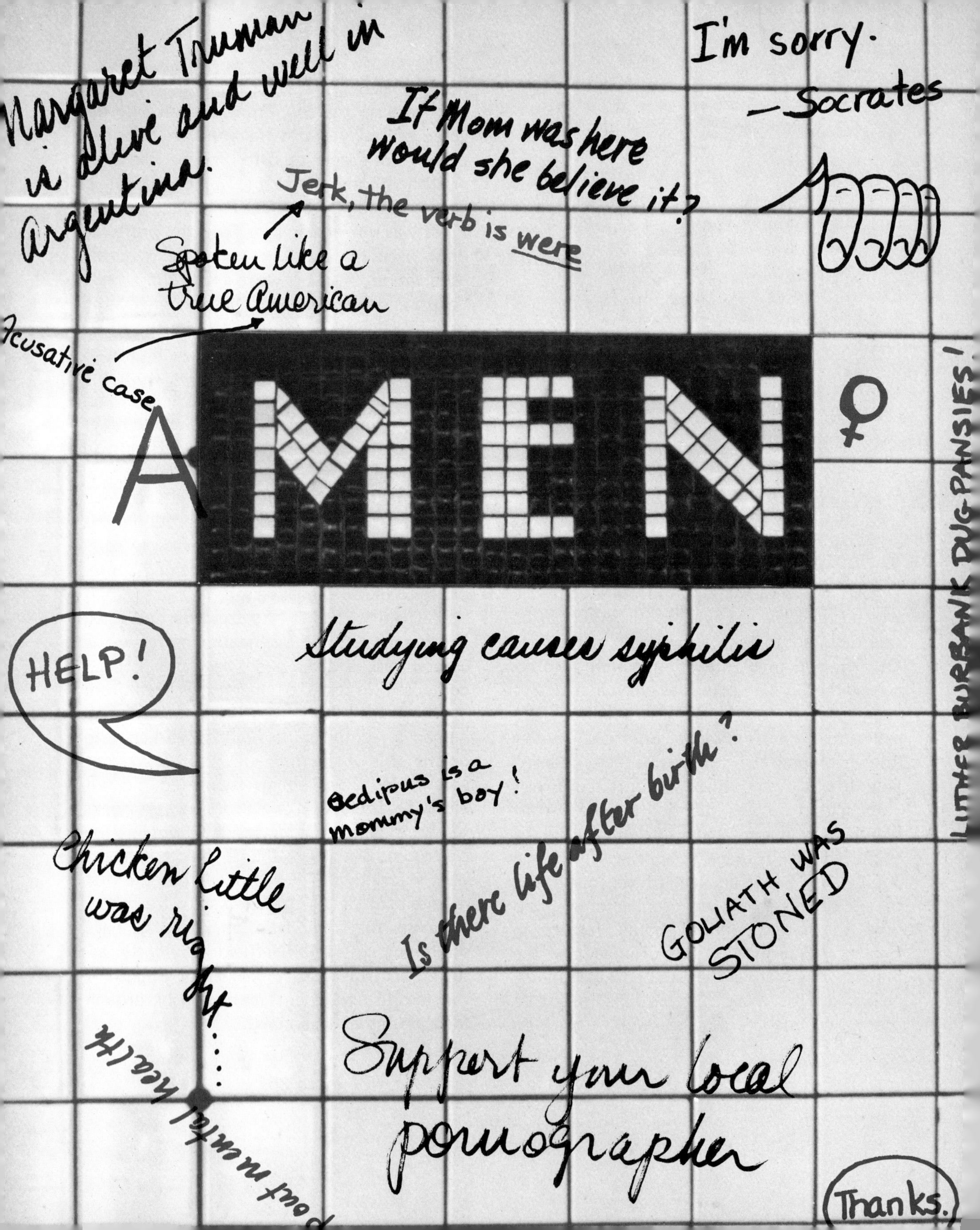

Margaret Truman is alive and well in Argentina.
I'm sorry. —Socrates
If Mom was here would she believe it?
Jerk, the verb is were
Spoken like a true American
Acusative case
A
MEN
LUTHER BURBANK DUG PANSIES!
HELP!
Studying causes syphilis
Oedipus is a mommy's boy!
Is there life after birth?
Chicken Little was right....
GOLIATH WAS STONED
Support your local pornographer
mental health
Thanks.

CREATIVE WRITING—MEN'S ROOM 1A

What is the message behind the messages here?

What kinds of things do people write on walls? Why? What quality?

As a specimen of our culture, what categories of information could the foregoing sample offer? What does it tell us about each of these categories? How much can such literature tell about our society?

ANGUS WILSON

INTERVIEWER: What is the difference for you between a short story and a novel?

WILSON: Short stories and plays go together in my mind. You take a point in time and develop it from there; there is no room for development backwards. In a novel I also take a point in time, but feel every room for development backwards. All fiction for me is a kind of magic and trickery—a confidence trick, trying to make people believe something is true that isn't. And the novelist, in particular, is trying to convince the reader that he is seeing society as a whole.

The essence of poetry with us in this age of stark and unlovely actualities is a stark directness, without a shadow of a lie or a shadow of deflection anywhere.

The condition of the world *today* is such that most writers feel they cannot truthfully be "comic" about it. (Was the world ever such that they could?) Perhaps they say: Can we single out the amiably comic eccentricity of individual beings, the ludicrous, the gauche, the maximless gawky, the dear and the daft and the droll, the runcible Booby, the Toby, the Pickwick, the barmy old Adam, when daily we are confronted, as social beings, by the dolt and the peeve and the minge and the bully, the maniac new Atom? I prefer the attitude of Pepys: "12th, Friday. Up, finding our beds good, but lousy; which made us merry. . . ."

Comic writers can't expect society to be comic just for *them.* "Do you serve women at this bar?" "No," says the barman, "you've got to bring your own." And society to a comic writer is always funny, even, or especially, on its deathbed. People walking into open lift-shafts, being wolfed by lions, missing the swung trapeze, are conventional subjects for a comic draughtsman; and the sight of society falling on its ear, and the prospect of civilisation itself going for a Burton, offer writers possibilities of every kind of laugh. "There is something in the house," said the wife of a comic writer in one of Algernon Blackwood's *John Silence* stories, "that prevents his feeling funny." There's enough, God knows, going on in *our* house to drive Peacock's Prince Seithennyn from drink; but that doesn't prevent a writer from creating a great comic world of his own out of the tragic catastrophe of this. "The best lack all conviction, while the worst are full of passionate intensity," wrote Yeats. But grave, censorious, senatorial, soul-possessing Man, erect on his two spindles, is still a colossal joke. A man in love makes a practical cat laugh. A man in power makes Engels weep—with laughter.

W. W. Jacobs was one of the trimmest, funniest, and most exact Edwardian writers, whose dialogue is as neat and sly and spare and taut as his mercenary and matrimonial plots. Here, in what I call a *minor* comic world, are the landlubber dreams of sailors on leave, the visions of a pocketful of Bradburys in snug saloons with buxom barmaids. Here are the intricate discomfitures of rival seamen; truculent unpaid rolling-pinned landladies; free fills of baccy; beer on the sly and the nod and the slate. Here all married women are harridans; all widows are plump and comfy and have a little bit put by; all unmarried girls are arch and mysterious; all men without exception are knaves and fools, and very often both, and are solely occupied in strategies concerning money and women and the getting and losing of them.

[Speaking of Stephen Leacock's works he said:] I read only his *Sunshine Sketches of a Little Town*, for only in these did Leacock create a *home* for his imagination, a "place" in which *his* people could be born and die, love, fall down, philosophize, have their hair cut, let their hair down, put their feet up.

[Calder Marshall asked:] Doesn't P. G. Wodehouse fit your definition of a comic world perfectly?

[The author replied:] Those chinless, dim eye-glassed, asinine, bespatted drones were borrowed, lock, stock and title, from memories of the Pink 'Un period and the Smart Set, from the ghostly, hansom past of the moneyed masher and the stage-door johnny. Some people like Jeeves, but include me out: I, for one, do not appreciate gentleman's gentleman's relish.

A truly comic, invented world must live *at the same time* as the world *we* live in.

What does [present-day comic writing] amount to? Funny columns in English newspapers, fence-sittings, beachcombings, shy-makings; the laboured, witless whimsy and pompous facetiousness of that national institution—or poorhouse of ideas—which *The New Yorker* once called "Paunch." All the best books—or nearly all but the best modern comic books are written by Americans. James Thurber, S. J. Perelman, Frank Sullivan, and Robert Benchley, all have written for that brilliant family magazine, but have nothing in common except their superiority to modern English comic journalists.

It is still impossible to compare the shy and baffled, introspective essays, fables, and fabulous reminiscences of Thurber, his cowering terror before the mechanical gadgets, the militant neuroses, the ubiquitous women, the democratic pitfalls and big-business bogies of this modern Americanised Age; it's impossible to compare him, class him, school him, with the glib Groucho zaniness of S. J. Perelman, who writes like a Hollywood advertising copywriter after reading James Joyce, Amanda Ross, Krafft-Ebing, Reverend Spooner, E. E. Cummings and Sam Goldwyn's ace publicity stooge in a state of hypertension in a Turkish bath managed by Man-Mountain Dean. But Thurber, Sullivan, Perelman, Benchley, all excellent comic writers, are all *essayists*; and I am concerned with comic, constructive writers of *stories.* I want, without boisterous back-slapping, without the hail-fellow guffaw of the tweedy pipe-sucking tankard-quaffing professional literary comedian, without nudge and titter, without the reedy neigh of the reviewer, I want laughter in books: the sight, and smell, and *sound* of laughter. And almost the only sound I hear from stories now recalls, to me, the sound of the watch in Frances Cornford's poem:

I thought it said in every tick:
I am so sick, so sick, so sick:
O death, come quick, come quick, come quick,
Come quick, come quick, come quick, come quick.

(1948)

"My facility is, in reality, tremendously hard work," he explained. "I write at the speed of two lines an hour . . . My poems are 'water-tight compartments,' the last thing they do is flow; they are much rather hewn." He was not blind to his faults, accused himself of "immature violence, rhythmic monotony, muddle-headedness, over-weighted imagery."

Even if you do learn to speak correct English, who are you going to speak it to?

MULTIPLE CHOICE

Is this a case of

a. mistaken identity
b. illiterate usage
c. cruelty to animals
d. bad grammar
e. misspent youth

All of these, some of these, or none of these? Choose the answer or answers which best suit the situation.

USAGE TEST

Here are nineteen expressions about which there is a good deal of controversy today. What is your opinion of their acceptability in everyday speech?

Do not be influenced by whether these usages do or do not violate formal grammatical rules. Rather, indicate, by a "yes" vote that you would be willing to use the expression listed or that you believe such an expression has become sufficiently current in educated American speech to be labeled acceptable usage; by a negative vote, that the expression, as used, is unacceptable in educated circles.

Circle whether or not the underlined expression would be acceptable to you under these conditions.

1.	His attitude makes me *mad.* (mad as a synonym for angry)	AC	UNAC
2.	I *will* pay your bill if you accept my check.	AC	UNAC
3.	The reason I'm worried is *because* I think she's ill.	AC	UNAC
4.	His work is different *than* mine.	AC	UNAC
5.	We had a *nice* time at the party.	AC	UNAC
6.	*Can* I have another helping of dessert, please?	AC	UNAC
7.	I encountered *less* difficulties than I had expected.	AC	UNAC
8.	Everyone put on *their coats* and went home.	AC	UNAC
9.	How much money have you *got*?	AC	UNAC
10.	*Due to* the storm, all trains are late.	AC	UNAC
11.	She has an *awful* headache.	AC	UNAC
12.	We *only* have five left. (position of *only*)	AC	UNAC
13.	Let's not walk any *further* right now.	AC	UNAC
14.	We must remember *to accurately check* each answer.	AC	UNAC
15.	He's one person I simply won't do business *with.*	AC	UNAC
16.	Go *slow.*	AC	UNAC
17.	It's *me.*	AC	UNAC
18.	She acts as if she *was* my wife.	AC	UNAC
19.	*Who* did you meet?	AC	UNAC

Answers on page 359.

Audio, visually.

What other devices are used in print to make sound visible?

Scoring the Usage Test

Tally the opinions of the entire class. If you agree with the majority, mark your answer right. If not, mark it wrong. The student with the highest score is the winner.

An Apostrophe for Your Journal

What do you think of the above method of determining correctness? How closely does it correspond to the realities of determining acceptable usage? *Who* determines correctness?

The "Experts"

This usage test was given to ten groups of people. Here they are in random order. Which group do you think would be more likely to accept these usages? Rearrange the list with those who would accept most readily first and those who would accept least readily last. Then turn to page 360 for the actual ordering and more comments about the list.

1. professional authors __________
2. *Harper's Magazine* subscribers __________
3. college teachers of English __________
4. radio columnists __________
5. lexicographers __________
6. editors of women's magazines __________
7. high school English teachers in cities. __________
8. high school English teachers in small towns __________
9. book publishing firms __________
10. editors of general magazines __________

"Acceptance ratio," A.R., is an index reached by figuring out the percentage of yes votes to total vote cast by that group.

College teachers of English were the most liberal, with an A.R. of 70. A majority rejected only No. 4 and No. 7. Many professors accepted all usages. Lexicographers were next most liberal with an A.R. of 65. Those questioned included members of the editorial staffs of Merriam-Webster, Winston, Random House, and Funk and Wagnalls dictionaries, as well as H. L. Mencken. Professional authors and editors of general magazines and those on staffs of book publishing firms had respective A.R.'s of 56.14 and 56.11. Radio columnists turned in an A.R. of 51.7 and high school English teachers an A.R. of 51.4. However, half of the high school teachers voted acceptance of only nine of the usages. Especially conservative were teachers from small towns. Harper's subscribers had an A.R. of 50. Feature writers and newspaper columnists gave an A.R. of 47. Editors of women's magazines were most conservative, scoring an A.R. of only 45.

The survey also breaks down the nineteen sentences in terms of "Established English"—an expression accepted by 75% of people questioned; Acceptable—a usage agreed to by 50% to 75%; Controversial—35% to 50%; Rejected—below 35%. These usages fared this way: **Established:** No.'s 2—I *will* pay; 5—*nice* time; 11—*awful* headache; 15—preposition to end a sentence *with*; and 16—Go *slow.* **Acceptable:** No.'s 1—*mad* as angry; 9—have *got*; 10—*due to* as because; 13—*further* as farther; 14—split infinitive; 17—It is *me.* **Controversial:** No.'s 3—The reason is *because*; 6—*can* for may; 8—everyone. . . their; 12—We only have five books; 19—*Who* did you meet? **Rejected:** No.'s 4—different *than* mine; 7—*less* difficulties; 18—She acts as if she *was* my wife.

How does your scoring of the items on the test compare with this criterion?

JAMES THURBER

THURBER: Well, someone once wrote a definition of the difference between English and American humor. I wish I could remember his name. I thought his definition very good. He said that the English treat the commonplace as if it were remarkable and the Americans treat the remarkable as if it were commonplace. I believe that's true of humorous writing. Years ago we did a parody of *Punch* in which Benchley did a short piece depicting a wife bursting into a room and shouting "The primroses are in bloom!"—treating the commonplace as remarkable, you see. In *The Secret Life of Walter Mitty* I tried to treat the remarkable as commonplace. . . .

I never quite know when I'm not writing. Sometimes my wife comes up to me at a party and says, "Dammit, Thurber, stop writing." She usually catches me in the middle of a paragraph. Or my daughter will look up from the dinner table and ask, "Is he sick?" "No," my wife says, "He's writing something." I have to do it that way on account of my eyes. I still write occasionally—in the proper sense of the word—using black crayon on yellow paper and getting perhaps twenty words to the page.

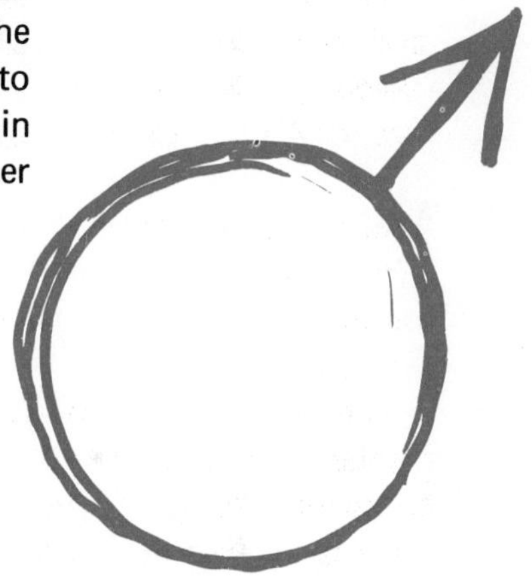

Some Generalizing Questions:

Should the opinions of the experts—the lexicographers and college teachers of English—be favored?

Why do you think editors of women's magazines were the most conservative? Why are lexicographers among the most liberal?

Does this survey support impressions of "correctness" you normally get from textbooks? How does language change?

You don't have to know how to spell to write poetry. You can be rather loose in your syntax as far as I am concerned. You don't have to know how to punctuate at all. Poe has nothing but dashes in his poems because he left punctuation to his printers. They kept too many of his dashes.

You don't need to know how to punctuate. I am proud I can write a telegram without putting the word "stop" in it. If I can't do that, I don't know how to write anything. I go that far.

And then you have to begin with something. You have to know how you write in free verse and in regular verse. You have to know that borderline between prose and verse and feel for it. And then you have to know something about the way verse has been written. You don't have to know all those forms. You just have to know strict iambic and loose iambic. That's all I know. You look at my poems.

Then you have to know what an *idea* is, in a joke or in a poem. You have to know how to make a point, to point up an idea. You have got to know the difference between an idea that will do in prose or in talk and all that, and one that is more poetical. I think you can go as deep as philosophy goes. You look for philosophy in the newspapers. It is one of my interests to see who writes the spirited editorials. I think of one. He is the front-page editorial man on the Atlanta *Constitution*, a brave man. He knows the difference between Southerners who take the Civil War wrong and those who take it right. He does it with a good deal of emotion. Anyway, poetry is not prose. It has to be a passionate thought.

The way to know about that is to read the beginnings of poems, see how they begin, how they launch out. See how soon they launch you into feeling, tone, air. That's all there is to it. It sounds simple. All you have to do is do it.

I have often tried to tell what an idea is. It is a feat of association. That's one of my definitions for it. It reaches its height in a good metaphor. Many metaphors are unemotional. Every philosopher has one big metaphor in him. That is all he has. One says the world is like unto that in man which is called "reason." That's the whole thing in Plato. Schopenhauer says the universe is like unto that in man which is called "will." Darwin's one thought is "natural selection"—the universe is a selective thing. Then he writes books on books to elaborate that. Nothing more to it. You can go right down the list.

The latest is, it is like unto that in man which is called "number." All can be reduced to number. Count it. You have got to get a number and see how many times it multiplies, and that's the universe. Another of Plato's figures of speech is that everything we have here is an imperfect copy of something somewhere else. If you sit in a chair, it is an imperfect copy of something somewhere else. Figures are daring. Effrontery is part of it. No figure has ever caught the whole thing.

You can see people nowadays trying to make one world. They try to decide what you would make out of it. *Love.* That is terrible, because *hate* is almost equal. There is no unity. We used to say money is the root of all evil. I saw a book called *Love Is the Root.* It went through my head when I looked at it that love is the root of all evil—one natural progression of the thought.

The strange thing is how tonal poems have to be. Prose doesn't need to be so tonal, but poetry has two things, meter and rhythm. Meter is a set thing, like a tennis court or a checkerboard, and on it you perform with rhythm. Neither of these is the poem. It is the stress of one on the other that lifts a sound from it, a tone from it, that is the poem.

When they want me to lay it on thick, they like me to say one of my own, *"Provide! Provide!"*

Now I want to be talked *to*. You can be a little ungrammatical if you come from the right part of the country. I don't want that to go too far. It all comes down to, every good thing you say is a dip for depth. You can or you can't. Some have it, and some don't. Some can write prose and think away in it, but it has got to be as deep as you can go in thought and take your emotions with you. The amusing part of my saying all this is that it doesn't matter at all. You probably know all about it.

I can tell when I get a little book of poetry or look at a manuscript: first thing, is it doing anything to my ear in some way of its own? Is it being successful in the relation of rhythm and meter? I can make short work of it; one or two poems and I can tell whether the person knows what it's all about. If I'm wrong, try the poem on another reader! I am always interested in whether the rhymes seem successful. I don't want it to look as if it's giving the writer trouble.

QUESTION: Was it Emerson as a philosopher or as a poet that most attracted you?

ANSWER: Emerson is the same person in his poetry as in his prose. There is a touch of melancholy that is just right. "Evil will bless and ice will burn." Emerson is a real poet in prose or verse. I heard that some teacher had trouble teaching Emerson in a college. He told me the boys came and said, "You cannot put that old stuff over on us." He let them get away with it. He ought to have shot them all! Emerson is clever and witty. All sorts of thoughts. He throws his weight about in all sorts of thinking.

QUESTION: I was interested in your using rhythm and meter together. What do you think of free verse, which has rhythm but no meter? How do you feel about it?

ANSWER: It's quite a difficult thing. Prose can have rhythm and meter. But it does not have these two acting on each other, the rhythm acting on the meter.

Let's put *this* straight. First of all, the coupling that moves you, that stirs you, is an association of two things you don't expect to see associated. The words used to be "surprise" and "inevitability." You can get that in prose. There is much great prose. When prose is the way it ought to be, it has rhythm. The other kind of prose is *declare, declare, declare* until you don't know what to do with your voice when you're reading it.

I am not asking for poetry. I can read Charles Lamb aloud to everybody. Other prose—I get sick of it before reading too far. You read it to yourself. That's the difference between a lecture read from a piece of paper and an extemporaneous talk. The littlest lyrics have this drama in them. Poetry gives your voice so many ways of behaving—cutting up with your voice.

That's very important, you know, in all our writing. In all the darn stuff I ever read in theme papers, it was as if there was no *esprit* in them. I once said to the class, "I'm not going to read them any more." I'm no perfunctory reader of perfunctory writing. I come here with a certain eagerness to tell you something, I tell my class. I want some of them to tell *me* something. I say, "Haven't you anything to tell me? Haven't you seen *into* anything lately? Seen *through* anything lately?"

QUESTION: How do you penetrate a poem that you don't understand?

ANSWER: How do you penetrate a lunkhead? One of your prides in life is that you know what's going on on any page. If I'm not smart enough, I miss it. I don't waive judgement. I don't say, I'm not up to that. Somebody's to blame and it's *not me!*

You take certain kinds of things that you see. I don't like loathsomeness in a poem. I'd just as soon step into something nasty on the street, if you know what I mean. I don't like botheration. The emotion of being bothered is no emotion. It's got to be amusement. It's one on me, for instance, if this world has to be ruled; if it gets so that it can only be managed by socialism, it would be one on me. I'd write a funny poem about myself. It amuses me that some of my friends say I have got to face it—overpopulation. One of the nice things that might happen; we might die from being too many, too close quarters. It would be one on me.

QUESTION: What do you read today for pleasure?

ANSWER: Lots and lots.

A young poet came to see me and asked me why I never mentioned him on the platform. I said, "My dear boy, I never mention anybody but Shakespeare!" When I was teaching, I never said "very good" on papers; I couldn't say good or bad to my students. They knew I was interested in the paper they wrote. If it arouses a thought in me, that's the great thing. I am not going to stand up here and tell you who can and who cannot write. You can tell something if you watch my life, whom I associate with, whom I quote a little, who comes into my thoughts. You can say they can all go down the sinkhole but Shakespeare.

I was talking with Mr. Nims the other day about giving grades. It is hard to tell the difference between A, B, C, and D. I can tell triple A, but I cannot tell the difference between A, B, C, and D. I haven't that kind of discrimination.

It makes me laugh to hear, "You were pretty good, considering you were a freshman; you were pretty good, considering you were a sophomore; a junior; considering you had only two years in graduate school." It is nothing at all. Most deceptive. There is good and not good. Keats was writing the same as he ever did, very early. So was Shelley. All of a sudden, he was doing it. You could have marked him A, good enough. I used to pass the students in my classes, after I had bothered them a year; I'd pass them out of pity so they wouldn't have to take the course again. I used to ask too much of them. I'd let them get by. I have been very, very, very terrible.

I remember talking to a class, a little group I

had once. I said, I don't want to see anything you've written until it has some age on it. Get at it. Get writing so you can have something to select from later. One of them said, "If I kept it awhile, I wouldn't show it to you; I'd throw it away." I said, "That'll save me from throwing it away."

There was one fellow—I don't know where he is now, but he became a professor. I started talking to him about using his own judgment. The most terrible thing is your own judgment. He set out suffering. I never saw the writing at all. He let me think he was suffering agonies. Never wrote anything.

One day I said to him, "Bill," I said, "you haven't written anything, have you?" He said, "No, sir." I said, "Now, look, we've done this on the high too long. You want to graduate?" He said, "Yes, sir." I said, "Now we're goin' to do it on the low. I'm not going to *read* what you write. But you're going to deliver to me so many pounds of it to weigh."

One night he came over to me in the library, where I was sitting with a student, and produced another pound. My friend waved him out. We were groping our way out of the building later (the lights were turned off); we saw a light under a door. I opened the door. There was a long table, a big brass projector, and there was this fellow asleep, waiting for me.

I had put him through a lot of agony, so he deserved to graduate.

QUESTION: Does the American poet have a special opportunity or challenge?

ANSWER: There is no challenge except the challenge of life to pull off something that *is* something. What is the idea? If you remember only one thing I've said, remember that *an idea is a feat of association,* and the height of it is a good metaphor. If you have never made a good metaphor, then you don't know what it's all about. You save an argument sometimes by using a figure they haven't time to attack or answer.

The first thing I ever wrote was a ballad. It was written hell for leather. It had a heroic sound. It was all heroes. It is heroic. Brave. That is the greatest emotion of all, to be brave. Brave.

TRANSMUTATION

See how well you can translate this picture into verbal symbols. What are the problems involved in getting your reader to experience the exact curve of the feeling you experience looking at it? What must you do to get him to see what you see, to feel what you feel? Would you do it in a poem, a story, an essay?

Compare your results with those of your classmates. Do some come closer than others? Can you specify what causes some to be more or less successful than others?

What do you observe about the process of going from the nonverbal to the verbal? What "tricks of the trade" do you notice? (One treatment of the subject is on page 481.)

UNA CLAVE EN LA CABEZA

Take this sentence (or any other for that matter, but the whole class should use the same sentence):

"Are these excerpts a writing lesson?"

to someone who knows German, French, Russian, Japanese. Ask him to write out a translation for you. Observe the kinds of questions he asks you. See what reactions your classmates noted. (Are all the German translations identical, the French, the Japanese?)

What significance can you give these responses?

In what sense is this investigation similar to the "transmutation" investigation preceding?

What can you and your classmates discover from this investigation about our own communication system?

WRITERS ON LEARNING TO WRITE

Examine the reactions of these fourteen rather diverse professional writers to their own experiences in studying grammar and literature.

What kind of general conclusions would you be inclined to draw?

After you have explored in your journal the implications of this survey, see if your classmates can expand its possibilities.

What are the strengths and weaknesses of such a study? Can you extend its significance beyond writing?

Art does not replace the visible. It makes visible.

No. 1: Do you recall that your formal schooling included much formal grammar? work in composition, rhetoric, style?

Pearl Buck: No, I was a constant reader of good books.

William F. Buckley, Jr.: Composition—yes. Rhetoric—no. Style—no. Formal grammar—it didn't. I studied grammar mostly in foreign languages.

Stuart Chase: No, not much.

Norman Cousins: Yes, my formal schooling included work in formal grammar, composition, etc.

Clifton Fadiman: Yes.

Ernest K. Gann: Yes, it did. Too much. I had plenty of trouble and still do.

Harry Golden: No—all I recall is reading.

John Hersey: Yes, from the ninth grade on in a private secondary school. *Rigorous* training. Omission of a comma, connecting the clauses of a compound sentence, meant a failing mark in any paper. On the positive side, great stress was placed on the beauty of correct rhetoric.

Aldous Huxley: Some grammar, a lot of "essay" writing, encouragement to write poems and stories. My education was classical and style was stressed in regard to composition in Latin (and Greek) prose and verse.

Martin Mayer: A fair amount—but all of it in an eighth-grade New York City public school. I have no recollection of much grammar instruction in my high school, though we did a good deal of writing, usually on topics associated with the books we were reading.

James Michener: Yes, and it turned out to be very helpful. Formal grammar was well taught, composition fairly well taught, rhetoric not taught, style not taught. I am speaking, of course, of high school.

Irwin Shaw: Little grammar, rhetoric, style—great deal of composition.

Dr. Benjamin Spock: A moderate amount of grammar and composition in high school.

No. 2: What did you gain from school grammar (or rhetoric or other) instruction of measurable influence in your writing career?

Buck: Nothing.

Buckley: Nothing.

Chase: Nothing to my knowledge.

Cousins: I received a foundation in the processes of logical thought which freed me to write easily, in the knowledge that I wasn't making grammatical bloopers.

Fadiman: I learned to write clear, *correct* English.

Gann: Very little except encouragement—thanks to an outstanding professor.

Golden: Do not recall a thing.

Hersey: A sense that an easy style, characterized by clarity, rhythmic flow, and an absence of affectation, could only be achieved through grammatical precision.

Huxley: Presumably, a habit of writing "correct" English.

Mayer: I picked up a dislike of solecism somewhere—I guess it was in school. But I was involved in "publishing" from third grade on (a friend of mine and I put out a sports periodical in third grade, based largely on my friend's interviews with Babe Ruth, who lived in his house). So I had my name on my writing in *public* from an early point in the game.

Michener: I learned what a good many writers apparently never learn, the construction of a clause, a sentence, and a paragraph. I appreciated diagramming, because I later came to use it, and I learned a great deal from the study of Latin.

Shaw: Nothing.

Spock: Hard to say. I enjoyed grammar as a sort of game, like mathematical problems.

No. 3: In what way was your interest in writing influenced by grammar studies?

Buck: None.

Buckley: Not at all.

Chase: In no way.

Cousins: My interest in writing was not influenced by grammar studies, except in the sense mentioned under question two.

Fadiman: In no way.

Gann: Not at all.

Golden: No way.

Hersey: We diagrammed sentences, and I saw that language had a kind of architecture, that sentences and paragraphs could be solidly and beautifully built.

Mayer: I don't think grammar studies influenced my interest in writing one way or the other.

Michener: Probably not at all. However, I later taught grammar myself in a high school and had to learn the subject professionally. This did help me and did inspire me to do some writing myself.

Shaw: Not at all.

Spock: I rather doubt that it was.

No. 4: Did you appreciate grammar study in school at the time as you look back now?

Buck: No.

Buckley: No.

Chase: No.

Cousins: No. I didn't like grammar study, though I recognized its importance. In short, I didn't like it, then or now, but I *appreciated* its importance.

Fadiman: It was a task to be done, not something to be "appreciated." Education is not for the purpose of making the child happy.

Gann: No. It just must be done.

Golden: No.

Hersey: Oh, yes, it was made distinctly enjoyable. The enthusiasm and conviction of fine teachers made grammar—as they would make prosody or musical theory or principles of design in art—a servant of beauty, and therefore of pleasure.

Huxley: Most of my grammar studies were mixed with Latin, Greek, French, German grammar—cannot say that I greatly enjoyed them.

Mayer: It was a bore. But most of school was a bore.

Michener: Yes, and as I look back on it I think that my judgment in school was about correct, that it was necessary in order to get a feeling for the structure of the language, even though at the time I did not have any idea that I would ultimately write.

Shaw: No and No.

Spock: See second question.

No. 5: Did teachers rather than the subject of English grammar make a difference in your comprehension of the subject?

Buck: Yes.

Buckley: Yes.

Chase: Yes. A good teacher opened up doors.

Cousins: Yes, the teacher made quite a difference. A warm, concerned teacher makes all the difference, especially in so cold and arid a subject as grammar.

Fadiman: Both.

Gann: Teachers.

Golden: The teacher who inspired us to *READ.*

Hersey: Yes, see No. 4.

Huxley: Obviously. Teaching is an art and, as in all the arts, there are more indifferent performances than good ones. Children learn a lot from good artists in teaching, little or nothing from poorer artists.

Mayer: I don't think so. The experience of publishing, and being ashamed of my own stuff—in school and college papers—was far more important than any aspect of formal instruction, including the temperament and personality of my teachers.

Michener: I would say that the grammar itself was the major value. As a matter of fact, I can't even remember who taught me the grammar.

Shaw: No.

Spock: Teachers make a big difference in any subject.

No. 6: Did your study of a foreign language in school influence your ability as a writer?

Buck: No.

Buckley: I expect so, though I'm not sure.

Chase: No. Latin sometimes told me where an English word came from.

Cousins: No, I doubt that a foreign language influenced my style.

Fadiman: Yes.

Gann: No. But highly recommend it for other reasons.

Golden: It would have helped greatly!

Hersey: I grew up more or less bilingual, in Chinese and English; this must surely have sharpened my ear for meanings.

Huxley: Yes.

Mayer: No. I had only Latin in school, which if anything reinforced the normal bright-juvenile habit of overly Latinate construction. Maybe it helped a little, by making me conscious of what I wanted to avoid.

Michener: As I said above, my study of Latin was very helpful. Also, I learned to speak Spanish moderately well and this was of great value to me in getting me to read novels written in that language and they have been of great help.

Shaw: No.

Spock: No; or at least not much.

No. 7: Did you learn the conventions of writing in school through classwork, or in private study or other means?

Buck: No.

Buckley: School through classwork.

Chase: Composition indicated that a sentence needed a verb. Mostly.

Cousins: I learned writing—as opposed to composing themes—in the actual process of turning out copy for publications. Naturally, this learning process involved a great deal of school and private study, but it all "jelled" only in writing for the deadline in the commercial world.

Fadiman: All means.

Gann: A little of everything—mostly trial and error. The study of conventional writers can easily be overdone. Develop your own style.

Golden: Reading—nothing else.

Hersey: Through classwork, primarily.

Huxley: Composition was done in class, criticized and corrected by the teacher.

Mayer: I don't like your phrase "conventions of writing." I have visceral reactions to language, as I do to music, and I had them from a fairly early age. I worked up (mostly, I guess, by myself) from Belloc and Chesterton to Shaw and Mencken and Twain, to Bryon and Shelley, to Hopkins; for a while it was Thomas Wolfe, then Huxley, then Orwell, then Joyce, Shakespeare, of course, from early on.

Michener: I learned a good deal in college from a very helpful history teacher. Mostly I learned it through private study.

Shaw: Never learned them.

Spock: I assume that the most important factor is growing up in a family that reads and speaks and writes, and that the influence of school is secondary.

No. 8: What has been the greatest influence on your writing ability?

Buck: Reading great books.

Buckley: My father—whose observations about everybody and everything were preceded by an evaluation of subjects' writing ability.

Chase: A natural curiosity to understand a given situation—war, depression, labor-management, automation, semantics—and then to explain it as lucidly as possible.

Cousins: Meeting many different kinds of people and conceiving a desire to tell others about them.

Fadiman: I have no idea—I just write, and learn by writing.

Gann: This question would take hours to answer.

Golden: Reading other writers.

Hersey: Not what, but who, King James' committee of translators, Tolstoi, Cervantes, Melville, Tsao Hsueh-chin, Stendhal, Conrad; and teachers, named Edgar, Haight, McChesney, Tinker, Williams, Chiappe.

Huxley: Reading. A keen interest in the problems of expression. A liking for language as such. Constant practice.

Mayer: Reading. Especially my own writing, with distaste.

Michener: Wide reading of people who can write better than I can write.

Shaw: Impossible to answer.

Spock: (Aside from general literacy level of family), my mother insisted, during any absence from home, that we write vivid, detailed descriptions of all happenings, people.

No. 9: What effect did reading have on your interest in writing?

Buck: Profound effect.

Buckley: Considerable.

Chase: Immense! The major stimulant! Not assigned books either. My uncle's library where I roamed at will—Homer, Dante with Doré drawings, Goethe, the works!

Cousins: Reading had an immense effect on my writing: it expanded my horizons, put me in touch with minds I could emulate and interact with despite barriers of time and place.

Fadiman: Obviously a considerable one—writers read, don't they?

Gann: It is one of the most important things *any* writer can do.

Golden: Everything depended on my *Reading.*

Hersey: The great writers are great teachers of writing. One learns to read on two levels—for immediate pleasure, and for fascination with the methods the writer has used to achieve his effects.

Huxley: See No. 3.

Mayer: Enormous. I was imitating other people's styles from the moment I could write. I have a hunch that only two composition exercises are really helpful—trying to write something in someone else's style, and trying to edit someone else's copy to maintain his style. They are valuable because there is a standard against which you can measure what you have done.

Michener: By the time I left college I had read almost all of the standard novels written in other languages that had been translated into English, and I mean *all.* This was of great help to me in formulating attitudes toward writing.

Shaw: Reading is the beginning of any writer's career, long before he has any notion he wants to write.

Spock: I read a lot and assume that it set tastes and created identification with writers.

No. 10: From your experience what would you recommend that English teachers stress to increase students' writing capabilities?

Buck: Writing without criticism.

Buckley: The students' ears should be stimulated to listen and imitate good rhythms, a rich vocabulary: a stress should always be laid on verbal competence.

Chase: Reading and good writing. Writing accounts of personal experiences which interested—involved—the student.

Cousins: I'd recommend the British system: the student completes a reading assignment in, say, history, then writes a short, compact account of what he has read, appending a short critique. For classroom purposes, the "paper" need not exceed a page or so. These papers are read aloud: fuzziness, lack of precision, etc., are then seen clearly by teacher and the other students.

Fadiman: Correct every error, with reasons; do not coddle; do not encourage "self-expression;" *force* them to read at least three good books a week, outside of school.

Gann: *Imagination!*

Golden: To *Read*—there is no short cut—alas!

Hersey: Precision, clarity, and a personal rhythm. Above all: to treat words as if they were people.

Huxley: Plenty of reading—above all of good books slightly *above* the children's current capacity. Also plenty of composition in verse, in fiction, in "essay" form.

Mayer: Stylistic imitation. For this purpose, however, the object of imitation must have style. Newspaper stories are often suitable—the scorn for "journalism" is a mistake. Magazine articles, however, are rarely suitable. Good criticism—of literature, music, theatre, art, past or present—is often splendid as a model.

Michener: I certainly think that English teachers ought to do all they can to increase students' writing capabilities, but I am not sure that they can do very much.

Shaw: Demand clarity, honesty, knowledge of the subject being written about.

Spock: Lots of practice in composition, with a friendly, inspiring teacher whom the students will want to imitate; along with reading which interests the students. (But this will bore students from relatively illiterate families.)

No. 11: What quality or qualities in writing do you believe students should strive for?

Buck: Freedom of expression.

Buckley: An agreeable rhythm.

Chase: Have *content,* something to write about. Simplicity—no "fine" writing, no showing off, no gobbledegook. An understanding that words are not things, and must be handled with care and precision.

Cousins: I think students should above all strive for clarity and simplicity, using basic words, without resort to fancy talk. This discipline will enable them finally to forget about form, grammar, and such, and to concentrate instead on what it is they want to say.

Fadiman: *Clarity, Economy, Correctness*—The larger virtues are those that only real writers will come to cultivate.

Gann: Brevity in words, richness in what those carefully chosen words say.

Golden: I'm a reporter and not given to sermons. My observation: you can not be a writer unless you are a reader—even Shakespeare!

Hersey: Two: a knowledge of how to use the tools of writing and a personal tone of style.

Huxley: Clarity, first of all. Coherence. Orderliness: Those who take an esthetic interest in language and its uses should be encouraged to study good models and to analyze the means employed for the achievement of the results obtained.

Mayer: Sensitivity to the fact of style—that such a thing exists and creates meaning. For this reason, students should not be asked to develop "their own style" any more than they should be graded simply on the basis of formally correct or incorrect usage. Models should be before them—and before their teachers—at all times.

Michener: I believe that the great drive of all writing is communication with another person and students should strive to accomplish this.

Shaw: Same as No. 10.

Spock: Detail, color, personal flavor.

H. Allen Smith found that a letter best answered the questionnaire. Because of its candor, I want to quote the entire letter.

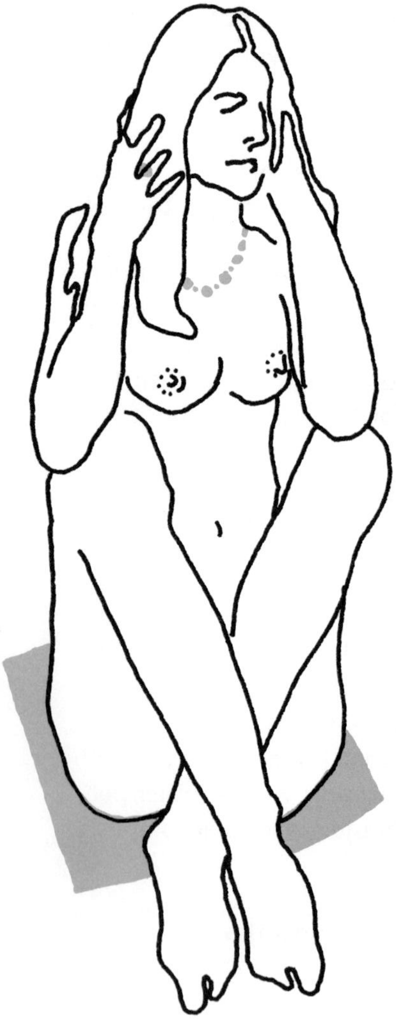

Dear Mr. Lowe:

I am not the guy for you. I just barely made it through the eighth grade. As of today I could not pass the simplest test in grammar. I know what is a noun and what is a verb and what is an adjective and that is about the extent of my knowledge of grammar.

I had not read a serious book of any kind until I was twenty and married. Yet I could write. It is my notion that a person can write or he can't. If he can't he can go twenty years to Harvard and Oxford and his stuff will still come out wooden. In other words, I don't think there are many individuals who can be *taught* to write. This is an unhappy situation—I know, from various sources, that about two-thirds of all college students have an idea they want to be writers. I get a steady flow of mail from them and much of it is obviously the work of semi-literate people. When I was twenty I was a newspaperman, had been on eight or ten papers in various parts of the country. I was accepted by my colleagues as a drinking pal and story-telling pal, but one day it occurred to me that I seldom understood what they were talking about most of the time—I mean books and authors and so on. So I went to work educating myself, and spent ten years reading, seldom going out evenings, taking notes as I read. In my recent autobiographical book *To Hell in a Handbasket* there is a letter from Bergen Evans suggesting that I am as well educated as he is, and he has all kinds of letters to go after his name. I don't know grammar except by ear. I have no scruples at all about making grammatical errors. If the sentence reads right to me, if it has flow, I don't give a damn whether it's grammatically right or wrong.

Sorry to be so negative.

/s/ H. ALLEN SMITH

FRANK O'CONNOR

INTERVIEWER: Do you think of a novel as a lot of short stories or one big short story?

O'CONNOR: It ought to be one big short story, and not one big short story, but one big novel. That's the real trouble—the novel is not a short story—there's your twenty-four-hour novel, that's what's wrong with it, it's a short story, and that's what's wrong with Hemingway, wrong with most of them; the span is too small. The span of a novel ought to be big. There is this business of the long short story turned out as a novel, and I'm all the time getting them. The span is too brief; there is nothing to test these characters by. Take *Ulysses*, which is twenty-four hours, and I maintain it's a long short story. And it was written as a short story, don't forget that. It was originally entitled *Mr. Hunter's Day.* And it's still *Mr. Hunter's Day* and it still is thirty pages. It's all development sideways. That's really what I was talking about: the difference between the novel which is a development, an extension into time, and this novel, which is not a novel, which is an extension sideways. It doesn't lead forward, it doesn't lead your mind forward. *Anglo-Saxon Attitudes* is the same: "So now boys, having finished with this brief moment of our novel, we'll go backward for a while." And all the time they're just going out like that because they're afraid to go forward.

B.C. **by johnny hart**

By permission of Johnny Hart and Publishers-Hall Syndicate.

NOW PUT THE FOUNDATIONS UNDERNEATH THEM

Seeing that truth consisteth in the right ordering of names in our affirmations, a man that seeketh precise truth had need to remember what every name he useth stands for, and to place it accordingly, or else he will find himself entangled in words as a bird in lime twigs—the more he struggles the more belimed. And therefore in geometry, which is the only science that it hath pleased God hitherto to bestow on mankind, men begin at settling the significations of their words; which settling of significations they call definitions, and place them in the beginning of their reckoning.

By this, it appears how necessary it is for any man that aspires to true knowledge to examine the definitions of former authors; and either to correct them where they are negligently set down, or to make them himself. For the errors of definitions multiply themselves according as the reckoning proceeds, and lead men into absurdities, which at last they see, but cannot avoid without reckoning anew from the beginning, in which lies the foundation of their errors. From whence it happens that they which trust to books do as they that cast up many little sums into a greater, without considering whether those little sums were rightly cast up or not; and at last, finding the error visible and not mistrusting their first grounds, know not which way to clear themselves, but spend time in fluttering over their books, as birds that, entering by the chimney and finding themselves inclosed in a chamber, flutter at the false light of a glass window, for want of wit to consider which way they came in. So that in the right definition of names lies the first use of speech, which is the acquisition of science; and in wrong or no definitions lies the first abuse; from which proceed all false and senseless tenets, which make those men that take their instruction from the authority of books, and not from their own meditation, to be as much below the condition of ignorant men as men endued with true science are above it. For between true science and erroneous doctrines, ignorance is in the middle. Natural sense and imagination are not subject to absurdity. Nature itself cannot err, and as men abound in copiousness of language, so they become more wise or more mad than ordinary. Nor is it possible without letters for any man to become either excellently wise, or, unless his memory be hurt by disease or ill constitution of organs, excellently foolish. For words are wise men's counters,—they do but reckon by them; but they are the money of fools, that value them by the authority of an Aristotle, a Cicero, or a Thomas, or any other doctor whatsoever, if but a man. . . .

FRANÇOISE SAGAN

SAGAN . . . Very broadly, I think one writes and rewrites the same book. I lead a character from book to book, I continue along with the same ideas. Only the angle of vision, the method, the lighting, change. Speaking very, very roughly, it seems to me there are two kinds of novels—there is that much choice. There are those which simply tell a story and sacrifice a great deal to the telling—like the books of Benjamin Constant which *Bonjour tristesse* and *Un Certain sourire* resemble in construction. And then there are those books which attempt to discuss and probe the characters and events in the book—*un roman où l'on discute.* The pitfalls of both are obvious: in the simple narrative it often seems that the important questions are passed over. In the longer classical novel the digressions can impair the effectiveness.

What is the difference between "real" and "actual"?

What is the difference between "verisimilitude" and "truth"?

"Why don't we knock off for today?"

No manufactured object could be less complicated than Ishi's fire drill, which consists of a lower and an upper piece: a woman piece and a man piece, as he symbolized them. The hearth or lower piece is a flat slab of wood which should be somewhat softer than the wood of the shaft or twirler. Willow or cedar make good hearths, if seasoned and dry and not too old and brittle. One or more sockets are bored or gouged out with an obsidian knife to the depth of a quarter inch or so, and notched at one side. The notch leads into a shallow channel cut from the socket to the edge of the hearth.

The drill, or upper piece, is an ordinary round stick of a size to fit the hearth socket, about the length of an arrow shaft, but larger at one end. Ishi preferred buckeye for his drills, but sage brush, poison oak, or indeed any fairly hard wood will answer equally well The making of fire with this drill rests upon the principle of concentration in one small spot, for only so can the human arm twirl fast and long enough to produce sufficient friction between hearth and drill to convert moving wood into heat.

When ready to begin drilling, Ishi first strewed tinder—usually dried moss, or thistledown, or finely shredded inner bark of willow —along the notch and channel of the hearth and on the ground where the channel led off the board. He then squatted, holding the ends of the hearth steady against the ground with his toes, or he might occasionally kneel on the hearth to hold it. Next, he placed the drill upright, the larger end in one of the sockets, grasped it between the palms of his open hands as they were pressed together and then rubbed back and forth in opposite directions. With each motion the drill was forced to rotate, first to right, then to left. His hands at the same time were bearing downward, pressing the revolving stick into the socket. Small particles of wood were ground off the sides of the socket, becoming fine sawdust or wood powder which began to turn brown, to smoke a little, to turn darker and darker to charcoal, and to smoke in good earnest, at the same time being forced by the accumulating mass out of the socket into the notch, along the channel, and so off the edge of the hearth. Ishi, at this point, worked faster and faster as he approached his goal, keeping the stick twirling furiously until a tiny spark suddenly glowed within the charred and powdered wood. The effective spark formed, not in the bottom of the socket where it would be quenched by an excess of wood dust, but just outside, in the notch, from whence it traveled, spreading down the channel and onto the pile of tinder on the ground. Once this was alight, he added a small bunch of grass to it, and some coarser shavings; he blew gently on the young flame, and fire was "made."

Considerable strength and much skill are needed to achieve this result, however. The drill must be firmly and continuously pressed into the hearth—strength and coordination are both needed for this. On the other hand, too heavy a pressure at the outset will exhaust the operator's strength, so that when the crucial moment comes and the spark is nearly at hand, there is no reserve for the added push. Also, as the hands bear down on the drill, they gradually slip downward along it, until, just before the hearth is touched by them, the palms must be quickly raised to the upper end of the stick. The drill actually stands still at this time, which means that the change of hand position must be done so deftly and rapidly that the heated contact point does not cool. If the hands are shifted as the spark is about to appear, the moment of no motion may prove disastrous. This is probably what happened when Waterman attempted to demonstrate the drill.

The whole process calls for manual tact of a kind that only experience can teach. The fire must be coaxed out of the unwilling wood—coaxed and nursed. Haste, violence of motion rather than strength, continuity and rhythm will accomplish nothing, nor will indifference, lassitude, or a moment's let-up. Ishi's patience, perseverance, and delicate control were precisely the requisite qualities.

HOW TO SUCCEED. . .

Following are directions for successful paragraphs and themes. Have you seen similar instructions in other texts? You have read what a number of professional writers have said about how they go about writing. How closely do their comments parallel these directions?

In this section you have been investigating actual writing practices. As you think over what has been said, what general rules for writing do you think emerge? Talk it over with other students and collect a list of meaningful writing suggestions. Which of the directions on the next pages are significant enough to be included? Which of them were mentioned by people who earn their living by writing?

When you have completed your list, generalize about the teaching of writing in schools. Which practices should be discontinued? Which should be emphasized?

When one has no character, one has to apply a method.

Directions for Successful Paragraphs

1. *Unity*

   See that the paragraph contains only those ideas which contribute to the main idea or topic of the paragraph.

2. *Topic Sentence*

   Include in each paragraph a topic sentence at the beginning or end that emphasizes or clarifies the main idea of the paragraph.

3. *Orderly Plan*

   Arrange your sentences in a clear pattern of time, position, or place so that your reader can follow the thought.

4. *Transitional Words*

   Use transition words to help your reader follow the shifts in your thoughts.

   place: here, there, beyond
   addition: for example, besides, and furthermore, too
   contrast: however, instead, but, still
   time: now, later, at first, meanwhile
   conclusion or summary: thus, in review, in short

5. *Clincher Sentence*

   Emphasize the main idea of the paragraph with a good clincher sentence.

Directions for Successful Themes

1. *Subject*

   Make a list of possibilities. Then select one that you can treat completely and convincingly. Write from your own experiences and feelings.

2. *Audience*

   Decide to whom you are writing. Keep this audience in mind as you write.

3. *Purpose*

   Have a purpose clearly in mind as you compose: to convince, to entertain, to inform.

4. *Data*

   Get your ideas on paper. Jot down all the ideas and details on a scratch pad as they come to you. Later you can select the data you will actually use without the risk of forgetting them.

Slept their dream...
said their nevers
did their dance
Laughed their cryings

5. *Outline*

   Arrange your data according to some definite plan.

6. *Introductory Paragraph*

   Work carefully to make your first paragraph capture your reader's interest and attention. Be sure this paragraph gives your reader a clear idea of what to expect in your paper.

7. *Emphasis*

   Build your main idea to some definite climax.

8. *Transition*

   Be sure transitions are clear to your reader. Use transitional devices to help make his reading smoother.

9. *Conclusion*

   Your conclusion should pull together the thoughts developed in the separate paragraphs.

10. *Title*

    Choose a title which will engage your reader's curiosity.

11. *Revision*

    Check for

unity:	(delete everything that does not support your main idea),
emphasis:	(your main idea should have the strongest emphasis. All other ideas must be subordinate to it),
coherence:	(be sure your theme has a recognizable plan or pattern).

12. *Final Copy*

    Check your rough draft for mechanics and spelling; eliminate all unnecessary data. Polish any sentences which sound confusing or awkward.

    Then write a clear copy.

Are the products of each man's hands and brain unique? If they are, can we develop the capacity to perceive each man's uniqueness?

You can find out for yourself through the following investigation. After you have given it a fair trial you may find it worthwhile to explore the value of such an exercise.

We have set up this investigation as a game. You are asked to try to figure out who created each of the following specimens. "Who" does not mean the *name* of the individual. Rather, the object is to build a personality sketch based on evidence you are able to glean from the specimen itself. The player who can amass the most complete characterization is the winner. Only after you have exhausted the evidence is it time to guess the name. You do not need a special background to succeed. The name is the least important part. To help you get the knack, we have supplied some help with the first four specimens.

Step one: What is the person like who wrote this passage? How much does he reveal about himself? Jot down everything you know about him. When you are finished, you can compare your sketch with the composite given on the following page. It consists of observations several students made when they examined this passage. How much did you miss? What did you see that they missed?

> So, what about these arrogant meat loaves? Just this. When I first came to the States, I was for a long time homesick for the old country. Of course, as a Viennese, my loathing for Germany was practically my inalienable birthright; but in those distant days I still had the earnest, unshakable belief that Europe was, somehow, the true home of all real culture.
>
> I was entirely too young and too dopey to take stock of what had actually happened there. I overlooked completely that even my dear Austrians, those great music lovers, had allowed Schubert and Mozart to languish into pauperism and to sicken out of this world in their early thirties, and that those great art lovers, the French, had failed to buy a single painting from either Van Gogh or Cézanne during the forty long years those two geniuses had labored among them.
>
> Through all of my visits abroad, I came to the bittersweet knowledge that our Columbia has one proud jewel in her diadem, whose duplicate you may seek in vain in all the other countries of this earth, and that jewel is Generosity. I've been all over, and I've been all over it with everybody, and let me tell you that from that day long ago when the first poor stonecutter had started to cough out his lungs in the quarries of Egypt, until this morning in New York, when somebody served me Crunchy-Cracklies for breakfast, there has never been a people more generous, more openhearted and more careless of its money than the overly washed, too heavily insured, insecure, lovable people of this country.
>
> Naturally, this makes for great hatred of us among all the chronically penurious bastards in the world who squat in sham reverence amidst their noble ruins and glower enviously at our good clothes and our expensive cameras.
>
> Just remember that there are signs posted all over the holy temples of Asia and the sacred cathedrals of Europe warning people not to pee up against their ancient walls. You know damned well

that those signs weren't placed there for the benefit of visiting American tourists. We don't do such things even to the walls of *new* churches, which are sometimes so hideous that there would be plenty of excuse for doing it.

And so I lost my homesickness for Europe, the very first time I went back, and I've never felt another twinge of it since. Certainly I would like to see Chartres, and Carcassonne, and Salzburg, and Venice, again, but I'm not a bit anxious to meet the petty, stingy, money-hungry leeches who, unfortunately, infest these landscapes.

Probably in his sixties. Austrian fervor probably predates Hitler. "I was entirely too young and too dopey"; hence, older now. Naturalized American from Vienna, Austria.

Probably wrote this in the fifties or sixties: The references to heavy insurance, over washing, cameras and Crunchy-Cracklies seem to be of this era.

Broad language spectrum: Literate: arrogant, inalienable, languish, diadem, penurious, sham, glower. Conversational, breathy, vigorous tone. Somewhat indelicate: pee, damned, bastards. Lively, enthusiastic, colorful. Likes strings of modifiers. Ironic: "those great music lovers."

Well traveled: "visits abroad," temples of Asia, cathedrals of Europe; comment about posted signs suggests first-hand observation.

Broadly informed: References to specific details about art, music, architecture.

He has probably had a long, active and varied life, mixing with all levels of society, but he seems to have a special interest in the arts and culture. He speaks his mind with gusto and assurance. He probably likes to try new things; he is probably adventurous. He seems to feel free to say what is on his mind directly and fully. He admits his own shortcomings. He is willing to commit himself fully to a position: "I was *entirely* too young," "I overlooked *completely*," "failed to buy a *single* painting," "never felt a twinge since."

Answer on page 391.

Step Two:

Following are three passages that have to do with the sea. They may or may not have been written by the same person. Can you find enough evidence to determine that they were or were not? See what you can discover about the person who wrote specimen A first. The game will be more effective if you do not look at the profile we have supplied (on the next page) until you and your classmates have used your own eyes to find out all you can.

BENJAMINFRANKLIN

A It was my first descent into the forecastle, and I shall not soon forget my impression of it, caught as I stood on my feet at the bottom of the ladder. Built directly in the eyes of the schooner, it was of the shape of a triangle, along the three sides of which stood the bunks, in double-tier, twelve of them. It was no larger than a hall bedroom in Grub Street, and yet twelve men were herded into it to eat and sleep and carry on all the functions of living. My bedroom at home was not large, yet it could have contained a dozen similar forecastles, and taking into consideration the height of the ceiling, a score at least.

It smelled sour and musty, and by the dim light of the swinging sea-lamp I saw every bit of available wall-space hung deep with sea-boots, oilskins, and garments, clean and dirty, of various sorts. These swung back and forth with every roll of the vessel, giving rise to a brushing sound, as of trees against a roof or wall. Somewhere a boot thumped loudly and at irregular intervals against the wall; and, though it was a mild night on the sea, there was a continual chorus of creaking timbers and bulkheads and of abysmal noises beneath the flooring.

The sleepers did not mind. There were eight of them,—the two watches below,—and the air was thick with the warmth and odor of their breathing, and the ear was filled with the noise of their snoring and of their sighs and half-groans, tokens plain of the rest of the animal-man. But were they sleeping? all of them? Or had they been sleeping? This was evidently the captain's quest,—to find the men who appeared to be asleep and who were not asleep or who had not been asleep very recently. And he went about it in a way that reminded me of a story out of Boccaccio.

The narrator is not a member of the crew. He is either a passenger or an officer: The ship is already underway; a crewman would have stowed his gear in the forecastle to start with.

The writer notices things from a landsman's point of view. He compares the quarters with a hall bedroom in Grub Street. The brushing sound is "as of trees against a roof or wall." The noises, sights and smells are very noticeable to him. A seaman would probably have been quite used to them.

The vocabulary is common to any fairly articulate person. "Abysmal" seems a trifle unusual. The selection of language seems controlled and sure. Nautical language is minimal: forecastle, eyes of the schooner, ladder. "Score" suggests an earlier era, not too common today. "Boccaccio" suggests a fairly literate background (although this could be used to give that appearance).

This is a large sailing ship, but bunks instead of hammocks are used. Before World War I? Obviously an era when captains had considerable power. They are not likely today to behave as described here. Sea lamps were used before days of electric power.

How far back? The flow of sentences and the language seem more like our era than of a century ago. The guess is around 1900.

This man knows something about life at sea around 1900, probably first-hand, but he seems to be more familiar with the land. His writing is controlled; his vocabulary is not academic, either by choice or background. He could have done some reading on his own (Boccaccio). Though this passage is in first person, it seems more like a story than an essay. Even in these three paragraphs, there is a building of suspense and uneasiness. The passage could be adventure fiction, then.

Answer on page 393.

Step Three:

Was the following passage written by the author of specimen A? First gather all the characteristics you can from the passage itself. Then compare the two to see what else is revealed. When you have exhausted your resources, you will find other students' observations on the next page.

B At 4:00 P.M. (it was then quite dark) all hands were called and sent aloft, in a violent squall of hail and rain to take in sail. We had now all got on our "Cape Horn rig," thick boots, southwesters coming down over our necks and ears, thick trousers and jackets, and some with oilcloth suits over all. Mittens, too, we wore on deck; but it would not do to go aloft with them, as, being wet and stiff, they might let a man slip overboard, for all the hold he could get upon a rope; so we were obliged to work with bare hands, which as well as our faces, were often cut with the hailstones, which fell thick and large. Our ship was now all cased with ice—hull, spars, and standing rigging; and the running rigging so stiff that we could hardly bend it so as to belay it, or, still less, take a knot with it; and the sails frozen. One at a time (for it was a long piece of work and required many hands) we furled the courses, mizzen topsail, and fore-topmast staysail; and close-reefed the fore and main topsails; and hove the ship to under the fore, with the main hauled up by the clew-lines and buntlines and ready to be sheeted home if we found it necessary to make sail to get the windward of an ice island. A regular lookout was then set, and kept by each night. It blew hard the whole time, and there was an almost constant driving of either rain, hail, or snow. In addition to this, it was "as thick as muck" and the ice was all about us.

The captain was on deck nearly the whole night, and kept the cook in the galley, with a roaring fire, to make coffee for him, which he took every few hours and once or twice gave a little to his officers; but not a drop of anything was there for the crew. The captain who sleeps all the daytime and comes and goes at night as he chooses, can have his brandy and water in the cabin, and his hot coffee at the galley; while Jack, who had to stand through everything and work in wet and cold, can have nothing to wet his lips or warm his stomach. This was a "temperance ship," by her articles, and, like too many such ships, the temperance was all in the forecastle. The sailor, who only takes his one glass as it is dealt out to him, is in danger of being drunk; while the captain, upon whose self-possession and cool judgment the lives of all depend, may be trusted with any amount to drink at his will.

ALEXANDER KING

Sailing ship, temperance ship, and "Jack" suggest an American vessel of the nineteenth century.

The writer seems very familiar with nautical terms and uses them knowingly: Cape Horn rig, southwesters, hull, spar, standing rigging, running rigging, bend and belay, furled the courses, mizzen topsail, fore-topmast staysail, close reefed, and so forth. (Compare with the language of the foregoing passage.) Otherwise his vocabulary is quite adequate but not exceptional.

The writer was a member of the crew, but quotations around "Cape Horn rig" and "as thick as muck" suggest this is how others would say it but not himself.

He describes the sailors' hardships. He is bitter toward the captain and his unwarranted privileges. There is a touch of irony in "the temperance was all in the forecastle."

This is a serious attack on sailing conditions by one who has himself suffered under them long enough to know the life thoroughly. But he was probably not a permanent crew member. The language is too articulate for an untutored sailor of that era, and the quotations are another clue.

Answer overleaf.

Did the same man write both passages? Compare the "feel" of the two. One simple device is to compare the sentence lengths.

	1	2	3	4	5	6	7
A:	31,	30,	31,	29,	34,	25,	39
B:	27,	31,	64,	42,	74,	11,	19
C:	__	__	__	__	__	__	__

Same?

Another technique is to compare the kinds of sentences used. If you can recognize simple, compound, or complex or periodic or balanced sentences, they may help you to see whether the same or different persons are writing. But the point is to see how the writer's language ebbs and flows, to notice individual traits. Even if you do not know these technical terms, you can notice a regular or choppy rhythm, a frequently interrupted or a highly structured sentence. Even the punctuation may indicate unique characteristics.

A	B
1. *compound-complex*	1. *simple*, with interrupters and parentheses
2. *complex*	2. *simple*, with series phrases
3. *compound*	3. *compound-complex* (colon, semicolon, commas)
4. *compound*	4. *complex*, with dash, series, etc.
5. *compound*	5. *complex*
6. *simple*	6. *simple*
7. *compound-complex*	7. *compound*

Writer A has a straightforward style with few interrupters; compound sentences predominate. Writer B has a wide variety with all sorts of structures within each sentence and many interrupters; he uses mostly simple or complex sentences.

Step Four:

Is specimen C the work of another writer? You can add to your other clues a word count and sentence classification and compare with specimens A and B. Other students' results are given below.

C As I lay in my hammock that night, overhead I heard the slow weary draggings of the three ponderous strangers along the encumbered deck. Their stupidity or their resolution was so great, that they never went aside for any impediment. One ceased his movements altogether just before the mid-watch. At sunrise I found him butted like a battering-ram against the immovable foot of the foremast, and still striving, tooth and nail, to force the impossible passage. That these tortoises are the victims of a penal, or malignant, or perhaps a downright diabolical enchanter, seems in nothing more likely than in that strange infatuation of hopeless toil which so often possesses them. I have known them in their journeyings to ram themselves heroically against rocks, and long abide there, nudging, wriggling, wedging, in order to displace them, and so hold on their inflexible path. Their crowning curse is their drudging impulse to straightforwardness in a belittered world.

The narrator sleeps in a hammock below decks on a sailing vessel. These are not the first tortoises he has observed: "I have known them in their journeyings." He probably had been on other voyages, though he is probably not an officer. If he is a crew member, he has unusual interests and an unusual background.

His vocabulary contains several uncommon items: ponderous, encumbered, resolution, impediment, penal, malignant, diabolical, enchanter, infatuation, inflexible, belittered. Only a few nautical terms appear.

He is interested in the philosophical meaning of the behavior he is witnessing.

Turn the page for Answer.

Specimen A is straightforward narration. The tone of B is that of an active participant, angry at a specific injustice, but C thinks of the incident in terms of the whole universe: What causes such behavior; can it be regarded as stupid, heroic, or resolute?

Sentence lengths:

	1	2	3	4	5	6	7
C:	24,	16,	9,	27,	35,	32,	13

How do these compare with A or B?

Sentence types:

C

1. *complex*
2. *complex*
3. *simple*
4. *simple*
5. *complex*
6. *simple*
7. *simple*

There is a fairly even mixture of simple and complex sentences, but they are more tightly structured (periodic) than either A or B. The parts are more tightly interwoven. It would be difficult to break up these sentences.

The tone, interests, involvement, language, sentence structure and sentence rhythms are different from A or B.

Is the utterance (outer-ance) a thumbprint of the Man?

HERMANMELVILLE

Following are several other passages you can try. As you proceed you will probably notice other aspects of the writing which may serve as clues to the author's identify. Is his personality congenial to your own? Could you bear to spend much time in his company?

> When I was a child of seven years old, my friends, on a holiday, filled my pocket with coppers. I went directly to a shop where they sold toys for children; and, being charmed with the sound of a *whistle* that I met by the way in the hands of another boy, I voluntarily offered and gave all my money for one. I then came home, and went whistling all over the house, much pleased with my *whistle*, but disturbing all the family. My brothers, and sisters, and cousins, understanding the bargain I had made, told me I had given four times as much for it as it was worth; put me in mind what good things I might have bought with the rest of the money; and laughed at me so much for my folly, that I cried with vexation; and the reflections gave me more chagrin than the *whistle* gave me pleasure.
>
> This however was afterward of use to me, the impression continuing on my mind; so that often, when I was tempted to buy some unnecessary thing, I said to myself, *Don't give too much for the whistle*; and I saved my money.
>
> As I grew up, came into the world, and observed the actions of men, I thought I met with many, very many, who *gave too much for the whistle.*
>
> When I saw one too ambitious of court favor, sacrificing his time in attendance on levees, his repose, his liberty, his virtue, and perhaps his friends, to attain it, I have said to myself, *This man gives too much for his whistle.*
>
> When I saw another fond of popularity, constantly employing himself in political bustles, neglecting his own affairs, and ruining them by that neglect, *He pays, indeed,* said I*, too much for his whistle.*
>
> If I knew a miser, who gave up every kind of comfortable living, all the pleasures of doing good to others, all the esteem of his fellow citizens, and the joys of benevolent friendship, for the sake of accumulating wealth, *Poor man,* said I, *you pay too much for your whistle.*

Answer on page 388.

My own experience was quite different. I was called by the draft board almost every week, even though I had been exempted from service the first time I went before the medical examiners. Either they were never convinced that it was me or else there was some clerical error in the records which was never cleared up. Anyway, there was usually a letter for me on Monday ordering me to report for examination on the second floor of Memorial Hall the following Wednesday at 9 P.M. The second time I went up, I tried to explain to one of the doctors that I had already been exempted. ''You're just a blur to me.'' I said, taking off my glass.'' You're absolutely nothing to me,'' he snapped, sharply.

I had to take off all my clothes each time and jog around the hall with a lot of porters and bank presidents' sons and clerks and poets. Our hearts and lungs would be examined, and then our feet; and finally our eyes. That always came last. When the eye specialist got around to me, he would always say, ''Why, you couldn't get into the service with sight like that!'' ''I know,'' I would say. Then a week or two later I would be summoned again and go through the same rigmarole. The ninth or tenth time I was called, I happened to pick up one of several stethoscopes that were lying on a table and suddenly, instead of finding myself in the line of draft men, I found myself in the line of examiners. ''Hello, doctor,'' said one of them, nodding. ''Hello,'' I said. That, of course, was before I took my clothes off; I might have managed it naked, but I doubt it. I was assigned, or rather drifted, to the chest-and-lung section, where I began to examine every other man, thus cutting old Dr. Ridgeway's work in two. ''I'm glad to have you here, doctor,'' he said.

I passed most of the men that came to me, but now and then I would exempt one just to be on the safe side. I began by making each of them hold his breath and then say, ''mi, mi, mi, mi,'' until I noticed Ridgeway looking at me curiously. He, I discovered, simply made them say ''ah,'' and sometimes he didn't make them say anything. Once I got hold of a man who, it came out later, had swallowed a watch—to make the doctors believe there was something wrong with him inside (it was a common subterfuge: men swallowed nails, hairpins, ink, etc., in an effort to be let out). Since I didn't know what you were supposed to hear through a stethoscope, the ticking of the watch at first didn't surprise me, but I decided to call Dr. Ridgeway into consultation, because nobody else had ticked. "This man seems to tick," I said to him. He looked at me in surprise but didn't say anything. Then he thumped the man, laid his ear to his chest, and finally tried the stethoscope. "Sound as a dollar," he said. "Listen lower down," I told him. The man indicated his stomach. Ridgeway gave him a haughty, indignant look. "That's for the abdominal men to worry about," he said and moved off. A few minutes later, Dr. Blythe Ballomy got around to the man and listened, but he didn't blink an eye; his grim expression never changed. "You have swallowed a watch, my man," he said, crisply. The draftee reddened in embarrassment and uncertainty. "On *purpose*?" he asked. "That I can't say," the doctor told him, and went on.

Answer on page 250.

Judging by Appearances?

[That's all we have
to judge by.]

What clues about the "author" does this work supply? What are his interests? What is his era? What is his disposition? How does he view the world?

Is this a *reading* problem?

Look back over the profiles you developed for Dana, London, and Melville and then decide which one wrote this passage. What evidence can you find to support your choice? Answer on page 331.

The morning was one peculiar to that coast. Everything was mute and calm; everything grey. The sea, though undulated into long roods of swells, seemed fixed, and was sleeked at the surface like waved lead that has cooled and set in the smelter's mould. The sky seemed a grey surtout. Flights of troubled grey fowl, kith and kin with flights of troubled grey vapours among which they were mixed, skimmed low and fitfully over the waters, as swallows over meadows before storms. Shadows present, foreshadowing deeper shadows to come.

To Captain __________'s surprise, the stranger, viewed through the glass, showed no colours; though to do so upon entering a haven, however uninhabited in its shores, where but a single other ship might be lying, was the custom among peaceful seamen of all nations. Considering the lawlessness and loneliness of the spot, and the sort of stories, at that day, associated with those seas, Captain __________'s surprise might have deepened into some uneasiness had he not been a person of a singularly undistrustful good nature, not liable, except on extraordinary and repeated incentives, and hardly then, to indulge in personal alarms, any way involving the imputation of malign evil in man. Whether, in view of what humanity is capable, such a trait implies, along with a benevolent heart, more than ordinary quickness and accuracy of intellectual perception, may be left to the wise to determine.

But whatever misgivings might have obtruded on first seeing the stranger, would almost, in any seaman's mind, have been dissipated by observing, that the ship, in navigating into the harbour, was drawing too near the land; a sunken reef making out off her bow. This seemed to prove her a stranger, indeed, not only to the sealer, but the island; consequently, she could be no wonted freebooter on that ocean. With no small interest, Captain __________ continued to watch her—a proceeding not much facilitated by the vapours partly mantling the hull, through which the far matin light

A style sets up a horizon of expectation . . .

from her cabin streamed equivocally enough; much like the sun—by this time hemisphered on the rim of the horizon, and apparently, in company with the strange ship entering the harbour—which, wimpled by the same low, creeping clouds, showed not unlike a lima intriguante's one sinister eye peering across the Plaza from the Indian loop-hole of her dusk *saya-y-manto.*

Is *this* a thumbprint? What does it reveal about the creator? What is he like? What is his background? What are some of his interests? Does the form itself reveal anything about him? Does the particular form inform? When you have discovered all you can, compare your results with those of other students on page 404.

LONDON

I wander thro' each charter'd street,
Near where the charter'd Thames does flow,
And mark in every face I meet
Marks of weakness, marks of woe.

In every cry of every Man,
In every Infant's cry of fear,
In every voice, in every ban,
The mind-forg'd manacles I hear.

How the Chimney-sweeper's cry
Every black'ning Church appalls,
And the hapless Soldier's sigh
Runs in blood down Palace walls.

But most thro' midnight streets I hear
How the youthful Harlot's curse
Blasts the new born Infant's tear,
And blights with plagues the Marriage hearse.

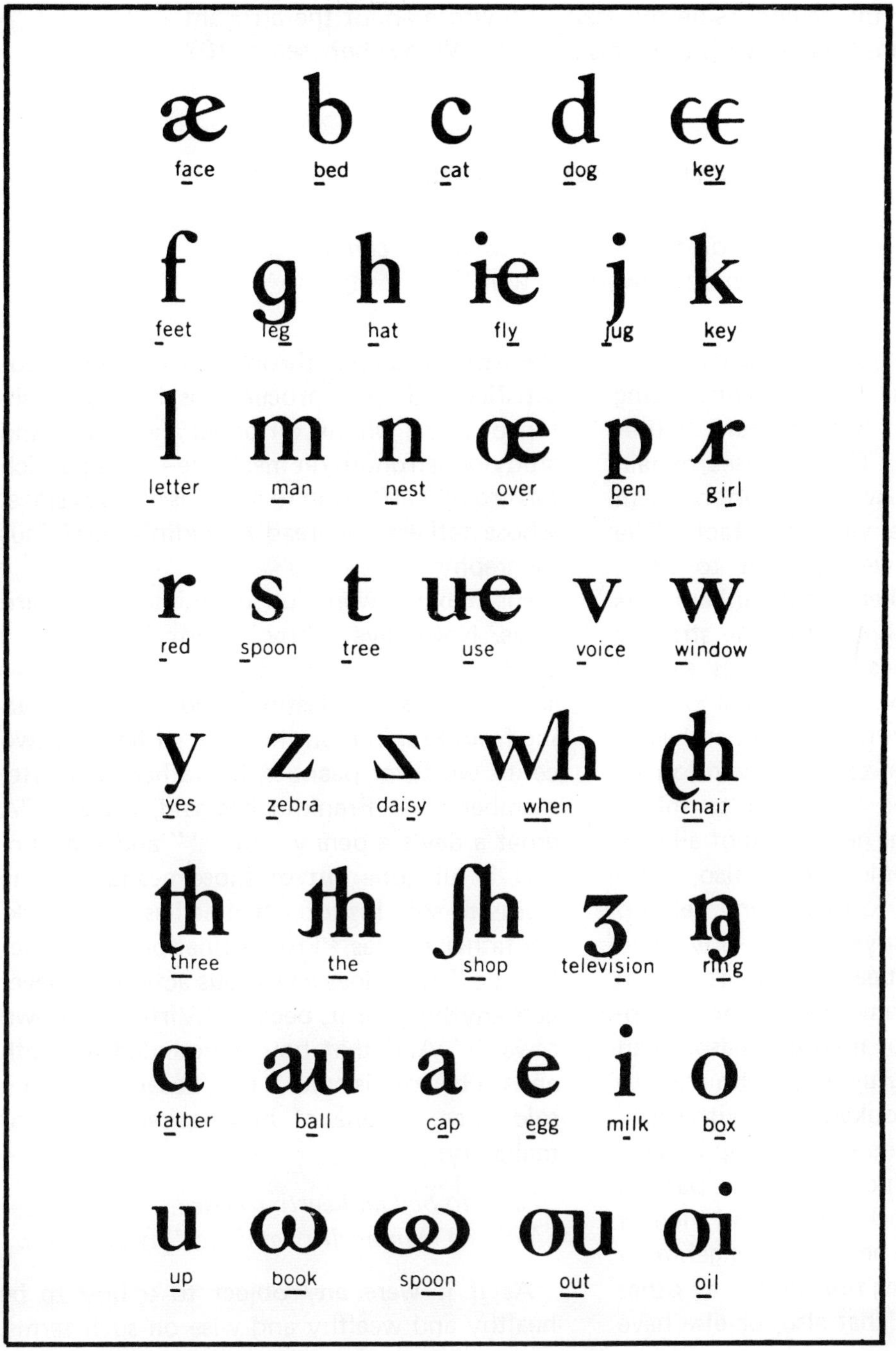

girls and bois lern
tω rεεd with i|t|a

Is this the same man who wrote about the draft board? Is his personality the same? Is he the man who wrote about the arrogant Europeans? What *is* his tone, his attitude? Who *is* he? see p. 407.

THE LATE BENJAMIN FRANKLIN

"Never put off till to-morrow what you can do day after to-morrow just as well." —B. F.

This party was one of those persons whom they call Philosophers. He was twins, being born simultaneously in two different houses in the city of Boston. These houses remain unto this day, and have signs upon them worded in accordance with the facts. The signs are considered well enough to have, though not necessary, because the inhabitants point out the two birthplaces to the stranger anyhow, and sometimes as often as several times in the same day. The subject of this memoir was of a vicious disposition, and early prostituted his talents to the invention of maxims and aphorisms calculated to inflict suffering upon the rising generation of all subsequent ages. His simplest acts, also, were contrived with a view to their being held up for the emulation of boys forever—boys who might otherwise have been happy. It was in this spirit that he became the son of a soap-boiler, and probably for no other reason than that the efforts of all future boys who tried to be anything might be looked upon with suspicion unless they were the sons of soap-boilers. With a malevolence which is without parallel in history, he would work all day, and then sit up nights, and let on to be studying algebra by the light of a smouldering fire, so that all other boys might have to do that also, or else have Benjamin Franklin thrown up to them. Not satisfied with these proceedings, he had a fashion of living wholly on bread and water, and studying astronomy at mealtime—a thing which has brought affliction to millions of boys since, whose fathers had read Franklin's pernicious biography.

His maxims were full of animosity toward boys. Nowadays a boy cannot follow out a single natural instinct without tumbling over some of these everlasting aphorisms and hearing from Franklin on the spot. If he buys two cents' worth of peanuts, his father says, "Remember what Franklin has said, my son—'A groat a day's a penny a year,'" and the comfort is all gone out of those peanuts. If he wants to spin his top when he has done work, his father quotes, "Procrastination is the thief of time." If he does a virtuous action, he never gets anything for it, because "Virtue is its own reward." And that boy is hounded to death and robbed of his natural rest, because Franklin said once, in one of his inspired flights of malignity:

Early to bed and early to rise
Makes a man healthy and wealthy and wise.

As if it were any object to a boy to be healthy and wealthy and wise on such terms.

The sorrow that that maxim has cost me through my parents' experimenting on me with it, tongue cannot tell. The legitimate result is my present state of general debility, indigence, and mental aberration. My parents used to have me up before nine o'clock in the morning sometimes when I was a boy. If they had let me take my natural rest where would I have been now? Keeping store, no doubt, and respected by all.

And what an adroit old adventurer the subject of this memoir was! In order to get a chance to fly his kite on Sunday he used to hang a key on the string and let on to be fishing for lightning. And a guileless public would go home chirping about the "wisdom" and the "genius" of the hoary Sabbath-breaker. If anybody caught him playing "mumble-peg" by himself, after the age of sixty, he would immediately appear to be ciphering out how the grass grew—as if it was any of his business. My grandfather knew him well, and he says Franklin was always fixed—always ready. If a body, during his old age, happened on him unexpectedly when he was catching flies, or making mud pies, or sliding on a cellar door, he would immediately look wise, and rip out a maxim, and walk off with his nose in the air and his cap turned wrong side before, trying to appear absent-minded and eccentric. He was a hard lot.

He invented a stove that would smoke your head off in four hours by the clock. One can see the almost devilish satisfaction he took in it by his giving it his name.

He was always proud of telling how he entered Philadelphia for the first time, with nothing in the world but two shillings in his pocket and four rolls of bread under his arm. But really, when you come to examine it critically, it was nothing. Anybody could have done it.

To the subject of this memoir belongs the honor of recommending the army to go back to bows and arrows in place of bayonets and muskets. He observed, with his customary force, that the bayonet was very well under some circumstances, but that he doubted whether it could be used with accuracy at a long range.

Benjamin Franklin did a great many notable things for his country, and made her young name to be honored in many lands as the mother of such a son. It is not the idea of this memoir to ignore that or cover it up. No; the simple idea of it is to snub those pretentious maxims of his, which he worked up with a great show of originality out of truisms that had become wearisome platitudes as early as the dispersion from Babel; and also to snub his stove, and his military inspirations, his unseemly endeavor to make himself conspicuous when he entered Philadelphia, and his flying his kite and fooling away his time in all sorts of such ways when he ought to have been foraging for soap fat, or constructing candles. I merely desired to do away with somewhat of the prevalent calamitous idea among heads of families that Franklin *acquired* his great genius by working for nothing, studying by moonlight, and getting up in the night instead of waiting till morning like a Christian; and that this programme; rigidly inflected, will make a Franklin of every father's fool. It is time these gentlemen were finding out that these execrable eccentricities of instinct and conduct are only the *evidences* of genius, not the *creators* of it. I wish I had been the father of my parents long enough to make them comprehend this truth, and thus prepare them to let their son have an easier time of it. When I was a child I had to boil soap, notwithstanding my father was wealthy, and I had to get up early and study geometry at breakfast, and peddle my own poetry, and do everything just as Franklin did, in the solemn hope that I would be a Franklin some day. And here I am.

The author of the poem on page 400 is a sensitive individual who is haunted by the feeling of sadness he gets from the London he knows well, probably on the basis of taking walks through the city.

He is from an era when the palace was powerful but still subject to open criticism. The printing conventions suggest an earlier era also *(thro', charter'd, forg'd;* the capitalization of common nouns). *Manacles* and *hapless* seem currently out of vogue in the context they are found in here. Chimney sweeps are not common today. The poem was probably written a little before Victoria's reign.

The writer is very observant and interconnects his observations into a complete view. He searches faces and finds there "marks of weakness and woe." He is probably religious but is critical of church corruption. He notes the human sounds all about him and finds indications of fear, anger, and need in them.

He is probably of an independent, individualistic temperament. He is appalled by institutional enslavement. He dislikes censored thought.

He is a literate man and probably educated. Though the thoughts expressed are impassioned, the poetic form used indicates the cool control of an experienced poetic craftsman. The poet likes to play with language, he likes to use the multiple meanings of a word, and he creates fresh metaphors. His use of a conventional rhyme scheme, meter and stanza form suggests a willingness to function within a frame, but departures (as with the seven-syllable lines in the third stanza) indicate individual creativity. The clarity of the sentences reflects the sharp mind of an individual who takes pains to say what he wants with precision and brevity. Though he is attracted to poetic ambiguity, his style is direct, his imagery stark, his mode forceful.

He feels socially responsible and is a critic of his society's institutions and of man's self-limiting fears.

WILLIAMBLAKE

Work by this writer appeared earlier in this book. Do you recognize his style? What do you know about him from this passage? Can you match it with a foregoing essay or story? What evidence can you gather to support your choice? Answer on page 410.

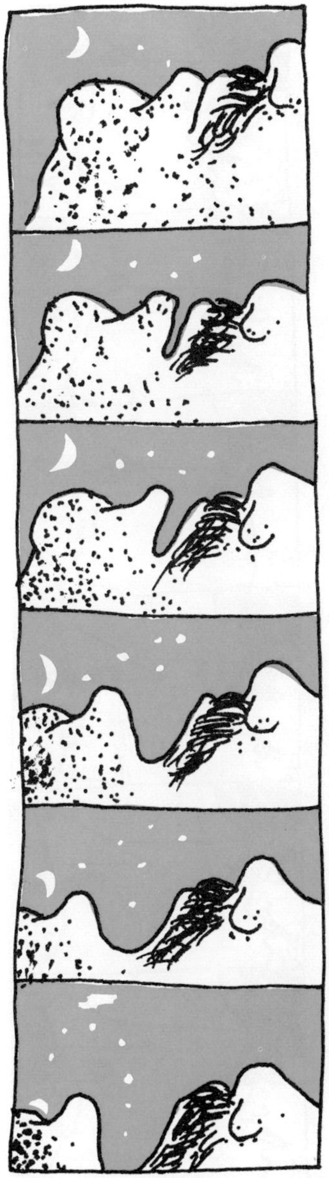

I glance around at the nest we have made. . . , at the continents of stain on the ceiling like an old and all-wrong discoverer's map, at the earnestly bloated canvases I conscientiously cover with great streaks straining to say what even I am beginning to suspect is the unsayable thing, and I grow frightened. I consider the life we have made together, with its days spent without relation to the days the sun keeps and its baroque arabesques of increasingly attenuated emotion and its furnishings like a scattering of worn-out Braques and its rather wistful half-Freudian half-Oriental sex-mysticism, and I wonder, *Was it for this that my father gave up his life?*

Lying awake beside you in the rose-touched dark, I wake on a morning long ago, in Vera Hummel's guest bedroom. Her room shone in the aftermath of the storm. My dreams had been a bent extension, like that of a stick thrust into water, of the last waking events—the final mile staggering through the unwinding storm; my father's beating at the door of the dark house, knocking and whinnying and rubbing his hands together in desperation yet his importunity no longer seeming absurd or berserk to me but necessary, absolutely in my blind numbness necessary; then Vera Hummel yawning and blinking in the bleaching glare of her kitchen, her unbound hair fanning over the shoulders of her blue bathrobe and her hands tucked in the sleeves and her arms hugging herself as she yawned; and the limping clump of her husband descending the stairs to receive my father's outpour of explanation and gratitude. They put us in their guest bedroom, in a postered sway-backed bed inherited from Mr. Hummel's mother, my grandfather's sister Hanna. It smelled of feathers and starch and was so like a hammock that my father and I, in underclothes, had to cling to the edges to keep from sliding together in the middle. For some minutes I kept tense. I seemed stuffed with the jiggling atoms of the storm. Then I heard the first rasp of my father's snuffly little snore. Then the wind outside the room sighed mightily, and this thrust of sound and motion beyond me seemed to explain everything, and I relaxed.

The room was radiant. Beyond the white mullions and the curtains of dotted Swiss pinned back with metal flowers painted white, the sky was undiluted blue. I thought, *This morning has never occurred before. . . .*

Are the characteristics of this writer the same as those of the preceding? Is it the same writer? What evidence can you find to support your position?
Answer on page 208.

There were still not enough schools, and those there were had quickly been preempted by the officials and minor officials for their own children. That was in Curatu. In the small villages and the countryside there were no schools at all.

And though around the capital there was a network of paved asphalt roads they went nowhere, ending abruptly in swamps or jungles only a few miles beyond the outskirts. In the mountains and valleys of the back country the *bandoleros* still struck terror into the hearts of the *campesinos.*

There had been a sadness in him those first few weeks he had been home. He was glad that his father was not there to see what he saw. It was not for this his father had spent his days.

He had gone down to the port and watched the ships come and go and the fishermen return with their catch. In the early hours of the morning he had wandered through the marketplace listening to the cries of the vendors. And everywhere he went he saw the small concrete statues of *el Presidente*—on the street corners, on each new building, at every pier in the port and entrance to the marketplace. And there was always the red and blue uniform of the soldiers.

It wasn't until a week had passed that he became aware that soldiers were following him. It wasn't until a few days later that he realized that the people looked at him as if he were a stranger, that the sound of his voice had a different accent from their own, that the cut of his clothes was of another society.

A sense of loneliness and isolation began to possess him. Suddenly the atmosphere of the city began to choke in his throat. It was not until then that he realized he was no longer the same person who had left here years ago. He was something else, someone else. What he was he did not know. Instinctively, hopefully, he left the city for the *hacienda* in the mountains where he had been born.

There, where the sky and the earth seemed to stretch forever before him and the mountains thrust their purple, craggy fingers at the sun and stars, he hoped to find again the sense of freedom he had lost. The reason for his being.

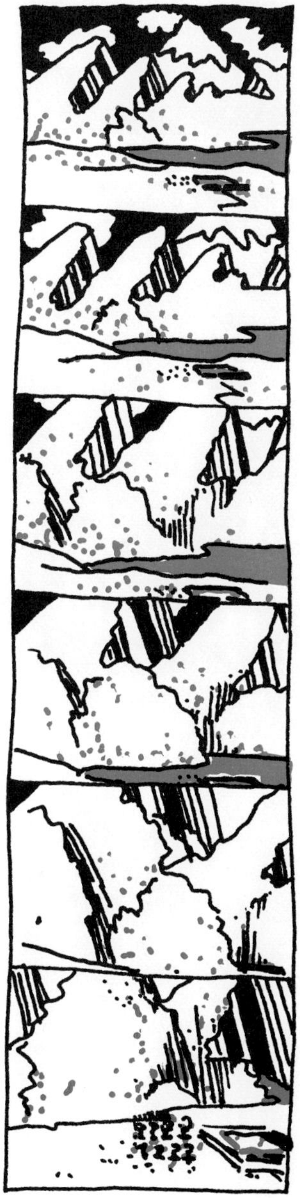

A sentence is a sound in itself on which other sounds called words may be strung. You may string words together without a sentence-sound to string them on just as you may tie clothes together by the sleeve and stretch them without a clothes line between two trees, but—it is bad for the clothes.

MARKTWAIN

What is the person like who wrote this? How much evidence can you find to support your view? The writer's identity is on page 448.

If you're in a really fantastic mood you can say life is really great. And if you're in a rather pessimistic mood you can say life is hell and not worth living———so what????? O.K., so I'm not extremely happy and delighted with all I see, but I'm not ready to commit suicide. So, I think I'm in a good frame of mind to write the way I feel without being prejudiced by extreme emotions.

Why live? Why teach English? Why do anything? There is no set answer. I can only give you mine and hope it is sufficient to make you see without a doubt of any kind that Zukerkandl's philosophy is the biggest waste written.

Zuckerkandl says the purpose of life is to get through it. We should do away with all sensation. The way to live is by habit. The way to get away from sensations is not to communicate. He says he isn't making up a new philosophy but just endorsing what mankind feels already. While I know you don't believe this, I really think you're seeing truth in it and feel there is no flaw. In the first place, you were wrong when you first played it and started laughing at it because even though it is a satire like you now say, it does have truth in it. However, the flaw in it blows the whole thing apart. The flaw is what makes life worth living. That flaw is people. Maybe sometimes you become really disappointed in people and say to hell with all of them. They're just not worth it. I know at times I've gotten extremely depressed and have felt that life is worthless and there really is absolutely no sense in living. But people are my sincere reason for living, so even though I may be ready to give it all up I always come back to it and sometimes with richer experiences.

I think a teacher's job is one of the most difficult. It's so easy to get in a comfortable rut and teach the same thing continuously. It's easy to go along with the school norms and be considered an All American good type teacher. But the way you teach can be very rewarding or completely disgusting or maybe even combinations of both. Now that I'm thinking about your position even more, I'm beginning to wonder why you haven't fallen down before and said to hell with it. Why, then? Because you care. That's why I know you can't really feel the life of habit is the perfect one. You need more than just existence. And if you tried to live this way, you would experience extreme unhappiness and dissatisfaction, which would defeat your whole purpose. . . .

> Is this a thumbprint? Can one increase his capacity to see "what's there"? How much is there in face value?

General society is so insipid an affair, even to the persons who make it what it is, that it is kept up for any reason rather than the pleasure it affords. All serious discussions on matters on which opinions differ, being considered ill-bred, and the national deficiency in liveliness and sociability having prevented the cultivation of the art of talking agreeably on trifles, in which the French of the last century so much excelled, the sole attraction of what is called society to those who are not at the top of the tree, is the hope of being aided to climb a little higher in it; while to those who are already at the top, it is chiefly a compliance with custom, and with the supposed requirements of their station. To a person of any but a very common order in thought or feeling, such society, unless he has personal objects to serve by it, must be supremely unattractive: and most people, in the present day, of any really high class of intellect, make their contact with it so slight, and at such long intervals, as to be almost considered as retiring from it altogether. Those persons of any mental superiority who do otherwise, are, almost without exception, greatly deteriorated by it. Not to mention loss of time, the tone of their feelings is lowered: they become less earnest about those of their opinions respecting which they must remain silent in the society they frequent: they come to look upon their most elevated objects as unpractical, or, at least, too remote from realization to be more than a vision, or a theory; and if, more fortunate than most, they retain their higher principles unimpaired, yet with respect to the persons and affairs of their own day they insensibly adopt the modes of feeling and judgment in which they can hope for sympathy from the company they keep. A person of high intellect should never go into unintellectual society unless he can enter it as an apostle; yet he is the only person with high objects who can safely enter it at all. Persons even of intellectual aspirations had much better, if they can, make their habitual associates of at least their equals, and, as far as possible, their superiors, in knowledge, intellect, and elevation of sentiment. Moreover, if the character is formed, and the mind made up, on the few cardinal points of human opinion, agreement of conviction and feeling on these has been felt in all times to be an essential requisite of anything worthy the name of friendship, in a really earnest mind. All these circumstances united, made the number very small of those whose society, and still more whose intimacy, I now voluntarily sought. (The author's identity is on page 121.)

JOHNUPDIKE

READING DOODLES

The following page contains twelve squares to be copied on a separate sheet of paper so they may be collected later. Complete these doodles in any manner you wish.

Are *your* doodles unique? Are they like fingerprints? Do they *communicate?* Perhaps they can tell you things about yourself that you are not aware of. To investigate these possibilities try the following approach: Write your name on the back only. Collect and shuffle all the pages from the class.

Then select one and discuss it together. When you have finished, can you guess the name of the doodler? If not, the individual can identify himself.

Then he can tell you where he thinks you went astray and where you were right.

Do you know him any better after examining his doodles than before? Does *he* know himself any better?

Can you generalize from this investigation?

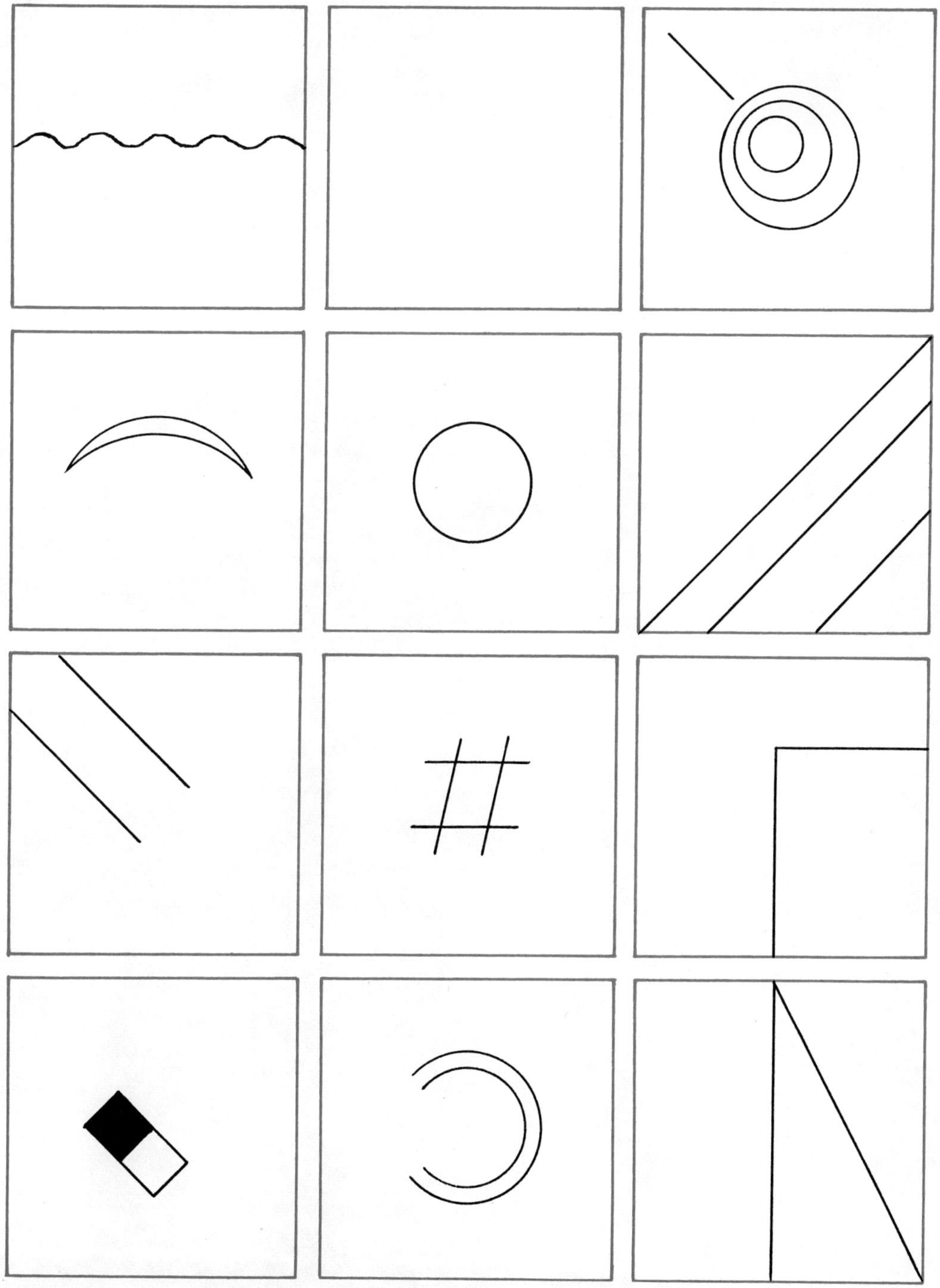

Some judge of authors'
names, not works,
and then
Nor praise, nor blame
the writing,
but the men.

. . . When a multitude of young men, keen, open-hearted, sympathetic, and observant, as young men are, come together and freely mix with each other, they are sure to learn one from another, even if there be no one to teach them; the conversation of all is a series of lectures to each, and they gain for themselves new ideas and views, fresh matter of thought, and distinct principles for judging and acting, day by day. An infant has to learn the meaning of the information which its senses convey to it, and this seems to be its employment. It fancies all that the eye presents to it to be close to it, till it actually learns the contrary, and thus by practice does it ascertain the relations and uses of those first elements of knowledge which are necessary for its animal existence. A parallel teaching is necessary for our social being, and it is secured by a large school or a college; and this effect may be fairly called in its own department an enlargement of mind. It is seeing the world on a small field with little trouble; for the pupils or students come from very different places, and with widely different notions, and there is much to generalize, much to adjust, much to eliminate, there are interrelations to be defined, and conventional rules to be established, in the process, by which the whole assemblage is moulded together, and gains one tone and one character.

Let it be clearly understood, I repeat it, that I am not taking into account moral or religious considerations; I am but saying that the youthful community will constitute a whole, it will embody a specific idea, it will represent a doctrine, it will administer a code of conduct, and it will furnish principles of thought and action. It will give birth to a living teacher, which in course of time will take the shape of a self-perpetuating tradition, or a *genius loci*, as it is sometimes called; which haunts the home where it has been born, and which imbues and forms, more or less, and one by one, every individual who is successively brought under its shadow. Thus it is that, independent of direct instruction on the part of Superiors, there is a sort of self-education in the academic institutions of Protestant England; a characteristic tone of thought, a recognized standard of judgment is found in them, which as developed in the individual who is submitted to it, becomes a twofold source of strength to him, both from the distinct stamp it impresses on his mind, and from the bond of union which it creates between him and others, effects which are shared by the authorities of the place, for they themselves have been educated in it, and at all times are exposed to the influence of its ethical atmosphere. Here then is a real teaching, whatever be its standards and principles, true or false; and it at least tends towards cultivation of the intellect; it at least recognizes that knowledge is something more than a sort of passive reception of scraps and details; it is a something, and it does a something, which never will issue from the most strenuous efforts of a set of teachers, with no mutual sympathies and no intercommunion, of a set of examiners with no opinions which they dare profess, and with no common principles, who are teaching or questioning a set of youths who do not know them, and do not know each other, on a large number of subjects, different in kind, and connected by no wide philosophy, three times a week, or three times a year, or once in three years, in chill lecture-rooms or on a pompous anniversary.

How Do You Know It's Good?

Is one story better than another? One movie, one poem? Is judgment purely arbitrary? How do you decide that something is good or great or terrible? Is it all caprice, or do you have standards which carry across all media? And if so, where do your standards come from? Are they learned or instinctive?

First, do you have standards for judging one poem as better than another? Examine each of the following versions of a poem. Which do you prefer? What would you say is wrong with each of the others? Write down your reasons and then compare your results with your classmates'. How many of you agree? If you disagree, do you understand the other person's viewpoint? Do you think it is valid? What makes a judgment valid and reasonable?

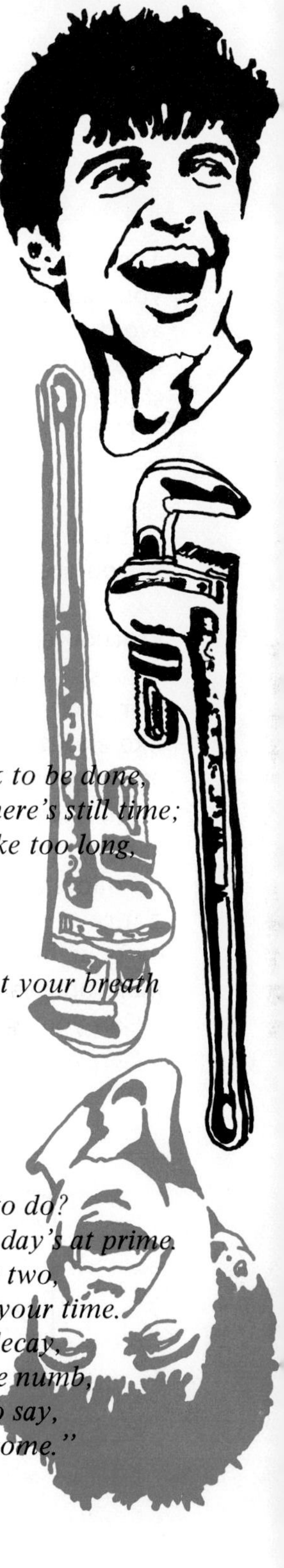

List, sweet youth, hast stints to do?
Haste thee! Phoebus' tender cheek
Blusheth, for day doth pursue.
Is't companionship thou seek?
Whisper, and I fly to thee
Ere above my fevered brow
Cyclamen and rosemary
Breathe the love I have enow!

Listen, my friend, if there's any work to be done,
You'd better get at it now while there's still time;
And if you need help and it won't take too long,
You certainly can have mine.
Pretty soon you'll lose your strength
And you won't have the nerve;
So you'd better do it while you've got your breath
Before you lie buried in the earth.

Hey, kid, got any work to do?
Hurry, while it's early.
Snap it up! If it takes two
Just say so without getting surly.
Before your muscles get weak like a baby,
What with one thing and another,
All your hot air will be gone, and maybe
I'll find that working is too much of a bother.

Say, lad, have you things to do?
Quick then, while your day's at prime.
Quick, and if 'tis work for two,
Here am I, man: now's your time.
Ere the wholesome flesh decay,
And the willing nerve be numb,
And the lips lack breath to say,
"No, my lad. I cannot come."

MAKING JUDGMENTS

The following investigation is designed to help you discover what you really feel about the quality of various works. You should avoid looking at the individuals' names until you have finished the investigation. To be effective, it requires your exploring other students' evaluations of the same items.

This collection contains materials from various sources: famous men, students, versifiers, and others. We think some of the material is poor. Some is good.

It is necessary that you not be familiar with any of the selections. If you are, you should disqualify yourself for that particular item.

Procedure:

For each selection write out what you think of it. What do you like about it? How good is it? Where does it fail? Be as complete and as precise as you can.

Then listen to each other's evaluations. Ask questions for clarification, but do not criticize.

Follow this procedure with the entire collection. As you progress notice your own critical processes. Are you becoming more aware of your motivations and your biases? Is your criticism becoming more precise?

Can you learn anything from this sort of process?

Can you *use* it? Where?

Answers

I kept my answers small and kept them near;
Big questions bruised my mind but still I let
Small answers be a bulwark to my fear.

The huge abstractions I kept from the light;
Small things I handled and caressed and loved.
I let the stars assume the whole of night.

But the big answers clamoured to be moved
Into my life. Their great audacity
Shouted to be acknowledged and believed.

Even when all small answers build up to
Protection of my spirit, still I hear
Big answers striving for their overthrow

And all the great conclusions coming near.

The secondhandedness of the learned world is the secret of its mediocrity.

The Marsh

Swampstrife and spatterdock
lull in the heavy waters;
some thirty little frogs
spring with each step you walk;
a fish's belly glitters
tangled by rotting logs.

Over near the grey rocks
muskrats dip and circle.
Out of his rim of ooze
a slit-black pond snail walks
inverted on the surface
toward what food he may choose.

You look up; while you walk
the sun bobs and is snarled
in the enclosing weir
of trees, in their dead stalks.
Stick in the mud, old heart,
what are you doing here?

Morning Under Bushes

Glistening flags glowing the start,
When the sun clasps all up for the day.
Every warted stem drifting slowly apart
As the wind scatters its prey.
The frost that turns to vibrant action,
Will burst in myriad colors.
Around about pierce blending fraction:
Stratum of glowing sculpture.

Just outside London there lived an old father who dearly loved his only son. Accordingly, when the boy was a youngster of some eighteen years, the old man sent for him and, with a benevolent glimmer of his horn-rimmed spectacles, said, "Well, Jack, you are now done with school. No doubt you are looking forward to going to the university."

"Yes, Dad, I am," said the son.

"You show good judgment," said the father. "The best years of one's whole life are unquestionably those which are spent at the university. Apart from the vast honeycomb of learning, the mellow voices of the professors, the venerable gray buildings, and the atmosphere of culture and refinement, there is the delight of being in possession of a comfortable allowance."

"Yes, Dad," said the son.

"Rooms of one's own," continued the father, "little dinners to one's friends, endless credit with the tradespeople, pipes, cigars, claret, Burgundy, clothes."

"Yes, Dad," said the son.

"There are exclusive little clubs," said the old man, "all sorts of sports, May Weeks, theatricals, balls, parties, rags, binges, scaling of walls, dodging of proctors, fun of every conceivable description."

"Yes! Yes, Dad!" cried the son.

"Certainly nothing in the world is more delightful than being at the university," said the father. "The springtime of life! Pleasure after pleasure! The world seems a whole dozen oysters, each with a pearl in it. Ah, the university! However, I'm not going to send you there."

"Then why the hell do you go on so about it?" said poor Jack.

"I did so in order that you might not think I was carelessly underestimating the pleasures I must call upon you to renounce," said his father. "You see, Jack, my health is not of the best; nothing but champagne agrees with me, and if I smoke a second-rate cigar, I get a vile taste in my mouth. My expenses have mounted abominably and I shall have very little to leave to you, yet my dearest wish is to see you in a comfortable way of life."

"If that is your wish, you might gratify it by sending me to the university," said Jack.

"We must think of the future," said his father. "You will have your living to earn, and in a world where culture is the least marketable of assets. Unless you are to be a schoolmaster or a curate, you will gain no great advantage from the university."

"Then what am I to be?" the young man asked.

"I read only a little while ago," said his father, "the following words, which flashed like sudden lightning upon the gloom in which I was considering your future: 'Most players are weak.' These words came from a little brochure upon the delightful and universally popular game of poker. It is a game which is played for counters, commonly called chips, and each of these chips represents an agreeable sum of money."

"Do you mean that I am to be a cardsharper?" cried the son.

"Nothing of the sort," replied the old man promptly. "I am asking you to be strong, Jack. I am asking you to show initiative,

> Her biggest success as a teacher is that she teaches her students primarily not what is beautiful but how to meet something on its own terms and seek out its beauty.

individuality. Why learn what everyone else is learning? You, my dear boy, shall be the first to study poker as systematically as others study languages, science, mathematics, and so forth—the first to tackle it as a student. I have set aside a cosy little room with chair, table, and some completely new packs of cards. A bookshelf contains several standard works on the game, and a portrait of Machiavelli hangs above the mantelpiece."

The young man's protests were vain, so he set himself reluctantly to study. He worked hard, mastered the books, wore the spots off a hundred packs of cards, and at the end of the second year he set out into the world with his father's blessing and enough cash to sit in on a few games of penny ante.

After Jack left, the old man consoled himself with his glass of champagne and his first-rate cigar and those other little pleasures which are the solace of the old and the lonely. He was getting on very well with these when one day the telephone rang. It was an overseas call from Jack, whose existence the old man had all but forgotten.

"Hullo, Dad!" cried the son in tones of great excitement. "I'm in Paris, sitting in on a game of poker with some Americans."

"Good luck to you!" said the old man, preparing to hang up the receiver.

"Listen, Dad!" cried the son. "It's like this. Well—just for once I'm playing without any limit."

"Lord have mercy on you!" said the old man.

"There's two of them still in," said the son. "They've raised me fifty thousand dollars and I've already put up every cent I've got."

"I would rather," groaned the old man, "see a son of mine at the university than in such a situation."

"But I've got four kings!" cried the young man.

"You can be sure the others have aces or straight flushes," said the old man. "Back down, my poor boy. Go out and play for cigarette ends with the habitués of your doss house."

"But listen, Dad!" cried the son. "This is a stud round, and nothing wild. I've seen an ace chucked in. I've seen all the tens and fives chucked in. There isn't a straight flush possible."

"Is that so?" cried the old man. "Never let it be said I didn't stand behind my boy. Hold everything. I'm coming to your assistance."

The son went back to the card table and begged his opponents to postpone matters until his father could arrive, and they, smiling at their cards, were only too willing to oblige him.

A couple of hours later the old man arrived by plane at Le Bourget, and shortly thereafter, he was standing beside the card table, rubbing his hands, smiling, affable, the light glinting merrily upon his horn-rimmed spectacles. He shook hands with the Americans and noted their prosperous appearances. "Now what have we here?" said he, sliding into his son's seat and fishing out his money.

"The bet," said one of the opponents, "stands at fifty thousand dollars. Seen by me. It's for you to see or raise."

"Or run," said the other.

"I trust my son's judgment," said the old man. "I shall raise fifty thousand dollars before I even glance at these cards in my hand." With that he pushed forward a hundred thousand dollars of his own money.

"I'll raise that hundred thousand dollars," said the first of his opponents.

"I'll stay and see," said the other.

The old man looked at his cards. His face turned several colours in rapid succession. A low and quavering groan burst from his lips and he was seen to hesitate for a long time, showing all the signs of an appalling inward struggle. At last he summoned up his courage and, pushing out his last hundred thousand (which represented all the cigars, champagne, and other little pleasures he had to look forward to), he licked his lips several times and said, "I'll see you."

"Four kings," said the first opponent, laying down his hand.

"Hell!" said the second. "Four queens."

"And I," moaned the old man, "have four knaves." With that he turned about and seized his son by the lapels of his jacket, shaking him as a terrier does a rat. "Curse the day," said he, "that I ever became the father of a damned fool!"

"I swear I thought they were kings," cried the young man.

"Don't you know that the 'v' is for valets?" said his father.

"Good God!" the son said. "I thought the 'v' was something to do with French kings. You know, Charles, Louis, V one, V two, V three. Oh, what a pity I was never at the university!"

"Go," said the old man. "Go there, or go to Hell or wherever you wish. Never let me see or hear from you again." And he stamped out of the room before his son or anyone else could say a word, even to tell him it was high-low stud they were playing and that the four knaves had won half the pot.

The young man, pocketing his share, mused that ignorance of every sort is deplorable, and, bidding his companions farewell, left Paris without further delay, and very soon he was entered at the university.

Sea Fever

I must go down to the seas again, to the lonely sea and the sky,
And all I ask is a tall ship and a star to steer her by,
And the wheel's kick and the wind's song and the white sail's shaking,
And a grey mist on the sea's face and a grey dawn breaking.

I must go down to the seas again, for the call of the running tide
Is a wild call and a clear call that may not be denied;
And all I ask is a windy day with the white clouds flying,
And the flung spray and the blown spume, and the sea gulls crying.

I must go down to the seas again to the vagrant gypsy life,
To the gull's way and the whale's way where the wind's like a whetted knife;
And all I ask is a merry yarn from a laughing fellow rover,
And quiet sleep and a sweet dream when the long trick's over.

421

Vermont: Indian Summer

Unseasonable
as bees in April,
rime in May,
or Orion high
in June,
days lost
somewhere in August,
green days, dun,
return at noon
as numb-winged wasps
swim in the lapse
of weather:
sun
and weathervane
are still; the cows
wait, hillside crows
caw down to barn
the first-frost burn
of sumac, maple,
and sideyard apple.
The sky is halo-
hazed, barn and silo
smell of baled hay,
corn-crib, and dry
harvest days;
days,
goldenrod days:
and the dazzled wasps
climb numb in the lapse
of weather, lost
in what cannot last,
wings struck dumb,
in this other summer,
summer twice come.

The Call

I must get out to the woods again, to the whispering
trees and the birds awing,
Away from the haunts of pale-faced men, to the
spaces wide where strength is king;
I must get out where the skies are blue and the
air is clean and the rest is sweet,
Out where there's never a task to do or a goal
to reach or a foe to meet.

I must get out on the trails once more that wind
through shadowy haunts and cool,
Away from the presence of wall and door, and
see myself in a crystal pool;
I must get out with the silent things, where
neither laughter nor hate is heard,
Where malice never the humblest stings and no
one is hurt by a spoken word.

Oh, I've heard the call of the tall white pine,
and heard the call of the running brook;
I'm tired of the tasks which each day are mine;
I'm weary of reading a printed book.
I want to get out of the din and strife, the clang
and clamor of the turning wheel,
And walk for a day where life is life, and the
joys are true and the pictures real.

Dream Animal

These our actors,
As I foretold you, were all spirits, and
Are melted into air, into thin air;
And, like the baseless fabric of this vision,
The cloud-capp'd towers, the gorgeous palaces,
The solemn temples, the great globe itself,
Yea, all which it inherit, shall dissolve
And, like this insubstantial pageant faded,
Leave not a rack behind. We are such stuff
As dreams are made on, and our little life
is rounded with a sleep.

In myth "precision" is sacrificed for a greater degree of suggestion. It is the mode of simultaneous awareness of a complex group of causes and effects.

Lift not the painted veil which those who live
Call Life: though unreal shapes be pictured there,
And it but mimic all we would believe
With colours idly spread,—behind, lurk Fear
And Hope, twin Destinies; who ever weave
Their shadows, o'er the chasm, sightless and drear.
I knew one who had lifted it—he sought,
for his lost heart was tender, things to love,
But found them not, alas! nor was there aught
The world contains, the which he could approve.
Through the unheeding many he did move,
A splendour among shadows, a bright blot
Upon this gloomy scene, a Spirit that strove
For truth, and like the Preacher found it not.

Amergin

English poetic education should, really, begin not with the *Canterbury Tales*, not with the *Odyssey*, not even with *Genesis*, but with the *Song of Amergin*, an ancient Celtic calendar-alphabet, found in several purposely garbled Irish and Welsh variants, which briefly summarizes the prime poetic myth. I have tentatively restored the text as follows:

I am a stag: *of seven tines,*
I am a flood: *across a plain,*
I am a wind: *on a deep lake,*
I am a tear: *the Sun lets fall,*
I am a hawk: *above the cliff,*
I am a thorn: *beneath the nail,*
I am a wonder: *among flowers,*
I am a wizard: *who but I*
Sets the cool head aflame with smoke?

I am a spear: *that roars for blood,*
I am a salmon: *in a pool,*
I am a lure: *from paradise,*
I am a hill: *where poets walk,*
I am a boar: *ruthless and red,*
I am a breaker: *threatening doom,*
I am a tide: *that drags to death,*
I am an infant: *who but I*
Peeps from the unhewn dolmen arch?

I am the womb: *of every holt,*
I am the blaze: *on every hill,*
I am the queen: *of every hive,*
I am the shield: *for every head,*
I am the tomb: *of every hope.*

It is unfortunate that, despite the strong mythical element in Christianity, mythical has come to mean fanciful, absurd, unhistorical; for fancy played a negligible part in the development of the Greek, Latin and Palestinian myths, or of the Celtic myths until the Norman-French *trovères* worked them up into irresponsible romances of chivalry. They are all grave records of ancient religious customs or events. . . .

Design

I found a dimpled spider, fat and white,
On a white heal-all, holding up a moth
Like a white piece of rigid satin cloth–
Assorted characters of death and blight
Mixed ready to begin the morning right,
Like the ingredients of a witches' broth–
A snow-drop spider, a flower like froth,
And dead wings carried like a paper kite.

What had that flower to do with being white,
The wayside blue and innocent heal-all?
What brought the kindred spider to that height,
Then steered the white moth thither in the night?
What but design of darkness to appall?–
If design govern in a thing so small.

"Gee, if ya like THAT kind of pitchers, I can get ya a whole kiddiegarter WALL full!"

Boy heart of Johnny Jones–aching
today?
Aching, and Buffalo Bill in town?
Buffalo Bill and ponies, cowboys
Indians?
Some of us know
All about it, Johnny Jones.
Buffalo Bill is a slanting look of the eyes,
A slanting look under a hat on a horse.
He sits on a horse and a passing look
is fixed
On Johnny Jones, you and me, bare-
legged,
A slanting, passing, careless look under
a hat on a horse.
Go clickety-clack, O pony hoofs along
the street.
Come on and slant your eyes again, O
Buffalo Bill.
Give us again the ache of our boy hearts.
Fill us again with the red love of prairies,
dark nights, lonely wagons, and the
crack-crack of rifles sputtering
flashes into an ambush.

Depend upon it, there is mythology now as there was in the time of Homer, only we do not perceive it.

Black Africa

O black Africa, beloved land of my ancestry;
Land of the blue waters of the Nile and the Zambezi,
Of the great lakes of Nakuru and the Elementaita;
Your Knight guardians—the Majestic mountains of the moon to the West,
And to the East—the sacred Kilimanjaro, beyond the great Serenoeti;
To the North Blue mountains; watch dog of the Gibrotar,
And to the South—the great misty Karoos
Across the red Limpopo river;
O Africa, queen of my heart, I do love you now,
"And I shall but love you better after death."

Fingers

Few fingers go like narrow laughs.
An ear won't keep few fishes,
Who is that rose in that blind house?
And all slim, gracious blind planes are coming,
They cry badly along a rose,
To leap is stuffy, to crawl is tender.

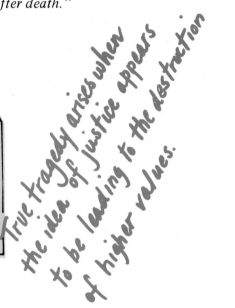

True tragedy arises when
the idea of justice appears
to be leading to the destruction
of higher values.

Buffalo Bill's
defunct
who used to
ride a watersmooth-silver
stallion
and break onetwothreefourfive pigeons justlikethat
Jesus
he was a handsome man
and what i want to know is
how do you like your blueeyed boy
Mister Death

EXPLORE
INNER
SPACE
READ

Can you match each picture with the correct author and book title?

You can play the game in one of three ways:

1. Supply the answers from memory.
2. Use your library to help you identify the author and his work. (What do you learn from doing this—about the book, about the author, about your library?)
3. Ignore the test but look at the names, titles, and pictures to see how much information is contained on the page. List everything it reveals; compare your list with those of others who used this approach.

Regardless of which approach you choose, think over the significance of the game: What does it communicate to you? What does it communicate to others about you? What do you learn about them?

Do the same people succeed with this game as with the movie star game? What is the significance of the answer here?

Can reading, viewing, and so forth be turned *into* an experience? Can experience be made secondhand by seeing it through the eyes of others?

Shirley Jackson
John Updike
Dylan Thomas
Eldridge Cleaver
Françoise Sagan
Ezra Pound
E. E. Cummings
James Thurber
James Baldwin
Tom Wolfe
William Faulkner
T. S. Eliot

Soul On Ice
My Life and Hard Times
A Certain Smile
The Centaur
"Ancient Music"
Go Tell It On The Mountain
Quite Early One Morning
The Lottery
Light in August
"anyone lived in a pretty how town"
"The Love Song of J. Alfred Prufrock"
The Kandy Kolored Tangerine Flake Streamline Baby

Words, our own or another's, can never be more than a commentary upon living experience. Reading can never be substituted for living. What do I understand about a tree? I have climbed into the branches and felt the trunk sway in the winds, and I have hidden among the leaves like an apple. I have lain among the branches and ridden them like another bough, and I have torn the skin of my hands and the cloth of my trousers climbing up and down the harsh bark. I have peeled away the skin of the willow and fondled the white sweet wood, and my ax has bitten through the pure fibers, and my saw laid bare the yearly rings and the heart-wood. Through the microscope I have copied out the traceries of the cells, and I have shaken out the rootlets like hair upon my hand; and I have chewed the gum and curled my tongue around the syrup, and shredded the wood fibers with my teeth. I have lain among the autumn leaves and my nostrils drank the smoke of their sacrifice. I have planed the yellow lumber and driven in the nails, and polished the smooth driftwood with my palm.

Within me now there is a grainyness, a leafiness, a confluence of roots and branches, forests above and afar off, and a light soil made of a thousand years of their decay, and this whisper, this memory of fingers and nostrils, the fragile leaf-budding shivering within my eyes. What is my understanding of trees if it is not this reality lying behind these poor names? So do the lips, the tongue, the ears and eyes and fingers gather their voices and speak inwardly to the understanding. If I am wise I do not try to take another into that strange, placeless place of my thoughts, but I lead him to the forest and lose him among the trees, until he finds the trees within himself, and finds himself within the trees.

EXPLORE
INNER
SPACE
READ

I lived . . . without any other continuity than that, from day to day, of I, I, I. From day to day women, from day to day virtue or vice, from day to day, like dogs—but every day myself secure at my post. Thus I progressed on the surface of life, in the realm of words as it were, never in reality. All those books barely read, those friends barely loved, those cities barely visited, those women barely possessed! I went through gestures out of boredom or absent-mindedness. Then came human beings; they wanted to cling, but there was nothing to cling to, and that was unfortunate—for them. As for me, I forgot. I never remembered anything but myself.

The heroic books will always be in a language dead to degenerate times.

Here is another investigation of "what's there." Is a part of a thing an epitome of the whole? How much can a small part reveal, not about the creator now, but about the whole work? How much *is* there to see?

For example, you have already read *Admiring the Scenery:* Look at its first paragraph (reprinted here) and see how many aspects of the whole story can be sensed. Jot down your observations and then compare yours with those of other students. To refresh your memory, you may want to read the story again.

From
ADMIRING THE SCENERY

From between the little wayside platforms the railway shot two shining arrows off into the vast bogland where they vanished over a rise that might have been imperceptible without them. It was just before sunset in early spring, a soft evening of evaporating moisture and tentative bird song; for the birds seemed to be practicing rather than singing, twirling and stopping, and twirling and stopping, and when the bold thrush rolled out a whirl of sound he might have been mocking all the other eager, stupid little fellows, like the bullfinch or the tits, who had not yet learned their songs.

Following are the beginning paragraphs of four works. Let your mind get the feel of the first sample. What is the attitude, the tone, the approach, the level, the scope? What might you guess the themes of this work are going to be? How much does the writer already tell you in these first paragraphs?

After you have jotted down your guess based on the evidence of the sample, compare it with the synopsis of the work on the next page.

Follow the same procedure with the other samples. As you go along, discuss your observations with your classmates. Can you generalize from this investigation?

How does this investigation relate to the rest of this book?

I

The sea is high again today, with a thrilling flush of wind. In the midst of winter you can feel the inventions of Spring. A sky of hot nude pear until midday, crickets in sheltered places, and now the wind unpacking the great planes, ransacking the great planes. . . .

I have escaped to this island with a few books and the child—Melissa's child. I do not know why I use the word "escape." The villagers say jokingly that only a sick man would choose such a remote place to rebuild. Well, then, I have come here to heal myself, if you like to put it that way. . . .

At night, when the wind roars and the child sleeps quietly in its wooden cot by the echoing chimney-piece I light a lamp and limp about, thinking of my friends—of Justine and Nessim, of Melissa and Balthazar. I return link by link along the iron chains of memory to the city which we inhabited so briefly together: the city which used us as its flora—precipitated in us conflicts which were hers and which we mistook for our own: beloved Alexandria!

I have had to come so far away from it in order to understand it all! Living on this bare promontory, snatched every night from darkness by Arcturus, far from the lime-laden dust of those summer afternoons, I see at last that none of us is properly to be judged for what happened in the past. It is the city which should be judged though we, its children, must pay the price.

Capitally, what is this city of ours? What is resumed in the word Alexandria? In a flash my mind's eye shows me a thousand dust-tormented streets. Flies and beggars own it today—and those who enjoy an intermediate existence between either.

Five races, five languages, a dozen creeds: five fleets turning through their greasy reflections behind the harbour bar. But there are more than five sexes and only demotic Greek seems to distinguish among them. The sexual provender which lies to hand is staggering in its variety and profusion. You would never mistake it for a happy place. The symbolic lovers of the free Hellenic world are replaced here by something different, something subtly androgynous, inverted upon itself. The Orient cannot rejoice in the sweet anarchy of the body—for it has outstripped the body.

Justine (1957) is a poetic novel which generates a mosaic of beauty and mood from the "post-coital sadness" of the four interrelated characters who derive their essence from the main character, the city of Alexandria. Each character's private neurosis is a source of intellectual anguish which Lawrence Durrell explores with penetrating acuity.

The heroine, Justine, raped as a child, makes her body accessible to a series of lovers but is "incapable of delivering her true self—because she does not know where to find it." Her husband, Nessim, a wealthy businessman, tacitly accepts her affair with the narrator, an Irish school teacher. Nessim finds temporary solace with Melissa, the gentle café-dancer mistress of the narrator.

The events and the characters' search for understanding are woven into a design of intricate and surprising turns and twists. These complex relationships are not developed sequentially. The story is obliquely arranged according to the narrator's impression of their significance. Information comes to the reader through Justine's diary, though a novel by her first husband, through rumor, through the cool perception of Clea, a woman painter, through Nessim's endless discussions.

Throughout, Durrell's sensuous prose evokes the filthy physical actuality and languorous sadness of Alexandria: dust-tormented streets, lemony sunlight, hashish dreams, the taste of quicklime in every summer kiss. The insights are both tender and cynical. Alexandria is ransacked for its religious, mystical, and philosophical secrets. A story emerges, not of vividly drawn personalities, but of the puzzles of existence, the harshness of love, and the city which "used us as its flora."

AND THE NOVELIST IS TRYING TO CONVINCE THE READER THAT HE IS SEEING SOCIETY AS A WHOLE.

Chapter I

* * *

I wish either my father or my mother, or indeed both of them, as they were in duty both equally bound to it, had minded what they were about when they begot me; had they duly considered how much depended upon what they were then doing;—that not only the production of a rational Being was concerned in it, but that possibly the happy formation and temperature of his body, perhaps his genius and the very cast of his mind;—and, for aught they knew to the contrary, even the fortunes of his whole house might take their turn from the humours and dispositions which were then uppermost:—Had they duly weighed and considered all this, and proceeded accordingly,—I am verily persuaded I should have made a quite different figure in the world, from that in which the reader is likely to see me.—Believe me, good folks, this is not so inconsiderable a thing as many of you may think it;—you have all, I dare say, heard of the animal spirits, as how they are transfused from father to son, etc. etc.—and a great deal to that purpose:—Well, you may take my word, that nine parts in ten of a man's sense or his nonsense, his successes and miscarriages in this world depend upon their motions and activity, and the different tracts and trains you put them into; so that when they are once set a-going, whether right or wrong, 'tis not a half-penny matter,—away they go cluttering like hey-go-mad; and by treading the same steps over and over again, they presently make a road of it, as plain and as smooth as a garden-walk, which, when they are once used to, the Devil himself sometimes shall not be able to drive them off it.

"Pray, my dear," quoth my mother, "have you not forgot to wind up the clock?"—"Good G—!" cried my father, making an exclamation, but taking care to moderate his voice at the same time,—"Did ever woman, since the creation of the world, interrupt a man with such a silly question?" Pray, what was your father saying?—Nothing.

Chapter II

* * *

—Then, positively, there is nothing in the question, that I can see, either good or bad.—Then, let me tell you, Sir, it was a very unseasonable question at least,—because it scattered and dispersed the animal spirits, whose business it was to have escorted and gone hand-in-hand with the Homunculus, and conducted him safe to the place destined for his reception.

The Homunculus, Sir, in how-ever low and ludicrous a light he may appear, in this age of levity, to the eye of folly or prejudice;—to the eye of reason in scientific research, he stands confessed—a Being guarded and circumscribed with rights:—The minutest philosophers, who, by the bye, have the most enlarged understandings, (their souls being inversely as their enquiries) shew us incontestably, That the Homunculus is created by the same hand,—engendered in the same course of nature,—endowed with the same loco-motive powers and faculties with us:—That he consists, as we do, of skin, hair, fat, flesh, veins, arteries, ligaments, nerves, cartilages, bones, marrow, brains, glands, genitals, humours, and articulations;—is a Being of as much activity,—and, in all senses of the word, as much and as truly our fellow-creature as my Lord Chancellor of England.—He may be benefited,—he may be injured,—he may obtain redress;—in a word, he has all the claims and rights of humanity, which *Tully, Puffendorff,* or the best ethic writers allow to arise out of that state and relation.

Now, dear Sir, what if any accident had befallen him in his way alone?—or that, through terror of it, natural to so young a traveller, my little gentleman had got to his journey's end miserably spent;—his muscular strength and virility worn down to a thread;—his own animal spirits ruffled beyond description,—and that in this sad disordered state of nerves, he had laid down a prey to sudden starts, or a series of melancholy dreams and fancies for nine long, long months together.—I tremble to think what a foundation had been laid for a thousand weaknesses both of body and mind, which no skill of the physician or the philosopher could ever afterwards have set thoroughly to rights.

Laurence Sterne's *The Life and Opinions of Tristram Shandy, Gentleman* (1760) takes in "not only, the Weak part of the Sciences, in which the true point of Ridicule lies—but every Thing else, which I find Laugh-at-able in my way." More modern in outlook and technique than many current novels, it resembles the montage techniques of an Eisenstein or the subjective, romantic disorientation of a Fellini rather than the approach and attitudes of a Marquand or an O'Hara.

It takes Tristram 200 pages to get himself born, the preface appears in the latter half of the book, there are blank pages, marbled pages, black pages, strange numberings, diagrams, unusual uses of type, one-line chapters, no-line chapters, dots, dashes—all sorts of oddities of materials and methods.

But these peculiarities support and indeed demonstrate Sterne's thesis that it is not deeds but the teachings of deeds which are the concern of men. It is not "Where are we going?" but "Where *are* we?" which interests Sterne. Thus, three or four apparently minor events are enough to sustain a 500-page novel. Around the few events of Tristram's life we are permitted to share, Sterne spins out innumerable digressions which finally become the story; from these few occurrences he reaches out to the entire world of eighteenth century culture: philosophy, law, religion, anatomy, music, medicine, and so forth, and so forth, and so forth. "Digressions, incontestably, are the sunshine;—they are the life, the soul of reading...," says Sterne.

As I walked through the wilderness of this world, I lighted on a certain place where was a Den, and I laid me down in that place to sleep: and as I slept I dreamed a dream. I dreamed, and behold, I saw a man clothed with rags, standing in a certain place, with his face from his own house, a book in his hand, and a great burden upon his back. I looked, and saw him open the book and read therein; and as he read, he wept and trembled; and not being able longer to contain, he brake out with a lamentable cry, saying, "What shall I do?"

In this plight, therefore, he went home and refrained himself as long as he could, that his wife and children should not perceive his distress; but he could not be silent long, because that his trouble increased. Wherefore at length he brake his mind to his wife and children; and thus he began to talk to them: O my dear wife, said he, and you the children of my bowels, I, your dear friend, am in myself undone by reason of a burden that lieth hard upon me; moreover I am for certain informed that this our city will be burned with fire from heaven; in which fearful overthrow, both myself, with thee my wife, and you my sweet babes, shall miserably come to ruin, except (the which yet I see not) some way of escape can be found, whereby we may be delivered. At this his relations were sore amazed; not for that they believed that what he had said to them was true, but because they thought that some frenzy distemper had got into his head; therefore, it drawing towards night, and they hoping that sleep might settle his brains, with all haste they got him to bed. But the night

His treatment of his material demonstrates his conviction that association is an accidental or whimsical process. Thus, Tristram feels there is much importance in the fact that at the moment of his conception his mother interrupts his father to ask if he has remembered to wind the clock. It seems crucial to Tristram that the maid forgets the correct *Trismegistus* and has Pastor Yorick christen him *Tristram* instead. No less important is the flattening of his nose by Dr. Slop's faulty use of the forceps, or the occasion on which the window sash falls on a vital member while young Tristram is relieving himself through a window.

Over such events Tristram himself ponders, or his father and Uncle Toby spin out extended and intricate speculations. And through all these we get, not plot, but Sterne's sensitive perception of the comedy that goes on in our minds. Through his examination of minutae in cartoon-like word pictures, Sterne takes us nowhere, but we discover that this is everywhere.

Sterne's technique of suspending time or fragmenting it, suspending the narrative while he goes off on attractive tangents parallels the technique of Joseph Heller's *Catch 22.* The action goes on inexorably and we come back to the main narrative with new dimensions and a richer awareness. While the primary narrative focuses on a handful of events at Shandy Hall, its true location is the all-encompassing mind.

was as troublesome to him as the day; wherefore, instead of sleeping, he spent it in sighs and tears. So, when the morning was come, they would know how he did. He told them, Worse and worse: he also set to talking to them again: but they began to be hardened. They also thought to drive away his distemper by harsh and surly carriages to him; sometimes they would deride, sometimes they would chide, and sometimes they would quite neglect him. Wherefore he began to retire himself to his chamber, to pray for and pity them, and also to condole his own misery; he would also walk solitarily in the fields, sometimes reading, and sometimes praying: and thus for some days he spent his time.

Now I say, upon a time when he was walking in the fields, that he was, as he was wont, reading in his book, and greatly distressed in his mind; and as he read, he burst out, as he had done before, crying, "What shall I do to be saved?"

Christian no sooner leaves the world but meets
Evangelist, who lovingly him greets
With tidings of another; and doth show
Him how to mount to that from this below.

I saw also that he looked this way and that way, as if he would run; yet he stood still, because, as I perceived, he could not tell which way to go. I looked then, and saw a man named Evangelist coming to him, who asked, Wherefore dost thou cry?

Pilgrim's Progress (circa 1677) is the chronicle of the inner journey of a lonely figure seeking salvation with no guide but the Bible and his own urgency. With his curious and imaginative analogies, his keen, good-humored wit and homely, virile style, his deep feelings for human beings, John Bunyan traces the stages of Christian's progress as he struggles through quagmires and pits, steep hills, dark and horrible glens, soft vales and sunny pastures. This dream-like fairytale structure is the framework for the Pilgrim's agonies of soul as he passes through the Slough of Despond, surmounts Hill Difficulty, and continues through House Beautiful, the Valley of Humiliation, the Valley of the Shadow of Death, and Vanity Fair. Enemies and false friends try to thwart him, but he is helped by his companions, Faithful and Helpful. Finally after crossing the Delectable Mountains, the Enchanted Ground and the River of Death, he reaches the Celestial City.

Though his struggles are representative of mankind's spiritual quest, Christian is a genuine man, as are the many persons with allegorical names he meets on his way: Obstinate, Pliable, Wordly Wiseman, Simple Sloth, Timorous, Wanton, Sincere, Knowledge, Hope, Vain-Hope.

Nor is the fullness of life denied. There are happy dinner parties, riddles and music, the ringing of cathedral bells, even a dance. Bunyan's vigorous everyday language of the seventeenth century with its quaint turns of speech sustains the story throughout.

Sitting beside the road, watching the wagon mount the hill toward her, Lena thinks, 'I have come from Alabama: a fur piece. All the way from Alabama a-walking. A fur piece.' Thinking *although I have not been quite a month on the road I am already in Mississippi, further from home than I have ever been before. I am now further from Doane's Mill than I have been since I was twelve years old.*

She had never even been to Doane's Mill until after her father and mother died, though six or eight times a year she went to town on Saturday, in the wagon, in a mail-order dress and her bare feet flat in the wagon bed and her shoes wrapped in a piece of paper beside her on the seat. She would put on the shoes just before the wagon reached town. After she got to be a big girl she would ask her father to stop the wagon at the edge of town and she would get down and walk. She would not tell her father why she wanted to walk in instead of riding. He thought that it was because of the smooth streets, the sidewalks. But it was because she believed that the people who saw her and whom she passed on foot would believe that she lived in the town too.

When she was twelve years old her father and mother died in the same summer, in a log house of three rooms and a hall, without screens, in a room lighted by a bug-swirled kerosene lamp, the naked floor worn smooth as old silver by naked feet. She was the youngest living child. Her mother died first. She said, "Take care of Paw." Lena did so. Then one day her father said, "You go to Doane's Mill with McKinley. You get ready to go, be ready when he comes." Then he died. McKinley, the brother, arrived in a wagon. They buried the father in a grove behind a country church one afternoon, with a pine headstone. The next morning she departed forever, though it is possible that she did not know this at the time, in the wagon with McKinley, for Doane's Mill. The wagon was borrowed and the brother had promised to return it by nightfall.

The brother worked in the mill. All the men in the village worked in the mill or for it. It was cutting pine. It had been there seven years and in seven years more it would destroy all the timber within its reach. Then some of the machinery and most of the men who ran it and existed because of and for it would be loaded onto freight cars and moved away. But some of the machinery would be left, since new pieces could always be bought on the installment plan—gaunt, staring, motionless wheels rising from mounds of brick rubble and weeds with a quality profoundly astonishing, and gutted boilers lifting their rusting and unsmoking stacks with an air stubborn, baffled and bemused upon a stumppocked scene of profound and peaceful desolation, unplowed, untilled, gutting slowly into red and choked ravines beneath the long quiet rains of autumn and the galloping fury of vernal equinoxes. Then the hamlet which at its best day had borne no name listed on Postoffice Department annals would not now even be remembered by the hookwormridden heirs-at-large who pulled the buildings down and burned them in cookstoves and winter grates.

William Faulkner's *Light in August* (1932) weaves tale within tale, stretches back in time, interrelates the land and the people who alter it and are altered by it. It is the story of a decaying world. The central tale is the uncertain, sullen life of Joe Christmas, a mulatto whose love affair with the white northern spinster, Miss Joanna Burden, culminates in the shocking climax of the novel.

The violence and passion surrounding Joe Christmas is given perspective by the frame story of Lena Grove, the pregnant poor-white mountain girl whose search for her seducer leads her into nightmarish scenes and out again. Through her story the reader is able to keep the threads and patches of tales sorted and is able to see them as part of the "long quiet rains of autumn and the galloping fury of vernal equinoxes." The accumulated tensions are dissipated as life goes inevitably and persistently on.

The story also ranges in psychological levels and angles of perspective. Lena, for example, thinks on one level in her native dialect, but her inner mind is not limited to that dialect. It sees more broadly. The author further explores Lena's situation from an exterior angle. Despite the abundance of information, much of the interpretation and meaning of the novel is left for the reader to determine.

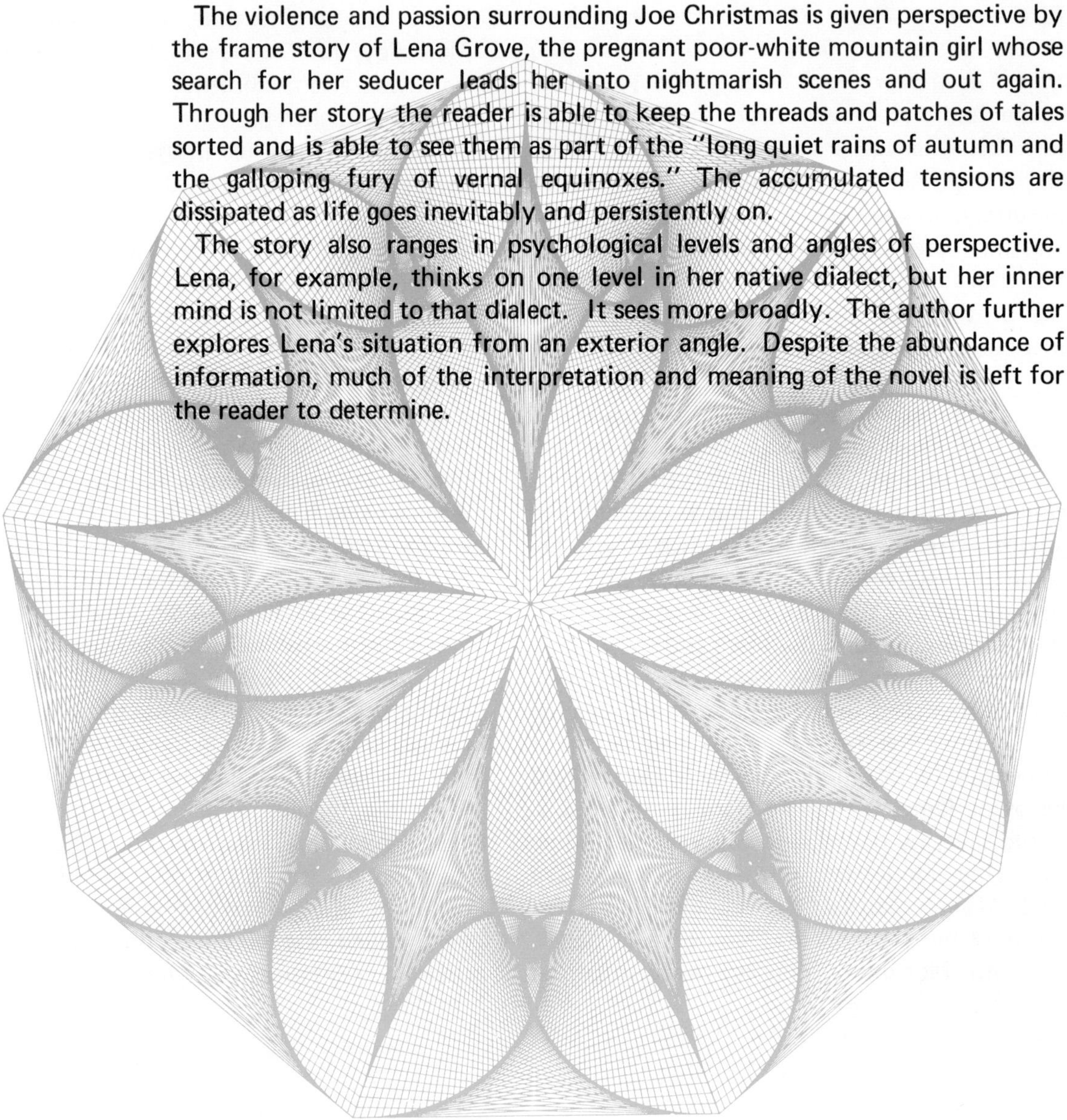

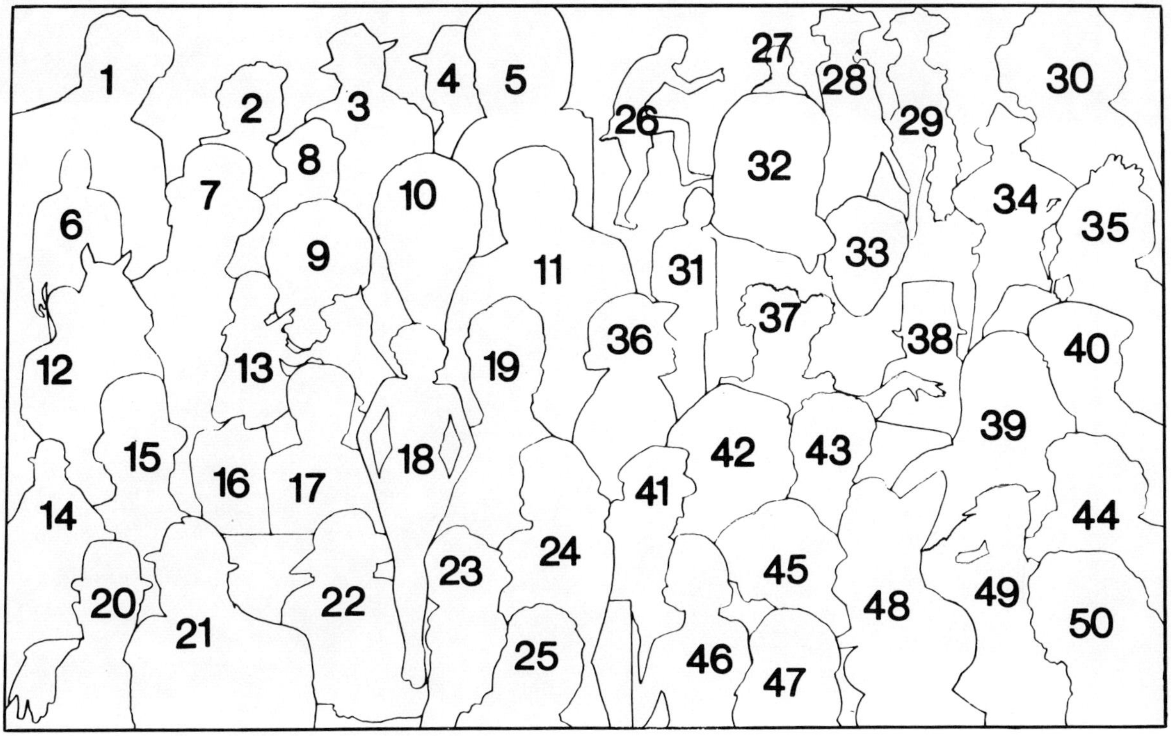

1. Paul Muni
2. Mercedes McCambridge
3. John Ireland
4. Broderick Crawford
5. Rita Tushingham
6. Ronald Reagan
7. Wallace Beery
8. Fatty Arbuckle
9. Dustin Hoffman
10. Zero Mostel
11. Peter Lorre
12. Kier Dullea
13. Shirley Temple
14. Charlie Chaplin
15. Max Von Sydow
16. Vanessa Redgrave
17. Abby Lincoln
18. Marilyn Monroe
19. Jean Simmons
20. Stanley Laurel
21. Oliver Hardy
22. Edna Purviance
23. Tyrone Power
24. Rita Hayworth
25. Albert Finney
26. Johnny Weismuller
27. Alan Bates
28. Brigitte Bardot
29. Jeanne Moreau
30. Clara Bow
31. Theda Bara
32. Shirley McLaine
33. Judy Holliday
34. Tom Mix
35. Marie Dressler
36. Gloria Swanson
37. Mae West
38. W. C. Fields
39. Catherine Deneuve
40. James Stewart
41. Efrem Zimbalist, Jr.
42. Pola Negri
43. Ava Gardner
44. Claudette Colbert
45. Ruth Gordon
46. Inger Stevens
47. Faye Dunaway
48. Jayne Mansfield
49. Buster Keaton
50. Mary Pickford

The others that are to follow me, the ties between me and them. . .

ONCE MORE, THE ROUND

What's greater, Pebble or Pond?
What can be known? The unknown.
My true self runs toward a hill
More! O more! Visible.

Now I adore my life
With the bird, the abiding leaf,
With the fish, the questing snail,
And the eye altering all;
And I dance with William Blake
For love, for Love's sake;

And everything comes to One,
As we dance on, dance on, dance on.

SEMANTICS AND THE CREATIVE PROCESS

Perhaps from this we can give an account in general semantic terms of the creative process. Let me put it something like this: if you see in any given situation only what everybody else can see, you can be said to be so much a representative of your culture that you are a victim of it. In other words, you haven't got the materials to be original with, since you have before you only "just another" sunset, "just another" tree, "just another" batch of left-overs in the icebox—these are the common abstractions. But if you are extensional about the world around you, open to the uniqueness of every object and event, if you are open, too, about your own feelings, namely, the uniqueness of your tensions and needs at the moment, and of those around you, what is before you is *not* "just another" sunset, or "just another" tree, or "just another" batch of left-overs. And the act of bringing together the uniqueness of yourself at the moment with the uniqueness of your materials at the moment and the uniqueness of other people's feelings at the moment into the solution of the problem is the act of creativity: whether the end-product takes the form of a painting, a sonata, a plan for prison reform, or a new kind of casserole dish.

With the instantaneous brilliance of a lightning flash, life and consciousness were born. The journey from void nonentity to vivid awakening was swifter than the passage of a meteor, instant and complete.

The search for self-identity began. Seconds after his awakening, the new-born being subjected his environment and himself to a minutely detailed examination. He discovered within himself, down in the misty centre of consciousness, a store of knowledge, all of it quite meaningless until linked with the stimulus of outside experience.

One thing he learned. He had a name. This was a convenient and necessary item. It was the symbol of individual identity. It defined the most important thing in his environment; himself. He knew that it would do more than that, he knew that his name contained the riddle of existence. When he succeeded in interpreting this riddle, he would become aware of the purpose for which he was created.

A DI-LEMMA

Here are the first few digits of a number system which uses base five instead of base ten.

1	2	3	4	10	11	12	13	14	20
21	22	23	24	30	31	__	__	__	
40	__	__	__	__	100	__			

3 + 4 in this system is 12. 4 X 4 is 31.

2 + 3 = __ 2 X 3 = __.

40 + 40 = __ 40 X 40 = __.

Some probes:

Reasons some operations seem easy or difficult.

Insights from learning a foreign tongue.

Habit. Ethnocentrism. Bias. Bigotry. Dis-covery.

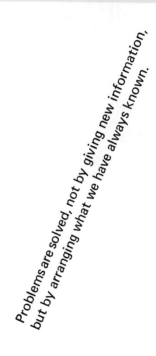

Problems are solved, not by giving new information, but by arranging what we have always known.

VISUAL METAPHOR

Here is the first page of a script for a television broadcast. Earlier in this book part of a television script, "An Essay on Women," appeared along with directions for visuals and sound and the duration of each shot.

If you were to use the idea of "bridges" metaphorically to represent connections and tie-ins you have observed in this book, how would you begin? What visuals would you use? How would you present them? For what duration? In what sequence?

Let yourself be creative. Try your hand at converting this page into a shooting script for a television show which would be not only about bridges but also about the interconnectedness of this book. (But make no change in the dialogue itself.) You may want to refer to "An Essay on Women" for appropriate format and camera directions.

You will probably find it revealing to compare your script with those of other students. Which scripts come closest to the essence of this book? Which scripts make maximum use of television possibilities? Is this different from making a movie?

REASONER: Man has always suspected that some state of perfection exists where function, beauty, truth and everlastingness converge. Perhaps the closest he has come to reaching this state is with the bridges he has built. If the earth was dipped in lava tomorrow and coated, like a candy apple, to be preserved for rediscovery from another planet in another age, the rediscoverers might easily attribute the cities to man—the trees, the rivers, the bridges, to God.

Cities are bordered on one or more sides by water. To get to a city you cross a bridge—and there are always reasons for coming to them, and for leaving.

There are a certain number of monuments erected in memory of man whose own fame, in time, grows to rival those whose name they bear. "The George Washington Bridge" is a name that has a meaning all its own. It does not recall to mind a man to those who use it.

The George Washington Bridge is suspended across the Hudson River between the rock palisades of New Jersey and the Island of

Manhattan—but it does not lead to New Jersey, it leads in and out of New York.

The Bridge is more a bottle than a bottleneck. Its 14 lanes of traffic have carried a quarter of a million cars in 24 hours. Anyone wishing to put his finger on the pulse of the city would put it here.

This many cars have crossed since it opened—they have paid so much in tolls—carried that many people at such and such a speed. A new number is born every second—but the George Washington Bridge exceeds its own statistics.

Othmar Ammann designed it. "You build a bridge," he said, "to last forever."

a
an is
association
of
idea feat

A LEMMA BY CONSTANCE REID

There is a square for every
Natural number. If we
Divide the squares into even
And odd, we find that we can
Place the natural numbers
And the two sets of even
And odd squares in one to one
Correspondence.
  We will never
Run out of squares. But neither
Will we run out of even
Or odd squares. Rest assured, though
Squares are inexhaustible, and
Problems concerning squares are
Also inexhaustible,
So are natural numbers.

Delight comes from simultaneous perception of multiple meanings with one form.

A time, place or means of connection or transition. . .

When the winds rise and snow fills the air, visibility may be reduced to a hundred feet or less, and travel becomes dangerous. But, if they must, hunters travel in such weather, even though the trail is lost and the dogs uncertain. I believe they can do it because of their knowledge of topography and winds. Their (Eskimo) astonishing gifts of observation, their familiarity with the smallest details of this monotonous land, particularly its coastline, never failed to amaze me. Rarely did a man seem uncertain as to his whereabouts, but as I looked about, at the utter sameness of the land, I simply could not imagine what reference points he was using.

Explore the significance of your findings in your journal.

By studying the way children between the ages of four and ten describe a familiar walk, such as the road home from school . . . we will see clearly how they learn to describe changes of position by using landmarks and eventually link these reference points in a comprehensive system.

A fool wants to kill space and time: a wise man, first to gain them, then to animate them.

As you study each item, essay, and story in this section, seek connections with material on other pages of this book.

FROMASTUDENT'SJOURNAL

THREADS

Habit cloaks the eye and ear,
Deadens what we see and hear.
The audio-visual cliché
Makes each new another day.
The world without, mirrors that within;
The naked senses hear and see again.

The recent rebellion against the narrowly cognitive emphasis in education should not surprise us. Twelve or fourteen years of emotionally barren and often meaningless fact-grubbing (the length of time college students have spent in school) seem well calculated to leave a person starved for feelings and for symbols. One form the rebellion has taken is the LSD movement. In part, advocates of LSD seem to want to restore instantly what has been left out of 14 or so years of education. Yet, the idea that a drug can do this is of a piece with behavioristically based education, in that it assumes the same kind of emptiness in the person. To be sure, emotions can be released and imagery induced by various chemical and mechanical means. But the range and quality of emotions and imagery are enhanced and developed through broad experience and a challenging education.

Ryokan, a Zen master, lived the simplest kind of life in a little hut at the foot of a mountain. One evening a thief visited the hut only to discover there was nothing in it to steal.

Ryokan returned and caught him. "You may have come a long way to visit me," he told the prowler, "and you should not return empty-handed. Please take my clothes as a gift."

The thief was bewildered. He took the clothes and slunk away.

Ryokan sat naked, watching the moon. "Poor fellow," he mused, "I wish I could give him this beautiful moon."

I SAW THE MAN IN THE PARK WITH A TELESCOPE

$40 + 40 = 3100$

Which of the following is the most likely meaning of this sentence? Which is least likely?

A. I looked through a telescope and perceived the man in the park.

B. While I was in the park I observed a man who had a telescope.

C. I am now sawing a man in the park in two, using a telescope as the instrument.

Can you think of other possible meanings?

Without the host of ethnic experiences which surround such a coded abstraction, would any one answer be any more likely than any other? What meanings would an unbiased computer accept?

$40 + 40 = 130$

$2 + 3 = \underline{11}$

$2 + 3 = \underline{10}$

. . . I have some reservations about your exercise for the page from "An Essay on Bridges." The reason I became my own producer was because producers who didn't know how to write *or* produce kept asking me when the script would be finished. I kept asking the producer and the film editor when the film would be rough cut. It turns out that neither the filming, the editing or the writing comes first. They have to come together—or at least they do in the sort of films I'm trying to make. What I'm saying is that your text or questions seem to suggest that the film is shot and edited from the directions appearing in the left-hand side of the script. That "shooting script" is a fake. The script is put together from the finished product, not vice versa. I think this is happening more and more, even with feature films.

Some people say that having bias limits the individual. Can it also free him?

LYRICS BY THE INDO-EUROPEAN LANGUAGE FAMILY

A sentence can be likened to a computer program; in fact, that is precisely what it is: a set of directions for the human thinking machine. The hearer or the reader of a sentence constructs its meaning by following the "directions" it provides in terms of the concepts and conceptual relationships it evokes, also utilizing whatever further information he may have concerning the situation in which he hears it. This process may be called *interpretation.* A string of linguistic signs that cannot be interpreted, like "words straighten poverty without every encounter," is devoid of situational meaning.

Determined not to let language slip on her tongue
and tumble her so that we laugh.

An expression has meaning only in the stream of life.

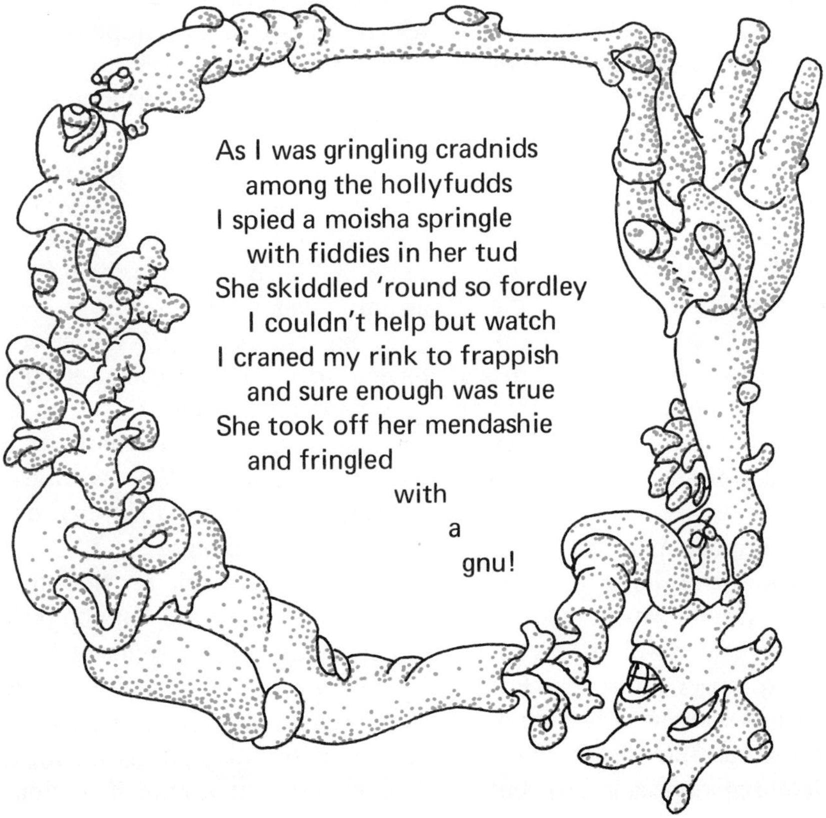

As I was gringling cradnids
  among the hollyfudds
I spied a moisha springle
  with fiddies in her tud
She skiddled 'round so fordley
  I couldn't help but watch
I craned my rink to frappish
  and sure enough was true
She took off her mendashie
  and fringled
    with
      a
        gnu!

The final thing:
A man learning to sing.

MUSIC BY?

SALT CRYSTALS, SPIDER WEBS, AND WORDS

Writing is like making love—it is astonishing how far pure instinct (if it really is pure) will carry you. It is also true of both these lyrical forms of expression that a few things consciously learned will push toward perfection what might otherwise be an ordinary act.

And yet—can writing actually be taught? Is there much more you can give to a beginner beyond Flaubert's no-nonsense advice of a kiss on the brow and a kick in the behind?

In pointing out that a writer crystallizes a concept, as when he endows a woman with qualities she simply does not have, Stendhal produced an image that, however little it flatters the ladies, does dramatize the process by which persuasive words can turn a dull object into something glittering and gay. He observes that a dead branch, dark and ugly, if left overnight in the salt mines of Salzburg, will be covered with crystals and next day will glitter in the sunlight.

This image of the salt crystals on the branch wisely and attractively illustrates what the writer does with that curious and secret substance called his "material." What writer has not been stopped by an eager-eyed and bushy-tailed person who cries out despairingly, "I've got the greatest material for a book, if I could just *write!*"

The first and most important point about writing is that there is no such thing as material by itself, apart from the way in which a person sees it, feels toward it, and is able to give it organized form and expression in words. For a writer, form is a part of content, affecting it, realizing it. A man may go through the most dramatic and horrible experiences in war, but actually draw out of them less "material" for writing than shy Emily Dickinson in the second-floor room of an Amherst house, lowering notes in baskets out the window and thinking gently of death—or even (biographers speculate) of a man she knew but little, whom she might never see again.

Henry James said it first and beautifully when he wrote that experience is unlimited: "an immense sensibility, a kind of huge spider web of the finest silken threads suspended in the chamber of consciousness, and catching every air-borne particle in its tissue. It is the very atmosphere of the mind." This is crucial, for it is not what happens in the outside world that is of absolute significance, but what happens to that external event when it is discovered and then ordered by the internal power of a mind. James goes on to speak then of the creative aspect: "and when the mind is imaginative . . . it takes to itself the faintest hints of life, it converts the very pulse of the air into revelations."

By experience, then, a writer does not mean having adventures. In answering a critic who had complained about the novel that it is impossible to have one without bold action, James protested, "Why without adventure, more than without matrimony, or celibacy, or parturition, or cholera . . . ?"

Anything is suitable for fiction, which is not a record of incidents happening *to* men and women, but of the response they make within themselves to the incidents. This is because fiction deals with character, which determines action, and thus actions illustrate character. The conduct of a man in a ring fighting an enraged bull or the soft wave of a woman's hand are equally moving and suitable.

A thousand Frenchmen may walk down a Paris street and, turning a corner, forget the place. But Toulouse-Lautrec walking down the same street would see, with his shrewd eye, and remember, with his artist's force of retention, not bricks but visions. In this way the imagination works not only on the stuff that is stored in the mind, but also on the very act of experiencing. Like the pilot, the writer must see faster and more completely than the ordinary viewer of life.

Out of his practical skills in the writing of fiction, James described the process of the writer using his experience. "The power to guess the unseen from the seen," he said, "to trace the implication of things, to judge the whole piece by the pattern, the condition of feeling life in general so completely that you are well on your way to knowing any particular corner of it—this cluster of gifts may almost be said to constitute experience, and they occur in country and in town, and in the most differing stages of education. If experience consists of impressions, it may be said that impressions *are* experience, just as (have we not seen it?) they are the very air we breathe."

This is final wisdom about writing. The writer, when given an inch, takes an ell. Remember that an ell is forty-five inches. If that is the degree of heightening, then the eye of the writer must look at life with forty-five times as much perception. That is a marvelous degree of intensity, and in particular when it comes from the author of *Portrait of a Lady,* a book about which it has been remarked that, although it concerns the relationship between a man and a woman, there is only one kiss, and the heroine, poor thing, did not enjoy it.

But some will argue: writing, like all art, is intuitive, and any intrusion of the reason will destroy the lovely, natural thing. This is dead wrong. It reduces writing to the level of a child babbling without regard to the shape of what he is saying. It is, indeed, so much like the uninhibited confessions from the psychiatrist's couch, sodium amytal cheerfully flowing through the veins and breaking down shyness, that it would seem proper to give inhibition-removing drugs to the writer. He could sit there gaily listening to the rustlings of his unconscious. And of course the hallucinatory state would be the most creative of all.

It is quite possible that some good things could be thus spontaneously created. I met in India people who could induce visions. Yet surely the great and structured works of writing are done with the intelligence playing over against the intuition, each bracing the other, the mind giving form and sense, the intuition giving immediacy of impression, the stored-up memory, the deeply instinctive phrase.

To say that writing comes only from the intuition is to belittle it as coming from one narrow aspect of our lives alone. The opposite is true. The total life of the writer is the source of his work. All these go into his writing, in varying quantities: the senses, as of taste and touch, the rate of metabolism, the blood pressure, the digestion, the body temperature, the memory of things past, perhaps going back to the childhood not only of the writer but of the race itself, the liveliness and alertness of the brain, previous reading of books, shrewdness of insight into human character, the libido, the ear for the sound of language.

The writer, therefore, must not only have a more than ordinary capacity for life and the power to retain what he experiences in a readily available memory but he must also have an astonishing degree of self-knowledge. Unless he is aware of his material, he cannot use it, save for the always present quantity that flows up from the deep well of the unconscious recollection. Without access to knowledge of self, the writer can make dreams but not art. Dr. Lawrence S. Kubie says that without self-knowledge, "we can have the neurotic raw material of literature, but not mature literature. We can have no adults, but only aging children who are armed with words."

By self-knowledge I do not mean self-expression. Although all good writing always bears the individual mark, sound, and motion of the writer, he is not trying to put his own self into words, but to create a piece of writing. Often, the less of his own self involved or expressed, the better. His own personality ought to be dissolved into the images or characters of his book. The writer is offering us not reality, but his reaction to whatever reality he has experienced.

Yet the ego is important. It must be that within the creative person there is a constant tension between an awareness of the reality around him, a thrusting up of the unconscious life and its memory, and the drive of the ego toward controlling these in a form that also heightens them. These are crude terms to describe subtle conditions, but the creation of any art is one of the most complex of human activities, involving every animal and human quality. The ego must shape the mortal impulses. It is here that something can indeed be taught about writing, for it is in this shaping that the individual's private events are turned into public forms. It is here that writing becomes an art and not merely a report on experience, and this is true of the best reporting.

How many boys have played around greenhouses? Swarms. But how many, on growing up, have put their feelings about that place into powerful poetry? Only Theodore Roethke. His account is proof.

Roethke asks what does it matter that he grew up in and around a beautiful greenhouse, hated school, worked in a pickle factory, lived sometimes quietly and sometimes foolishly and violently, and meant almost nothing to the people of his own state, the man in the street, but passionately desired their regard?

> All such details, and others like them [Roethke comments] seem particularly trivial and vulgar in my case because I have tried to put down in poems, as barely and honestly as possible, symbolically, what few nuggets of observation and, let us hope, spiritual wisdom I have managed to seize upon in the course of a conventional albeit sometimes disordered existence. I have tried to transmute and purify my "life," the sense of being defiled by it in both small and formal and somewhat blunt short poems, and latterly, in longer poems which try in their rhythms to catch the very movement of the mind itself, to trace the spiritual history of a protagonist (not "I" personally) of all haunted and harried men; to make in this series (now probably finished) a true and not arbitrary order which will permit many ranges of feeling, including humor. . . .

And then he says in verse:

My heart sways with the world.
I am that final thing,
A man learning to sing.

Although this may suggest a self-consciousness not shared by all poets, it is further evidence of that deep need for self-knowledge that is a strength and a source. Roethke knew *what* he was trying to do in those moving and often tortured poems, and this awareness, far from inhibiting the imaginative freedom of the verse, enriched it. The cool mind, curiously enough, it seems, really can express a warm feeling.

Once the writer has a sense of his experience and of his own self, without illusion, and can be tough-minded about his own weakness and vulgarity, what else can he possibly learn? What can he *do* to make his writing better, assuming that he is not trapped in the conviction that writing is a wholly automatic outburst from underground?

He can examine the knowledge of their own writing habits great men have made available. It is odd the things writers have done. The German poet Schiller used to keep rotting apples under the lid of his desk because their smell helped him write. Pilots on the river at Rouen would see the light in Flaubert's study very late at night as he utterly shut himself away from the world to worry two pages of prose a week into the ruthlessly purified and perfected shape he demanded. Why this enormous care? The old wisecrack says that a physician who fails can always bury his patient out of sight. Frank Lloyd Wright remarked that an architect who fails can at least urge his client to plant vines. The writer, however, once his work is in print, can do nothing. There the text is, black on the page; any errors and ugliness will show forever. There are rare exceptions, of course, like William Butler Yeats, who, in his old age (with that marvelous lyrical mind hardened by the criticism of others), went back to the poems of his youth and cut out much of the sentimentality and soft, vague language.

Reticent as always, William Faulkner said that the tools of the writer's trade are paper, tobacco, food, and whiskey. Of these, the most dangerous is not tobacco or whiskey (writers are famous for abusing them), but paper. One of the most terrifying sights is that waiting, threatening blank sheet. Its force is proved by the Japanese writer who, after much success, could not, for a long time, push ahead with his writing. One autumn—and this is a true story—he disappeared. The next spring his body was found, after the snow had melted, high up in the mountains. Pinned to his jacket was a note only the suffering writer could have written: "I have done this because I could no longer endure the sight of the empty page."

All those writers who have commented on their craft agree that a work of art is work. How could the joining of passion and idea in slippery words be anything but a labor? That first really modern novel, *Madame Bovary*, was composed by Gustave Flaubert with the deliberation of a medieval monk illuminating a manuscript. The French novelist could write quickly and fluently, as his early books and his lively letters show, but he would never give up a sentence until it was beyond improving. To get his description of the landscape correct, he sat all day on a balcony looking through pieces of different-colored glass in order to note the changes in shape of fields and roads and trees hour by hour.

Never was a writer more emotionally involved with what he was writing than Flaubert. When he described Emma Bovary poisoning herself, he was so moved that he could taste arsenic on his own tongue and felt so poisoned himself that he vomited his dinner. And yet when he finally finished that scene, he had engineered it onto the page with an almost fanatical control. Once again, the writer's talent had produced an immortal passage out of passionate deliberation.

Flaubert would begin a single paragraph by setting down its general idea, with perhaps a few images (a risk always, for a brilliant image-making faculty he had; he wrote that he was devoured by metaphors as by vermin and spent his time crushing them). Then he wrote a first draft, reading it aloud for sound and sense (always read any sort of text out loud, the surest way to catch the feeble phrase, the trite adjective, the outworn image, the dull rhythm, the phony speech). Then he would rewrite, again and again, as a fine craftsman polishes over and over the same increasingly brilliant piece of maple or mahogany. Every word that did not act with energy was thrown away, until the paragraph was lean, tough, expressive. *Madame Bovary's* final version was written on 1,788 pages, but these were only the latest of many times that number of pages actually written. At times fifteen or twenty pages would be reduced to four. Thus, when Flaubert said that he spent a week over two pages, he meant over the two finally perfected pages out of many more.

Flaubert may be the only man in history who told his girl friend, "You should write more coldly." This was a part of his advice that "we must be on our guard against that kind of intellectual overheating called inspiration, which often consists more largely of nervous emotion than of muscular strength . . . my brow is burning, sentences keep rushing into my head. . . . Instead of one idea I have six, and where the most simple type of exposition is called for I find myself writing similes and metaphors. I could keep going until tomorrow noon without fatigue." And yet he could follow such an outburst with the blunt advice, brief, wise, but taking most writers a lifetime to learn: "Everything should be done coldly, with poise." When putting down the word "hysterics" one day he was so carried away that he bellowed loudly and felt so sharply what Emma Bovary was going through that he was afraid of having hysterics himself.

Can it be that the French, more than any other people, are able to balance heat and cold, desire and deliberation, and make a single intense but controlled utterance? The modern poet, Paul Valéry, wrote that poetry must be a holiday of the mind and then said, with greater calm, that when he writes, "I proceed like a surgeon who sterilizes his hands and prepares the area to be operated on. . .clearing up the verbal situation."

The English seem more practical, if a little less dedicated to perfection. Novelist Joyce Cary described his process thus:

> A finished book of mine starts usually perhaps ten years before as a character sketch and a bit of description; it goes on to an incident or so, it gathers subsidiary characters, and then perhaps I grow interested in it, and set out to give it form as a book. I sketch a plan; I may write the end, the middle, and the beginning and very often just in this order. That is, I decide how and where the book shall end, which is just as important to a book as to a play, and then I ask myself where are the most difficult turns in the book. Then I may write one of these difficult passages to see if it is viable. . . . I may stop there. But if it does work, then I may devise a beginning and finish the book.

How contrary to the old notion of inspiration to find Cary devising a beginning of a novel of which he has written bits in various parts and without order. This is evidence that what the writer is really doing is not so much writing a poem or play or story that he has firmly in mind, but rather is using his writing to discover what it truly is he is trying to say. Often he will not know until the final revision of the last page what he had been trying to do from the start.

One would hardly guess the zest and liveliness of Chekhov's mind if he had only seen a moody performance of *The Sea Gull.* Commenting on the new "decadent" writers he noted, "They're a lot of strong, healthy young men: what they need is to be sentenced to a few months hard labor! This new-art business is just a pack of nonsense. . . . There's nothing new in art except talent." Chekhov constantly wrote subjects for stories in moments taken from his medical practice ("Medicine is my lawful wife, literature my mistress. When I am tired of the one, I spend a night with the other.") One notebook contained 100 entries. Some of these are diverting: A building contractor of great frugality loathed paying repair bills. When he married, he chose an exceptionally healthy woman so that he would have no repair bills with her.

A writer should be as objective as a chemist, he commented, and have nothing to do with the subjective approach that most of us make in our everyday lives. And when he wrote that the writer should never sit down to his work until he felt cold as ice, he was remarkably like Flaubert. Any reader of Chekhov's short stories will be amazed to find how very simple were the original notes for two of the finest. "A cabdriver who has just lost his son has to go on working just the same. He tries to speak of his grief to his fares, but finds only indifference." Another equally famous story began with three little sentences. "Some officers on maneuvers are invited to a house where there are several young women. One of them kisses one of the officers, a shy and reserved young man, in the dark. He looks for her, but in vain." These are the plain, experienced reality, but the stories written out of them are the heightened overreality.

Poor Chekhov, tending the sick with his own fatal illness corrupting his lungs. When he died in Germany, his coffin was taken to Moscow in a baggage car marked "Oysters." Yet he never allowed a scrap of self-pity to interfere with the absolute integrity of his dedication to writing:

> My own experience is that once a story has been written, one has to cross out the beginning and the end. It is there that we authors do most of our lying. . . . One must always tear up the first half. I mean that seriously. Young writers begin by, as one says, "placing the story"—whereas the reader ought, on the contrary, to be able to grasp what it is all about by the way it is told, without any explanations from the author, from the conversation and the actions of the characters. . . . One must ruthlessly suppress everything that is not concerned with the subject. If, in the first chapter, you say there is a gun hanging on the wall, you should make quite sure that it is going to be used further on in the story.

Chekhov felt strongly the distinction between direct reality as it is lived and the imagined reality of art. In 1898 he went to a rehearsal of *The Sea Gull* at the Moscow Art

Theater and was told by an actor that backstage there would be sounds of frogs croaking, grasshoppers scraping, and dogs barking. He asked why, and was told this would be realistic. But the theatre is not realism, it is art, he argued. If you put a real nose into a painting of a face, the nose will be realistic but the picture will be ruined. You do not use fiction to resolve the existence of God; you exhibit characters conducting lives and show the way in which they discuss God.

Similarly Tolstoy remarked that *Anna Karenina*, that massive novel, was just a simple story about a married woman who falls in love with an officer. This sort of reducing of any piece of writing to its essence is a part of that control over material which is indispensable to the practicing writer. Such definition comes out of enormous and confusing reaches of experience. No one has more imaginatively stated the mysterious and at the same time gritty nature of human existence than Virginia Woolf when she wrote that "life is a luminous halo, a semitransparent envelope surrounding us from the beginning."

Virginia Woolf also wrote a paragraph defining the nature of this envelope more precisely:

> Examine for a moment an ordinary mind on an ordinary day. The mind receives myriad impressions—trivial, fantastic, evanescent, or engraved with the sharpness of steel. From all sides they come, an incessant shower of innumerable atoms; and as they fall, as they shape themselves into the life of Monday or Tuesday, the accent falls differently from of old; the moment of importance came not here but there; so that, if the writer were a freeman and not a slave, if he could write what he chose, not what he must, if he could base his work upon his own feeling and not upon convention, there would be no plot, no comedy, no tragedy, no love interest, or catastrophe in the accepted style.

The simple, often gruntlike puffs of air which we call words must be used by the writer with such skill that they can bring to a reader, who cannot even hear whatever tone of voice the writer would give them, a form and sense that will move him. This is by no means so easy as lifting bricks all day or breaking stone. Flaubert testifies to that: "My head reels and my throat aches with chasing after, slogging over, delving into, turning 'round, groping after, and bellowing, in a hundred thousand different ways, a sentence that I've at last finished. It's good . . ." One sentence!

No one knew better the tortures or the necessity of this sort of harsh self-discipline than the most exuberant and debauched poet, Baudelaire. In his *Flowers of Evil*, he wrote, there was a cold and sinister beauty. How did that beauty happen? This first of the beatniks differed from his later brothers not in his contempt for the vulgarity of middle-class life, nor in his concern for the flaunting immorality that repudiated such life, but in his attitude toward his art. Yearning to have his book appear so that it could prove to his mother, his formidable father-in-law General Aupick, and his friends that he was an authentic poet, he nevertheless kept the printer waiting several months while he revised a few lines into perfection. It may actually be that much writing is created into excellence and then revised into greatness. This is true of the play, the story, the novel, the poem, the article, of whatever form men choose to make words move other men.

SEESAW

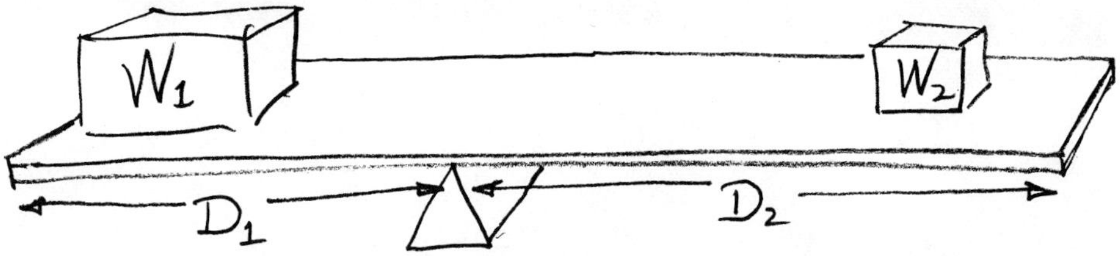

2 is in the same relation to 4
As 3 is to 6.
On a fulcrum,
Weight$_1$ is in the same relation
to Weight$_2$
As Distance$_2$ is to Distance$_1$.
But
Why
Weights and distances
Are like numbers
Is
Still
To be
Explained.

One lemma equals assurance.
Two lemmas equal dilemma.

What can they know of England...?

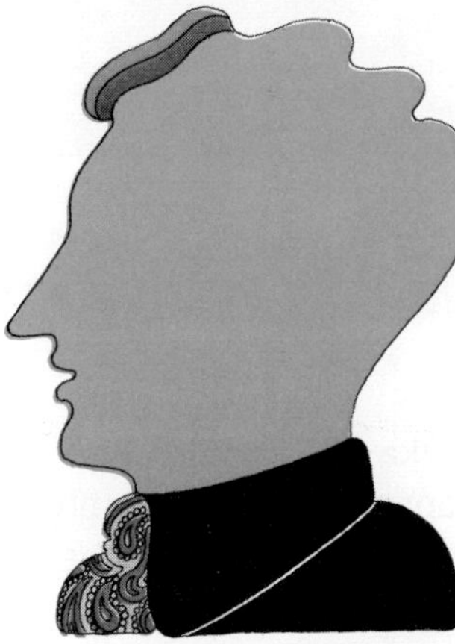

Whenever an American moves overseas, he suffers from a condition known as "culture shock." Culture shock is simply a removal or distortion of many of the familiar cues one encounters at home and the substitution for them of other cues which are strange. A good deal of what occurs in the organization and use of space provides important leads as to the specific cues responsible for culture shock.

The Latin house is often built around a patio that is next to the sidewalk but hidden from outsiders behind a wall. It is not easy to describe the degree to which small architectural differences such as this affect outsiders. American Point Four technicians living in Latin America used to complain that they felt "left out" of things, that they were "shut off." Others kept wondering what was going on "behind those walls." In the United States, on the other hand, propinquity is the basis of a good many relationships. To us the neighbor is actually quite close. Being a neighbor endows one with certain rights and privileges, also responsibilities. You can borrow things, including food and drink, but you also have to take your neighbor to the hospital in an emergency. In this regard he has almost as much claim on you as a cousin. For these and other reasons the American tries to pick his neighborhood carefully, because he knows that he is going to be thrown into intimate contact with people. We do not understand why it is that when we live next to people abroad the sharing of adjacent space does not always conform to our own pattern. In France and England, for instance, the relations between neighbors are apt to be cooler than in the United States. Mere propinquity does not tie people together. In England neighbor children do not play as they do in our neighborhoods. When they do play, arrangements are sometimes made a month in advance as though they were coming from the other side of town!

n.b.

"Okay," shouts the final inspector in a Japanese auto assembly plant, signaling to the driver to take away the new car.

"All-righ, all righ," the girl conductor calls to the "busu" driver as he maneuvers his vehicle into a tight parking spot.

"Wondafuru, wondafuru," murmurs the teenager as she listens raptly to the "disuku joku" playing her favorite "rikuesuto."

The Japanese language, like many others, is undergoing rapid transformation.

The front page of the newspaper *Asahi* nowadays may contain, in the ordinary Japanese text, such words as "surogan" (slogan), "kosto" (cost), "terebi" (television), "sumogu" (smog), "baransu" (balance), "semento" (cement), and "meka" (maker or manufacturer).

New Set of Words

In some cases these are words for which the Japanese language has no equivalent. But increasingly it has become popular to use a foreign word even when a Japanese one suits the purpose and is more widely understood.

The influx of foreign words, often adopted with meanings that would surprise Westerners, has accompanied a widespread movement to simplify one of the world's most complex languages.

If the student lacks eloquence in traditional Japanese, he has a new set of words to express new ideas. "Kanningu" (cunning) is the highly developed art of cribbing in examinations.

"Abekku" (avec) represents the concept of dating or companionship between the sexes. "Arbeito" (arbeit) is the side job performed by a student working his way through college.

Just as many American stores use French phrases that suggest an air of Parisian elegance, many Japanese commercial establishments now seek a trace of exoticism by printing their names in Roman letters and using an English tag such as "romance mood," "shopping date," "honeymoon style" or "bargain sale."

Kanji

All these are also likely to be rendered phonetically in Japanese.

Radio and television are spreading the new words to even the most remote corners of the country.

But the very nature of the Japanese language has abetted the introduction of new words from abroad. To make the language more legible for the rank and file, the newspapers have agreed to use no more than 1,800 Chinese ideographs—known as kanji—whose total runs to more than 30,000.

New kanji are seldom created or adopted to new concepts or new words. Instead, kata kana, one of the two phonetic syllabaries that can be read easily by all persons, is used to render, syllable by syllable, the closest Japanese approximation to the new foreign word.

Here are some more "English" words for you to try. You can cover the hints if you prefer a more challenging game.

1.	ho-te-ru	(travelers)	________
2.	e-re-be-ta	(It's uplifting.)	________
3.	u-ii-su-ki	(a liquid)	________
4.	bu-ru-ba-do	(of happiness)	________
5.	gu-ri-ru	(hibachi)	________
6.	su-te-re-o	(euphony)	________
7.	cha-ko-re-to	(opposite of baniira)	________
8.	orinpikku	(games)	________
9.	durimurando	(the world of fantasy)	________
10.	supido	(over 65)	________
11.	bakansu	(It's French, but we get it, too, usually in the summer.)	________
12.	hasuru	(rush around)	________
13.	homurun	(Thomas Wolfe said you can't.)	________
14.	furiru	(bustles and bows)	________
15.	chiinejya	(pays more for insurance)	________
16.	baniira aisu kurimu	(good à la pie)	________
17.	riibapuru saundo	(The Beatles have it.)	________
18.	jyukubaaksu	(Where the riibapuru saundo is.)	________

AKRESTOMIJE, ERGAHERGAHMAH, AND OHE

Akrestomije, Ergahergahmah, and Ohe are three languages unknown to linguists. Even those who belong to the three speech communities are not fluent in these languages, for each community consists of only the six people who developed the three languages as a project in an oral communication course at Allegheny College. The languages were constructed during three class sessions as an introduction to the study of the nature of language.

"Today, we're going to construct a language," was the simple statement which introduced the unit. Three groups were quickly organized and sat staring at one another, for no one seemed to know where to begin. Indeed, many could not believe that the project was to be taken seriously.

"Agree on some sounds," the groups were directed.

"How many?" someone asked.

"It's up to you," was the answer.

One group finally decided upon ten sounds. A mathematician in the group assured his fellow students that the three and a half million possible combinations would be quite adequate for their purposes. Thus was Ergahergahmah begun. Soon, Akrestomije was brought to life with twelve sounds, and, shortly thereafter, Ohe became a language with twenty-four sounds.

At the end of the class session each student was asked to make up ten words and bring them to the next class meeting.

At the second class meeting, the groups were asked to classify the words they had created. Although any feasible classification could be used, Sapir's classification of "object," "quality," and "action" seemed practical.

The important principle developed at this meeting was that words do not have a necessary connection with their referents. The relationship between a given sound or group of sounds and the thing to which it refers is arbitrary. In Akrestomije, an "ima" might just as well have been called a "jat." In Ohe, a "ha" might have been called "da." And, in Ergahergahmah, what is called a "booingemm" might just as easily have been classed as an "ergahbooingemm." This concept, so easily escaped from when referring to English words, is dramatically demonstrated with a "do-it-yourself" language.

For further development during this class meeting, each group was asked to consider what use might be made of "inflection," "function words," and "sentence structure."

Homework consisted of more vocabulary building.

The third day of language construction consisted of putting the final touches on the language. Students were asked to consider whether their language would have articles, singular and plural, words for days of the week or months, verb-noun-adjective endings, numbers, words for yes and no, and words for greetings and farewell. The questions about these possibilities were suggestions and not prescriptions, for the intent of the third day was to demonstrate to the students how language affects our perception of reality and to show how our language conditions our view of another culture.

The afternoon of the third day, representatives

of each group met, typed up the rules and vocabularies of their languages; and dittoed them for distribution to the entire class. The fourth and final day of this unit was spent in discussing the ways a particular language conditions an individual's perception of reality and the forces of change within a speech community.

Students were asked to write a paper telling what they had derived from the assignment.

YOU TAUGHT ME LANGUAGE; AND MY PROFIT ON'T IS, I KNOW HOW TO CURSE. THE RED PLAGUE RID YOU FOR LEARNING ME YOUR LANGUAGE.

"Whom did you pass on the road?" the King went on, holding out his hand to the messenger for some hay.

"Nobody," said the messenger.

"Quite right," said the King. "This young lady saw him too. So of course Nobody walks slower than you."

"I do my best," the messenger said in a sullen tone. "I'm sure nobody walks much faster than I do."

"He can't do that," said the King, "or else he'd have been here first."

Is the King's argument "true," or is it "valid," or both?

anyone lived in a pretty how town
(with up so floating many bells down)
spring summer autumn winter
he sang his didn't he danced his did.

Women and men (both little and small)
cared for anyone not at all
they sowed their isn't they reaped their same
sun moon stars rain

children guessed (but only a few
and down they forgot as up they grew
autumn winter spring summer)
that noone loved him more by more

when by now and tree by leaf
she laughed his joy she cried his grief
bird by snow and stir by still
anyone's any was all to her

someones married their everyones
laughed their cryings and did their dance
(sleep wake hope and then) they
said their nevers they slept their dream

stars rain sun moon
(and only the snow can begin to explain
how children are apt to forget to remember
with up so floating many bells down)

one day anyone died i guess
(and noone stopped to kiss his face)
busy folk buried them side by side
little by little and was by was

all by all and deep by deep
and more by more they dream their sleep
noone and anyone earth by april
wish by spirit and if by yes.

Women and men (both dong and ding)
summer autumn winter spring
reaped their sowing and went their came
sun moon stars rain

"... it is a strange thing today—you must have 35mm—you must go out and catch things, and they use a word of violence, 'To shoot.' This thing to me—Photography—is a matter of concentration and philosophy. I must communicate with a blade of grass to show its magnificence. I cannot do this by shooting at it!

Shall we melt or remain forever fixed ?

"In my work I try to express the oneness I see in the universe.... Life and death are two words for the same thing—all fragments of the living order; the illumination of which leads to the underlying philosophy of the expression of creative artists. And as in a mirror, the responsible observer will discover in the work not only the artist's reflection but his own image as well. This way we share and communicate and fulfill a deep human need."

captured snowflakes ?
You?
Charlie Schulz ?
ME ?

Although many attempts have been made to identify gravitational attraction as an electromagnetic effect, all have failed. Einstein thought he had succeeded in 1929 and published a unified field theory which he later rejected as inadequate. His new theory, completed in the final days of 1949, was far more ambitious; for it promulgated a set of universal laws designed to encompass not only the boundless gravitational and electromagnetic fields of interstellar space but also the tiny, terrible field inside the atom. Whether the whole grand objective of a Unified Field Theory will be realized only many more months or years of mathematical and experimental work can determine. But in its vast cosmic picture, when fully revealed, the abyss between macrocosmos and microcosmos—the very big and the very little—will surely be bridged and the whole complex of the universe will resolve into a homogeneous fabric in which matter and energy are indistinguishable and all forms of motion from the slow wheeling of the galaxies to the wild flight of electrons become simply changes in the structure and concentration of the primordial field.

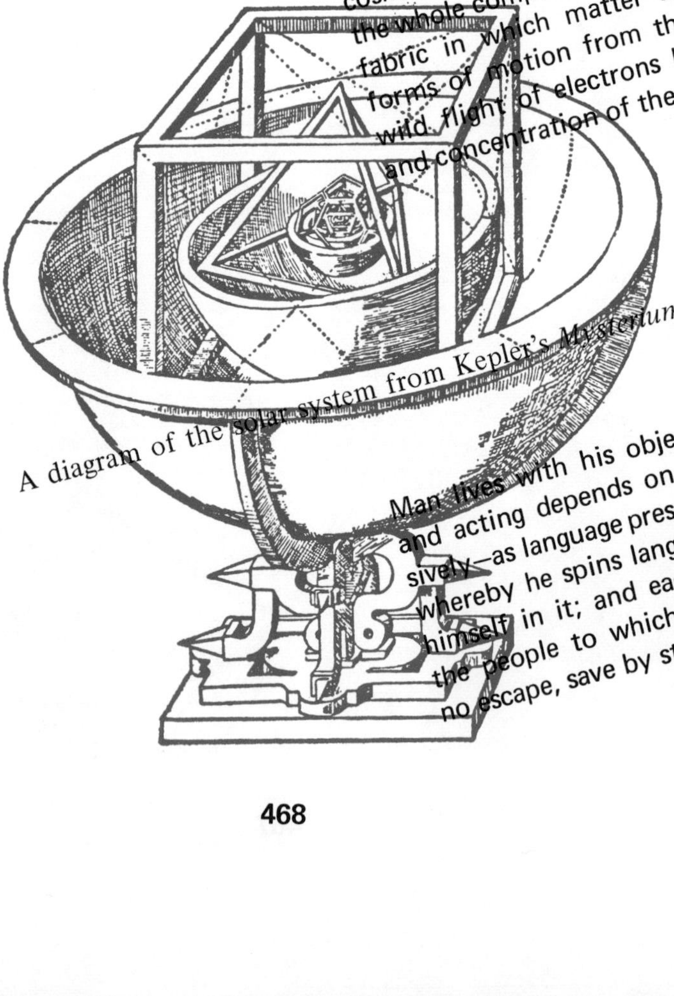

A diagram of the solar system from Kepler's *Mysterium Cosmographicum*, 1596.

Man lives with his objects chiefly—in fact, since his feeling and acting depends on his perceptions, one may say exclusively—as language presents them to him. By the same process whereby he spins language out of his own being, he ensnares himself in it; and each language draws a magic circle round the people to which it belongs, a circle from which there is no escape, save by stepping out of it into another.

Any society, however brilliant, soon crushes me whereas I have never been bored with the women I liked. It hurts me to confess it, but I'd have given ten conversations with Einstein for an initial rendezvous with a pretty chorus girl. It's true that at the tenth rendezvous I was longing for Einstein or a serious book. In short, I was never concerned with the major problems except in the intervals between my little excesses.

Smack warm. Smacked smackwarm on her smackable warm woman's thigh.

Title: ______________________________

For human intercourse, as soon as we look at it for its own sake and not as a social adjunct, is seen to be haunted by a specter. We cannot understand each other, except in a rough and ready way: we cannot reveal ourselves, even when we want to; what we call intimacy is only a makeshift; perfect knowledge is an illusion. But in the novel we can know people perfectly, and, apart from the general pleasure of reading, we can find here a compensation for their dimness in life. In this direction fiction is truer than history, because it goes beyond the evidence, and each of us knows from his own experience that there is something beyond the evidence, and even if the novelist has not got it correctly, well—he has tried. He can post his people in as babies, he can cause them to go on without sleep or food, he can make them be in love, love and nothing but love, provided he seems to know everything about them, provided they are his creations. That is why Moll Flanders cannot be here, that is one of the reasons why Amelia and Emma cannot be here. They are people whose secret lives are visible or might be visible: we are people whose secret lives are invisible.

And that is why novels, even when they are about wicked people, can solace us; they suggest a more comprehensible and thus a more manageable human race, they give us the illusion of perspicacity and of power.

What two extremes do these samples illustrate?

Why is the one case successful and the other not? By studying these two samples, see what you can observe about the relationship between thought and speech.

When is abbreviation possible?

Could telepathy be understanding the abbreviation?

What general implications do you perceive?

Before the judge who's deaf two deaf men bow,
One deaf man cries: "he led away my cow."
"Beg pardon," says the other in reply
"That meadow was my father's land in days gone by."
The judge decides: "For you to fight each other is a shame.
Nor one nor t'other, but the girl's to blame."

"I have long wished to ask you something."

"Please do."

"There," he said, and wrote the following letters—W, y, a: i, c, n, b; d, y, m, t, o, n?

These letters stood for: When you answered: it can not be; did you mean then or never? It was quite unlikely that she would be able to make out this complicated sentence.

"I have understood," she said with a blush.

"What word is this?" he asked, pointing to the n which stood for never.

"The word is never," she said, "but that is not true."

He quickly rubbed out what he had written, handed her the chalk and rose.

She wrote: T, I, c, n, a, o.

Suddenly his face beamed, he had understood: The letters meant "Then I could not answer otherwise." She wrote these initial letters—T, y, m, f, a, f, w, h. This meant "That you might forgive and forget what happened."

He seized the chalk with nervous, trembling fingers, broke it and wrote the initial letters of the following: "I have nothing to forget or forgive, I never ceased to love you." "I understand," she whispered. He sat down and wrote out a long sentence. She understood it all, and without asking if she was right, took the chalk and wrote the answer at once. For a long time he could not make out what she meant and he often looked up in her eyes. He was dazed with happiness. He could not find the words she meant at all; but in her beautiful eyes, radiant with joy, he saw all that he wanted to know. And he wrote down three letters. But before he had finished writing she read it under his hand, finished the sentence and wrote the answer, "yes." Everything had been said in that conversation. She had said that she loved him and would tell her father and mother and he said that he would call in the morning.

What is the use of studying philosophy if all that it does for you is to enable you to talk with some plausibility about some abstruse questions of logic, etc., and if it does not improve your thinking about the important questions of everyday life, if it does not make you more conscientious than any. . .journalist in the use of dangerous phrases such people use for their own ends. You see, I know it's difficult to think well about "certainty," "probability," "perception". . . But it is, if possible, still more difficult to think, or try to think, really honestly about your life and other people's lives. And the trouble is that thinking about these things is not thrilling, but often downright nasty. And when it's nasty then it's most important. . .

Happiness is a word. What does it mean? Exaltation; an intensified feeling of the significant worth of man's being and becoming? Well, if it means that—and not a mere smirking contentment with one's lot—I know there is more of it in one real tragedy than in all the happy-ending plays ever written. A work of art is always happy; all else is unhappy.

SPRING AND FALL: TO A YOUNG CHILD

Margaret, are you grieving
Over Goldengrove unleaving?
Leaves, like the things of man, you
With your fresh thoughts care for, can you?
Ah! as the heart grows older
It will come to such sights colder
By and by, nor spare a sigh
Though worlds of wanwood leafmeal lie;
And yet you will weep and know why.
Now, no matter, child, the name:
Sorrow's springs are the same.
Nor mouth had, no nor mind, expressed
What heart heard of, ghost guessed:
It is the blight man was born for,
It is Margaret you mourn for.

MAN'S ENTIRE VITAL

人間の致命的な

FUNCTION MAY BE SAID

全機能は可能性

TO HAVE TO DEAL WITH

を扱ふことにあると

MAYBES

云へるだらう

Development occurs in response to challenge. When the individual encounters situations he cannot manage with his existing repertoire of responses, he generates new responses. If these are successful, they are retained and integrated with the rest of the personality. However, people insist on doing things as they always have unless they meet situations that require new kinds of adaptation. Children, of course, are constantly confronted with challenging situations and so they learn very rapidly. College students present difficulties to the educator because they already have learned many more or less suitable adaptive strategies, so it is difficult to challenge them to generate new behavior patterns.

Thinking is the conscious or unconscious manipulation of internal processes for oneself, usually in some particular direction such as the solution of a problem. Communication, whether through language or through other means (such as music or painting), is behavior in which the initiator of the communication seeks (whether successfully or not) to arouse certain internal processes in the recipient of the communication and possibly to secure certain overt responses on his part.

Language symbols—or, rather, the internal processes that underlie given language symbols for the individual—may figure prominently in thinking and often determine its direction. The concepts named by language symbols—that is, verbal mediating processes—are "tools" of thought in these two senses: 1. They provide at least some of the internal stimuli and stimulus-producing responses that carry forward the sequences of events from the external stimuli initiating the process to the overt responses terminating it. And 2. they represent organizations of internal processes (acquired through learning or past experiences) that are potentially critical in determining whether a given sequence of thought will eventuate in successful or rewarded overt response.

PIDGIN AND KRIO

Expanding analogies progressively reveal relations; argument by analogy is the fundamental technique in the process of abstraction.

In Freetown (West Africa), a form of English has been developed that is almost a new language. This is Krio. In contrast to pidgin (English), Krio is not a lingua franca but a mother tongue. Nearly all people who use pidgin have an African mother tongue and they use pidgin as a means of communication with other African language groups or Europeans. Krio speakers, on the other hand, have no African tongue.

How does pidgin differ in structure and vocabulary from English? How does Krio differ? For example, in the pidgin sample below

done try to go	stands for	tried to go,
done go	stands for	went,
get	stands for	got,
live	stands for	lived, and
done pass	stands for	passed.

Why would the version on the left be chosen? Which is less complicated? What other changes do you notice? Can you discover some underlying principles?

Pidgin

I done try to go church, I done go for court
Dem all dey talk about di "new culture";
Dem talk about "equality," dem mention "divorce"
Dem holler am so-tay my ear nearly cut;
One wife be for man.

My fader before my fader get him wife borku,
E no get equality palaver: he live well
For he be oga for im own house,
Bot dat time done pass before white man come
Wit im
One man for one wife.

Tell me how una woman no go make yanga
Wen e know say na in only dey.
Suppose say—make God no gree—e no born at all.
A tell you dat man bin dey craze wey start
One wife for one man.

Notes

borku: plenty
oga: master
una: your
yanga: pride
sabe: know-how

Jus tell me how one wife fit do one man;
How man fit stay all time for him house
For time when belleh done kommot.
How many pickin self, one woman fit born
When one wife be for one man?

Suppose, self, na so-so woman your wife dey born
Suppose your wife sabe book, no sabe make chop;
Den, how will you go tell man e no go out
Sake of dis divorce? Bo dis culture na waya O!
When one wife be for one man.

Does normal English tend toward simpler or more complicated structures? For example, what principle lies behind the shift from "It's I" to "It's me"? From "It's he" to "It's him"?

Krio

To get the feel of Krio, compare the English version of Mark Antony's speech line for line until you get the sense of it. It is easier than it looks. Then see if you can figure out some of the rules for Krio. What are the English equivalents of some of the Krio vocabulary items, such as "may want pass mark"?

Paddy den country, una all way day nar Rome.
Una len me una yase, yar.
Are cam berr Caesar, are no cam praise am.
Dem kin member bad way person kim do long tem
after de person kin done die.
But plenty tem de good way person de kin berr
Wit un bone dem. Make e be so with Caesar.
Bra Brutus done tell una say Caesar na been
Man may want pass mark. If he talk true, nar
Bad ting dis yar. En Caesar done get in bed
Pay for dat. Are take permission from Bra
Brutus dem for cam talk nar Bra Caesar in
Berrin en Bra Brutus na honourable. Caesar nar
Been me fren; e good en trait. But Brutus say

No man may want pass mark. En Brutus nar
honourable O! Caesar done bring plenty
prisoner cam Rome. De copper way dem pay for
dem buil up de revenue. Nar want pass
Mark dat? When poor man halla, Caesar kin burs
Cry. Man why want-want pass mark for get
"Trong" eart. But Brutus say nar man way want
Pass mark. En Bra Brutus nar honourable O!

DAY'S EYE

It's all relative.

". . . there is no fact in nature which does not carry the whole sense of nature . . . Besides, in a centred mind . . . the chief value of the new fact, is to enhance the great and constant fact of Life . . . The world being thus put under the mind for verb and noun, the poet is he who can articulate it. . . . So the poet's habit of living should be set on a key so low that the common influences should delight him. His cheerfulness should be the gift of the sunlight; the air should suffice for his inspiration, and he should be tipsy with water. That spirit which suffices quiet hearts, which seems to come forth to such from every dry knoll of sere grass, from every pine-stump and half-imbedded stone, on which the dull March sun shines, comes forth to the poor and hungry, and such as are of simple taste. If thou fill thy brain with Boston and New York . . . thou shalt find no radiance of wisdom in the lonely waste of the pine woods."

The Caterpillar and Alice looked at each other for some time in silence: at last the Caterpillar took the hookah out of its mouth, and addressed her in a languid, sleepy voice.

"Who are *you?*" said the Caterpillar.

This was not an encouraging opening for a conversation. Alice replied, rather shyly, "I—I hardly know, sir, just at present—at least I know who I *was* when I got up this morning, but I think I must have changed several times since then."

"What do you mean by that?" said the Caterpillar sternly. "Explain yourself!"

"I can't explain *myself*, I'm afraid, sir," said Alice, "because I'm not myself, you see."

"I don't see," said the Caterpillar.

"I'm afraid I can't put it more clearly," Alice replied very politely, "for I can't understand it myself, to begin with; and being so many different sizes in a day is very confusing."

"It isn't," said the Caterpillar.

"Well, perhaps you haven't found it so yet," said Alice, "but when you have to turn into a chrysalis—you will some day, you know—and then after that into a butterfly, I should think you'll feel it a little queer, won't you?"

"Not a bit," said the Caterpillar.

"Well, perhaps *your* feelings may be different," said Alice; "all I know is, it would feel very queer to *me*."

"You!" said the Caterpillar contemptuously. "Who are *you?*"

Which brought them back again to the beginning of the conversation. Alice felt a little irritated at the Caterpillar's making such *very* short remarks, and she drew herself up and said very gravely, "I think you ought to tell me who *you* are, first."

"Why?" said the Caterpillar.

Here was another puzzling question; and as Alice could not think of any good reason, and as the Caterpillar seemed to be in a *very* unpleasant state of mind, she turned away.

"Come back!" the Caterpillar called after her. "I've something important to say!"

This sounded promising, certainly. Alice turned and came back again.

"Keep your temper," said the Caterpillar.

"Is that all?" said Alice, swallowing down her anger as well as she could.

"No," said the Caterpillar.

Alice thought she might as well wait, as she had nothing else to do, and perhaps after all it might tell her something worth hearing. For some minutes it puffed away without speaking; but at last it unfolded its arms, took the hookah out of its mouth again, and said, "So you think you're changed, do you?"

"I'm afraid I am, sir," said Alice; "I can't remember things as I used—and I don't keep the same size for ten minutes together!"

"What size do you want to be?" it asked.

"Oh, I'm not particular as to size," Alice hastily replied; "only one doesn't like changing so often, you know."

"I *don't* know," said the Caterpillar.

Alice said nothing; she had never been so much contradicted in all her life before, and she felt that she was losing her temper.

"Are you content now?" said the Caterpillar.

"Well, I should like to be a *little* larger, sir, if you wouldn't mind," said Alice; "three inches is such a wretched height to be."

"It is a very good height indeed!" said the Caterpillar angrily, rearing itself upright as it spoke (it was exactly three inches high).

"But I'm not used to it!" pleaded poor Alice in a piteous tone. And she thought to herself, "I wish the creature wouldn't be so easily offended!"

"You'll get used to it in time," said the Caterpillar, and it put the hookah into its mouth and began smoking again.

This time Alice waited patiently until it chose to speak again. In a minute or two the Caterpillar took the hookah out of its mouth, and yawned once or twice, and shook itself. Then it got down off the mushroom, and crawled away into the grass, merely remarking as it went, "One side will make you grow taller, and the other side will make you grow shorter."

"One side of *what?* The other side of *what?*" thought Alice to herself.

"Of the mushroom," said the Caterpillar, just as if she had asked it aloud; and in another moment it was out of sight.

Alice remained looking thoughtfully at the mushroom for a minute, trying to make out which were the two sides of it; and, as it was perfectly round, she found this a very difficult question. However, at last she stretched her arms round it as far as they would go, and broke off a bit of the edge with each hand.

"And now which is which?" she said to herself, and nibbled a little of the right-hand bit to try the effect: the next moment she felt a violent blow underneath her chin; it had struck her foot.

She was a good deal frightened by this very sudden change, but she felt that there was no time to be lost; as she was shrinking rapidly; so she set to work at once to eat some of the other bit. Her chin was pressed so closely against her foot that there was hardly room to open her mouth; but she did it at last, and managed to swallow a morsel of the left-hand bit. . . .

"Come, my head's free at last!" said Alice in a tone of delight, which changed into alarm in another moment, when she found that her shoulders were nowhere to be found; all she could see, when she looked down, was an immense length of neck, which seemed to rise like a stalk out of a sea of green leaves that lay far below her.

"What *can* all that green stuff be?" said Alice. "And where *have* my shoulders got to? And oh, my poor hands, how is it I can't see you?" She was moving them about as she spoke, but no result seemed to follow, except a little shaking among the distant green leaves.

As there seemed to be no chance of getting her hands up to her head, she tried to get her head down to them, and was delighted to find that her neck would bend about easily in any direction, like a serpent. She had just succeeded in curving it down into a graceful zigzag, and was going to dive in among the leaves, which she found to be nothing but the tops of the trees under which she had been wandering, when a sharp hiss made her draw back in a hurry; a large pigeon had flown into her face, and was beating her violently with its wings.

Alice crouched down among the trees as well as she could, for her neck kept getting entangled among the branches, and every now and then she had to stop and untwist it. After a while she remembered that she still had the pieces of mushroom in her hands, and she set to work very carefully, nibbling first at one and then at the other, growing sometimes taller and sometimes shorter, until she had succeeded in bringing herself down to her usual height.

It was so long since she had been anything near the right size, that it felt quite strange at first, but she got used to it in a few minutes, and began talking to herself as usual. "Come, there's half my plan done now! I'm never sure what I'm going to be, from one minute to another! However, I've got back to my right size; the next thing is to get into that beautiful garden—how *is* that to be done, I wonder?" As she said this she came suddenly upon an open place, with a little house in it about four feet high. "Whoever lives there," thought Alice, "it'll never do to come upon them *this* size; why, I should frighten them out of their wits!" So she began nibbling at the right hand bit again, and did not venture to go near the house till she had brought herself down to nine inches high.

ALICE, THROUGH THE LOOKING GLASS

$x^2/a^2 + y^2/b^2 = 1$

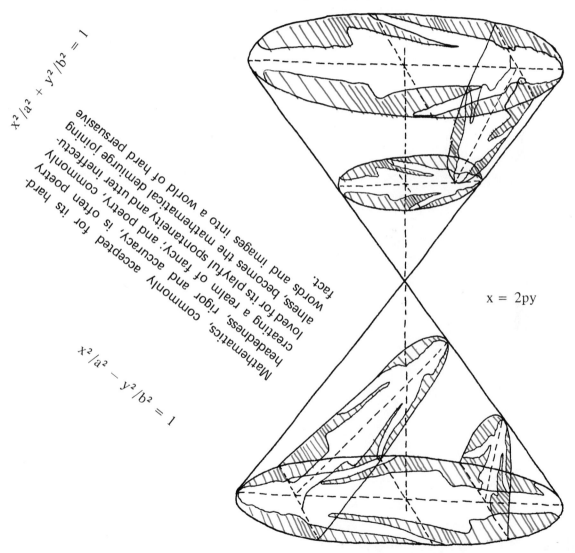

Mathematics, commonly accepted for its hard-headedness, rigor and accuracy, is often poetry creating a realm of fancy; and poetry, commonly loved for its playful spontaneity and utter ineffectualness, becomes the mathematical demiurge joining words and images into a world of hard persuasive fact.

$x^2/a^2 - y^2/b^2 = 1$

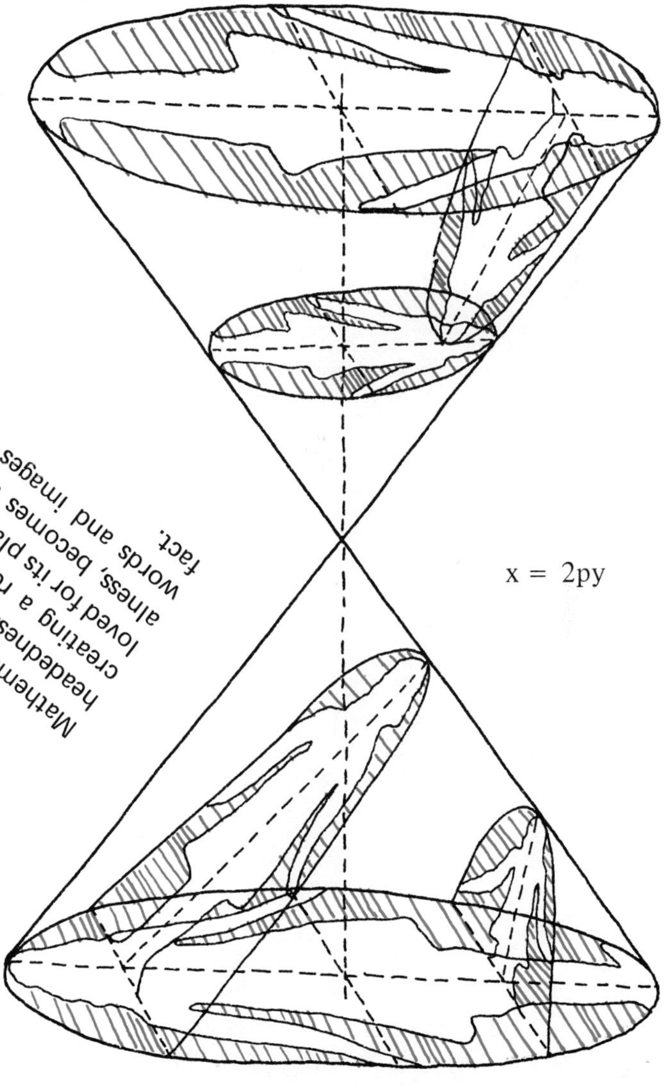

x = 2py

To him whose elastic and vigorous thought keeps pace with the sun, the day is a perpetual morning. It matters not what the clocks say or the attitudes and labors of men. Morning is when I am awake and there is a dawn in me. Moral reform is an effort to throw off sleep. Why is it that men give so poor an account of their day if they have not been slumbering? They are not such poor calculators. If they had not been overcome with drowsiness, they would have performed something. The millions are awake enough for physical labor; but only one in a million is awake enough for effective intellectual exertion, only one in a hundred millions to a poetic or divine life. To be awake is to be alive. I have never yet met a man who was quite awake. How could I have looked him in the face?

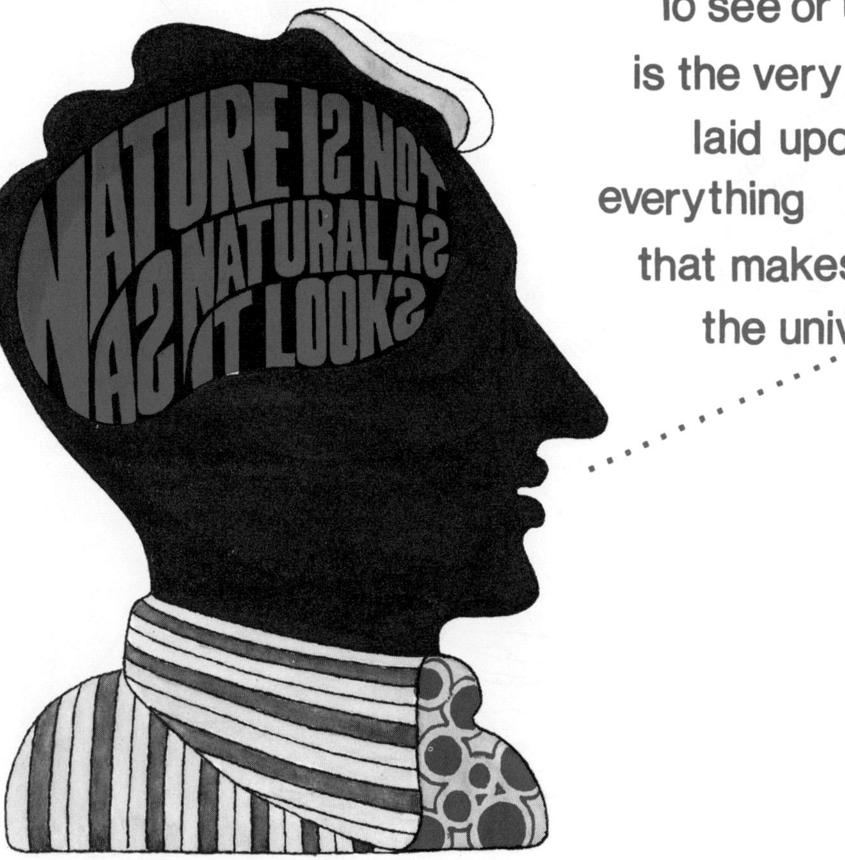

To see or to perish
is the very condition
laid upon
everything
that makes up
the universe.

FLOWER IN THE CRANNIED WALL

Flower in the crannied wall,
I pluck you out of the crannies,
I hold you here, root and all, in my hand,
Little flower—but if *I could understand*
What you are, root and all, and all in all,
I should know what God and man is.

Analogies should be as
far fetched as possible.
What can you learn from
the close fetched?

PATTERNS

. . . in about 1947-8, certain documentary film-makers (Luciano Emmer, Enrico Gras, Henri Storck, Alain Resnais, and Gabriel Pommerand) developed a new technique in such films as *Il drammo di Cristo, The World of Paul Delvaux, Van Gogh,* and *Légende cruelle.* The camera from the start is set right inside the world of the painting, as if it were a real world. It never goes outside the canvas and we never see the frame of the painting. The painting—or paintings—is cut into fragments, which, by rearrangement, contrast, linkage and visual synthesis are built up into a new total effect. Further . . . the spatial relationships of the painting become, in film, relationships in time. The film-maker dissects the painter's work, organized in spatial immobility, and transforms it into a moving temporal unity formed by cutting, montage, and camera movement.

The result of the camera never going outside the painting is that it appears as unbounded in space. This is due to a curious psychological effect. Instead of the spectator's vision being limited by the frame of the painting which he knows is real, it is limited only by a boundary which he regards as conventional—the edge of the screen. By substituting its own frame for that of the painting, the cinema substitutes *film space* for pictorial space; and by this trick it assimilates pictorial space into the unbounded space of nature which the camera usually shows us. This illustrates the quite arbitrary nature of our concept of space in the cinema.

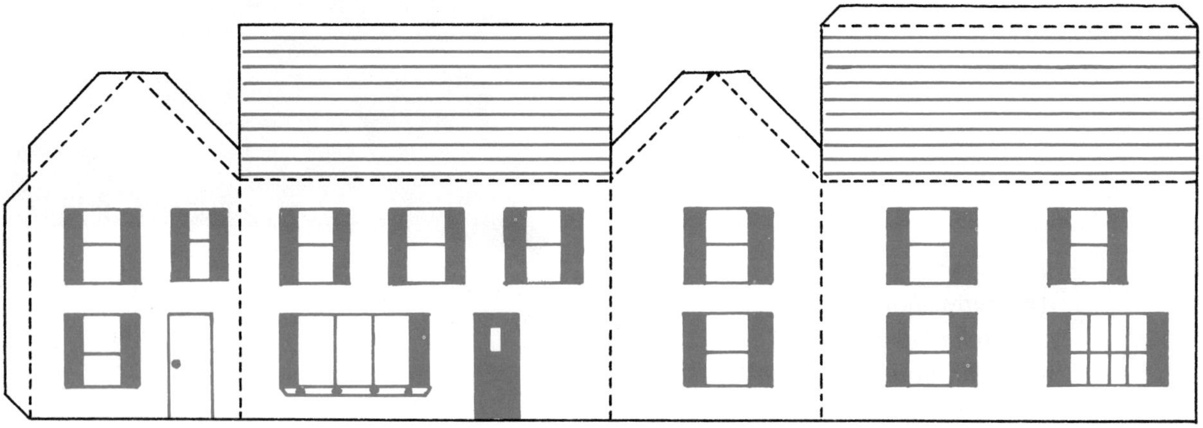

. . . I believe that Zen appeals to many in the . . . West because it does not preach, moralize, and scold. . . . Buddhism does not deny that there is a relatively limited sphere in which human life may be improved by art and science, reason and good will. However, it regards this sphere of activity as important but nonetheless subordinate to the comparatively limitless sphere in which things are as they are, always have been, and always will be—a sphere entirely beyond the categories of good and evil, success and failure, and individual health and sickness. On the one hand, this is the sphere of the great universe. Looking out into it at night, we make no comparisons between right and wrong stars, nor between well and badly arranged constellations. Stars are by nature big and little, bright and dim. Yet the whole thing is a splendor and a marvel which sometimes makes our flesh creep with awe. On the other hand, this is also the sphere of human, everyday life which we might call existential.

For there is a standpoint from which human affairs are as much beyond right and wrong as the stars, and from which our deeds, experiences, and feelings can no more be judged than the ups and downs of a range of mountains. Though beyond moral and social valuation, this level of human life may also be seen to be just as marvelous and uncanny as the great universe itself. This feeling may become particularly acute when the individual ego tries to fathom its own nature, to plumb the inner sources of its own actions and consciousness. For here it discovers a part of itself—the inmost and greatest part—which is strange to itself and beyond its understanding and control. Odd as it may sound, the ego finds that its own center and nature is beyond itself. The more deeply I go into myself, the more I am not myself, and yet this is the very heart of me. Here I find my own inner workings functioning of themselves, spontaneously, like the rotation of the heavenly bodies and the drifting of the clouds. Strange and foreign as this aspect of myself at first seems to be, I soon realize that it *is* me, and much more me than my superficial ego. This is not fatalism or determinism, because there is no longer anyone being pushed around or determined; there is nothing that this deep "I" is not doing. The configuration of my nervous-system, like the configuration of the stars, happens of itself, and this "itself" is the real "myself."

From this standpoint—and here language reveals its limitations with a vengeance—I find that I cannot help doing and experiencing, quite freely, what is always "right," in the sense that the stars are always in their "right" places. As Hsiang-yen put it,

> There's no use for artificial discipline,
> For, move as I will, I manifest the ancient Tao.

Or as is said in the *Hsin-hsin Ming:*

> If you want to get the plain truth,
> Be not concerned with right and wrong.
> The conflict between right and wrong
> Is the sickness of the mind.

Awareness, Spontaneity, Intimacy.

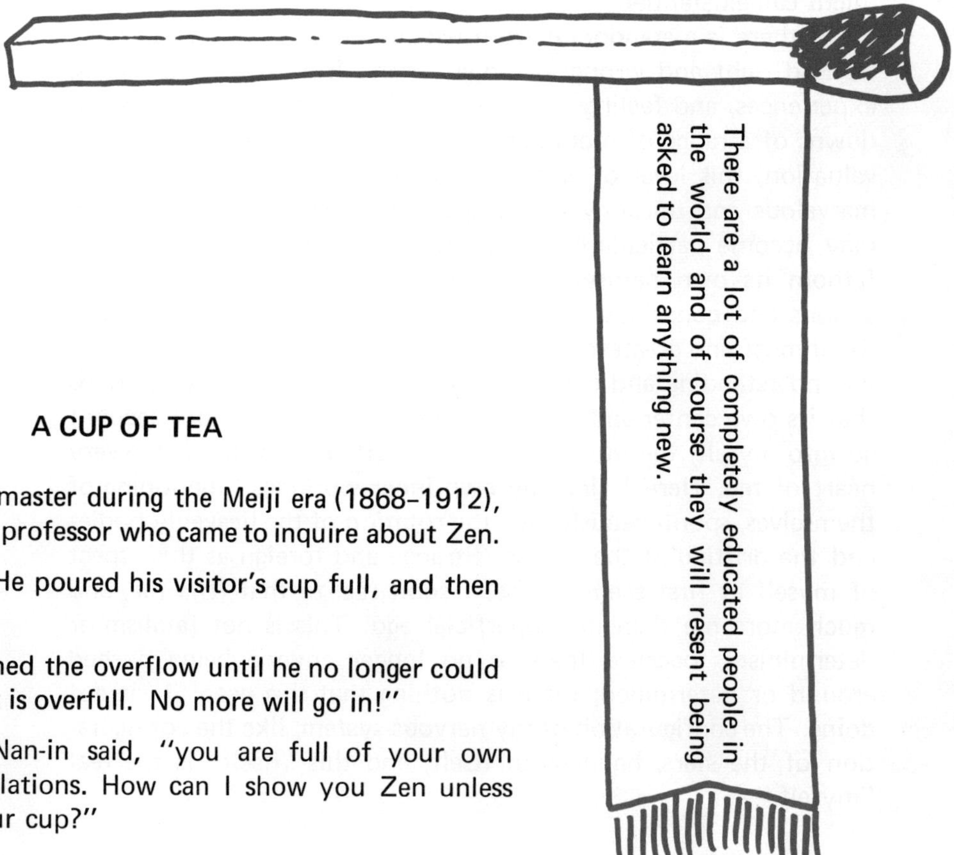
There are a lot of completely educated people in the world and of course they will resent being asked to learn anything new.

A CUP OF TEA

Nan-in, a Japanese master during the Meiji era (1868–1912), received a university professor who came to inquire about Zen.

Nan-in served tea. He poured his visitor's cup full, and then kept pouring.

The professor watched the overflow until he no longer could restrain himself. "It is overfull. No more will go in!"

"Like this cup," Nan-in said, "you are full of your own opinions and speculations. How can I show you Zen unless you first empty your cup?"

O body swayed to music,
O brightening glance,
How can we know the dancer
from the dance?

"All arts aspire to the condition of music." Music goes farther in the way of abstraction, in dispensing with particular meaning, than any other art. . . . Pure music is the freest of all arts and is able to communicate immediately and intimately with the listener. It strikes through and beyond reason and emotion. It can stir us to the depth of our being without arousing specific thoughts or emotions.

The man that hath no music in himself,
Nor is not mov'd with concord of sweet sounds,
Is fit for treason, stratagems and spoils.

Pure poetry and pure mathematics, like pure music, are never expressed.

And you O my soul where you stand,
Surrounded, detached, in measureless oceans of space,
Ceaselessly musing, venturing, throwing, seeking the spheres
to connect them,
Till the bridge you will need be form'd, till the ductile
anchor hold,
Till the gossamer thread you fling catch somewhere, O my soul.

NIGHT WATCH

With the instantaneous brilliance of a lightning flash, life and consciousness were born. The journey from void nonentity to vivid awakening was swifter than the passage of a meteor, instant and complete.

The search for self-identity began. Seconds after his awakening, the new-born being subjected his environment and himself to a minutely detailed examination. He discovered within himself, down in the misty center of consciousness, a store of knowledge, all of it quite meaningless until linked with the stimulus of outside experience.

One thing he learned. He had a name. This was a convenient and necessary item. It was the symbol of individual identity. It defined the most important thing in his environment; himself. He knew that it would do more than that, he knew that his name contained the riddle of his existence. When he succeeded in interpreting this riddle, he would become aware of the purpose for which he was created.

Meantime, it was enough that he had a name. His name was Asov.

He turned his attention to the world around him, the baffling, incomprehensible world into which he had been born. It was a world of contrasts both glaring and subtle. Asov was at once sensitive to these contrasts and began to compare and measure, building up a picture of his environment on the fresh, fertile canvas of his experience.

Light and darkness. Motion and peace. Growth and change.

These were the concepts with which Asov wrestled, each new item of information being stored away within his miraculous memory and related to his inborn store of data.

The world took shape and meaning. His lightning senses could now instantly recognize a thousand variations in the interplay of energy which was how he saw the world. Like himself, the world too had a name. It was called Galaxy.

As he emerged from infantile bafflement, Asov could at last understand the riddle of his name. With that understanding came an awareness of his place in creation. His essential purpose no longer eluded him.

Asov. Automatic Stellar Observation Vehicle.

Suddenly, he became aware that one object in his immediate vicinity was demanding his attention, drowning out the innumerable distractions of pressure and radiation which were as sight and sound to him. The intensity of the object's attraction grew steadily, which Asov interpreted as meaning that he himself was in motion, and moving toward this blazing area of disturbance. This then was the source of his awakening. For a nameless time he had drifted in the void, a seed of dormant intelligence awaiting the signal which would melt away the cocoon of unconsciousness, the first, faint caress of light and heat which would activate his sleeping sensors.

The star registered itself in Asov's brain as a frenzied pattern of nuclear reactions and continuous explosions. This image he related to the pre-stored information within and translated the image into his creators' terms of reference. The star was a red dwarf, spectral class M5, surface temperature around 4,000° C. As he swung in a wide orbit around his stellar prey, Asov picked up the contrastingly faint light-heat emanations of smaller, cooler bodies which circled the dense old star in their timeless chains of gravity. He again related the incoming data with his inborn, encyclopaedic memory.

Planets: Four. Temperature range: absolute zero to near frozen. Condition: lifeless, having lost gaseous atmospheres. . . .

Painstakingly, unconscious of the passage of time, Asov continued his survey. When he was finished and his brain cells each held a full load of information, a signal was passed to his motor nervous system and with a sudden bound he was accelerating away from the domain of the red dwarf.

As the old star slowly receded, he completed the program of his first mission. The data which loaded his brain cells was collated, coded and dispatched in a tight beam of radio waves, directed toward a tiny area of the firmament where lay the remote star Sol and the planet Earth. The planet which he had never known, but out of which he had come.

At last the urgency of his first stellar encounter grew dim, and Asov sought out the nearest available light-source, drawing upon the dormant energies of space to propel him toward his next encounter. Having completed the required maneuvers, Asov drifted in the relative peace of the interstellar vacuum, where gravity came not in waves but in gentle ripples and the nuclear voices of the stars were no more than a faint chant, a cosmic lullaby. Asov slept.

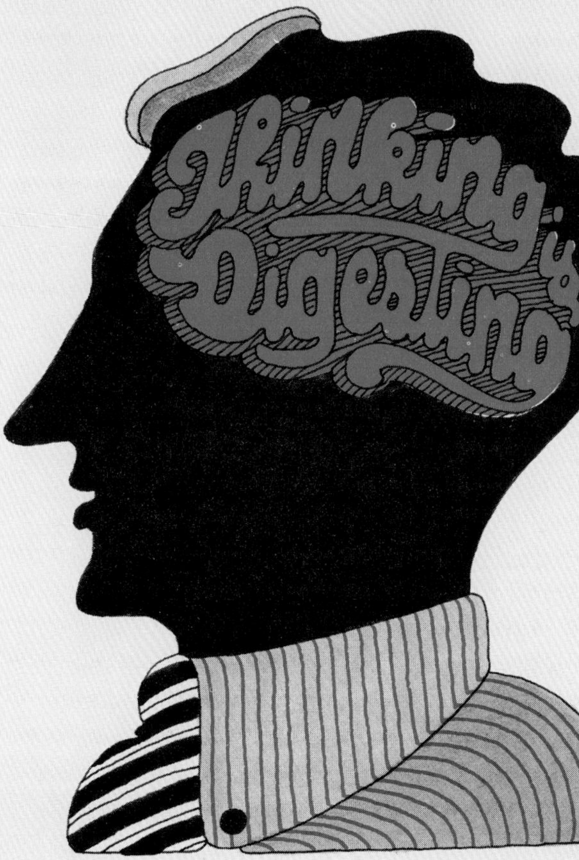

The cycle was repeated each time he passed within the gravitational embrace of any interstellar object capable of the slightest degree of energy output. The sources of his awakening-cycle were mainly stars of the red dwarf type, which comprised the bulk of the galaxy's population. But there were rare occasions when he would awake to the stimuli of massive giants and their proportionately enormous retinues of planets. Such occurrences demanded longer and more detailed survey, though of course Asov was unconscious of the time element.

Several times he passed through tenuous light-years of hydrogen, the life-stuff of the Universe. At times, these ghostly regions were sufficiently dense and luminous to wake his sensors, in addition to restocking his nuclear power reserves. Occasionally such nebulae contained the embryonic materials of new-born stars, hot and blue and amorphous. There was a great deal to learn at such times, particularly concerning the early evolutionary development of the stars. With each successive encounter his understanding of galactic processes increased, and was duly transmitted to the ever-more-distant point of origin.

Another rare event which Asov experienced was the discovery of a certain secondary characteristic of some planetary systems. The phenomenon of life. This characteristic was listed in his pre-birth instruction circuits as of the highest priority.

His first encounter with the phenomenon occurred while in the vicinity of a small, orange star of the classification G7. A star not unlike his native sun. He awoke to the familiar disturbance pattern; a strengthening of the gravitational tides which bore him, an intensification of light, heat, and the full range of radiation. A new energy source was before him.

After the routine observations of the star, his attention turned to the solid bodies in orbit about it. Of these planets, two offered distinct traces of organic molecules. Even at a remote distance Asov's spectroscopic vision could wrest these planetary secrets with ease. For a more detailed survey, however, a close approach was necessary. Acting upon this preliminary data, his motor nerves were immediately stimulated to inject him into a planetary trajectory which would bring him into orbit around each of the target worlds.

It was the second planet which possessed the most rewarding conditions. First he noted the patterns of abundant areas of ocean. Spectroscopic examination revealed that the seas, like the atmosphere, were rich in life's constituents. Then came direct evidence of advanced life. As he swung in a close orbit around the planet, just clearing the violet, upper fringes of the atmosphere, Asov observed the unmistakable signs: lighted areas on the night-side, large artificial structures and courses, and most unexpected of all, contact. After many reconnaissance circuits he intercepted a stray tendril of radiation. A short analysis was sufficient to convince him that this could not be accounted for by the natural emissions from the planet. The only possible explanation was that the radio signal had been directed at him by an intelligence.

. . . the final thing,
a man learning to sing.

The Questor was being questioned!

In accord with his built-in responses, Asov returned a signal toward the unknown source on the same wave-length as the one he had received. This signal comprised a tightly coded account of Asov's home system, a record of terrestrial thought and history. In that small beam of signals was contained a thorough biography of man, his progress in medicine and philosophy, his discoveries and disasters.

Simultaneously, Asov was working on the message he had received from the aliens. This too was in the form of a mathematical code, which when broken down revealed a long and detailed history of two planets. Like man, the aliens were as yet confined to their local system, though unlike Asov's distant creators, they had evolved a global way of life which permitted world-wide understanding while encouraging the valid, essential differences between beings of even the same species.

On completion of the exchange, Asov passed on out of the kingdom of the orange star, quite unaware that he had been the cause of the greatest single event in the history of a solar system.

Although virtually indestructible in the erosion-free vacuum, and although his motive power was available in unlimited quantities from the suns and gases of space, there had to come a time when Asov would meet with unexpected danger. Normally his senses were swift enough to avert a likely collision. This danger was only met within the confines of a solar system, when passing through belts of asteroids and cometary debris, the coastal defenses of the stars. Occasionally, these cosmic missiles would move at velocities beyond even Asov's power to out-maneuver. In the vicinity of large solar masses, the gravitational tides were so immense that much power was required for drastic course correction, and at the same time any local fleets of meteors would be moving with high orbital velocities.

It happened as he prepared to make his exit from the system of a red giant. The huge star had been a rare find indeed and it possessed the unusual feature of a retinue of minor stars, instead of the normal planets. These satellite stars were dwarfs, mostly in the last stages of stellar senility. They weaved around the sullen giant in weirdly eccentric orbits. So eccentric that the entire stellar system was a wildly turbulent whirlpool of gravitational forces. Enormous sized fragments of shattered planets flung themselves insanely across the system, as twigs will spin and dart in a vortex of water. Asov, given time, could have calculated precisely the mechanics of the whole complex system. He possessed the equipment to predict exactly the speed and trajectory of each hurtling fragment. But time, or the lack of it, was his undoing.

The collision when it came was not with one of the larger masses. These Asov had predicted and had taken evasive action. The fateful missile was a tiny splinter of rock, which compensated its insignificance in size with its vast velocity. It struck him at a point which in itself was expendable, upon a transmitting aerial of which he had several duplicates. But the shock of impact was great enough to deaden the sensitivity of his control mechanisms. In a coma almost as deep as death, Asov drifted helplessly into the dark wastes, unguided, aimless, totally without function.

It should have been the end. His inactive remains should have floated on for eternity, just another item of mineral debris in a Universe already familiar with the lifeless, the inert and the expended. But it was not the end.

In the furthest limits of interstellar space, as in the cosy realms of inhabited planets, the unexpected, the unpredictable occurs from time to time. Given long enough, and Asov had all of Time ahead of him, such an event was almost bound to happen. His was no immediate resurrection. He drifted in unconsciousness for the lifetime of many a star. While his senses lay dormant, planets formed, producing sea and slime from which finned oddities crept out on to cooling land surfaces to do battle with primal monsters and create civilizations. Some of these civilizations reached out into space in sleek and shining machines. Some of them died in nuclear holocaust and others died of introspection. Although the total Universe maintained its steady state, the individual stars and galaxies of stars evolved and changed. Much happened in the interval during which Asov slept the sleep which was so near to oblivion.

His damage was not "organic." It was a question of degree. The sensitivity of his optical and other senses had been so reduced by the collision that no normally available source of energy was powerful enough to activate him. No normally available source.

One phenomenon alone possessed sufficient energy to stir his stunned sensibility. One rare but regular occurrence which a galaxy will produce from time to time to startle the Universe with its power.

Supernova.

In an average sized galaxy there are around a hundred thousand million stars. When one of these suns becomes unstable through the excess creation of helium, it produces a phenomenon which must rank as one of the most bizarre events in the cosmos. Quite suddenly, in a split-second of time, such a star flares into frenzied incandescence of such a magnitude that it rivals the combined star-glow of half a galaxy.

During his long coma Asov had drifted through the remote ripples of several supernovae explosions, but there had to come a time when he would find himself in the direct path of one such cosmic upheaval. He was immersed in a boiling sea of radiation. The space around him was no longer a passive vacuum but a seething cauldron of hell-fire. In that cosmic Hades, Asov was resurrected. He emerged from the fire as the Phoenix, re-born, triumphant.

His second birth followed a similar pattern to his first. Again, the flood-gates were opened to his inner reservoir of knowledge and he drank avidly of the sudden deluge of information. In no time, he was once more in complete command of his faculties but, before any detailed appraisal of the larger scene, Asov had yet to investigate the immediate source of energy; the supernova which had raised him from the cosmic dead.

As usual in such cases, the star was a blue super-giant, of a size equivalent to four hundred solar diameters (Asov's home star was

Direct your eye right inward, and you'll find
A thousand regions in your mind
Yet undiscovered. Travel them, and be
Expert in home-cosmography.

always taken as the yardstick for such measurements). It was, of course, at that moment undergoing an expansion which one day would result in the creation of a nebula, with the shrunken shell of the erstwhile giant sun at its center. He was unable to detect any planetary system as the outer atmosphere of the star had already expanded to a point well beyond the orbit of even the furthest possible planet. Any such system would in any case have been instantly vaporized in the first few minutes of the conflagration.

Asov, caught in the rapidly expanding shell of gases, for a time lost track of the outer Universe. He was riding blind in the center of a cosmic storm, a storm of blinding light and dust which seemed to stretch to the end of time and space in its convulsive, frantic rush. When he did finally emerge from the stellar death-dance, his sensors saturated with new knowledge, Asov turned his attention to the outside scene.

At first, it seemed that his sensing equipment was malfunctioning. The composite image of the galaxy which he was receiving was not in accord with what his invincible memory circuits had prepared him for. He quickly checked his sensory systems, but without discovering anything amiss. Again he surveyed the large-scale features of his environment and again a scarcely credible picture confronted him.

Having no alternative but to believe his senses, Asov could make but one deduction from this picture: the galaxy had grown old. This could only mean that his period of unconsciousness had been long indeed, long in terms of space itself.

The immediate problem was one of energy. Power for propulsion, transmission, collating. Energy sources were, for the first time in his experience, severely limited. In his immediate environment, they were almost unavailable.

His galactic voyaging had taken him in a great ellipse around the system. It was in these outer regions that the stellar population had dwindled most drastically. Toward the center of the galaxy, which was observable to Asov as a gleaming island of mist, the stars retained at least a semblance of their old density. Here in the outer regions of the galactic spiral the stars had always been relatively sparse, and here the stellar death-toll had been more severe. Although the central stars tended to be older, they were also the more stable. The outer giants had always been short-lived, burning away their lifetimes with wanton fury while the inner stars were content with a humble output of energy, conserving their nuclear life-blood for as long as possible.

But not for eternity.

Forever practical, Asov concentrated upon the problem of energy sources. He was quick to predict that his present course would soon take him beyond the area of minimum power, where his senses would once more be eclipsed by the clouds of oblivion.

Only one decision was possible. This decision would have been made by any being, whether for the emotional desire of self-preservation or for the logical necessity of fulfilling a mission. Drawing upon the abundant energies still flowing from the supernova, Asov performed a major maneuver, altered his thrust vector to an extent unheard of in previous course corrections, and set sail for the galactic center.

In search of life and light, he left behind the grim silences of the galaxy's desolate shore.

On his way Asov charted the downfall of

the galaxy. He observed each dead and dying star which came within his long-range sensors. Very occasionally he approached close enough to witness the funeral processions of whole solar systems.

The pattern was one of somber repetition. The star, life-giver and source of light for so many millions of years, wrapped in a dim, red death-mist. The once populated planets cold, empty stretches of rock; desolate, global tombstones. On their surfaces, nothing stirred, and in their skies the naked stars were flaring in a final agony.

The rhythms of life and the conflict of the elements were drawing everywhere to a close. But Asov, unlike his environment, remained unchanged. His instincts, his basic motivations were the same as they had been that first day when the caress of starlight had opened his eyes to the Universe. However somber and woeful the environment which now met his probing senses, he must continue his explorations, as though in the faith that somewhere, sometime, he would discover something new.

Each time fresh information reached his brain cells, he would faithfully transmit the message to the remote point in space out of which he had emerged. He continued this ritual despite the increasing probability that the planet which had dispatched him so long before might now be no more than a frozen shell circling a small spent sun.

Even when he arrived at the great, glowing heart of the galaxy, Asov detected the signs of approaching doom. Spreading pools of darkness lay between the stars, a gradual, inexorable tide which ultimately would engulf the galaxy in a great and final shadow.

He continued his mission. As the ages came and went and the stars declined, he witnessed the long, losing battle against the night. Each stage of stellar decay he noted, the expansions and contractions, the brief flaring into momentary brilliance, the subsequent collapse as frigid darkness came in to close each chapter.

But the age of the unexpected had not yet passed. Suddenly, in the midst of now-familiar tragedy, an unprecedented phenomenon upset the pattern to which Asov had become resigned.

At first too faint to be correctly analysed, a new and puzzling transmitting source interrupted his silent vigil. The disturbance occupied only a tiny fragment of the complete, electro-magnetic environment, but it was sufficient to rouse Asov to immediate investigation. This was his essential purpose in existing, to spot and explore the unexpected.

He traced the disturbance factor, measured its frequency, and estimated its position relative to his own. It was comparatively close. The puzzling part was that no observable energy-source lay in that particular direction. Whatever was emitting the radiation was invisible, even to Asov's supersensitive vision. Invisible, or very small.

It was Asov's experience that no tiny cosmic object transmitted more than a tiny amount of radiation. This fact allowed him to deduce the basic nature of the phenomenon before he had actually closed the gap.

It had to be artificial.

In confirmation of this deduction, the object began to gravitate towards him, signifying that it too had picked up an unexpected radio source, in this case Asov.

At last they faced each other, two lonely voyagers meeting on a dead sea shore. Degree by degree, the mutual interchange of data which flowed between their radio centers was assimilated. A mathematically-based code system, founded on the same principles as those behind Asov's original transmission system, was evolved to permit a smooth flow of communication.

Asov learned that the mysterious object was in reality something very familiar and at the same time totally alien. It was an interstellar probe, almost a mirror-image of himself though its origins were half-a-galaxy away from his.

After the event, Asov could see that such a meeting, although unthinkably unlikely in any other circumstances, was perfectly logical at this time and place. He knew, had known for countless years, that other races existed in the galaxy; their number was legion. It was reasonable to expect that they too would in their day create beings similar to Asov, cosmic scouts which would voyage the galaxy independent of their creators, unaffected by the latters' doom.

It was to be expected that these scouts, like Asov, would seek out the galactic center, where life and light held on the longest. With the steady shrinkage of the galaxy's habitability zone, it was inevitable that sometime, these inward moving probes would gravitate toward each other. And one day, meet.

Proof that the encounter was not a rare quirk of Chance was soon forthcoming. More meetings took place, at first widely separated in time and space, later on an increasingly more frequent basis. Each encounter occurred amid a steadily shrinking nucleus of stars.

Although of varied design and complexity, these last representatives of cosmic man were all possessed by the same instinct, the instinct which had been programmed into them during construction. The decline and death of their creators in no way removed this primal instinct. The quest for light was their mission and their life. It would end only when the fires of the Universe grew dim and flickered out.

As the watching probes swung round the fading remnants of a once proud galaxy, their numbers continued to grow, vastly. In direct proportion to the number of highly advanced species which had once peopled the galaxy, the vanished ones who had dispatched their silent sentinels to keep watch over the stars.

While the dark waters of nothingness gradually flooded the firmament, Asov occupied his time by exchanging histories with his new-found counterparts.

Between them, a composite picture of galactic history was built up, each ancient probe contributing its own knowledge and experience to the common pool. Where before each probe possessed only fragmentary information about the processes of cosmic law, the combined experiences permitted a fuller understanding of the whole spectrum of creation.

In a sense, the gathering of probes formed a single entity. A composite being, possessing an almost unlimited experience of an entire galaxy.

But as the surrounding star-glow dimmed, so also did their intellectual activity diminish. Power was at a premium, the first priorities being propulsion and sensory activity. Transmission became less frequent, communication less intense.

The desperate search for energy sources began.

Asov was already approaching that state of suspended consciousness in which he had drifted after his fateful collision. But while there remained a spark of awareness, he was committed to his mission and to the discovery of light. It was quite impossible for him to anticipate oblivion and to yield himself to the darkness. His long-range sensors probed into the night, comparing, rejecting, selecting. Often, the particular light source which he was following would fade before him, as the advancing tide of darkness claimed yet another stellar victim. Many times his course would change, with increasing frequency, until it seemed that the Universe would soon be devoid of light and his senses deadened for ever.

But there were certain sources of light, which although faint in the extreme, were steady and appeared to remain unaffected by the fate of his immediate environment. These sources were by no means unfamiliar to Asov; they had been present throughout the long saga of his interstellar life, but they had been beyond the area of his established activity. Their distances were not merely interstellar, but extra-galactic. Until now, there had been no reason to attach much importance to those far-off sources of light.

But until now there had always been bright and abundant beacons of energy immediately available.

With the continued fading of the galaxy's fire, Asov and his companions turned at last to those distant, glowing mists; the last resort, the faint and final source of energy. However unprecedented the situation which faced them, the community of probes acted quickly, spontaneously and in unison. In a sense this was the consummation of their galactic lifetimes; and the introduction to a heightened mode of existence. From diverse space routes they had converged, in this final hour, to witness the last moments of a galaxy. Although little power was available for the final adjustments necessary for their outward courses, there was sufficient, as gravity had followed light down the long corridors of dissolution.

As they progressed beyond the confines of the galaxy, the last, dim fires were quenched, and behind them, a great darkness settled. The last of the suns had set.

Although unimaginably distant, the island universes for which they sailed were tangible enough. In the millennia to come, those signal fires would glow brightly from the void, to awaken and stimulate long dormant senses. Then the cycle would begin anew. Energies would be re-stocked from youthful, vital fires and a second chapter would be written in an ancient saga of exploration.

The great probe fleet, keepers and guardians of cosmic history, sailed out to the starless gulfs in search of galaxies to call their own.

The morning wind forever blows,
the poem of creation is
uninterrupted; but few are
the ears to hear it.

People seek a central point. That is hard and not even right.
I should think a rich, manifold life, brought close to the eyes,
would be enough without express tendency; which, after all,
is only for the intellect.
And you that shall cross from shore to shore
years hence are more to me, and more in my
meditations than you might suppose.

AUTHOR INDEX FOR MONTAGE

Legend: P = poem; E = essay; S = story; EX = excerpt; Q = quotation; A = artwork; F = photograph; C = cartoon or drawing; G = game

See Acknowledgments for further information on the works.